Privileging the Press
Confidential Sources, Journalism Ethics, and the First Amendment

D0143787

A book in the series:

Law and Society: Recent Scholarship
Edited by Melvin I. Urofsky

Privileging the Press
Confidential Sources, Journalism Ethics, and the First Amendment

Jason M. Shepard

LFB Scholarly Publishing LLC
El Paso 2013

First published 2011 by LFB Scholarly Publishing LLC.
First printing in paperback, 2013
All rights reserved.

Library of Congress Cataloging-in-Publication Data

Shepard, Jason M., 1976-
  Privileging the press : confidential sources, journalism ethics and the
First Amendment / Jason M. Shepard.
      p. cm. -- (Law & society)
  Includes bibliographical references and index.
  ISBN 978-1-59332-464-3 (hardcover : alk. paper)
  1. Confidential communications--Press--United States. 2. Press law--
United States. 3. Journalists--Legal status, laws,etc.--United States. 4.
Freedom of the press--United States. 5. Journalistic ethics--United
States. 6. United States. Constitution. 1st Amendment. I. Title.
  KF8959.P7S52 2011
  342.7308'53--dc23

                                                2011017857

ISBN 978-1-59332-464-3 (casebound)
ISBN 978-1-59332-635-7 (paperback)

Printed on acid-free 250-year-life paper.
Manufactured in the United States of America.

Table of Contents

v

Acknowledgements

The ideas in this book grew from my experiences as a working journalist. My love of newspapering was cemented early. I no doubt caused many headaches for my high school journalism teacher and adviser Roxanne Biffert, but she sparked my love affair with journalism and defended my rabble-rousing ways when her thin-skinned colleagues wanted me reeled in. Loni Lown as editor of the weekly *Wisconsin Dells Events* hired a 17-year-old cub reporter to cover the local school board in my hometown of 2,200 people, riddled with scandal. Dave Hutchison, the publisher of the upstart 300-circulation *Dells-Delton Daily*, lured me away as the schools beat reporter, replacing Gail Gunderson, a competitor turned friend.

When I moved to Madison for college, the newsroom of *The Capital Times* quickly became my journalistic home. Assistant city editor Anita Weier plucked me as a college freshman and guided me from freelancer to intern to staff writer. I aimed to please my supportive editors on the city desk, Charles Sherman and Ron McCrea, as well as the editor-in-chief and journalistic legend Dave Zweifel. John Nichols, the political and editorial writer, and Mike Miller, the veteran courts reporter, were important peer role models. The *Cap Times* was a great place to begin a life in journalism, with its feisty and progressive traditions and fascinating cast of characters.

When I returned to Madison for graduate school after a three-year stint as a New York City public-school teacher as part of Teach for America, Marc Eisen as editor and Vince O'Hern as publisher were generous enough to give me a regular gig at *Isthmus*, Madison's superb alternative newsweekly. I wrote an education column and periodic pieces about crime, media and politics. It was at *Isthmus* that I got to work for the finest editor of them all, Bill Lueders, the archetype crusading watchdog. As a reporter he is fearless and dogged, and as an editor he made my copy sing. He is proof that the pen still has power.

I owe a lot to University of Wisconsin-Madison, where I earned my bachelor's, master's and doctoral degrees. The School of Journalism and Mass Communication awarded me its top undergraduate award, four years of teaching assistant support, multiple research grants, selection as its 2008 Teaching Fellow, and a year-long fellowship to complete my dissertation. The entire faculty was supportive, particularly Professors Stephen Vaughn, James Baughman, Doug McLeod, Sue Robinson and Stephen J.A. Ward. Professor Katy Culver had an infectiously optimistic spirit who became a professional mentor and friend. Fellow graduate students provided intellectual and moral support, particularly Wendy Swanberg, Julie Lane, Phil Glende and Lucy Atkinson. My biggest debt of gratitude goes Professor Robert E. Drechsel. Drechsel was the faculty advisor every graduate student dreams of – patient, thoughtful, rigorous and generous. More than anyone else, he helped develop and shape the ideas in this book, gave me the encouragement and help to meet tough deadlines, and provided detailed edits and suggestions throughout the process. In so many ways, he is the type of teacher and scholar I aspire to emulate.

One of the great things about the University of Wisconsin is its commitment to interdisciplinary study. In the political science department, Professor Donald Downs was an important mentor during both my undergraduate and graduate years, and I was lucky to serve as a teaching assistant for Professor Howard Schweber. At the University of Wisconsin Law School, where I received a Ph.D. minor, Professors Linda Smith and Anuj Desai sharpened my legal research skills.

Several colleagues at California State University, Fullerton, deserve mention for helping make an easy transition from Ph.D. student to assistant professor: Genelle Belmas, Andi Stein, Paul Lester, xtine burrough, Emily Erickson, Tom Clanin, Jeff Brody, Tony Fellow, Irene Matz and Rick Pullen. And my students at the *Daily Titan* student newspaper have made sure I still have fun in a newsroom.

I also want to thank my grandmother, Helene Morse, and my parents, Mike and Tammy Shepard, for their love and support; and friends who have inspired me along the way: Shira Diner, Mike Verveer, Lesley Rogers, Loreto Ansaldo, Adam Rosen, Melissa Jones, Ashmeed Ali and Emily Pope.

Finally, some research presented in this book was first published in the academic journals *Communication Law and Policy* and the *Journal of Media Law & Ethics*.

Preface

The first time I was leaked federal grand jury documents for a newspaper story, I had no idea of the perilous legal environment I was entering. As a young police reporter for *The Capital Times*, a metro afternoon daily in Madison, Wis., I was eager to get my byline on the front page, please my editors and force my competition at the larger morning daily to cite my reporting in their follow-up to our scoops. Little did I know that my investigation into cocaine purchases at Jocko's Rocket Ship, a seedy downtown bar just off State Street on the edge of the University of Wisconsin-Madison campus, would eventually spark a book about the ethics and laws of journalists and their confidential sources.

The initial hints of a big story came when I got tipped off about a secret police raid of Jocko's in which a number of patrons were injured by more than two dozen heavily armed cops. Official police sources wouldn't tell me anything, but eventually through ambulance and 911 records I tracked down a man who was sent to the hospital. He gave me some tantalizing details about the raid before calling back and leaving me a voice mail threatening to kill me if I reported his name in the paper. The intrigue continued. At a press conference announcing that the bar owner and eight others were indicted for operating an "indoor open-air drug market" for a decade, federal prosecutors stated that a number of city firefighters were among the regular clientele. Among Madison's chattering political class, rumors also implicated other prominent people, including high-profile attorneys and even members of the Police Department. Some of the police reports from the investigation were provided to the Fire Department, which then had no choice but to launch its own investigation into how widespread cocaine use was in its ranks. Secret suspensions fueled criticism about the investigation, and my newspaper's editorial board crusaded against the secrecy and the rising costs associated with the investigations. Provocatively, the editors even ran a box on the front-page each day tallying the amount of taxpayer money being spent on the salaries of suspended employees and excoriating the mayor for the secrecy surrounding the case. The city's legal fees alone eventually topped $500,000. The official streams of information – the police, the mayor, the district attorney, and the U.S. attorney's office – were maddeningly silent. So when a source connected with the case offered to let me read the case file (thanks in part to the source's connections with a senior columnist whose desk was next to mine), I leapt at the opportunity to learn more about the investigation. It was, frankly, a journalist's dream come true: shedding light on the secrets of government and holding public officials accountable for their actions.

I was given two days to read more than 2,000 pages of investigative reports, and subsequent stories reconstructed the roots of the drug investigation, discussed the elaborate operations of the bar owner and his associates, named for the first time the firefighters who were suspended, and documented admissions of regular cocaine use by a number of additional firefighters. There were also racial overtones; all of the suspended firefighters were black while the other drug users still on the job were all white. Hours after the initial story based on the documents was published, city officials pledged to investigate its firefighting ranks and later went to court seeking access to the documents as part of their own internal investigation. Later, I sat in a federal courtroom and listened to a judge condemn the leak and encourage the U.S. attorney to investigate my source. "There is no excuse for anyone who had legitimate access to the grand jury's materials to pass them to the media. The breach of (federal rules) by someone connected with this federal prosecution was egregious and this court expects the U.S. attorney actively to pursue this matter,'" Magistrate Judge Stephen Crocker said.

At the time, I did not realize how perilously close I came to be confronted with the choice of facing serious jail time or breaking my promise of confidentiality to my source. I avoided a subpoena in the city's attempt to get the documents released by a federal judge, but I did receive a subpoena to testify before the city's Police and Fire Commission, a quasi-judicial body that was holding hearings about the discipline and firing of several firefighters. Thankfully, our newspaper's attorney, Bob Dreps, was able to get the subpoena tossed out, and nothing, to my knowledge, ever came of the U.S. Attorney's investigation into the leak.

The U.S. magistrate judge had a point when he said my reporting was a result of a breach of federal rules. Should I have been allowed to read the grand jury documents? No. Did I do what good journalists do? Yes. I was a 23-year-old reporter who with hard work and some luck got a major scoop about *the* major local news event of the day. But what I did not know then was that the law generally wasn't on my side.

The Jocko's story wasn't the first, nor was it the last, that required promises of confidentiality. My first real investigative coup – while I was an intern at *The Capital Times* – was a report about the University of Wisconsin's secret use of monkeys that were born at the local zoo but subsequently used in invasive and often deadly research projects, in violation of written agreements not to use zoo-born monkeys in such projects. The university denied such practices until they learned that I was provided with internal monkey birth and transport records, something I received from an employee who demanded anonymity. University officials almost got away with it but for a courageous employee who leaked evidence of malfeasance to a reporter.

I can still recall working the initial story on deadline, rushing to a hotel bar on the east side of Madison to receive a stash of critical documents. I agreed to the meeting spot before realizing that I was not yet 21 years old and therefore couldn't legally get into the bar. I was too embarrassed to admit this to my source, fearing that the source would rethink trusting someone so green. I skirted by the doorman, found my source, got the documents, and raced back to the newsroom to add some new details to the story. The city editor had cancelled his Friday night dinner plans to vet the story and edit the copy. "Zoo monkeys secretly killed" screamed across Saturday morning's front page, and the competition the next day ran a big Sunday story quoting extensively from mine. It was the first of more than 50 news stories I wrote about the university's killing of monkeys born at the local zoo and its cover-up and subsequent fallout.

As a police and crime reporter, there were many law enforcement stories I wrote that were the result of unauthorized disclosures of information. A police source upset with preferential treatment provided me with details about an assistant district attorney's husband who wasn't arrested after being found drunk, with a loaded gun in his car, after threatening to kill a cop. The A.D.A. had called the cops after the husband threatened to kill a male officer who danced with her at a wedding earlier in the night. The sergeant who oversaw the incident took the man to a detox center instead of jail, didn't file any charges, and subsequently lied about the incident to supervisors. I also spent months unraveling a missing-persons case that cops believed was a drug homicide. My stories based on leaked police records provided a grieving mother for the first time with new facts about what might have happened to her son. Amos Mortier is still missing more than four years later.

But perhaps my most important pieces of reporting to stem from a confidential source came in 2008 when I reported that a murder victim called 911 as she was being attacked but the 911 dispatcher never sent her any help. Brittany Zimmermann was a pre-med student at the University of Wisconsin-Madison when she walked home to her campus-area apartment around noontime after an exam. Hours later, her fiancé came home to discover her dead, having been brutally beaten and stabbed multiple times. Police worked on the theory that she was killed by a stranger, but no suspect was identified. Hers was the third unsolved campus-area murder within a year, and the cops were under tremendous public pressure to solve the case. Several weeks after her murder, I was provided a tip by a familiar source that Brittany had called 911 as she was being attacked and that the 911 center botched the handling of the call. I tried to confirm this through routine methods, including reviewing a 911 dispatch log that was routinely available to reporters. The call was not there. I also filed public-records requests for basic 911 call information, which were denied. Interviews with officials went nowhere, and the 911 center director dodged all my queries. I went back to my original source, pieced a few things together from other sources, and then presented two other police sources with a draft of my story. Those subsequent sources knew more than I did and provided some key confirming details and also corrected an error. The story, under the headline "Brittany Zimmermann called 911, but no one came," sparked immediate outrage. The police chief and the 911 center director held dueling news conferences and provided contradictory facts, while the county executive was busy defusing criticism about short staffing and mismanagement inside the 911 center. Eventually, the story and several follow-ups resulted in the resignation of the 911 center director, several lawsuits, and significant budget increases to the center. None of this would have happened but for confidential sources trusting journalists.

I relay these stories to show that my interest and experience in journalists' uses of confidential sources originated in my own practices over a decade as a journalist. Confidential sources were crucial to some of my most important pieces of public-service journalism. Some of these tips and leaks were the result of luck and happenstance; others took weeks and months to develop. Some came from sources who I knew for years, while others took a chance in trusting a journalist to blow the whistle on perceived malfeasance or injustice. Almost all of my sources violated some kind of law or policy by providing me with information. They risked a lot in talking to me. Despite their lawlessness, I view them as courageous and important. What does that say about me and my view of journalism? These were among the questions I often thought about when I transitioned from life as a journalist to life as an academic.

This book is a result of that transition. It examines how confidential sources in journalism have long presented ethical and legal problems. Today, 49 states and the District of Columbia recognize some form of a journalist's privilege, a legal right to protect the identity of confidential sources and newsgathering information. Protections under federal law remain murkier, which is one of the reasons why I, in retrospect, could have been in deep trouble with my Jocko's Rocket Ship stories. The Supreme Court's 1972 decision in *Branzburg v. Hayes* rejected a First Amendment-based journalist's privilege, although dozens of lower courts subsequently reinterpreted *Branzburg* and recognized a qualified privilege in common law.

While scholars have examined the journalist's privilege from a legal doctrinal perspective, problems of ethical practice have garnered little attention. Those ethical questions are crucial in understanding the justifications of the privilege and in thinking about appropriate limits and exceptions, as matters of law and of ethics. This book dissects the relationship between the ethics and laws of confidential source protection and places the concept of journalistic duty to protect sources in the broader historical context of the development of the journalism profession and journalism ethics discourse.

This book began as a Ph.D. dissertation that set out to answer four primary research questions: (1) How did it come to be that journalists believe they are morally and ethically justified to go to jail to protect the identity of confidential sources? (2) How did this professional duty develop in American journalism? (3) How have journalists' ethical and legal arguments changed over time? and (4) Why is confidential-source protection a continuing problem in journalism ethical practice and law?

In examining these questions, I found a dynamic interaction between journalism ethics, free-press theory and legal jurisprudence. Over time, journalists developed ethical doctrines rooted in their developing practices and the emerging values of the profession. Journalists transformed these ethical principles and values into free-press arguments, and the law has responded, in terms of First Amendment theory, judicial doctrine and statutory rules, to both reject and embrace the ethical claims as legal rules. This book tells the story of this evolution.

By providing a historical study of an important journalistic practice, this research contributes to a small field of scholarship on the history of journalistic ethics, practices and professionalization. Professor Hazel Dicken-Garcia noted in her groundbreaking 1989 book *Journalistic Standards in Nineteenth-Century America* that "no literature deals to a significant degree with the history of journalism ethics," and calls this scholarship gap "conspicuous and limiting." Writing in 2005, Professor Patrick Lee Plaisance asserted that "documentation of the evolution of how ethics came to be applied within American journalism remains sketchy." Professor Stephen J.A. Ward's *The Invention of Journalism Ethics*, published in 2004, is a recent significant contribution to filling this gap, positioning the philosophy of journalism ethics in the context of several distinct historical periods. The concept of source protection, however, is absent from Ward's history. This work fills that gap and also contributes to the law and society scholarship by showing the complex relationship among professional ethics, constitutional theory and positive law.

This research shows how the practice of cultivating and protecting confidential sources was an essential element of the journalism professionalism movement that emerged in the late 19th century, and it remains a central tenet of journalism practice 150 years later. It is important to understand that the ethical claims of journalistic duty predated much of the modern understanding of the First Amendment and journalism ethics. In tracing the history of this professional ethic from its ideological roots in the practices of colonial newspaper editors through the most recent confrontations between the press and the government in the George W. Bush and Barack Obama administrations, this research examines the core values and beliefs that have given rise to the journalist's privilege. The history of this ethical discourse reveals that journalists have emphasized that their moral obligations to uncover truth and expose corruption, misconduct and incompetence sometimes require them to make promises of confidentiality and subsequently deal with difficult consequences. The study emphasizes the dynamic relationship between law and ethics in the context of the journalist's privilege and the ways in which different legal mechanisms have changed in response to pressures from the journalism profession. By tracing the privilege from the 19th century, when it had no acceptance in law, through its statutory, constitutional and common law incarnations of the 20th century, the research reveals how journalists successfully "legalized" one of their key ethical canons, at least in part. The legal debates over the privilege's purposes, standards and limits also show how social and political concerns affect legal development and views of the constitutional free-press doctrine. And the debates over the legal foundation of the privilege – in constitutional, common or legislative law – show that principles and policies can take multiple legal shapes.

In sum, this book argues that journalistic duty to protect confidential sources has been a central ethical norm in the professional development of journalism with roots as far back as the colonial era; that this ethical norm has been transformed into legal principles of statutory, constitutional and common law to varying degrees; and that these ethical norms support the basis for a broadly recognized journalist's privilege in law, although one that is less than absolute. The historical development of these ethical norms also provide guidance for resolving modern legal problems, including the limits of the privilege, how judges might conduct "public-interest" balancing, and in determining who should be recognized as a journalist eligible for the privilege.

Methodologically, this research utilizes traditional legal history methods and analyzes and explains how and why the law has changed in social and political context. The study draws on a diverse range of primary and secondary sources. More than 100 court decisions were analyzed, showing how judges apply legal theory and rules to cases. Legal briefs and affidavits showcase the arguments journalists advanced. Transcripts of hearings and depositions offer further insights into the thinking of journalists and those seeking material from journalists. Murray Waas's 584-page compilation of primary documents is an important source for the Valerie Plame case. Editions of James Franklin's *New England Courant* from the 1720s were analyzed at the Wisconsin Historical Society to understand the content and practices of the first truly defiant colonial newspaper editor. The *New York Times* database provided access to articles about several privilege cases beginning in the late 19th century. *Editor & Publisher* was a key source regarding privilege cases in the early 20th century, at a time when the law reports were largely void of discussions of the issue. Legislative documents were helpful. A 1949 report by the New York Law Revision Commission provided a definitive account of early privilege cases and legislative proposals. An examination of the congressional hearings of the 1970s draws from thousands of pages of congressional hearing transcripts and the archives of Robert Kastenmeier, the U.S. Representative who chaired a series of hearings debating shield legislation, housed at the Wisconsin Historical Society. More than a hundred law review articles were also reviewed to assess the evolution of the judicial doctrine.

Personal interviews were conducted with several journalists and media lawyers, including Floyd Abrams, the attorney for Judith Miller and Matt Cooper often described as the most respected First Amendment attorney in the United States; attorney James Goodale, described as the "father" of the modern journalist's privilege; Josh Wolf, the videoblogger who spent 226 days in jail; Lance Williams of the *San Francisco Chronicle,* who narrowly avoided jail in 2006 after his source was identified; Tom Robbins of the *Village Voice,* who came forward about a key witness's potential perjury, based on discrepancies in his confidential interview with her, in the middle of a murder trial; Dave McGraw, deputy general counsel of the *New York Times*; Robin Bierstedt, deputy general counsel for Time Inc.; Lee Levine, a distinguished Washington, D.C. media lawyer and adjunct professor at Georgetown University Law Center; and Lucy Dalglish, executive director of the Reporters Committee for Freedom of the Press. Personal and institutional accounts also provided context to these and other cases.

The book is divided into three parts. Part one, comprising the first three chapters, explains the modern journalist-subpoena problem and includes several case studies of recent controversies. Part two constructs the historical development of the journalist's privilege in the profession and in law. Part three proposes solutions to several contemporary ethical and legal problems.

CHAPTER 1

The Journalist-Subpoena Problem

On the morning she went to jail for refusing to identify a confidential source, Judith Miller, a reporter for the *New York Times*, told a federal judge that "if journalists cannot be trusted to guarantee confidentiality, then journalists cannot function and there cannot be a free press." Controversially, Miller articulated a nearly absolutist view of the journalist's privilege principle. She argued that the American concept of freedom of the press implies both a legal right and ethical duty of journalists to withhold the identity of confidential sources. As a distinguished but controversial reporter on national-security issues, Miller argued that citizens would be deprived of important news and information if she could not protect the identity of her sources, many of whom held sensitive jobs and spoke to her only under well-established ground rules of journalistic confidentiality. Arthur Ochs Sulzberger Jr., the *Times'* publisher, said Miller was "doing her job as the founders of this nation intended." Federal judges disagreed. District and appellate courts ruled against Miller, and the Supreme Court of the United States declined to hear her appeal. In an act of civil disobedience both heralded for its courageousness and chided for its appearance of martyrdom, Miller defied the court order and spent 85 days in jail before she negotiated a waiver of confidentiality from her source and testified in court as a prosecution witness against her source – the chief of staff to the vice president of the United States.

At about the same time Miller's case was exposing the backchannels of communication between reporters and government officials in Washington, across the country in San Francisco federal prosecutors were seeking to imprison Josh Wolf. Wolf, then a 24-year-old self-described "artist, activist, anarchist and archivist," had attended and videotaped a protest in San Francisco where a police officer was injured and a squad car set on fire. When FBI agents showed up at his apartment days later, Wolf declined to turn over his tape and hired a lawyer. A federal grand jury then issued a subpoena for the videotape and his testimony. After losing his legal appeals, Wolf spent 226 days in jail. A judge told Wolf at his sentencing, "Every person, from the president of the United States down to you and me, has to give information to the grand jury if the grand jury wants it." On his blog, Wolf proclaimed himself to be "longest jailed journalist in U.S. history" for "committing journalism" and for "protecting his sources' confidentiality and defending the First Amendment." But the case did not involve confidential sources, nor was Wolf working for any news organization. His footage was filmed on a public street; he occasionally posted video clips on a blog; and because of the newsworthiness of the event, he sold some footage to local television stations. "When you're an activist cavorting with the people you're chronicling, then you are not a journalist," wrote *San Francisco Chronicle* columnist Debra Saunders. But other journalists recognized Wolf as one their "new media" peers, and the Reporters Committee for Freedom of the Press paid for part of Wolf's legal fees.

In serving jail sentences longer than any previous journalists in American history based on their conceptions of journalistic duty and responsibility, Miller and Wolf highlighted one sphere of longstanding tension between the press and the state and one of the most perplexing problems of communications law. But they are not alone. In the first decade of the 21st century, the threat of government subpoenas has sharpened at a perilous time for journalism, when journalistic independence, credibility and authority have come under attack by profound economic and social changes that have left some wondering whether the profession of journalism can even survive. At the same time, new technologies have eliminated the gate-keeping function that traditional journalists have long served in deciding when to publish secrets, as evidenced by the publication of more than 400,000 classified documents by the website Wikileaks in late 2010.

Miller and Wolf are but two of an unprecedented number of journalists who have been threatened with increasingly coercive tactics for refusing to cooperate with law enforcement and the judiciary seeking information obtained during newsgathering. These unprecedented coercive attempts by government threaten a journalistic tradition to protect confidential sources rooted in conceptions of moral and professional duty that journalists have articulated since colonial times. Subsequent chapters establish that the journalist's privilege to protect confidential sources has roots in the independent ideology of the earliest colonial newspapers and developed as an ethical duty as newspapers "professionalized" in the late 19th century. Over 150 years, scores of journalists have been successful in transforming their conceptions of ethical duty into legal protections. Today, some form of a legal privilege for journalists exists in many jurisdictions through a patchwork of state statutes, state and federal common law and constitutional provisions, and administrative rules.

This chapter explores some foundational questions about the press and the state in American constitutional democracy that are raised by the journalist's privilege. When journalists invoke ethical claims of duty to violate court orders demanding the identity of their sources, they often argue that the principle of source protection serves broader public interests. In developing a response to these claims, the state is confronted with two choices: potentially diminish the press's watchdog function, that has important social and political value, by not recognizing a privilege to protect sources, or, on the other hand, provide special rights to journalists by legalizing a professional ethic that could hamper law enforcement and the judiciary, be abused by journalists and be redefined at the will of lawmakers and judges. First, this chapter examines the nature of confidential sources in journalism, finding that confidential sources are commonplace and important in journalism. Second, the chapter positions source protection within the broader context of journalism ethics discourse, showing that source protection is supported by core journalistic functions, principles and practices. Third, the chapter discusses how confidential source decisions raise questions about First Amendment values. Finally, the chapter briefly sketches out the issues and questions examined in the rest of the book.

SUBPOENAS AND JOURNALISTS' CONFIDENTIAL SOURCES

Confidential sources are commonplace in news stories. In his book on the Valerie Plame CIA leak case, Time Inc. editor Norman Pearlstine said that "anonymous sources have become embedded in journalism; they are a critical part of coverage in small towns and large cities, and for national newspapers, magazines, cable news channels and television networks."[1] Two studies conducted in 1971 and 1985 found that confidential sources were used in roughly one in four news stories.[2] Professor Vince Blasi's 1971 study on journalist subpoenas found that confidential sources were relied upon in 22.2 percent to 34.4 percent of stories by the reporters surveyed. Professor John E. Osborn's 1985 study found that 31.25 percent of respondent reporters relied on confidential sources for their news stories. In a brief to the Supreme Court of the United States in the *Cohen v. Cowles Media* case, which ruled that journalists can be sued by sources for breaking promises of confidentiality, one lawyer cited studies that showed confidential sources were found in 80 percent of newsmagazine stories and two-thirds of Pulitzer Prize nominations.[3]

Confidential sources appear more regularly in certain types of reporting, such as political reporting, crime reporting, national security reporting, military reporting and investigative reporting. As veteran *Washington Post* investigative journalist Bob Woodward said, "The job of a journalist, particularly someone who's spent time dealing in sensitive areas, is to find out what really happened. When you are reporting on inside the White House, the Supreme Court, the CIA, or the Pentagon, you tell me how you're going to get stuff on the record. Look at the good reporting out of any of those institutions – it's not on the record."[4] Sometimes, a promise of confidentiality is the price journalists are willing to pay for access to information they otherwise could not obtain. Some promises of confidentiality result in explosive scoops, but more often they allow sources to talk frankly so journalists can better understand issues and context.

Generally, information that is attributed to an identifiable source has more credibility to readers than information sourced to anonymous or confidential sources, and most news organizations therefore encourage reporters to try to persuade sources to be "on the record," meaning that any information provided by the source can be attributed transparently directly to the source, by name and title.[5] Norman Pearlstine's proposed guidelines for Time Inc. developed after the Valerie Plame case, for example, say, "Reporters should make every effort to gather information and conduct interviews that are on the record. When we used an unnamed source, we risk undermining the credibility of the information we are providing. We must be certain in our own minds that the benefit to readers is worth the cost of credibility."[6] The *New York Times'* policy states that the "use of unidentified sources is reserved for situations in which the newspaper could not otherwise print information it considers reliable and newsworthy."[7]

Because many sources prefer not to be publicly identified, journalists often must negotiate with sources the rules of their interviews. The significance and nature of the information is an important criteria to determine if a source "deserves" confidentiality. Pearlstine's proposal lists several situations in which confidential sources should not be used: for material that is "trivial, obvious, or self-serving;" for quotations that just add "color" to a story; or to voice "speculation." The *New York Times'* policy states that anonymous sources should be used only "as a last resort" and not for personal or partisan attacks, and readers should be told why the source was granted anonymity.[8] Generally, reporters have varying degrees of confidential relationships with sources, ranging from "off the record" conversations, often meaning that the information cannot be used at all, to conversations on "on background," meaning the information may be used without identifying the source. *Time's* Matt Cooper, for example, noted in an e-mail to his editor that his conversation with Karl Rove, one of his sources for learning the identity of CIA agent Valerie Plame, was on "super secret background." Journalists sometime grant sources confidentiality implicitly, while others negotiate detailed confidentiality rules without which reporters would lose important information. Sometimes, the rules set by politicians and government officials require anonymity as a ground rule, including briefings by government officials. Other times, reporters grant promises of confidentiality to protect the source from the repercussions that would come from being identified as the provider of information.

"Leaks," meanwhile, can describe different types of information provided by confidential or anonymous sources. Professor Elie Abel, a former dean of Columbia University's Graduate School of Journalism, distinguished between "true leaks," such as a premeditated act by a source that occurs without prodding by a reporter, and other types of information reporters sometimes receive from sources after promises of confidentiality. [9] Sometimes, these are "plants" authorized by higher ranking officials to advance a person's interests or goals. Other subjects of reporter-source conversations result from questions by reporters who use various methods to convince sources to disclose information they might otherwise not disclose.[10] The distinction might be important to journalists who later must decide whether the source's motives should factor into decision-making about the ethics of using the information.

Individuals provide journalists with information after promises of confidentiality for several reasons. Researcher Stephen Hess has identified seven categories to describe the motives of leakers.[11] The "ego leak" is done to increase the self-importance of the leaker. A "goodwill leak" is done to build rapport or earn good will with the reporter. A "policy leak" aims to get more attention to particular proposals. An "animus leak" is done to criticize or attack an opponent. A "trial balloon leak" floats a particular idea or strategy to test its favorability. A "whistle-blower leak" is attempting to fix what the leaker perceives as a wrong.[12]

Especially in national political reporting, leaks and promises of confidentiality are routine. One study conducted by the Institute of Politics at Harvard's Kennedy School of Government found that 42 percent of surveyed former federal policymaking officials said they leaked information to reporters while in office. Four in five of them said they did so to counter false or misleading information. Three in four respondents said they leaked to direct attention to a policy issue, while half leaked to force action on an issue. One in three said they leaked information in response to a reporter's skill or persistence.[13]

Abel argued in a 1987 study that news leaks are generally beneficial to society by helping people understand the complexities of government and making officials more accountable.[14] Abel concluded that leaks are unlikely to diminish because there is so much secrecy surrounding government facts and initiatives, too many government officials have access to classified and secret material, and tensions and factions in government provide incentives to leaking. On the journalistic side, editors allow reporters to use confidential sources and the journalistic profession looks favorably on journalists who break important stories based on confidential sources.[15]

Subpoenas seeking confidential information from journalists are troublesome for a number of reasons. First, subpoenas can undermine the policy justifications for privileges in general. The law recognizes some privileges from compelled disclosure, such as the doctor-patient, priest-penitent, therapist-patient and spousal privileges, because the costs to the legal system do not outweigh the important societal benefits from protecting confidentiality. Sources may be chilled from talking to journalists if they fear being unmasked by a subpoena. Journalistic autonomy may be threatened if the government can subpoena journalists at will. In his dissent in *Branzburg v. Hayes*, Justice Potter Stewart succinctly summarized the problems with subpoenas to journalists:

> The right to gather news implies, in turn, a right to a confidential relationship between a reporter and source. This proposition follows as a matter of simple logic once three factual predicates are recognized: (1) newsmen require informants to gather news; (2) confidentiality – the promise or understanding that names or certain aspects of communications will be kept off the record – is essential to the creation and maintenance of a news-gathering relationship with informants and (3) an unbridled subpoena power – the absence of a constitutional right protecting, in any way, a confidential relationship from compulsory process – will either deter sources from divulging information or deter reporters from gathering and publishing information.[16]

Accurate data on subpoena frequency is difficult to find, in part due to the diffuse nature of both journalism and law enforcement. A study in 2006 concluded that more than 7,000 subpoenas were received by all daily newspapers and network-affiliated broadcast news stations in the United States during the past year. The study, conducted by Professor RonNell Andersen Jones, found that about half of news organizations received at least one subpoena, while about eight percent received 10 or more subpoenas.[17] Andersen found a "dramatic increase" in the number of subpoenas seeking confidential information. Newspaper reporters were more likely to receive complicated subpoenas for confidential information, while television news organizations were more likely to receive subpoenas for non-confidential information, such as outtakes and videos of broadcasts. And as a result of the negative judicial precedents discussed in later chapters, one-third of editors surveyed said they believed sources were less willing to speak to journalists on a condition of confidentiality than they were five years earlier.

The use of confidential sources can be problematic for journalists and news organizations in other ways. Too much reliance on confidential sources can diminish the credibility of news stories. One 1979 study found that 81 percent of newspaper editors considered unnamed sources less believable, and one-third said they were unhappy with how anonymous sources were handled at their paper.[18] In some cases, journalists using confidential sources can be burned by printing incorrect information, such as when, during the sensational O.J. Simpson murder trial, a reporter falsely reported that the murder victim's blood had been found on a sock found at Simpson's home.[19] After the erroneous O.J. Simpson story, Michael Gartner, editor of the *Daily Tribune* in Ames, Iowa, said, "The lesson is this: Beware anonymous sources. They can lie without accountability. They can fudge without responsibility. They can hide behind anonymity. They can strain readers' credulity and damage journalists' credibility."[20] And reliance on a questionable confidential source led to the forced early retirement of Dan Rather, the venerable anchor and managing editor of the CBS Evening News. In 2004, CBS retracted a story that accused President George W. Bush of lying about his National Guard service, a story that was apparently based on forged documents and other information provided to CBS on the condition of confidentiality.[21]

Occasionally, uses of confidential sources can also cover up journalistic misconduct. The *New York Times'* policy was revised in 2004 after one of its reporters, Jayson Blair, was determined to have plagiarized and made up details in a number of news stories, some with the reliance on anonymous sources. Columbia University graduate students who read six months of news stories before and after the policy change, which required editors to be more vigilant in challenging reporters when anonymous sources appeared in news stories, found that the number of anonymous sources cited in stories dropped by half.[22] The *Washington Post* had its own scandal several years earlier, when reporter Janet Cooke used claims of confidentiality to cover up the fact that she made up a story, for which she won a Pulitzer Prize, about a young boy addicted to drugs. The case provoked widespread criticism of the newspaper's failures to police its reporters.[23]

The reporter-source relationship has been the subject of journalism codes of ethics since they first were developed. Journalism codes of ethics almost universally compel journalists to keep their promises of confidentiality. The American Society of Newspaper Editors states that "pledges of confidentiality to news sources must be honored at all costs, and therefore should not be given lightly."[24] The Society of Professional Journalists' code of ethics says journalists should "always question sources' motives before promising anonymity," but says journalists must "keep promises" once given.[25] One national study of journalists, conducted in each of the past three decades, has found consistent evidence that protecting confidential sources is a fundamental journalistic value, with fewer than 10 percent of journalists saying that it is ever justifiable to name a confidential source. "If there is a bedrock principle among journalists, it is that a commitment to a source' anonymity must be honored at all costs," the study concluded.[26]

Individual reporters have also developed their own standards over time for when anonymous source material should appear in their stories. Walter Pincus, the national security reporter for the *Washington Post*, said he uses at least three standards to evaluate when to publish information from confidential sources.[27] First, the information must be credible and verifiable, and information attributed to anonymous sources "has to be checked more closely than any other type of material." Second, Pincus said the information must be newsworthy, and not published just because it is a secret. Third, the potential harm of publishing classified material, especially regarding national security, must be considered. And journalists need to be concerned that overuse of anonymous sources can undermine the credibility and importance of protecting sources in important cases. Pincus wrote:

> Journalists should pause before handling information received from people who demand anonymity. Reporters should avoid promising anonymity to sources if it is being offered simply to encourage the source to say something in a dramatic or damaging way that the source would not say on the record. This use of anonymity harms the profession and diminishes the value of the confidentiality given to those who are whistleblowers – people who risk their jobs and jail for what they may believe is a higher cause.[28]

WATERGATE AND THE ROMANCE OF "DEEP THROAT"

Memorialized in journalism history is the role of "Deep Throat" in the resignation of President Richard Nixon – the archetype confidential source helping a journalist expose the truth. Because of his ability to protect his source's identity, Bob Woodward won a Pulitzer Prize, convinced countless government officials to answer his questions about some of the most secretive aspects of government, and garnered a reputation as one of the best journalists of his generation.[29] For three decades, Woodward and his reporting partner Carl Bernstein refused to reveal the identity of the notorious government official who leaked damaging information about President Richard Nixon and his administration to *The Washington Post* during the Watergate investigation in the early 1970s. The duty Woodward felt toward his source reaped subsequent professional benefits, as countless other sources over the years cooperated with Woodward's book-length investigative projects about the inner workings of government.[30] "You'll protect sources," individuals explained to Woodward in rationalizing their willingness to talk to him.[31] Sometimes, particularly with reticent sources, Woodward recalled:

> I would even say at times that this was a "Deep Throat" conversation, and some of those in the most sensitive positions or best-placed crossroads of the American government would nod and then talk in remarkable detail, plowing through security classifications and other barriers as if they did not exist, including private conversations with a president. Deep Throat, or the concept of rigid source protection, became the unstated part of the conversation.[32]

In 2005, Woodward wrote about his relationship with Deep Throat in his book *The Secret Man: The Story of Watergate's Deep Throat*, after the family of Mark W. Felt identified him as Deep Throat in an article published by *Vanity Fair*.[33] Felt, who had been the second in command of the FBI during the Watergate investigation, was suffering from dementia and had few specific memories of the Watergate era. The book provided the public with a fascinating window into one of the most significant reporter-source relationships in American history, probing as well the complex motives of a government leaker who helped the public learn about the crimes of a president and his men.

As Woodward recalled, he first met Felt when, as a 27-year-old Navy lieutenant assigned to the office of the chief of naval operations, he and Felt had a chance encounter in a hallway of the White House, where Woodward was waiting to hand-deliver files.[34] Woodward later sought out Felt for career advice, and the two developed something of a friendship. When Woodward was hired at the *Post*, he continued to nurture his relationship with Felt. And as Woodward and his reporting partner Carl Bernstein first began to cover the conspiracy behind the break-in of the Democratic Party's headquarters in the Watergate building, Felt was an obvious source for Woodward, although Woodward at first had no idea how Felt would respond to his questions about the peculiar Watergate investigation. As Woodward described it in 2005:

> (Felt) was relatively open with me but insisted that he, the FBI and the Justice Department be kept out of anything I might write or pass on to others at the paper ... He was stern and strict about those rules, which he issued with a booming, insistent voice. I promised. He said that it was essential I be careful. The only way to ensure total confidentiality was that I tell no one – no one – that we knew each other or had talked, or that I knew anyone in the FBI or Justice.[35]

Certainly, Woodward was not the first reporter who reaped professional success from cultivating relationships with sources and convincing them to talk out of school. Woodward's reliance on Felt shaped the *Post's* coverage of Watergate by allowing the reporters to confirm key details with a top government official who also pushed the reporting in new directions, even if Felt wasn't regularly providing Woodward with new facts. Felt was careful to avoid detection from leak investigations, both by his actions, such as detailed tactics to throw off potential surveillance while the two met in an underground parking garage at two in the morning, as well by the piecemeal approach Felt took in providing Woodward with information.[36] By making reporters go elsewhere for initial information and by limiting what he confirmed to Woodward, Felt was also distancing himself from the leak investigations that were ongoing at the White House.[37] Woodward knew he couldn't contact Felt too often for fear of scaring him off, but Woodward also pushed Felt beyond their established ground rules, calling Felt at times and places when Felt told him not to, and occasionally brazenly violating the ground rules of attribution.[38]

One of the most interesting aspects of *The Secret Man* is Woodward's reflection on Felt's motives. Woodward wrote that at the time he did not think deeply about the reasons Felt might be helping him. "What was important was whether the information checked out and whether it was true," Woodward wrote.[39] But as the years passed,

Woodward often wondered why the second-in-command of the FBI would take such enormous risks to help a young reporter. Woodward said Felt "had clearly been torn, and even uncertain – not fully convinced that helping us was the proper course, wanting both to do it and not do it. Like many if not most confidential sources he wanted to be free of the ramifications of his actions and words. He wanted to be protected at nearly any cost, and he had gone to extraordinary lengths to conceal his identity."[40] Woodward concluded that Felt was acting in part on his belief that he was protecting the FBI "by finding a way, as clandestine as it was, to push some of the information from the FBI interviews and files out to the public, to help build public and political pressure to make the president and his men answerable."[41]

Woodward said that Felt understood the political power of newspaper stories, especially as he watched the White House effectively shut down lines of FBI inquiries in the early stages of the Watergate investigation.[42] In assessments after Nixon's resignation of the role of journalism in the Watergate affair, the impact of Woodward and Bernstein's reporting was downplayed by historians and the FBI, who claimed that investigators working outside of the public eye deserved the credit for unraveling the conspiracy.[43] Journalism historian Michael Schudson offered some evidence to the contrary, although his balanced assessment of the "myth" of Watergate seemed to suggest that the social and political effects of Woodward and Bernstein's reporting was something of an anomaly.[44] Woodward, as well as Felt, disagreed that the reporting was inconsequential. "Felt understood," Woodward wrote, "that the information wasn't going anywhere until it was public," adding:

> While the tapes prove that Nixon regularly ordered criminal action and abused government power, Mark Felt is important less for his name than for the position he held as No. 2 in the FBI. The system of justice had been so polluted and corrupted and politicized by Nixon and his men that the FBI could never get to the bottom of Watergate. The law and the rules had been set aside and subverted. Mark Felt was driven to expose what was going on. He had to do it his way. But without him, and it must be said, without countless others who talked as confidential sources and the prosecutors and Judge Sirica and the Senate and House, you never would or could have gotten to the Nixon tapes.[45]

Woodward and Watergate, in many ways, represent the idealized vision of journalistic duty to protect confidential sources. Woodward's careful navigation of his relationship with Felt helped the *Post* break important stories that helped the public better understand the extent of corruption inside the Nixon White House. Woodward's adherence to what he called "rigid source protection" established his journalistic bona fides with colleagues and sources alike. The clandestine, if not bizarre, meetings between Woodward and Deep Throat, shaped a romantic vision of the crusading investigative journalist and the meritorious whistleblower. A generation of journalists sought their own Deep Throats in their attempt to be the last and best hope for the public airing of truth and justice. As Alicia C. Shepard wrote in the introduction to her book, *Woodward and Bernstein: Life in the Shadow of Watergate*: "Over and over in reporting this book, I heard men and women say they had gone into journalism solely because of what Woodward and Bernstein accomplished. There's a nary a journalism class that does not tell the tale of what many call journalism's finest hour or show the movie *All the President's Men*."[46]

ETHICAL DIMENSIONS OF CONFIDENTIALITY

Journalism ethics serve several purposes. They support normative ideals of democracy, set forth the obligations journalists have to advance those ideals, and provide parameters for practical decision-making. When journalists speak of a duty and a right to protect confidential sources, they enter an interrelated discourse of journalism ethical theory, free-press theory and democratic theory. A brief discussion of the ethical sphere is important to show how interrelated legal and political problems are when it comes to using and protecting confidential sources. In arguing that protection of confidential sources is central to key normative social and political functions of journalism in American democracy, journalism ethical discourse provides a common language for discussing the values and appropriate practices with using and protecting confidential sources.

Several scholars have argued that one of the most important purposes of journalism ethics is in justifying journalism's importance to democracy.[47] The idea that journalists have responsibilities to the public related to enhancing democratic ideals is a critical tenet of Walter Lippmann's influential critiques in the 1920s of the press's failure to serve as expert mediators between the public and decision-makers. Professor Stephen J.A. Ward treats the history of journalism ethics as part of a "rhetorical theory of value change" in which journalism ethics establish, maintain and enhance journalistic credibility during different historical periods. Dave Iggers emphasizes the "public interest" values of journalism ethics and suggests that "the most fruitful work in the field of journalism ethics" is "not in the area of abstract moral theory, but in the area of politics: creating an alliance between journalists and the public."

One journalism ethics framework in examining journalistic duty looks at the *functions, principles and practices* of journalism as the concepts have emerged in the field of journalism ethics. Separately, Professor Louis W. Hodges suggests there are "three levels of responsibility" that "can be seen to encompass journalism ethics in its entirety." The first level involves the functions or social roles of journalism. The second level involves the principles that should guide the press to serve its proper functions, and the third level examines the actions that journalists should or should not take to serve the principles. This framework of functions, principles and practices lets us think about journalism in general and the journalist's privilege in particular.

Functions. In examining the responsibilities of journalists as they relate to the functions of journalism, Hodges identifies four journalism functions or roles.[48] The first is the political function. By informing citizens about government and other centers of power, and scrutinizing the activities of those in power, journalists are themselves an important part of the political process. The second function is an educational one. By reporting on and promoting discussion of ideas, opinions and facts, journalists serve as facilitators of a metaphorical town meeting. The third function of journalism is as a "utility" that serves as society's "bulletin board." The fourth function is as a "mirror" of society that "reflects the kind of people we are" by showing people "our heroes and villains" and "our shared values."[49] Hodges' functions framework helps us consider what types of journalistic standards can help journalists serve democratic, information-dissemination, bulletin board or mirroring functions.

Other articulations of journalistic functions focus on the political and social roles of journalism. In an important collection of essays published in 2005 as part of Oxford University Press's series titled *Institutions of American Democracy*, Professor James Curran argues that the media generally "need to be understood in relation to the wider political environment" and suggests that the media are one of several "intermediary" systems that can enhance and support democratic values of representation, deliberation, conflict resolution, accountability, and information dissemination.[50] Journalism, and the media more broadly, has been examined for its contributions to the "marketplace of ideas,"[51] of "agenda setting,"[52] in serving as "watchdogs,"[53] in informing the public of news,[54] and in mobilizing citizen participation.[55] Notably, many of the articulations of journalistic duty to protect sources invoke these functional ideals.

Principles. Ideas about these social and political functions of journalism have created principles and values to guide journalistic decision-making. Some of these principles have developed as a result of the professionalization of journalism. Journalistic "objectivity," for example, became a common expectation of American newspaper reporters beginning in the late 19th century as a result of both commercial and professional developments.[56] Although there are significant definitional debates, the idea of journalistic objectivity remains a central tenet of modern journalism ethics.[57] Some of these definitions emphasize balance and fairness in content; others suggest that readers should be able to see the possibility of different conclusions based on the presentation of facts and evidence.[58]

Professor Edmund Lambeth's synthesis of key journalistic principles helps us examine when source protection is appropriate, and when competing interests may dictate less than absolutist protections. For example, the principles of truth-telling and justice are central to a journalist's responsibility; they are ingrained in the moral compass of the ideal journalist. In the context of assessing a response to attempts at compelled disclosure of confidential sources, should a journalist consider whether breaking a confidential promise ultimately serves the principles of truth telling and justice? A discussion of the *Cohen v. Cowles Media* case later in this chapter illustrates this tension between principles.

While journalists generally agree upon the existence of a principle of duty to protect confidential sources, there is not universal agreement about its appropriate limits. Later chapters will show how journalists have occasionally argued for an absolute legal right to protect sources. For example, many journalist organizations pushed hard for absolutist protections during the congressional debates over shield legislation in the 1970s, refusing to support bills calling for limited qualifications to the privilege.[59] Quite separate from the legal absolutism is the question of when, as a matter of ethics, journalists can, or should, break promises of confidentiality.

Practices and standards. From these concepts of responsibility and functions, we can begin to assess key norms and practical standards of journalism. If ethics is generally the evaluation of what is good, codes of ethics provide firmer advice that governs journalistic practices and establishes professional norms. The Society of Professional Journalists code of ethics summarizes a journalist's four primary ethical principles: Seek truth and report it. Minimize harm. Act independently. Be accountable.[60] The primary responsibility of journalists, according to the preamble, is to serve justice and democracy by "seeking truth and providing a fair and comprehensive account of events and issues."[61] Professor Robert M. Entman articulated five "defining standards and behavioral traits of traditional journalism activity" that focus on accuracy, balance, journalistic autonomy as separate from profit maximization, democratic accountability, and separation between news and opinion.[62] In *Elements of Journalism: What Newspeople Should Know and the Public Should Expect,* an often-cited study of the principles of journalism, Bill Kovach and Tom Rosenstiel argue that the first principle is that the "purpose of journalism is to provide people with the information they need to be free and self-governing."[63] The authors' study, which drew from testimony of 300 journalists at 21 public forums, more than 100 three-and-a-half hour interviews, and two national surveys, articulated nine corresponding principles of journalism: (1) journalism's first obligation is to the truth; (2) journalism's first loyalty is to citizens; (3) journalism's essence is a discipline of verification; (4) journalists must maintain an independence from those they cover; (5) journalists must serve as an independent monitor of power; (6) journalism must provide a forum for public criticism and compromise; (7) journalism must strive to make the significant interesting and relevant; (8) journalism must keep the news comprehensive and proportional; and (9) journalists must be allowed to exercise their public conscience.[64]

In articulating these principles, Kovach and Rosenstiel offer both a description of conventional journalism practices and a justification for those principles based on democratic values and ideals of citizenship. While these descriptions may provide the definition of the ideal form of journalism, at least in terms of civic virtue, in practice, principled journalistic decision-making often involves a balancing of interests, because in many situations one can find competing principles. Scholars Jay Black, Bob Steele and Ralph Barney, for example, see three guiding principles often at odds with one another:

> (1) seeking and reporting as much truthful, accurate, and significant news as possible using honest, fair, and courageous newsgathering and reporting methods;
> (2) acting independently from sources, subjects, and others who would unfairly manipulate the news coverage to their own advantages and counter to the public interest; and
> (3) minimizing the harm and discomfort that journalism often entails, and treat sources, subjects and colleagues as human beings deserving of respect, not merely as means to journalistic ends.[65]

Ethics, generally, can be thought of as a process of determining what is "right" or "good." Professor Ward defines ethics as "the analysis, evaluation and promotion of correct conduct and/or good character, according to the best available standards."[66] Ward's articulation of an ethical journalist is as "an impartial communicator of important news and views to the public and from the impartial perspective of the public; using responsible and accurate methods of newsgathering, for the sake of a self-governing citizenship."[67]

Hodges' framework of functions and Lambeth's framework of principles provide one basis for an analysis of the journalist's privilege as an ethical construct that allows us to better understand the process of moral reasoning by journalists in their uses and defenses of confidential sources, and encourages us to raise questions about the competing values that might sometimes be minimized or overlooked by journalists seeking to avoid legal entanglement in compelled disclosure cases.

Hodges categorizes responsibility into three types: assigned, contracted and self-imposed. Journalists are not assigned responsibilities by the government beyond "negative" duties, such as the responsibility not to be libelous or to invade personal privacy. Certainly, news organizations assign responsibilities to journalists, and these employment conditions can also be viewed as contractual responsibilities. Journalists can also view their responsibility to society generally, or their readers specifically, as contractual. Journalists can also set high standards of responsibility for themselves, often framed in terms of personal identity. Hodges offers as an example an individual who describes himself as "I am a journalist" rather than "I work for the newspaper" as demonstrative of this concept.

Ultimately, questions requiring serious ethical debate by journalists can be answered only through rigorous analysis, reflection and justification. Writing in 1992, Lambeth suggested the following guidelines for ethical decision-making: (1) identify the principle or principles and the probable consequences considered and how they are weighted in reaching a decision; (2) assess the stakes of the parties affected by ethical choice: sources, public, the journalists involved, peers, and the profession at large; (3) minimize the chance that choices are based on mere personal impression, style, or whim; (4) show, in cases of conflicting principles or ambiguous forecasts of consequences, what values guide ethical choice; and (5) create, in truly major cases, a record on which others can draw and reflect, so as to make the benefits of dialogue cumulative.[68]

Viewing ethics as the evaluation of "good" or "right" conduct and behavior, we can see how journalism ethics can be used to explain and justify journalistic practice to society. But because ethics is the application of principles and values, we can also see how competing visions of "right" behavior can result in different outcomes. We can look to principles and values, at a more abstract level, and look to the process of decision-making and the actions of journalists in particular circumstances. Almost immediately, we can see how principles clash with one another, how values are articulated differently, and how competing principles and values lead journalists to different conclusions.

In the journalist's privilege context, we can begin to see that journalistic duty to protect confidential sources can help journalists fulfill their social and political functions. Ultimately, the journalist's moral, ethical and legal claims are strongest when they can justify their work in the public interest. Demonstrating how confidential sources generally, and individual cases specifically, are beneficial to journalism's functions will be increasingly important in a skeptical legal environment, not to mention a social environment where journalism is increasingly shrinking as a forum of public information. Journalists need to acknowledge greater ethical ambiguities in journalist's privilege cases and recognize that history should require a healthy dose of skepticism about the importance of protecting all sources at all costs. While personal conscience may propel journalists to violate court orders and go to jail to protect sources, journalistic principles and values are complex and occasionally contradictory; the messy nature of confidential sources even further muddy the search for clear ethical guidelines and standards.

Consider the case of *Cohen v. Cowles Media* as an example of how journalists' conceptions of functions and principles led them to different decisions regarding confidential source protection. In the final days of the 1982 gubernatorial race in Minnesota, Dan Cohen, a political operative, leaked to four reporters documents showing that one candidate for lieutenant governor had been charged in 1969 with three counts of unlawful assembly and convicted in 1970 for petit theft, a conviction that was later vacated.[69] Cohen was unusually explicit in securing a promise of confidentiality from the journalists, having received advice from a journalism professor prior to making contact with the journalists.[70] His prepared comments included the following:

> I have some documents which may or may not relate to a candidate in the upcoming election, and if you will give me a promise of confidentiality – that is, that I will be treated as anonymous source, that my name will not appear in any material in connection with this, and you will also agree that you're not going to pursue with me a question of who my source is – then I'll furnish you with documents.[71]

The Associated Press ran a story about the documents abiding by its reporter's promise of confidentiality, while WCCO-TV, the CBS affiliate in Minneapolis, declined to air any story about them. The two daily newspapers, the Minneapolis *Star Tribune* and the St. Paul *Pioneer Press*, published stories about the documents – but also included the fact that they were leaked by Dan Cohen.[72] The campaign for which Cohen was working denied any involvement, and Cohen was fired by his employer.[73] By identifying Cohen, the newspapers broke the promises of confidentiality made by their reporters. Editors argued that newspapers have a duty to be honest with its readers. Publishing the allegations without revealing that they came from the opponent's camp would have led readers astray, the editors argued.[74] There was a clear conflict between a newspaper's obligation to publish full and accurate information on political affairs and its responsibility to honor promises of confidentiality. Cohen later recalled several phone calls from the newspaper reporters prior to publication, telling Cohen that the newspaper editors were second-guessing the reporters' promises of confidentiality. Reporters for both newspapers told Cohen they disagreed with their editors' decisions.[75]

The decision to "burn" their source, justified as being in the public interest, split the journalistic community. Floyd Abrams called the newspapers' behavior "reprehensible and damaging to all journalists," and legal affairs reporter Lyle Denniston said the editors' decisions to break reporter promises "is a straightforward, baldfaced ethical violation."[76]

Cohen sued the newspapers, alleging fraudulent misrepresentation and breach of contract. A jury ruled in Cohen's favor and awarded him $200,000 in compensatory damages and $500,000 in punitive damages.[77] The Minnesota Supreme Court reversed the lower courts, ruling that reporter-source agreements were not contracts in the legal sense, but, "what we have here, it seems to us, is an 'I'll-scratch-your-back-if-you'll-scratch mine' accommodation."[78] The appeal made its way to the Supreme Court of the United States, which ruled 5-4 that the First Amendment did not prohibit Cohen from suing on the grounds of *promissory estoppel,* a state-law cause of action that presumes responsibilities similar to contractual agreements in the absence of an explicit contract.[79]

The case presented the novel question of whether journalists could be held legally culpable for breaking promises of confidentiality to sources. The newspapers argued that the decision to name Cohen was made after considerable debate among many editors, and that "sometimes, however, journalists reluctantly will conclude that they must break a promise to a source in order to fulfill their obligation to their readers."[80] Many other journalists, however, argued that the Minnesota newspapers violated ethical standards by breaking a promise to a source. In their reply brief to the Supreme Court, the newspapers argued that ethical standards should not be relevant to the legal argument, citing the proposition in *Hustler v. Falwell,* a case involving a First Amendment defense to the intentional affliction of emotional distress tort, that while "a bad motive may be deemed controlling for purposes of tort liability in other areas of law, we think the First Amendment prohibits such a result in the area of public debate about public figures."[81]

The *Cohen* precedent created something of a paradox for journalists. The law and ethics of making and breaking promises were intertwined in a novel way. Journalists had long sought a legal right to protect sources based on their ethical duty; here a plaintiff was using evidence of ethical violations to support his legal claim. The divergent views of the editors and reporters clearly show the complexities of ethical decision-making when it comes to confidential sources. The reporters saw the issue in black-and-white terms – they knowingly and intentionally gave a promise of confidentiality to a source, and there was no overriding reason to break their promise.

The editors prioritized their duty to be truthful to readers. They viewed Cohen's leak as a political dirty trick that would unfairly tarnish the reputation of a political candidate days before an election. The principles of justice and truth, in the editors' eyes, required disclosure of Cohen's identity as the leaker. While couched in altruistic aims, the editors' decision underscored one major problem of journalism ethics, namely that almost any journalistic decision could be defended, albeit perhaps unpersuasively, as ethical so long as it had a tangential explanation in one of journalism's functions, principles, or values. Ethics, for all its value as a rhetorical and decision-making device, created very different views on the importance of absolutist confidential source protection.

THREATS TO FIRST AMENDMENT VALUES

Thus far, I've established that confidential sources are widely used in journalism and that despite the costs associated with using confidential sources, journalists believe confidential sources are important to their work. Journalists explain and justify their reliance on confidential sources using journalism ethical theory about the proper functions, principles and practices of ethical journalism. But these ethical ideals are closely connected with principles and values from free-press theory. Given the clashes that have arisen between journalists and the courts over the "right" to protect confidential sources, modern debates about confidential source protections are more often framed in legal theory.

Two legal theories of freedom of the press create a dichotomy between two key values: autonomy rooted in libertarian free-press values and social responsibility that is an essential component of journalism ethics. Among free-press theorists, that journalists have social responsibilities can itself be a controversial claim. In terms of questions of government regulation, for example, some media law scholars are uneasy about articulations of responsibility for fear that accountability measures will subsequently undermine free-press values.[82] The journalist's privilege draws on professional standards and practices and free-press values to assert a legal right that would enhance journalistic practice. In this sense, it is a call for legal recognition of a professional ethic. The privilege also is based entirely on concepts of journalistic responsibility: in order for journalists to properly fulfill their societal and political functions, they need to be able to gain information from confidential sources. The worry of some free-press advocates is that ethical and legal realms should be viewed separately, for fear that the law will be used to compel ethics and therefore undermine the libertarian tradition of freedom of the press.[83]

The theory that journalists have responsibilities to the public was most importantly articulated in 1947 in a report titled *A Free and Responsible Press,* written by the Commission on Freedom of the Press. Central to the Commission's report was the belief that the news media have a duty to provide citizens with the information they need to be actively engaged in self-government, and that failure to serve the public interest may require intervention of the state. In the influential *Four Theories of the Press,* a landmark 1956 study of competing views of press rights, social responsibility theory was contrasted with libertarian theory, creating one theoretical dichotomy for assessing the role of regulation in the press. Several scholars, including Professors Robert E. Drechsel and William Van Alstyne, have argued that the assertion that journalists have special responsibilities, and therefore deserve special legal rights, will invite government regulation when journalists fail to live up to those responsibilities. They have warned against embracing social responsibility theory because of its invitation for greater government regulation of expression. When speech and press are not related to the "public interest," for example, does that make the expression vulnerable to regulation as a constitutional question?

The constitutional theories of freedom of the press are useful in examining the role of law in advancing journalism's functions and principles. Whether the First Amendment creates a journalist's privilege was the subject of a flurry of scholarship in the 1970s that examined the meanings of the press clause and considered whether the press clause was an individual right, largely viewed the same conceptually as the speech clause, or whether it provided some special rights to the institutional press, whether defined by "status" or "function." Decisions of the U.S. Supreme Court are important documents in this debate, as are analyses of Supreme Court decisions emphasizing press responsibility, including the work of Elizabeth Blanks Hindman and John C. Watson. Professors David Anderson and Leonard Levy have contributed significant historical analyses of press freedom that provide different views on the question of the original intent of the press clause, while a 1974 speech by Justice Potter Stewart is an influential call justifying an institutional rights view of the press clause. Alexander Meiklejohn's theory of the First Amendment as being essential for self-government and Vince Blasi's articulation of the checking value of the First Amendment are important to understanding journalism's functional roles. As elements of constitutional theory, this scholarship provides deeper understanding of *Branzburg v. Hayes,* the 1972 U.S. Supreme Court case that ruled journalists do not have a First Amendment right to avoid testifying before grand juries. In *Branzburg,* which is discussed in detail later, journalists had sought the transformation of their ethical duty into a constitutional right, which the Supreme Court declined to do.

Despite the Supreme Court's rejection of a constitutional journalist's privilege, over time the ethical duty has been conferred, at least in part, into law as a matter of legislation and through the common law. In terms of statutory law, legislative history and the text of legislation provide a framework for studying competing visions of the privilege and its legally defined limits. Equally important are judicial decisions expounding on the principles and functions of journalists. Judicial decisions also show the extent to which ethical and legal principles of the journalist's privilege clash with other important values, and offer some solutions that while intended as legal solutions also can aid in thinking about the ethical problems. For example, Judge David Tatel of the District of Columbia Circuit proposed a common law privilege in the Judith Miller case that included a "public-interest balancing" prong in the analysis, which required judges to balance the interest in compelled disclosure, measured by the harm the leak caused, against the public interest in newsgathering, measured by the leaked information's value. Judge Richard Posner of the Seventh Circuit, on the other hand, has ruled that the journalist's privilege has no foundation in the law, either as constitutional principle or as a common law rule. A number of judicially created tests clarify the competing interests posed by different types of journalist-source relationships.

Over the years, scholars have offered several reasons for protecting freedom of speech and press. Among them are that free expression furthers the search for truth, enables a true marketplace of ideas, results in self-fullfillment, serves as a "safety valve" for individuals, and acts as a "check" on those in power. One of the key roles of journalism – with roots in colonial newspaper practices and articulated as an ethical function as part of its professionalization movement in the late 19th century – is that of the institutional "watchdog," in which the journalist's privilege to protect confidential sources contributes to "right to know" and "checking value" theories of the press.

The importance of citizen access to government information is central to Alexander Meiklejohn's theory, which describes freedom of speech as a prerequisite to self-government and is as much a theory about American democracy as it is about the First Amendment. In 1897, Meiklejohn earned a Ph.D. in philosophy from Cornell University. He served as Amherst's president for 10 years before taking a faculty job at the University of Wisconsin-Madison in 1926, where he created the Experimental College. Later, he taught at the University of California-Berkeley, and became active in civil liberties issues. Meiklejohn first articulated his First Amendment theory in three lectures at the University of Chicago and published it in 1948 with the title *Free Speech and Its Relation to Self-Government*. In 1963, Meiklejohn was awarded the Presidential Medal of Freedom.[84]

Meiklejohn's theory has several components. He posited absolutist protection for speech about political affairs based on the notion that the government, as subordinate to the people, has no authority over the people to prohibit the discussion of political ideas. Understanding this dichotomy between the "rulers and the ruled" is important. The people as sovereign have ultimate power to make political decisions and therefore must be free to hear all ideas, no matter how threatening to political stability. Meiklejohn elaborated on the process of political decision-making through a metaphor of a town hall meeting. Finally, his theory labeled speech unrelated to self-governance as "private" speech governed not by the First Amendment but by the due process clause of the Fifth Amendment.

Meiklejohn developed his theory in response to the emerging interpretation of the First Amendment by the U.S. Supreme Court in the early part of the 20th century. Meiklejohn opposed the "clear and present danger" standard that was being used by the Supreme Court beginning with the 1919 *Schenck v. U.S.* decision. He wrote at the time that the ruling in the case "annuls the most significant purpose of the First Amendment" and "destroys the intellectual basis of our plan of self-government."[85] The Supreme Court's attempt to define "the line" between protected and unprotected speech ran afoul of basic self-governing values, Meiklejohn argued. The Constitution, he said, allows for unqualified debate among legislators on the floors of Congress. They would not be arrested and prosecuted for criticizing the draft, as was Schenck, because the concept was germane to self-government. The public discussion by citizens "shall have the same immunity," Meiklejohn concluded. "In the last resort, it is not our representatives who govern us. We govern ourselves, using them."

This concept of sovereignty over political discussion is central to understanding Meiklejohn. As sovereign, the people come together to govern themselves. Here, Meiklejohn draws on an extended metaphor of a town hall meeting, where the purpose is not that every person is able to talk as much as he or she wants, but that every idea gets a fair hearing. In one of Meiklejohn's most quoted lines, he says, "What is essential is not that everyone shall speak, but that everything worth saying shall be said."[86] Meiklejohn's theory is closely related to the "marketplace of ideas" theory of the First Amendment because both advance an argument that speech is a means to more fruitful end, either as a tool in the search for truth among competing views or as a tool to further the collective governing interests through reasoned analysis and debate.

Under both the "right to know" and "marketplace of ideas" theories, the role of journalists can be explained as helping citizens further their goals of searching for truth and maintaining an informed electorate. The "checking value" theory of the First Amendment also underscores the social and political functions of journalism as a watchdog of government and society. In a 1977 essay entitled "The Checking Value in First Amendment Theory," Professor Vince Blasi argued that a core purpose of the First Amendment's speech and press clauses was to prevent the abuse of official power.[87] The checking value theory presumes a more cynical view than other First Amendment theories by asserting that political power often breeds corruption, and free speech can be an antidote to abuses of power. Blasi compiled a wide range of historical and empirical evidence to support his theory, including rooting in the practices of colonial America and in the original intent of the Framers. Blasi recounted the role newspapers and opposition political parties played in politics in 18th century England, which served as a powerful basis for the Framers of Constitution to value freedom of the press. Such skepticism of government, and the need for external checks, is present in many of the underlying philosophers and theorists whose work inspired the Constitution. It also had a presence in England during colonial times. John Wilkes, a member of the British parliament, published a journal in the 1760s attacking the king, and concluded: "The liberty of the press is a birth-right of a Briton, and is justly esteemed the firmest bulwark of liberties in this country. It has been the terror of all bad ministers" by exposing misdeeds to the public.[88] From "Cato's Letters," the influential collection of essays, to James Madison's Virginia Report of 1799-1800, it is clear that skepticism of powerful government officials was an important value in colonial American times. James Madison's arguments in particular show that among the primary purposes of the First Amendment is to allow scrutiny of public officials by the press. Blasi concludes: "Indeed, if one had to identify the single value that was uppermost in the minds of the persons who drafted and ratified the First Amendment, this checking value would be the most likely candidate."[89]

The checking value theory is thoroughly rooted in modern Supreme Court constitutional doctrine as well. Blasi noted that in *Miami Herald v. Tornillo*, when striking down a Florida statute that required newspaper editors to print replies from candidates for public office who were attacked in print, Justice White noted that the press must act "as a powerful antidote to any abuses of power by government officials and as a constitutionally chosen means for keeping officials elected by the people responsible to all the people whom they were selected to serve."[90] The justices, Blasi wrote, recognized that government intervention into editorial decisions on what to print in newspapers "would strike at the heart of some important values implicit in the concept of freedom the press."[91] In *Near v. Minnesota*, the court struck down a law allowing a judge to stop the publication of a newspaper deemed to be a public nuisance. The court noted the press's special role in society as checking government abuses:

> Meanwhile, the administration of government has become more complex, the opportunities for malfeasance and corruption have multiplied, crime has grown to most serious proportions, and the danger of its protection by unfaithful

officials and of the impairment of the fundamental security of life and property by criminal alliances and official neglect, emphasizes the primary need of a vigilant and courageous press, especially in great cities.[92]

As professional watchdogs of government, journalists serve as an important exemplar of the checking value theory. He further argued that abuse of official power by the government is a particularly grave evil that is important to guard against. Blasi argued that this evil is separate from other society and business evils in part because of government's ability to exercise ultimate control over its citizens by legitimized violence: "The threat posed by the totalitarian state represents, to my mind, the overriding problem of twentieth-century politics."[93] In addition to the ability to throw a person in jail indefinitely, government has the ability to covertly investigate people, subpoena them, search their homes and businesses, and collect vast amounts of data about them. The public employees who are given this ability to control others can "acquire an inflated sense of self-importance, often a critical first step on the road to misconduct."[94] Blasi went so far as to suggest that most of human suffering is caused by the misconduct of public officials who work in a vast and complex government bureaucracy. To avoid totalitarianism, critics of government must be given access and audience. Blasi posited a positive view of journalists in which he argued that the press's reporting of misconduct will spark public outrage, which will in turn right the wrongs of the misconduct. An obvious outcome of Blasi's theory is the view that journalists should have some special rights under the constitution to fulfill their important social and political functions. Blasi wrote, "A proponent of the checking value should treat requests by journalists to view government activities and inspect official records as embodying First Amendment interests of the highest order."[95] One First Amendment scholar, David A. Anderson, noted: "(Blasi's) view of the press clause seems so thoroughly supported by the legislative history that one may wonder why it has not been universally accepted."[96]

Meiklejohn and Blasi's theories suggest that journalism ethics, through its articulation of functions, principles and appropriate practices, serves to enhance First Amendment values.

Thus far, this chapter has provided an introduction to the concept of journalistic duty to protect sources by examining the nature of confidential sources in modern journalism and related ethical and legal theories. The chapter has described the professional benefits as well as perils of using confidential sources and argued that journalistic duty to protect confidential sources is rooted in conceptions of journalism's social and political functions, which can be viewed through different frameworks of journalism ethics and First Amendment theory. These frameworks provide a means for further analysis of the ethical and legal problems that can arise when journalists use and protect confidential sources.

INVESTIGATION OF HISTORICAL, LEGAL AND ETHICAL QUESTIONS

So far, we can see that no "one-size-fits-all" theory can explain how journalists should respond to attempts to identify confidential sources. The typology of sources and leaks make generalizations difficult, and the value of confidential sources is undermined, at least in public opinion, by journalistic abuses of confidential sources. In cultivating and protecting confidential sources in their roles as watchdogs of government and in keeping the public informed about public affairs, reporters and editors are acting on fundamental journalistic principles. But at times, journalists are confronted with competing principles and values, as well as professional and personal questions about the limits of duty to protect source confidentiality when confronted with legal orders.

Leaks and unauthorized disclosures of information raise a number of thorny issues. Recent cases reveal both the absolutist tendencies of journalists and the difficult ethical and legal questions associated with them. For example, some news organizations have resisted attempts to force journalists to simply verify in court the veracity of facts they reported in news stories. Journalists have gone to jail for refusing to help open criminal investigations, including one who refused to reveal the location of a woman the journalist interviewed who was accused of defying a custody order and kidnapping her 8-year-old daughter. Journalists have fought attempts to turn over material that the initial sources wanted made public. Josh Wolf spent seven months in jail over a videotape of events on a public street. In other cases, journalists have sought to keep secret information that could prove the guilt or innocence of an individual on trial. For example, the initial investigation in the Valerie Plame leak case sought to establish whether high-ranking officials in the administration of President George W. Bush broke the law in intentionally unmasking the identity of a CIA agent in an attempt to undermine a critic of the administration's rationale for invading Iraq.

However, journalists are not of one mind about these questions. In the Valerie Plame case, for example, some journalists cooperated with prosecutors after being presented with so-called waivers of confidentiality, signed by their government sources at the request of prosecutors. Judith Miller rejected the waivers as meaningless, but after 85 days in jail, she had a change of heart and had her attorneys negotiate a waiver with her source. News organizations and editors issued new policies stating their willingness to reveal sources after legal appeals are exhausted. One news organization turned over a reporter's notes revealing a confidential source, against the wishes of the individual journalist.

The cases raised a number of questions of historical and normative questions of journalism ethics. How is that journalists generally share an ethical code that justifies ignoring a valid court order? Are all confidential source promises the same, or should journalists make distinctions based on the content of the leaked material or the motives of leakers? Should journalists be more willing to break promises if the leak itself was a potential crime? How should journalists react when their sources lie about their communication publicly or in court? When should journalists agree to identify a source after the source has "waived" a promise? Questions about the ethics of media institutions were also raised. How should journalists communicate about confidential sources with their editors and corporate owners? How should journalists organize their notes and store materials that might identify confidential sources?

Many of the questions became even more difficult to grapple with when confronted with an ambiguous legal environment. What does a promise of confidentiality require of journalists and their employers? What is expected of journalists when the law compels them to provide testimony? How should journalists go about evaluating situations in which they are called upon to break promises? What range of approaches might be used? How should journalists balance the potential legal vulnerabilities with the duty to publish important stories? If the privilege is not absolute as an ethical matter, is still appropriate as an ethical matter to violate a final court order and go to jail in contempt? Is jail ever *required* as an ethical matter?

The legal protections that have been established, dating to the earliest cases of the 19th century and the first state statute in 1896, are largely a result of the social and political utility of the privilege as a concept that developed in the realm of journalism ethics. In assessing the how legislative and judicial remedies developed, we can see how journalists and legal players have advanced ideas about journalism's functions and principles to support their decisions to protect confidentiality. We can see, for example, how the typology of the leak might factor into the analysis, as did the public interest in the content of the information. When the confidential source can be justified in terms of journalism's fundamental principles, source protection may be strongest, at least politically. But there are many legitimate and necessary types of confidential sources beyond the paradigm example of the whistleblower who provides journalists with important information of high public value that might otherwise remain secret. The uncertainty over protections does have some social value by allowing for an evolutionary assessment of the journalists' claims in the political and judicial branches of government, an assessment that requires journalists to justify their work in broader societal and political terms.

While journalistic independence, keeping promises and protecting confidential sources are important values, so too are judicial principles of truth-seeking and justice. How do journalists reconcile their principles and values with those of other institutions? For starters, they can recognize that the ethical domain is not absolutist either. Several journalists and scholars, including Jack Fuller, Anthony Lewis, Lillian BeVier, and Geoffrey Stone, have supported legal protections but have criticized journalists' absolutist proclivities as unreasoned and troubling. If as a matter of ethics confidential source protection is not an absolutist ideal and can be betrayed with a final court order without ethical violation, then such absolutisms are a bad idea in law. Because of the importance of confidential source protection to democratic and free press values, the state must put up with some forms of abuse, while journalists have a responsibility to minimize abuse or risk retreat in legal protections. This is a delicate balance.

Ultimately, this book makes the claim that in recognizing a qualified right of journalists to protect confidential sources – similar to testimonial privileges that exist for doctors, lawyers and therapists –

judges and legislators have sanctified in law a concept that first emerged in the ideology of journalism ethics and practice. By examining the history of journalistic duty that underlies the legal framework, this research suggests that concepts of journalistic ethics should figure more prominently in resolving modern disputes. The research finds that journalists have historically framed their uses of confidential sources in utilitarian and public-interest defenses – a finding important to recent debates over public-interest balancing at the center of current common law and statutory proposals. Journalism ethics and standards will be crucial in defining the contours of this balancing.

Exploring these legal, policy and ethical questions related to the journalist's privilege – and the difficult balancing that can occur in those realms – is the goal of subsequent chapters. The next two chapters set forth modern dilemmas. Chapter four examine the historical development of the journalist's privilege, investigating how the concept developed in the profession in the late 19th century and was used in courts and legislatures to advocate a corresponding legal right. Chapters five, six and seven trace the evolution of the journalist's privilege in constitutional, common and statutory law. Chapter eight asks whether bloggers are journalists for purpose of protection and how the relationship between ethics and law will inform the future of the journalist's privilege.

Chapter 1 Notes

---

[1] NORMAN PEARLSTINE, OFF THE RECORD: THE PRESS, THE GOVERNMENT, AND THE WAR OVER ANONYMOUS SOURCES 259 (2007).

[2] Vince Blasi, *The Newsman's Privilege: An Empirical Study,* 70 MICHIGAN LAW REVIEW 229 (1971-1972) and John E. Osborn, *The Reporter's Confidentiality Privilege: Updating the Empirical Evidence After a Decade of Subpoenas,* 17 COLUM. HUM. RTS. L. REV. 57 (1985).

[3] ELLIOT C. ROTHENBERG, THE TAMING OF THE PRESS: COHEN V. COWLES MEDIA COMPANY 167 (1989), citing 73 Minn. L. Rev. 1553 (1989).

[4] Alicia C. Shepard, *Anonymous Sources,* AMERICAN JOURNALISM REVIEW, December 2004.

[5] Sherrie L. Wilson, William A. Babcock and John Pribek, *Newspaper Ombudsmen's Reactions to Use of Anonymous Sources,* 18 NEWSPAPER RESEARCH JOURNAL 143 (1997).

[6] NORMAN PEARLSTINE, OFF THE RECORD: THE PRESS, THE GOVERNMENT, AND THE WAR OVER ANONYMOUS SOURCES 259 (2007).

[7] New York Times Company, Confidential News Sources Policy, March 1, 2004, *available at* http://www.nytco.com/company/business_units/sources.html (last visited June 1, 2009).

[8] *Id.*

[9] ELIE ABEL, LEAKING: WHO DOES IT? WHO BENEFITS? AT WHAT COST? 2 (1987).

[10] *Id.*

[11] STEPHEN HESS, THE GOVERNMENT/PRESS CONNECTION: PRESS OFFICERS AND THEIR OFFICES (1984).

[12] Abel, *supra* note 9, at 20.

[13] *Id.* at 62.

[14] *Id.*

[15] *Id.*

[16] Branzburg v. Hayes, 408 U.S. 665, at 728.

[17] RonNell Andersen Jones, *Avalanche or Undue Harm? An Empirical Study of Subpoenas Received by the News Media,* 93 MINN. L.R. 588 (2008).

[18] See Shepard, *supra* note 4.

[19] *Id.*

[20] *Id.*

[21] Dick Thornburgh & Louis D. Boccardi, *Report of the Independent Review Panel, On the September 8, 2004 60 Minutes Wednesday Segment "For*

the Record" Concerning President Bush's Texas Air National Guard Service, January 5, 2005, *available at* http://wwwimage.cbsnews.com/htdocs/pdf/complete_report/CBS_Report.pdf (last visited July 15, 2009).

[22] Clark Hoyt, *Culling the Anonymous Sources*, N.Y. TIMES, June 8, 2008.

[23] JEREMY IGGERS, GOOD NEWS, BAD NEWS: JOURNALISM ETHICS AND THE PUBLIC INTEREST 38 (1999) at 11.

[24] American Society of Newspaper Editors, Statement of Principles, *available at* http://www.asne.org/index.cfm?ID=888 (last visited June 1, 2009).

[25] Society of Professional Journalists, Code of Ethics, available at http://www.spj.org/ethics_code.asp (last visited June 1, 2009).

[26] DAVID H. WEAVER, THE AMERICAN JOURNALIST IN THE 21ST CENTURY 162 (2007).

[27] Walter Pincus, *Anonymous Sources: Their use in a time of prosecutorial interest*, Nieman Watchdog, July 6, 2005, available at: http://www.nieman.harvard.edu/reportsitem.aspx?id=101098 (last visited June 1, 2009).

[28] *Id.*

[29] ALICIA C. SHEPARD, WOODWARD AND BERNSTEIN: LIFE IN THE SHADOW OF WATERGATE xi (2007).

[30] BOB WOODWARD, THE SECRET MAN: THE STORY OF WATERGATE'S DEEP THROAT 184 (2005).

[31] *Id.*

[32] *Id.*

[33] John D. O'Connor, *I'm the Guy They Called Deep Throat*, VANITY FAIR, July 2005.

[34] Woodward, *supra* note 30, at 17.

[35] *Id.* at 39-40.

[36] *Id.* at 106.

[37] *Id.*

[38] *Id.*

[39] *Id.* at 104.

[40] *Id.* at 5.

[41] *Id.* at 104.

[42] *Id.* at 186.

[43] *Id.*

[44] *See* MICHAEL SCHUDSON, WATERGATE IN AMERICAN HISTORY: HOW WE REMEMBER, FORGET, AND RECONSTRUCT THE PAST 103 (1992).

[45] Woodward, *supra* note 30, at 121.

[46] Shepard, *supra* note 29, at xiii.

[47] Journalism's potential to serve democratic ideals has been the subject of a number of recent books, including JEFFREY SCHEUER, THE BIG PICTURE: WHY DEMOCRACIES NEED JOURNALISTIC EXCELLENCE (2008), and MICHAEL SCHUDSON WHY DEMOCRACIES NEED AN UNLOVABLE PRESS *(2008)*. Both make the case that journalism, as defined by modern conceptions of ethical and professional standards, is important to the quality of democracy.

[48] Louis W. Hodges, *Defining Press Responsibility: A Functional Approach,* in DENI ELLIOT, RESPONSIBLE JOURNALISM 13 (1986).

[49] *Id.* at 21.

[50] James Curran, *What Democracy Requires of the Media*, in GENEVA OVERHOLSER AND KATHLEEN HALL JAMIESON (eds), THE PRESS 120 (2005).

[51] Robert Schmuhl and Robert G. Picard, *The Marketplace of Ideas,* in GENEVA OVERHOLSER AND KATHLEEN HALL JAMIESON (eds), THE PRESS 141 (2005).

[52] Maxwell McCombs, *The Agenda-Setting Function of the Press,* GENEVA OVERHOLSER AND KATHLEEN HALL JAMIESON (eds), THE PRESS 156 (2005).

[53] W. Lance Bennett and William Serrin, *The Watchdog Role,* in GENEVA OVERHOLSER AND KATHLEEN HALL JAMIESON (eds) THE PRESS 169 (2005).

[54] Thomas Patterson and Philip Seib, *Informing the Public,* in GENEVA OVERHOLSER AND KATHLEEN HALL JAMIESON (eds), THE PRESS 189 (2005).

[55] Esther Thorson, *Mobilizing Citizen Participation,* in GENEVA OVERHOLSER AND KATHLEEN HALL JAMIESON (eds), THE PRESS 203 (2005).

[56] DAVID T.Z. MINDICH, JUST THE FACTS: HOW 'OBJECTIVITY' CAME TO DEFINE AMERICAN JOURNALISM (1998).

[57] *Id.*

[58] *See generally* STEPHEN KLAIDMAN AND TOM L. BEAUCHAMP, THE VIRTUOUS JOURNALIST (1987).

[59] *See generally infra* chapter six.

[60] JEREMY IGGERS, GOOD NEWS, BAD NEWS: JOURNALISM ETHICS AND THE PUBLIC INTEREST 38 (1999).

[61] *Id.* at 38.

[62] Robert M. Entman, *The Nature and Sources of News*, in GENEVA OVERHOLSER AND KATHLEEN HALL JAMISON (eds), THE PRESS 54 (2005).

[63] BILL KOVACH AND TOM ROSENSTIEL, THE ELEMENTS OF JOURNALISM: WHAT NEWSPEOPLE SHOULD KNOW AND THE PUBLIC SHOULD EXPECT 12 (2001).

[64] *Id.* at 12-13.

[65] Iggers, *supra* note 60, at 23.

[66] Stephen J.A. Ward, *Researching Ethics, available at:* http://journalismethics.ca/research_ethics/approaches_to_ethics.htm (last visited Aug. 1, 2009).

[67] Stephen J.A. Ward, *Researching Ethics, available at:* http://journalismethics.ca/research_ethics/nature_of_journalism_ethics.htm (last visited August 1, 2009).

[68] EDMUND B. LAMBETH, COMMITTED JOURNALISM: AN ETHIC FOR THE PROFESSION 181-182 (1986).

[69] Cohen v. Cowles Media, 501 U.S. 663 (1991).

[70] *Id.*

[71] Rothenberg, *supra* note 3, at 2.

[72] *Id.*

[73] Cohen v. Cowles Media, 501 U.S. 663, at 666 (1991).

[74] Rothenberg, *supra* note 3, at 52-53.

[75] DAN COHEN, ANONYMOUS SOURCES: AT WAR AGAINST THE MEDIA, A TRUE STORY. 43 (2005).

[76] Petition for Writ of Certiorari to the Supreme Court of the State of Minnesota, Cohen v. Cowles Media Company, at 6.

[77] Cohen, 501 U.S. at 666.

[78] *Id.*

[79] Cohen, 501 U.S. at 668.

[80] Brief of Respondent Cowles Media Company, U.S. Supreme Court, October Term, 1990, at 22.

[81] *Id.* at 19.

[82] See, for example, Robert E. Drechsel, *Media Ethics and Media Law: The Transformation of Moral Obligation Into Legal Principle,* 6 NOTRE DAME J.L. ETHICS & PUB. POL'Y 5 (1992); Robert E. Drechsel, *Media Malpractice: The Legal Risks of Voluntary Social Responsibility in Mass Communication,* 27 DUQ. L. REV. 237 (1988); Robert E. Drechsel, *The Paradox of Professionalism: Journalism and Malpractice,* 23 UALR L. REV. 181 (2000) and William Van Alstyne, *The Hazards to the Press of Claiming a Preferred Position,* 28 HASTINGS L.J. 761 (1977).

[83] *Id.*

[84] PALLAVI GUNIGANTI, ALEXANDER MEIKLEJOHN: TEACHER AND CITIZEN (excerpted in VINCENT BLASI, IDEAS OF THE FIRST AMENDMENT 743 (2006).

[85] ALEXANDER MEIKLEJOHN, POLITICAL FREEDOM (1960) (This book contains the text of Meiklejohn's 1948 version of FREE SPEECH AND ITS RELATION TO SELF-GOVERNMENT), at 30.

[86] *Id.* at 26.

[87] Vince Blasi, *The Checking Value in First Amendment Theory*, 1977 AM. B. FOUND. RES. J. 521 (1977).

[88] *Id.* at 531.

[89] *Id.* at 527.

[90] *Id.* at 619, quoting Mills v. Alabama 384 U.S. 214, 219 (1966), and Miami Herald Publishing Co. v. Tornillo, 418 U.S. 241, 260 (1974).

[91] *Id.* at 621.

[92] Near v. Minnesota 283 U.S. 697 at 720.

[93] Blasi, *supra* note 87, at 538.

[94] *Id.* at 540.

[95] *Id.* at 610.

[96] David A. Anderson, *The Origins of the Press Clause,* 30 UCLA L. REV. 455 (1983).

CHAPTER 2

Modern Legal and Ethical Case Studies

The rights of journalists to protect the confidentiality of news sources grew in spurts and fits throughout the 20th century, including, paradoxically, immediately after the 1972 *Branzburg v. Hayes* ruling by the Supreme Court of the United States. But between 2001 and 2007, a clear retreat in legal protections occurred as six decisions by federal Courts of Appeals rejected journalists' arguments for the protection of confidential sources or other information acquired during newsgathering[1] As a result of court orders, some journalists identified their sources.[2] Several journalists were jailed, while others faced staggering fines for their defiance of legal orders.[3] Media lawyers decried the swift accumulation of negative precedent and lamented, not for the first time, that judicial decisions would have a chilling effect on journalists' ability to gather news, to the detriment of the free flow of information and the ability of the press to serve as a watchdog of government.[4] In short, journalists and their lawyers believed the failure of the law to embrace the journalist's privilege principle would undermine key social and political functions of journalism.

Read collectively, the decisions by the Courts of Appeal halted the slow but steady expansion of legal protections for journalists seeking to protect confidential sources in the federal courts. In 1972, journalists appeared to lose their legal fight to protect confidential sources, when the Supreme Court of the United States in *Branzburg v. Hayes* declined to create a First Amendment right of journalists to avoid testifying before grand juries.[5] But between 1972 and 2003, dozens of federal appellate decisions created a qualified constitutional privilege under some circumstances.[6] Somewhat separate from the constitutional privilege, many lower courts have also recognized a common-law privilege under the federal rules of evidence.[7] Additional statutory, constitutional and common law protections at the state level expanded after *Branzburg*. These developments, seemingly unlikely after *Branzburg*, were the result of a deeply ingrained journalism ethical doctrine of confidential source cultivation and a cadre of organized media lawyers to litigate cases. As a result, journalists only sporadically were compelled to reveal confidential information, and journalists who refused legal orders often received relatively minor sanctions and the support of their news organization. The upside of fighting a subpoena was the professional fame that came with becoming a martyr for freedom of the press.

The first signs of worry about the qualified federal privilege in recent times emerged in 2001 when federal prosecutors in Texas jailed Vanessa Leggett, a freelance writer and college English teacher who refused to turn over to the FBI every document related to a book she was writing about a high-profile murder.[8] Leggett spent 168 days in jail after the Fifth Circuit Court of Appeals refused to overturn her civil contempt holding and was released only after the expiration of a grand jury term.[9]

Then, in 2003 influential federal appellate Judge Richard Posner issued a peculiar decision in a case involving subpoenas to three Chicago journalists emanating from a domestic terrorism trial occurring in Ireland.[10] The defendant sought to use the reporters' notes and interview transcripts to impeach the credibility of a government witness who had granted interviews to the reporters. Posner's decision in *McKevitt v. Pallasch* dismissed the legal protections that had developed in most federal circuits as "skating on thin ice," and his decision rejecting any concept of a privilege gave ammunition to government and plaintiff attorneys in several other pending cases.[11] The decision was interpreted as eliminating a privilege in the Seventh Circuit, comprising Illinois, Wisconsin and Indiana, and quickly became cited by courts in other circuits not bound by its precedent but nonetheless drawn to it.[12]

A flurry of journalist privilege cases grabbed headlines following the *McKevitt* decision. In 2003, six reporters based in Washington, D.C., were subpoenaed to reveal sources who leaked them information about the espionage investigation of Wen Ho Lee, a nuclear scientist who was sensationally charged with espionage only to have a judge later release him and apologize for what he underwent at the hands of the government and media.[13] In 2004, Judith Miller and Philip Shenon of *The New York Times* had their phone records subpoenaed in a leak investigation regarding a terrorist plot, and the Second Circuit Court of Appeals upheld the subpoenas.[14] Rhode Island television journalist James Taricani was sentenced to six months of home confinement in 2004 after he refused to identify a confidential source who provided him with a videotape documenting a public corruption.[15] The subpoenas in the Valerie Plame case began in 2004, ensnarling nearly a dozen Washington reporters.[16] In 2005, federal prosecutors subpoenaed journalists for evidence against New York City defense attorney Lynne Stewart on charges of aiding terrorism, and one was forced to testify in Stewart's trial.[17] Also in 2005, federal prosecutors subpoenaed Lance Williams and Mark Fainaru-Wada of the *San Francisco Chronicle* for the identity of a confidential source who provided them with grand jury information about steroid use by professional baseball players, and they avoided jail sentences only after their source was identified by a third party.[18] In 2006, a *Detroit Free Press* reporter was subpoenaed by a former federal prosecutor who was seeking to learn who leaked criticism of his job performance in a terrorism trial.[19] In 2007, Steven Hatfill, in his lawsuit against the federal government for unlawful leaking of private information, subpoenaed six journalists, several of whom were held in contempt until the case was settled. [20] In 2008, James Risen was subpoenaed by a federal grand jury for the identity of sources related to a book about the history of the CIA, an effort that continued well into 2010.[21]

If the list of cases seems long, it is because the quick succession of publicized subpoenas was unprecedented, and with rare exception journalists lost their cases in the courts. While no data exist that precisely measure the numbers of subpoenas American journalists receive, one survey estimated that in 2006, more than 7,000 subpoenas were issued to American journalists, averaging almost 20 subpoenas a day. The study also concluded that the number of subpoenas had indeed increased from prior years.[22]

For journalists and media lawyers, the message from the courts was startling. Because media lawyers had been successful in quashing many subpoenas, many journalists had misconceptions about their legal vulnerabilities when dealing with confidential sources. "Many reporters didn't fully understand that the law wasn't necessarily on their side," said David McGraw, deputy general counsel for the *New York Times*.[23]

Robin Bierstedt of Time Inc., agreed. "Today the legal presumption is that the journalist loses. Before, the presumption was that the journalist would ultimately be left alone to protect his or her sources."[24] From the newsroom perspective, *New York Times* columnist David Carr noted that "within the news business, there is a consensus that the roof is caving in on the legal protections for working journalists."[25] Up until the mid 2000's, according to Lucy Dalglish, executive director of the Reporters Committee for Freedom of the Press, "journalists thought there'd be no problem in protecting a source, and if in a blue moon if they had to, if they were asked to reveal a source, they would gladly go to jail, and they were thinking of jail in terms of hours or days at most. Now we're in a completely different ball game."[26]

In addition to the increase in the number of subpoenas, the legal sanctions were becoming harsher. The three longest jail terms in American history for journalists refusing to turn over newsgathering material have all occurred since 2001: Vanessa Leggett served 168 days, Judith Miller served 85 days, and Josh Wolf spent 226 days in prison. The Valerie Plame case saw the use of the contempt power against a publicly held corporation as an influential coercive tool, not to mention the effective use of jail time to compel journalists to ultimately comply with subpoenas. Threats of personal bankruptcy also raised the stakes for journalists in new ways. For example, *USA TODAY* reporter Toni Locy was fined $500 a day for seven days, $1,000 a day for the next seven days, and $5,000 a day after that, and the judge ruled that no one else – including *USA TODAY* – could help Locy pay the fines.[27] The tactic was subsequently adopted by other prosecutors.[28] While the fines in the Locy case were stayed pending an appeal, and the case was settled before the subpoena appeal was heard, the case startled journalists and media lawyers because of its draconian novelty.[29]

The increase in subpoenas, the judicial hostility toward privilege claims, and the harsher coercive tactics raised not only legal problems for journalists, but ethical problems as well. Journalists were confronted with waivers of confidentiality and struggled with whether or not to accept them as meaningful waivers of their ethical obligation to protect confidential sources. Were journalists prohibited from talking to their sources about the source's wishes, or was that inappropriate after they made their initial promise of confidentiality? Was talking to a source after the issuance of a subpoena a form of obstruction of justice that would bring more legal problems?

The meanings of confidentiality also prompted editors to second-guess their reporters about what obligations are owed to news sources. Could a promise of confidentiality be implied as part of the conventions of journalist-source interactions, especially in areas of political, law enforcement, military and national security reporting? Do implicit promises require the same things of journalists as explicit promises? At *Time*, editor and reporters publicly disagreed about this question. Journalists also worried about the strength of their news organizations' support of their decisions. Some reporters faced dire personal consequences for violating court orders, including threats of personal bankruptcy and indefinite jail sentences, that required them to rationalize their decisions to both professional and personal expectations.

These were the "new" ethical questions, but there were also longstanding ones. Dating back to colonial times, journalists have gone to jail as an act of civil disobedience, arguing that an ethical duty justified the evasion of a valid and final court judgment. Just when, and if ever, are journalists morally justified in violating final court orders to protect confidential sources, or only some kinds of confidential sources? This question of a "right" to violate a final court order plagued the analysis inside Time Inc. during the Plame case. Another central question inside Time Inc., was to what extent confidential promises required different things from corporations and individuals. The distinctions here have important implications for reporter-editor relations, since most news organizations require that at least one editor know the identity of confidential source. Those policies may actually place editors and corporations in greater legal jeopardy in privilege cases. How should journalists balance their professional obligations with personal ones? In other words, ultimately what do journalists owe to their sources? To their employers? To the public? To themselves?

These and other questions and problems arose in the actual and threatened jailing of journalists between 2003 and 2007. This chapter presents three case studies as a window into the ethical issues raised by confidential source relationships, underscored here by the complex intersection with the law. This chapter does not present clear answers to these questions. Rather, the case studies that follow show why and how confidential source relationships can create difficult ethical and legal problems.

This chapter examines three cases in more detail. First, I discuss subpoenas to the *San Francisco Chronicle* and a Rhode Island television reporter, both involving the leak of information regarding grand jury investigations. The first case discussed here involved an investigation into the illegal use of steroids by elite athletes; the second case involved allegations of municipal public corruption. Second, I discuss two cases in which individuals subpoenaed journalists as part of civil cases against the government alleging inappropriate disclosure of private information. Third, I discuss the jailing of videoblogger Josh Wolf and discuss some of the issues associated with bloggers claiming privilege protection.

THE GRAND JURY LEAK CASES

Reporters for the *San Francisco Chronicle* smelled a story right away, when, on September 3, 2003, nearly two dozen law enforcement agents armed with rifles and handguns and monitored by police helicopters overhead, raided the offices of the Bay Area Laboratory Cooperative (BALCO), near the San Francisco airport on the outskirts of the city.[30] "The city desk was having a hard time getting anywhere on the story, and the government wouldn't tell anyone what they were doing down there," recalled reporter Lance Williams.[31] But the sports desk received tips linking the raid to a wider steroids investigation involving high-profile professional athletes, and within weeks, reporters had linked the raid to an investigation being conducted by the U.S. Anti-Doping Agency. An elementary web search had provided some juicy possibilities, as the BALCO website listed some of its most famous customers, including a number of top athletes in different sports.[32] The lab would later be accused of providing various types of performance-enhancing drugs, with names like The Cream and The Clear, that would not be detected by drug tests.[33]

At the time, professional baseball was under scrutiny for its failure to institute rules prohibiting steroid use, and anonymous steroid testing introduced in 2003 showed that seven percent of major league players were using steroids. So it was a big scoop when *Chronicle* sports reporter Mark Fainaru-Wada learned almost immediately after the BALCO raid that a federal grand jury had subpoenaed Barry Bonds, the San Francisco Giants left fielder dubbed the "Homerun King" and one of the most accomplished Major League players of all time. Other athletes, like Jason Giambi and Gary Sheffield of the New York

Yankees, would soon be connected with the investigation. "Almost immediately, Mark heard that Bonds had used steroids, and that's what this was about," Williams recalled. "And within a few days of me getting involved, I was introduced to a sort of universe of sources that Mark had not known about, who knew quite a bit about Bonds' use of steroids. So we were hearing about this from two totally different places almost immediately."

The two reporters worked together to develop separate lists of sources, many of whom provided tips and gossip in exchange for promises of confidentiality. Some were lawyers representing potential witnesses, while others were connected with law enforcement. The reporters and their editors decided early in their investigation that they would not use anonymous sources to accuse athletes of using performance-enhancing drugs, because such sourcing would make the allegations less credible to readers. They decided they needed the allegations on the record, or from documents. But early on, the confidential sources provided the context and gave them important clues on where to look for answers about the investigation. In an interview, Williams was hesitant to discuss in detail the quantity of confidential sources during the fall of 2003, but said there were more than fifty.[34]

In February 2004, four individuals associated with BALCO were indicted on several drug-conspiracy charges. There was no official mention of impropriety by any athletes, but, signaling the significance of the prosecution, the indictment was announced in Washington D.C., at a press conference by Attorney General John Ashcroft.[35] The trial judge issued a protective order prohibiting lawyers and the defendants from releasing to anyone discovery material, including grand jury transcripts.

The first stories linking Bonds and other high-profile professional athletes to the BALCO case appeared on March 2, 2004, in the *Chronicle*. By any journalism standards, the *Chronicle's* reporting was a major scoop. More than 200 newspapers reported the story the next day.[36] The *Chronicle* story reported that Bonds and six other professional athletes had obtained drugs from BALCO.[37] The next edition of *Sports Illustrated* carried a picture of Bonds on the cover with the headline, "Is Baseball in the Asterisk Era?" Within weeks, the revelations sparked a congressional investigation into professional baseball's steroid policies, and Arizona Senator John McCain said in one hearing that baseball was on the verge of "becoming a fraud."[38] A month later, the *Chronicle* obtained an investigative report that alleged BALCO had provided Olympians Marion Jones and Tim Montgomery with banned substances, and stories about their cheating dominated sports coverage leading up to the 2004 summer Olympics in Athens. But the most explosive headlines came in December 2004, when the *Chronicle* published stories based on the athletes' grand jury testimony.[39] The Yankee's Giambi was quoted as describing to the grand jury how he injected himself with human growth hormone, even though Giambi had publicly stated that he never used the substance.[40]

Throughout their reporting on the story, the reporters used dozens of sources who were promised confidentiality. "Very few people wanted to go on the record," Williams said.[41] The reporters spent hours talking to people loosely connected with the case, sharing tidbits about who knew what. The court record and subsequent stories about the case showed a wide network of potential sources – from lawyers to defendants to witnesses, as well as government agents. "The appeal to everyone we talked to was, Do you really think it's fair that the dope dealers have 42 felony counts and the millionaire athletes didn't even get their names in the paper?" said Williams.[42] At the time, it appeared that the BALCO owners would get lengthy jail sentences and the athletes would be left untouched – a fundamental injustice in the minds of many who were closely following the case. While few of the stories used anonymous quotes, promises of confidentiality were crucial to understanding the big picture of the investigation. "Usually it was an anonymous source giving us documents or tapes or pointing us to other things," Williams said.[43]

While their journalistic peers were envious of their scoops, others did not look kindly on the journalists' disclosure of confidential court information. The judge overseeing the BALCO prosecutions asked the Department of Justice to investigate the December 2004 leak of the grand jury transcripts, and agents raided the home of BALCO's owner under the suspicion that he had provided the transcripts to the reporters. But by the spring of 2005, the reporters hadn't been contacted and they thought nothing more would come of the investigation. They also took comfort in praise from President George W. Bush, who they met at a White House press corps' reception held to honor award-winning reporting. "We introduced ourselves, and he knew our reporting and immediately said, 'You've done a service,'" Williams recalled.[44] The president, himself a former baseball team owner, talked to the reporters about steroids in baseball and the recent disclosures of steroid use by Jose Conseco, who had just published a tell-all book. The president had also drawn attention to the steroid problem in his 2004 State of the Union speech, in which he criticized professional athletes for sending the message to kids that cheating is acceptable in sports. After the president again complimented their reporting at the end of their conversation, "We thought, well, certainly they won't come after us now," Williams said.[45]

The reporters were wrong. In May 2006, the U.S. Attorney in San Francisco issued subpoenas to Fainaru-Wada and Williams seeking the identity of their source of the grand jury transcripts. At the time the stories ran, the reporters had only limited discussions about how they might respond to subpoenas, mostly because they thought the possibility was unlikely. "At the time, it was a different world," Williams said. "*Branzburg* was still on the books, of course, but the Justice Department was still reticent about subpoenaing reporters. We didn't have a particular concern." In fact, as Williams remembers, most of the legal discussions with editors revolved around defamation issues and the libel liability from sourcing information to non-public government-produced documents. "We knew it was grand jury material and we knew they'd be mad, but we didn't think we'd get a [subpoena] out of it," Williams recalled.[46] After receiving the subpoenas, the reporters discussed how to respond. They decided against hiring their own attorneys separate from the newspaper, in part for fears of prosecutors wedging the reporters against the Hearst Corporation, the *Chronicle's* owners. The paper's editor, Phil Bronstein, knew the identity of the source, but reporters were thankful that they were careful enough never to put the source's name in an e-mail, so subpoenas for the corporation's e-mail records did not turn up any evidence for prosecutors.[47]

The reporters had heard from some sources that prosecutors were requiring potential leakers to sign, under the penalty of perjury, documents denying any role in the leaks and waiving any promises of confidentiality made to reporters. "One of my first questions was, had the rules all changed? Some of the greatest journalists of our generation had just testified against their sources in the Plame case under this theory that they got a waiver. So we had to talk about what we would do if our sources came in with waivers. I knew they were coerced in the Plame case. Is this the industry standard now?" Williams wondered.

Still, he said he knew none of the sources in the BALCO case would voluntarily waive their promises, so the reporters agreed to "pay no attention" to the waiver issue if it came up in their case.

The Hearst Corporation filed a motion to dismiss the subpoenas and coordinated unprecedented support from government officials in the form of *amicus* briefs. The newspaper argued that a federal common-law and First Amendment privilege provided protections for journalists. Hearst argued that evidence of a federal common-law privilege could be found in the consensus of state legislation, and they even filed an amicus brief from the attorneys general of 23 states supporting their position. The newspaper also argued that the Justice Department was not following its own internal journalist-subpoena guidelines. A former public affairs director for the Justice Department, Mark Corallo, filed an affidavit in support of the journalists, saying that subpoenas would not have been issued under former Attorney General John Ashcroft's tenure because they failed to comply with internal Department of Justice regulations that limited prosecutor discretion in subpoenaing journalists.[48]

At a hearing in August 2006, Judge Jeffrey S. White denied the reporters' motion to quash the subpoena.[49] The *Chronicle's* attorneys argued that the Ninth Circuit's interpretation of *Branzburg* required the court to conduct a balancing test of interests in evaluating the subpoenas, emphasizing Justice Powell's concurrence opinion in *Branzburg* that called for a case-by-case balancing. They argued that the judge should balance the "public harm that might come from the leak" against the "public benefit that is derived from the reporting."[50] The government argued that no privilege existed for journalists in criminal cases, and the subpoena should not be treated differently because journalists were the recipients. "We have reporters who are firsthand receptors or participants in the criminal conduct," the government attorney argued.[51]

The journalists were convicted of civil contempt in September 2006 and sentenced to jail, which was stayed pending appeal.[52] Once the reporters were held in contempt, they had conversations about how much in fines the cash-strapped Hearst Corporation could afford before its board would compel disclosure. "As we got into this thing, after we were sentenced, they were talking about $50 million in fines," Williams said. Williams said he went into Bronstein's office once day and asked, "What's going to happen when the fines get too much?" Bronstein's response was that when the corporation came to him and ordered him to reveal the source, he'd quit, and "we'd all go to jail together."

The collective march to jail was averted when the source was outed by a disgruntled former colleague. Just before the Ninth Circuit Court of Appeals was to hear the appeal, a lawyer representing one of the BALCO defendants publicly acknowledged being the source of the leak and was later sentenced to two and half years in prison.[53] The lawyer, Troy Ellerman, was outed as the leaker by a former attorney colleague.[54] As part of his plea agreement, Ellerman admitted that he leaked the materials and then filed an affidavit in court complaining of the prejudicial nature of the leaks, suggesting that the government was involved in the leaks. This raised some questions about whether the reporters were used as pawns by an attorney. But to the journalists, the motives of the source were largely irrelevant. "In some cases, confidential source motives are really important, and you have to learn them. If a guy tells you heard something, and there's no way to verify it, just his word, you really have to know why he's telling you this," said Williams. But being provided documents is something entirely different, Williams argued. "In this case, the material spoke for itself and it was offered without any strings attached," he said. The motives were irrelevant to the newsworthiness of the information. The real public value of the information was in unmasking the cheaters in elite sports, he argued. "If you don't expose the cheaters, nothing happens," Williams said, and it increasingly appeared, especially after the BALCO defendants pleaded guilty, that the athletes might go unpunished. This, Williams implied, helped justify the news stories "outing" the athletes as drug abusers.

The public naming of the reporters' sources did not immediately bring a dismissal to the reporters' subpoenas, and the journalists were left to continue to worry about being jailed. Behind the scenes, journalists and lawyers also lobbied members of Congress about the case during the ongoing congressional debates over journalist shield legislation. Williams described himself as a "moving exhibit" among lawmakers on his trips to Washington, and he believes that the Justice Department was pressured in part to drop the subpoenas after receiving letters from a number of members of Congress, including newly elected Speaker of the House, Representative Nancy Pelosi of California. The political and public campaigns justifying the importance of confidential sources was one important component in ultimately having the subpoenas dismissed, Williams believed. Journalists also rallied around the *Chronicle* reporters more aggressively than in other privilege cases. An organization called Sports Writers for Freedom of the Press rallied sports columnists around the country to write articles about the case. "Sports pages around the country, from little weekies to *Sports Illustrated*, were running columns about us and the First Amendment," Williams recalled.[55] Sports columnists generally have greater editorial freedom, and the tone of the stories was highly critical of the Bush administration and his Justice Department. The *Chronicle's* reporting was described by a journalist for the *New York Daily News* as "a hymn to everything that I still want my business to be."[56]

A similar case of leaked grand jury material had more dire consequences for the journalist. Between 1999 and 2001, several city officials in Providence, Rhode Island, were indicted in federal court on a variety of corruption charges in what was locally described as the "Plunder Dome" scandal.[57] While the charges were pending and a grand jury investigation continued, a federal judge issued a "gag rule" barring lawyers from disclosing evidence turned over during discovery. Despite this, James Taricani, an investigative reporter for the local NBC affiliate WJAR-TV, obtained and broadcast a video purporting to show a witness giving a cash bribe to the mayor's deputy. A special prosecutor was appointed to determine the source of the leak, and after interviewing more than a dozen witnesses without discovering the source, the prosecutor issued a subpoena to Taricani. Taricani refused to identify the source, asserting a "newsman's privilege" based in the First Amendment, and the prosecutor then sought a motion to compel Taricani to testify.[58] The district court rejected Taricani's First Amendment claims, asserting that the *Branzburg* case definitively ruled on the question of subpoenas related to grand jury investigations.[59] Then, in synthesizing the lower court cases in the First Circuit, the district court rather contradictorily asserted that no First Amendment privilege exists for confidential information relevant to a legitimate criminal investigation, although a "lesser degree" of First Amendment protection exists for "the confidentiality of a journalist's sources when those sources are utilized in gathering news to be disseminated to the public." In determining whether disclosure is required, courts "must balance the potential harm to the free flow of information that might result from the disclosure against the asserted need for the requested information." The judge ruled that the special prosecutor was acting in good faith investigating the willful violation of a protective order. On

March 16, 2004, Taricani was held in civil contempt and issued a $1,000-a-day fine, which was stayed pending an appeal to the First Circuit Court of Appeals. In total, more than $85,000 in fines were levied against WJAR.[60]

The First Circuit ruled against Taricani, dismissing arguments that the special prosecutor should have been bound by Department of Justice regulations and that the First Amendment protected him from revealing the source of the leak. Just before a district court was to sentence Taricani for the criminal contempt conviction, the FBI and the special prosecutor identified Taricani's source as an attorney for one of the defendants, and the attorney acknowledged his role. The source, attorney Joseph A. Bevilacqua, told prosecutors he was the source after they indicated they were planning to issue him a subpoena for testimony regarding the leak. Bevilacqua claimed that he never sought confidential source protection from Taricani, and in 2002 signed a "waiver" of confidentiality after being asked for one from the special prosecutor. "Contrary to Mr. Taricani's repeated assertions, both publicly and before this court, Mr. Bevilacqua, the 'source,' did not request any promise of confidentiality in exchange for the videotape," the special prosecutor wrote in a court filing. Taricani said he would never have "jeopardized my health and reputation and put my family and my company through this ordeal if my source had not required a promise of confidentiality." Taricani said Bevilacqua "repeatedly insisted that I keep his name in confidence, despite the fact that he had signed a waiver. He told me he had to sign the waiver, otherwise it would have raised suspicions that he was my source."[61]

In the end, Taricani was sentenced to six months of home confinement despite the unmasking of his confidential source. He escaped jail only because the 55-year-old had a heart transplant and thus had serious health concerns about serving his sentence in jail.[62] In sentencing Taricani, Judge Ernest C. Torres identified five "myths" surrounding the case, which summarized some of the competing judicial interests with a journalist's privilege.[63] Judge Torres said it was a myth that Taricani's reporting uncovered any corruption in city hall, since the broadcast of the tape showing the bribe had no impact on the police investigation or in uncovering any new misconduct, and had been scheduled to be played in an upcoming trial. Judge Torres also called it a myth that that compelled disclosure by Taricani would have a chilling effect on a reporter's ability to gather news. The judge said the chilling effect would only be in deterring lawyers from violating gag orders and therefore committing a crime, which Judge Torres said was an appropriate chilling effect. Judge Torres also ridiculed the argument that the courts were not equipped to be the final arbiters of the limits of journalist-source promises of confidentiality:

> The fourth myth is that every reporter has an absolute right to be the sole arbiter of whether and under what circumstances the identify of the source should remain confidential no matter what the law or the court may say ... [Taricani's lawyers] apparently recognize that that proposition is completely indefensible, it has been disclaimed. They purport to recognize that there may be circumstances under which a reporter should reveal the identity of the source, and they suggest or imply that those circumstances might include cases in which national security is involved or lives are at stake. But that doesn't alter the fact that what they are really claiming is that a reporter has a right to unilaterally decide what those circumstances are.
>
> They concede that those circumstances might include cases, as I've said, in which national security is involved or lives are at stake, but they claim to be the sole arbiter of when those circumstance exist. And apparently some of their colleagues do not believe that national security was involved or lives were at stake in the Valerie Plame case, for example, where it was alleged that the life of an undercover CIA agent was threatened when a confidential source illegally revealed her identity to reporters as a means of getting back at her husband. They do not believe that punishing and deterring criminal acts that threaten the fundamental constitutional rights of others provide a sufficient reason for revealing the identity of a source. And I think that provides an apt illustration of why it is contrary to the public interest to vest such exclusive and unreviewable authority in individual reporters. Our system of constitutional government ultimately vests that authority in the courts, just as it does with every other legal issue of public importance. Despite the great respect that I have for those many reporters who conscientiously seek to gather the news and report it fairly and accurately, it is not and should not be up to individual reporters to make the ultimate decision in cases where it

becomes an issue for a number of reasons; one is that not all reporters live up to those standards. Fortunately, most do, but there's some who don't. And if the ultimate decision is made by each individual reporter, we would have as many standards as there are reporters. Also, it's a bad idea because reporters are required to act on the spur of the moment, they're under competitive pressure to get a story or a scoop, and they might not know all of the relevant facts. It defies logic and common sense, as well the law, to say that a promise of confidentiality made under such circumstances should be absolute and unreviewable by a court or anyone else. In cases where the issue arises, the question of confidentiality is one of that must be reviewable by a court. The court is in a position to hear all of the facts. The court is in a position to determine the applicable law and to balance any competing public interests that would be implicated by disclosure versus non-disclosure. And a court's decision is reviewable, in turn, by a higher court.[64]

Judge Torres's statement at Taricani's sentencing hearing revealed some of the complexities of journalism ethics and law. Both Taricani and the *Chronicle* reporters published information that the courts wanted to remain secret, for legitimate reasons. Grand jury and pre-trial discovery materials are not considered public records and their secrecy is justified by several important interests, including protecting individuals' reputations from false allegations and in protecting the rights of criminal defendants from pre-trial publicity. Still, those interests are often at odds with other interests, including the interests of the public in receiving newsworthy information. Judge Torres's comments made clear that leaving the ultimate decision as to what journalists should publish up to individual journalists is troubling. But so too is it troubling to leave the ultimate decision of publication to the government. The two cases here show that different conceptions of the public interest dominate both the ethics and legal questions.

THE PRIVACY CASES

A legal strategy by civil litigants suing the federal government has emerged as yet another problem for the journalist's privilege. In several cases, individuals suing the government for violations of the Privacy Act of 1974,[65] a law passed to protect employee personnel records after abuses were uncovered in the Nixon administration, have issued subpoenas to journalists to help bolster their cases. The Privacy Act created a civil cause of action when a government agency improperly discloses government records pertaining to individuals. To identify the specific government employees responsible for leaks allegedly in violation of the law, litigants have subpoenaed journalists to reveal their sources. In an attempt to coerce reporters into talking, judges have levied significant fines, as much as $1,500 a day, and in some cases ordered the fines must be paid by the reporters individually, rather than by outside groups or news organizations. "The ramifications of criminalizing the dissemination of this information is breathtaking," said Washington D.C., media attorney Lee Levine.[66]

One case, still pending in 2010 after more than three years of litigation, is that of *Detroit Free Press* reporter David Ashenfelter, who was subpoenaed by former U.S. attorney Richard Convertino as part of a lawsuit Convertino filed against the federal government for allegedly unlawful disclosures made about his potential misconduct during a post-September 11, 2001, terrorism trial in Detroit. A federal judge denied the journalist's motion to quash the subpoena, ruling that no federal privilege exists in the Sixth Circuit. Ashenfelter subsequently invoked the Fifth Amendment, arguing that he is vulnerable to prosecution for several crimes as the recipient of the leak, including conspiracy, perjury, false statements, obstruction of justice, theft, and state laws that criminalize possession of stolen material.

The first of the recent high-profile Privacy Act cases arose in 2003, when as part of a lawsuit filed against the federal government by former government scientist Wen Ho Lee, a federal judge ordered five reporters to reveal who leaked to them information about Lee. In 1999, the government indicted Lee, who worked on nuclear weapon designs at the Los Alamos National Laboratory in New Mexico, on 59 counts of mishandling classified information. Several reporters were leaked information about Lee for stories they wrote about the arrest. For example, James Risen and Jeff Gerth wrote a story in the *New York Times*, with the headline "China Spy Suspect Reportedly Tried to Hide Evidence," that alleged Lee was suspected of spying for China and tried to hide evidence of illegal downloading of nuclear secrets two days after he failed an FBI polygraph.[67]

In dramatic fashion, the prosecution of Lee unraveled, and in September 2000 Lee accepted a plea deal under which he was convicted on one count of mishandling classified information and was released with time served, during which Lee was subjected to "demeaning, unnecessarily punitive conditions," in the words of the federal judge overseeing the case. Judge James A. Parker decried the government's handling of the case in open court:

> I am truly sorry that I was led by our executive branch of government to order your detention last December ...
>
> It is only the top decision makers in the executive branch, especially the Department of Justice and the Department of Energy and locally, during December, who have caused embarrassment by the way this case began and was handled. They did not embarrass me alone. They have embarrassed our entire nation and each of us who is a citizen in it.
>
> I might say that I am also sad and troubled because I do not know the real reasons why the executive branch has done all of this. We will not learn why because the plea agreement shields the executive branch from disclosing a lot of information that it was under order to produce that might have supplied the answer.[68]

Lee then sued the federal government, alleging among other things that officials had leaked information about him in violation of the Privacy Act. Lee's lawyer argued that Clinton administration officials engaged in an illegal effort to frame and smear his client, and reporters were willing participants. "What they were doing was not journalism, it was a rush to judgment. We want accountability for the leakers," attorney Brian Sun said. "There's a distinction between the press reporting on someone who is revealing government misbehavior and someone who is engaged in just plain bad conduct. In this case the officials were trying to slant the public's perception of the case in an unlawful manner, and for a crime Dr. Lee didn't commit, and the question is, how do you control the leakers and the journalists rushing to publish?"[69]

The district court ordered the journalists to testify, saying Lee had overcome a qualified privilege by showing he had exhausted reasonable attempts at identifying the sources and that the information was "of central importance" to his case.[70]

A three-judge panel of the D.C. Court of Appeals upheld the district court decision. Judge David Sentelle narrowly construed two previous appellate precedents that ruled in favor of journalist source protection in civil cases.[71] The full court declined to review the decision on a 4-4 vote.[72] In dissent, Judge David S. Tatel argued that the panel had not properly applied the common-law privilege test that emerged from a 1981 case in the circuit, *Zerilli v. Smith*, by failing to properly weigh the public's interest in protecting reporter's sources against the private interests at stake in compelling disclosure.[73] Another judge in dissent, Merrick Garland, wrote, "The significance of the court's decision in this case should not be underestimated" because it eases limits on the ability of leak investigations to turn to journalists for the identity of leakers.[74] While the case was being considered for appeal to the U.S. Supreme Court, Wen Ho Lee agreed to settle the case after several media companies agreed to pay Lee $750,000 to drop his subpoenas against journalists.[75] The settlement was controversial.

A lawsuit filed against the government by Steven Hatfill had similar facts, although the tactics against journalists were even harsher. In 2003, Hatfill filed a lawsuit under the Privacy Act as a result of being implicated in the FBI investigation into anthrax attacks that occurred in several U.S. cities just after the September 11, 2001, terrorist attacks.[76] Anthrax that was mailed to various locations killed five people, sickened 17 more, and sparked alarm across the country. Hatfill, a former government researcher in "germ warfare," was publicly identified as a "person of interest" by then Attorney General John Ashcroft. He was later cleared, although he claimed the notoriety ruined his life and career. As part of his lawsuit, he subpoenaed several reporters who wrote stories about the FBI investigations in an attempt to establish the motives of the leakers. In November 2008, the lawsuit was settled after the government agreed to pay Hatfill $4.6 million.[77]

In each of these cases, journalists reporting on matters of intense public interest relied on government employees as confidential sources of information. As Clark Hoyt, the *New York Times'* public editor, wrote, "Hatfill's case poses uncomfortable journalistic questions that do not have easy answers. In reporting on a major criminal investigation, how do you balance the interests of the public in knowing as much as possible with the rights of individuals who come under suspicion, especially when the information comes from sources –

often anonymous – whose motives aren't clear?"[78] The journalist's function in informing the public necessarily encourages them to assemble as many facts as possible, and the public interest is heightened in important, high-profile criminal investigations. But journalists' skepticism must also lead them to tread cautiously when relying on confidential sources for information about criminal defendants. In these types of cases, source motives must also be considered, including questions about whether journalists are being used as pawns by prosecutors.

THE BLOGGER CASES

In each of the cases described thus far, the individuals seeking journalist-privilege protection were undoubtedly journalists. Most worked for traditional, mainstream news organizations, had years of professional expertise, and were trained in journalism schools. No one questioned whether they were entitled to seek privilege protections that existed. However, the question of who qualifies for protection has been one of the most perplexing problems in the common law, constitutional and public policy debates over a journalist's privilege. The Supreme Court majority in *Branzburg* said that defining who qualifies for protection "would present practical and conceptual difficulties of a high order," and since the 1972 decision academics, lawyers, judges, journalists, and members of Congress have struggled to articulate the best definition of "journalist."[79] In the Judith Miller case discussed in the next chapter, Appellate Judge David Sentelle suggested no distinction could be drawn between professional journalists and the "stereotypical 'blogger' sitting in his pajamas at his personal computer."[80] During the 2007 and 2008 congressional debates over a statutory privilege, the Justice Department argued that "(d)efining who is entitled to invoke a 'reporter's privilege' is a very difficult, if not intractable, problem," and predicted "bloggers and MySpace users" would flood the courts with journalistic claims to avoid subpoenas if Congress passed a law.[81]

The two cases discussed in this section show some of the legal and ethical difficulties that can arise when bloggers make journalist privilege claims. The case of Josh Wolf raises questions about what criteria can be used to define journalists and journalism, while the case involving bloggers covering the Apple corporation shows how the decentralized nature of the blogosphere might facilitate the leaking of new types of information that may not have been a serious problem before the rise of the Internet.

The jailing of Josh Wolf occurred just after the Miller decision and heightened the concerns about definitional clauses in the congressional debates.

On July 8, 2005, Wolf was a 22-year-old psychology student at San Francisco State University when he attended an anarchist demonstration in the city's Mission District, organized in protest of the Group of Eight economic summit taking place in Scotland. Wolf said he had attended and filmed "just about every major protest and quite a few minor protests" that occurred in San Francisco between September 2003 and July 2005, and said his intent was to videotape the protest and post the footage on his blog.[82] Wolf had been a participant in previous protests and acknowledged that he "attended a few organizing meetings" for the July 8 protest. "It's difficult to determine that I was an active participant, but I definitely wasn't passive like a traditional journalist," Wolf said. "I wasn't bringing signs over or working out strategies dealing with the police. But there wasn't a wall between me and them."[83]

The FBI's Joint Terrorism Task Force opened an investigation into the protest after a police squad car was set on fire and two police officers were injured, including one who suffered a skull fracture that left him unable to work for one year.[84] Wolf posted edited video on his blog, and made about $2,000 selling the footage to local San Francisco television stations as a freelancer. A few days after the protest, two FBI agents appeared at Wolf's apartment and asked to interview him and obtain the full video footage in an attempt to identify individuals who engaged in violence. After Wolf called an attorney, the FBI subpoenaed Wolf for his testimony and video. Despite Wolf's declaration that his video showed nothing helpful to the police investigation, he refused to comply with the subpoena on the grounds that the First Amendment protected him from compelled disclosure.[85] "What I thought would happen is that I would have gone in there, they would have played the tape and pressed pause whenever a new person entered the shot, and they would say, 'Do you know that person?' The last thing I wanted to do was to be put in that position," Wolf said. The FBI justified its involvement because it provided federal funds to the San Francisco Police Department and therefore had jurisdiction to investigate the vandalism of a city police car. Wolf believed the reason the FBI was involved was because of a broader effort to monitor anarchist groups. "They had an anarchist rally and they wanted to identify more anarchists. (I thought) the FBI was seeking to inject themselves into this to gather broad information about civil unrest in the Bay Area," Wolf said.[86]

Wolf lost his attempts to quash the subpoena. In April 2006, a magistrate judge in the District Court for the Northern District of California rejected Wolf's arguments that the subpoena was unreasonable or oppressive and that the grand jury investigation was being conducted in bad faith.[87] The judge also rejected Wolf's claim that the California state shield law offered him protection and instead applied what she described as a qualified First Amendment privilege against compelled testimony. Nonetheless, she ruled that the privilege did not apply in cases of federal grand jury subpoenas, consistent with the central holding in *Branzburg.*[88]

Wolf went to federal prison four months later, on August 1, 2006, when U.S. District Judge William Alsup found Wolf in contempt of court and ordered him immediately jailed for the 11-month remainder of the grand jury term.[89] "Every person, from the president of the United States down to you and me, has to give information to the grand jury if the grand jury wants it," Alsup said during the court hearing.[90] Wolf was released on bail on August 31, 2006, while his case was on appeal, but a three-judge panel of the Ninth Circuit Court of Appeals upheld the lower court's contempt order in an unpublished decision issued on September 8, 2006.[91] The appeals court said the *Branzburg* decision was unambiguous in holding that no privilege exists for journalists in the context of a good-faith grand jury investigation. The court rejected arguments that the grand jury was being misused to investigate a crime outside of federal jurisdiction and that Wolf's tape was relevant to the investigation. As an aside, the court also noted that because Wolf was neither connected with nor employed by a news organization, he may not have qualified for privilege protection even if California law was binding.[92]

Wolf's jailing became a cause célèbre of journalists. Wolf was named "journalist of the year" by the Northern California chapter of the Society of Professional Journalists, and dozens of press organizations signed on to *amicus* briefs and editorialized for his release.[93] "He may not have the clout or journalism credentials of some of the other government targets, but Josh Wolf is no less entitled to First

Amendment protection," the *San Francisco Chronicle* wrote in an editorial headlined, "Free Josh Wolf."[94] The Reporters Committee for Freedom of the Press, which was founded in the *Branzburg* era in part as a reaction to the threatened jailings of a number of newspaper reporters, helped pay for Wolf's legal defense.[95] In a court filing in January 2007, Assistant U.S. Attorney Jeffrey Finigan said Wolf's "resolve to remain confined rather than comply with the grand jury subpoena is apparently fueled by his anointment as a journalistic martyr."[96]

Wolf was released from the federal prison in Dublin, California, on April 3, 2007, after court-ordered mediation resulted in an agreement between Wolf and the federal prosecutors in which Wolf would turn over the entirety of his footage but not have to testify before a grand jury. He did agree to answer two questions under oath, in writing, regarding whether he saw anyone vandalize the police car or injure the police officer. He said no to both questions.[97] He spent 226 days in jail, the longest jail term on record for an American journalist in a privilege case.

But was Wolf a journalist? After his release, Wolf ran as a fringe candidate for San Francisco mayor and worked at a public-access television station before being hired as a reporter for the *Palo Alto Daily News*, where he was one of three full-time reporters and covered local government. When he filmed the anarchist protest in 2005, he viewed himself as something of an alternative journalist whose beat was political dissent in San Francisco, although he preferred the label of documentarian rather than journalist. Now, he was as mainstream of a journalist could get. "It doesn't get more traditional journalism than our newspaper," Wolf said in December 2008. He expressed some frustrations at the conventions of daily news reporting, including at his editor's insistence of objectivity. "There's this struggle where frequently you'll come to a conclusion, and it's a logical conclusion, but you can't say it (as the reporter), you have to go out and find other people to say it and draw the connection with their quotes. Now, does that really make me more neutral to find someone who says what I think?" But Wolf said his traditional reporting job reinforced his desire to work in journalism, albeit in a different venue than covering government meetings for a local daily. He traced the roots of his aspirations to a "curiosity award" he won as a kindergarten student. One of his favorite classes at San Francisco State was Issues in Free

Speech. He worked on his college newspaper and landed an internship at an alternative newsweekly.

Why did Wolf persist in staying in jail for so long? "The role of the journalist is to be a checks and balances on a system of checks and balances – to be in a sense outside of the government, and outside of the government's control. When a journalist goes to jail, it's our way of saying, no, you can't exert your control and influence over me." Wolf also believed that the government should have limits on what it compels its citizens to say. He lumps together principles of the journalist's privilege with an individual-rights philosophy. "You can say there needs to be a key distinction between journalists and non-journalists, and in my case we're dealing with the footage I was gathering as a reporter. But as I see it, the idea of coercive custody does not seem to be in line with the First Amendment itself, or the idea of a free society. Utilizing coercion to obtain a confession of a crime is not an admissible confession. If I was involved in the act, I could invoke the Fifth Amendment. But I wasn't, so they could jail me to force me to talk."

Wolf's case helped intensify the effort in 2007 and 2008 for the passage of a federal shield statute by the U.S. Congress, and bloggers watched closely as policymakers debated various proposals. [98] The bill passed by the U.S. House would not have covered many bloggers. It would have protected "a person who regularly gathers, prepares, collects, photographs, records, writes, edits, reports or publishes news or information that concerns local, national or international events or other matters of public interest for dissemination to the public for a substantial portion of the person's livelihood or for substantial financial gain and includes a supervisor, employer, parent, subsidiary, or affiliate of such covered person."[99] Bills advanced in the Senate did not include the requirement that a person be financially supported by his or her work, and therefore were likely to protect more bloggers. Wolf said he was glad the bill failed to become law because of the substantial financial gain provision, which he said would fail to protect bloggers, student journalists and interns as well.

As a matter of law, judges sometimes skirt the definitional question and assume without analysis that bloggers qualified for protection. This is because most jurisdictions provide for a qualified, rather than absolute, privilege, so judges have assumed that the individual is indeed a journalist for purposes of the law but ruled that the blogger must nonetheless reveal sources or provide testimony.

The most extensive judicial treatment thus far of the definitional question as it relates to bloggers came in May 2006 in the case of *O'Grady v. Superior Court*, in which a California appeals court overturned a lower court's ruling that three bloggers had to reveal their sources.[100] The appeals court determined that the bloggers who regularly reported about Apple Computer, Inc., qualified for protection under the state shield law because they were involved in the "gathering and disseminating of news."[101] Apple had sought the identity of individuals who leaked to the bloggers information about unreleased Apple products. Relying on the statutory language that protects a person "connected with or employed" by a "newspaper, magazine or other periodical publication," the court distinguished the bloggers from anonymous Web posters by determining that their Web sites "reflect a kind and degree of editorial control that makes them resemble a newspaper or magazine far more closely" than other online web sites.[102] The court also distinguished the blogs from paid advertisements and said "in no relevant respect do they appear to differ from a reporter or editor for a traditional business-oriented periodical."[103] The essential element of distinction was the degree to which the bloggers employed traditional journalistic methods and values in their work. The decision was the first decisive victory for bloggers invoking the journalist's privilege.[104]

Other cases suggest that individuals who post information to the Web in a variety of formats may describe themselves as "bloggers" and also "journalists" for purposes of legal protections. In September 2008, a Montana judge ruled that a newspaper did not have to reveal the identities of two anonymous posters to its Web site, determining that anonymous "bloggers" to the Web site were protected under a state statutory privilege that protected "any person connected with or employed by a [news organization] for the purpose of gathering, writing, editing or disseminating news," but made no attempt to distinguish the anonymous posters from journalists or reporters and instead relied on the commonalities between confidential sources and anonymous posters.[105] Other judges have made opposite rulings, suggesting that the question of who is a journalist will continue to be a matter of legal dispute. One possible solution to this morass lies in evaluating an individual's commitment to the purposes, processes, and product. A line of federal court decisions evaluating privilege claims by non-traditional journalists, such as book authors, trade publications, and freelancers, shows that judges have often looked toward a person's commitment to journalism ethical standards and principles as a benchmark for determining the definitional hurdle. The implications of this are discussed in chapters seven and eight.

CONCLUSION

When journalists agree to go "on background" or "off the record," rarely do they consider what that means beyond an agreement not to publicly identify the source in a news story. As a matter of professional standards and ethics, the first and second chapters have described the existence of a professional ethic to protect sources. Journalists have cultivated and protected confidential sources to obtain information they have deemed newsworthy, which is often unable to be obtained elsewhere. On occasions in which journalists are served with subpoenas, they have adopted various strategies. Because journalists view their promises of confidentiality as sacrosanct, most have fought in court attempts to unmask confidential sources. Legal tactics of coercion have increased, making journalists more vulnerable and making it more difficult for them to protect confidential sources in the face of court orders for compelled disclosure.

Journalists, then, are faced with difficult questions about their duty to protect sources. Do they have a duty to comply with court orders, or cooperate in exposing potential crimes of leakers? Or is their allegiance to their sources and their promises, regardless of the seriousness of the source's misconduct or potential value of the journalistic testimony to legal proceedings? For journalists, the case studies in this chapter – and the Valerie Plame leak case discussed in the next chapter – demonstrate that the legal status of confidential source protection remains in a state of flux, especially as a question of federal law. As a legal matter, the journalist's privilege presents both old and new problems. If First Amendment interests are raised by compelled disclosure, how should judges prioritize those interests? Does *Branzburg* allow for a First Amendment-based privilege, and if so, what are its standards? Quite separate from the constitutional principle is the claim that a journalist's privilege exists in common law. Here, disparate federal circuit holdings point in different directions. The recent cases suggest in the circuits that recognize a common-law privilege, its contours are unclear and changing. The lack of theoretical and foundational coherence demonstrated by recent judicial decisions is but one of the many problems of law with the journalist's privilege.

This uncertainty has very real ramifications to journalists and their reporting practices. The case studies also highlight some competing views of the purposes and limits of source protection as a matter of law, but also raise a number of questions and problems about journalism ethics and practice. How should journalists view their obligations after promising sources confidentiality? What are journalists' obligations to their employers, especially as cash-strapped media companies are more likely to surrender to subpoena threats because of little likelihood of succeeding in court challenges?

Journalists are encouraged to adopt "drug dealer" methods to avoid leaving a trail of records that might be the subject of subpoenas, such as e-mail and phone logs. Notes stored on company computers and e-mails to editors also expand the vulnerability for journalists trying to protect confidential sources. Technology has also given prosecutors more avenues to identity a journalist's sources by using subpoenas to telephone and Internet service providers, sometimes without telling the journalists or news organizations. No longer could journalists rely on what former *Washington Post* editor Ben Bradlee once called the "gray-haired widow" defense, referring to the *Post's* policy that all reporters' notes belonged to the newspaper, and a judge would have to ultimately jail publisher Katherine Graham to compel disclosure.[106]

Journalists also need to be careful about who in the news organization knows about the confidential source. Sometimes this is a Catch-22, since many ethics codes require reporters to identify confidential sources to editors. Corporate liability and shareholder responsibility led *Time* magazine to turn over documents against the wishes of its reporter in the Valerie Plame leak case, discussed in the next chapter, signaling to reporters the possibility of internal threats as well as external threats. Time Inc. editor Norman Pearlstine said this was the most "difficult decision" of his 40 years in journalism. The *New York Times* has a policy that its editors who know the identity of confidential sources are ethically bound by the reporter's initial promise. In some cases, disputes have risen over the ownership of reporters' notes.

Journalists are also confronted with more skeptical sources who have seen reporters turn on their sources. Journalists who try to be up front with their sources about the extent to which they will protect the source risk scaring off the source entirely. Journalists also must consider how to treat a source after receiving a subpoena for his or identity. When should journalists agree to identify a source after the source "waived" a promise? Officials leading leak investigations have also asked government employees to sign releases indicating that they have "waived" whatever promises journalists might have made to keep their identities secret. In the Plame case, special prosecutor Patrick Fitzgerald obtained documents from a number of Bush administration officials waiving their promises of confidentiality to any journalists. Presented with these waivers, some journalists viewed them as a release of their promise of confidentiality and agreed to talk to prosecutors. Judith Miller and Matt Cooper, on the other hand, believed the waivers were worthless because they were coercive and not voluntary. But both reporters ultimately cooperated after they became convinced, upon questioning their original sources, that the sources wanted the reporters to cooperate with prosecutors. Journalists are right to be skeptical about "waivers," although strict rejection of the concept presents its own problems. Walter Pincus, the veteran national-security reporter for *The Washington Post,* explained his reasoning on the question this way: "It is called a reporter's privilege, but once I publish the information from a confidential source who has risked firing or even jail to give me the information, I believe the privilege of keeping his or her name secret belongs both to the source and to me. That source, after getting a confidentiality pledge from me, can disclose that same information within hours to another reporter for attribution. The source could also go to a prosecutor in private, disclose that he or she has talked to me and provide the substance of the conversation. I could hardly claim a privilege to that same prosecutor, if I am directly assured that the source is releasing me from my pledge."[107]

As it relates to the functions and principles of journalism briefly outlined in chapter one, the journalist's privilege is a structural provision designed to ensure a level of scrutiny of government, even if it comes with the price of occasional abuse. While it is impossible to measure the "chilling effect" of journalists' inability to protect sources, on occasion evidence can be found. For example, the *Cleveland Plain Dealer* took its lawyers' advice and killed an investigative story that it claimed had valuable public interest because it could not guarantee protection to its confidential sources.[108] The editor, Doug Clifton, called the stories "profoundly important," but said that "publishing the stories would almost lead to a leak investigation and the ultimate choice: talk or go to jail. Because talking isn't an option and jail is too high a price to pay, these stories will go untold for now. How many more are out there?"[109]

Chapter 2 Notes

---

[1] In re Grand Jury Subpoenas (Leggett), 29 Med. L. Rptr. 2301 (5th Cir. 2001); McKevitt v. Pallasch, et al., 339 F.3d 530 (7th Cir. 2003); In re: Special Proceedings (Taricani), 373 F.3d 37 (1st Cir. 2004); Lee v. U.S. Dep't of Justice, 413 F.3d 53 (D.C.Cir. 2005); In Re Grand Jury Subpoena (Miller), 397 F.3d 964 (D.C. Cir. 2005); In re Grand Jury Subpoena, Joshua Wolf, No. 06-16403, D.C. No. CR-06-90064-MMC (9th Cir. 2006); and New York Times v. Gonzales, 459 F.3d 160 (2nd Cir. 2006).

[2] Matt Cooper of Time Magazine and Judith Miller of the New York Times, for example, revealed their sources after the District of Columbia Court of Appeals ruled against them.

[3] Toni Locy of USA Today faced a threat of personal bankruptcy. See *Locy appeal dismissed, contempt order vacated*, Reporters Committee For Freedom of the Press, Nov. 17, 2008, available at http://www.rcfp.org/newsitems/index.php?i=7137, (last visited June 1, 2009).

[4] *See, for example*, Rachel Smolkin, *Waivering*, AMERICAN JOURNALISM REVIEW, February/March 2006, at 32, and Lori Robertson, *Kind of Confidential*, AMERICAN JOURNALISM REVIEW, June/July 2007, at 26.

[5] Branzburg v. Hayes, 408 U.S. 665 (1972).

[6] *See infra* chapter seven.

[7] *Id.*

[8] *See generally* Guillermo X. Garcia, *The Vanessa Leggett Saga*, AMERICAN JOURNALISM REVIEW, March 2002; Skip Hollandsworth, *The Inmate: Why Has Vanessa Leggett Been in Jail Longer Than Any Journalist in U.S. History? Herein Lies the True Crime*, TEXAS MONTHLY, December 1, 2001; Daniel Scardino, *Vanessa Leggett Serves Maximum Jail Time, First – Amendment Based Reporter's Privilege Under Siege*, 9 COMM. LAWYER 4 (2002), Joshua Lipton, *Vanessa Leggett: Why She Wouldn't Give Up Her Notes*, COLUMBIA JOURNALISM REVIEW, March 2002.

[9] In re Grand Jury Subpoenas, 29 Med. L. Rptr. 2301, (5th Cir. Aug. 17, 2001). *See also* David B. Kopel and Paul H. Blackman, *Abuse of Power: Jailing Journalists*, NATIONAL REVIEW ONLINE, January 22, 2002, *available at* http://nationalreview.com/kopel/kopel012202.shtml (last visited April 8, 2009).

[10] McKevitt v. Pallasch, et al., 339 F.3d 530 (7th Cir. 2003).

[11] *Id.*

[12] *See infra* chapter seven.

[13] These included James Risen and Jeff Gerth of *The New York Times,* Bob Drogin of the *Los Angeles Times,* Pierre Thomas, formerly of CNN, Josef Hebert of the Associated Press and Walter Pincus of *The Washington Post.*

[14] New York Times v. Gonzales, 459 F.3d 160 (2nd Cir. 2006).

[15] In re: Special Proceedings (Taricani), 373 F.3d 37 (1st Cir. 2004).

[16] *See infra* chapter three.

[17] Esmat Salaheddin of Reuters, Patricia Hurtado of *Newsday* and Joseph Fried and George Packer of *The New York Times* received subpoenas.

[18] Forrest Wilkinson, *Call to the Bullpen: The Mark Fainaru-Wada and Lance Williams Story,* RealGmBaseball.com, August 21, 2006, *available at* http://www.realgmbaseball.com/src_calltothebullpen/55/20060821/reporting_in _shadows_the_mark_fainaru_wada_and_lance_williams_story/ (last visited June 1, 2009).

[19] See *Locy appeal dismissed, contempt order vacated,* Reporters Committee For Freedom of the Press, Nov. 17, 2008, available at http://www.rcfp.org/newsitems/index.php?i=7137, (last visited June 1, 2009).

[20] These include *Newsweek*'s Michael Isikoff and Daniel Klaidman, ABC's Brian Ross, *The Washington Post*'s Allan Lengel, CBS's James Stewart and *USA TODAY*'s Toni Locy.

[21] Charlie Savage, *U.S. Subpoenas Times Reporter Over Book on C.I.A.,* N.Y. TIMES, Apr 28, 2010, and Philip Shenon, *Times Reporter Subpoenaed Over Source of Book,* N.Y. TIMES, Feb. 1, 2008.

[22] RonNell Andersen Jones, AVALANCHE OR UNDUE ALARM? AN EMPIRICAL STUDY OF SUBPOENAS RECEIVED BY THE NEWS MEDIA, 93 MINN. L. REV. 585 (2008).

[23] Personal interview, conducted on Nov. 12, 2007.

[24] Personal interview, conducted on Nov. 13, 2007.

[25] David Carr, *Subpoenas and the Press*, N.Y. TIMES, Nov. 27, 2006.

[26] Personal interview, conducted on Nov. 6, 2007.

[27] See *Locy appeal dismissed, contempt order vacated,* Reporters Committee For Freedom of the Press, Nov. 17, 2008, available at http://www.rcfp.org/newsitems/index.php?i=7137, (last visited June 1, 2009).

[28] *Id.*

[29] *Id.*

[30] Personal interview.

[31] *Id.*

[32] *Id.*

[33] *Id.*

[34] *Id.*

[35] Jonathan Littman, *The Persecution of Barry Bonds*, PLAYBOY, April 2009, *available at* http://www.playboy.com/magazine/features/barry-bonds-2009/barry-bonds.html (last visited April 7, 2009).

[36] Mark Fainaru-Wada and Lance Williams, GAME OF SHADOWS: BARRY BONDS, BALCO, AND THE STEROIDS SCANDAL THAT ROCKED PROFESSIONAL SPORTS 219 (2006).

[37] *Id.* at 219.

[38] *Id.* at 221.

[39] *Id.* at 239.

[40] *Id.*

[41] Personal interview.

[42] *Id.*

[43] *Id.*

[44] *Id.*

[45] *Id.*

[46] *Id.*

[47] *Id.*

[48] Bree Nordenson, *The Shield Bearer,* COLUMBIA JOURNALISM REVIEW, May/June 2007.

[49] District Court decision: In Re Grand Jury Subpoenas to Mark Fainaru-Wada and Lance Williams, No. CR 06-90225 (D.N.Cal., August 15, 2006).

[50] Transcript of Proceedings, In Re: Grand Jury Subpoenas to Mark Fainaru-Wada and Lance Williams, No. CR 06-90225, Aug. 4, 2006, at 48 (on file with author).

[51] *Id.* at 54.

[52] District Court decision: In Re Grand Jury Subpoenas to Mark Fainaru-Wada and Lance Williams, No. CR 06-90225 (D.N.Cal., August 15, 2006).

[53] Bob Egelko, *Judge sends leaker to slammer, chides Bush,* S.F. CHRONICLE, July 13, 2007.

[54] Justin Scheck, *Balco's Singing Cowboy*, THE RECORDER, March 14, 2007, *available at* http://law.com/jsp/law/pubarticleprinterfriendly.jsp?id=1173776617352 (last visited April 1, 2009).

[55] Personal interview.

[56] Forrest Wilkinson, *Call to the Bullpen: The Mark Fainaru-Wada and Lance Williams Story*, RealGmBaseball.com, August 21, 2006, *available at* http://www.realgmbaseball.com/src_calltothebullpen/55/20060821/reporting_in

_shadows_the_mark_fainaru_wada_and_lance_williams_story/ (last visited June 1, 2009).

[57] Ian Donnis, *The Trials of Jim Taricani*, THE PROVIDENCE PHOENIX, *available at* http://www.providencephoenix.com/features/top/multi/documents/04319945.asp (last visited June 1, 2009).

[58] *Id.*

[59] *Id.*

[60] *Id.*

[61] *Lawyer comes forward as convicted reporter's confidential source*, ASSOCIATED PRESS, December 2, 2004, available at http://www.firstamendmentcenter.org/news.aspx?id=14461 (last visited April 1, 2009).

[62] Pam Belluck, *Reporter Granted Release From Sentence*, N.Y. TIMES, April 7, 2005 at A19.

[63] *Transcript of Judge Torres's remarks regarding "five myths" he says emerged from the case*, PROVIDENCE JOURNAL, Dec. 10, 2004, *available at* http://www.projo.com/extra/2004/taricani/ (last visited June 1, 2009).

[64] *Id.*

[65] Privacy Act of 1974, 5 U.S.C. § 552a (1974).

[66] Casey Murray, *Journalists in the Privacy Crosshairs*, NEWS MEDIA & THE LAW, Fall 2005, p. 16.

[67] James Risen and Jeff Gerth, *China Suspect Reportedly Tried to Hide Evidence*, N.Y. TIMES, April 30, 1999 at A6.

[68] *Statement by Judge in Los Alamos Case, With Apology for Abuse of Power*, N.Y.TIMES, Sept. 14, 2000 at A1.

[69] James Sterngold, *Wen Ho Lee Wants Reporters to Reveal Sources Who Alleged He Was a Spy*, S.F. CHRONICLE, Nov. 6, 2005.

[70] Wen Ho Lee v. DOJ, 287 F. Supp. 2d 15 (D.D.C., Oct. 9, 2003).

[71] Wen Ho Lee v. DOJ, 413 F. 3d 53 (D.C. Cir. 2005).

[72] Lee v. Department of Justice, 428 F.3d 299 (D.C. Cir. 2005).

[73] *Id.*

[74] *Id.*

[75] *Settlement reached in Lee case involving reporter's subpoenas*, Reporters Committee for Freedom of the Press, June 2, 2006, *available at* http://www.rcfp.org/news/2006/0602-con-settle.html (last visited June 1, 2009).

[76] *Reporter subpoenas approved in anthrax suit*, Reporters Committee for Freedom of the Press, Oct. 28, 2004, *available at* http://www.rcfp.org/news/2004/1028hatfil.html (last visited June 1, 2009).

[77] *Locy appeal dismissed, contempt order vacated*, Reporters Committee For Freedom of the Press, Nov. 17, 2008, *available at* http://www.rcfp.org/newsitems/index.php?i=7137, (last visited June 1, 2009).

[78] Clark Hoyt, *Headlines and Exonerations*, N.Y. TIMES, Aug. 16, 2008, *available at* http://www.nytimes.com/2008/08/17/opinion/17pubed.html (last visited June 1, 2009).

[79] Branzburg v. Hayes, 408 U.S. 665, 703 (1972). *See generally* Scott Neinas, *A Skinny Shield is Better: Why Congress Should Propose a Federal Reporters' Shield Statute That Narrowly Defines Journalists*, 40 U. TOL. L. REV. 225 (2008); Mary Rose Papandrea, *Citizen Journalism and the Reporter's Privilege*, 91 MINN. L. REV. 515 (2006); Joseph S. Alonzo, *Restoring the Ideal Marketplace: How Recognizing Bloggers as Journalists Can Save the Press,* 9 N.Y.U. J. LEGIS. PUB. POL. 751 (2006); Stephanie J. Frazee, *Bloggers as Reporters: An Effect-Based Approach to First Amendment Protections in a New Age of Information Dissemination,* 8 VAN. J. ENT. & TECH. L. 609 (2005); Linda L. Berger, *Shielding the Unmedia: Using the Process of Journalism to Protect the Journalist's Privilege in an Infinite Universe of Publication,* 39 HOUS. L. REV. 1371 (2003); Laurence B. Alexander, *Looking Out for the Watchdogs: A Legislative Proposal Limiting the Newsgathering Privilege to Journalists in the Greatest Need of Protection for Sources and Information,* 20 YALE L. & POL'Y REV. 97 (2002); Clay Calvert, *And You Call Yourself a Journalist? Wrestling With a Definition of "Journalist" in the Law,* 103 DICK. L. REV. 411, (1999); Daniel A. Swartwout, *In Re Madden: The Threat to New Journalism,* 60 OHIO ST. L.J. 1589 (1999); Kraig L. Baker, *Are Oliver Stone and Tom Clancy Journalists? Determining Who Has Standing to Claim the Journalist's Privilege*, 69 WASH. L. REV. 739 (1994).

[80] In Re: Grand Jury Subpoena, Judith Miller, 397 F.3d 964 (D.C. Cir. 2005).

[81] Letter from Brian A. Benczkowski, Principal Deputy Assistant Attorney General, to Rep. Lamar S. Smith (July 31, 2007), *available at* http://www.usdoj.gov/opa/mediashield/odni-view-ltr-hr2102-092707.pdf (last visited Sept. 5, 2008).

[82] Personal interview.

[83] Personal Interview.

[84] Debra J. Saunders, *Josh Wolf – blogger – has no press pass*, S.F. CHRONICLE, Feb. 27, 2007 at B7 and In re: Grand Jury Investigation, No. CR 06-90064 MISC MMC (MEJ) (N.D. Cal., April 5, 2006).

[85] Bob Egelko, *Cameraman jailed for not yielding tape,* S.F. CHRONICLE, Aug. 2, 2006 at A1.

[86] Personal interview.

[87] *Id.*

[88] *Id.*

[89] *Id.*

[90] *Id.*

[91] In re Grand Jury Subpoena, Joshua Wolf, No. 06-16403, D.C. No. CR-06-90064-MMC (9th Cir., Sept. 8, 2006).

[92] *Id.*

[93] *Free Josh Wolf,* SAN FRANCISCO CHRONICLE, August 3, 2006, at B6.

[94] *Id.*

[95] Dana Hull, *Lone Wolf,* AMERICAN JOURNALISM REVIEW, April/May 2007.

[96] Bob Egelko and Jim Herron Zamora, *The Josh Wolf Case: Blogger freed after giving video to feds,* S.F. CHRONICLE, April 4, 2007, at B1.

[97] *Id.*

[98] Walter Pincus, *Senate Panel Freezes Bill on Legal Protections for Reporters,* THE WASHINGTON POST, Sept. 24, 2006. For an analysis of prior federal attempts, see Anthony L. Fargo, *Analyzing Federal Shield Law Proposals: What Congress Can Learn from the States,* 11 COMM. L. & POL'Y 35 (2006).

[99] H.R. 2102, 110th Cong. (2007). For a comparison of the major bills in the 109th and 110th Congress, *see Journalist's Privilege: Overview of the Law and Legislation in the 109th and 110th Congress,* C.R.S. Report for Congress, (July 29, 2008), *available at* http://www.fas.org/sgp/crs/secrecy/RL34193.pdf (last visited Sept. 20, 2008).

[100] O'Grady v. Superior Court, 44 Cal. Rptr. 3d 72 (Cal. Ct. App. 2006), *overturning* Apple Computer, Inc. v. Doe, No. 1-04-CV-032178 (Cal. Super. Ct., Mar. 1, 2005). *See also* Matthew Bloom, *Subpoenaed Sources and the Internet: A Test for When Bloggers Should Reveal Who Misappropriated a Trade Secret,* 24 YALE L. & POL'Y REV. 471 (2006); *Protecting the New Media: Application of the Journalist's Privilege to Bloggers,* 120 HARV. L. REV. 996 (2007).

[101] *Id.* at 70.

[102] *Id.* at 49.

[103] *Id.* at 70.

[104] While the O'Grady case was a victory for online journalists, an earlier Apple lawsuit resulted in a settlement in which Apple dropped its attempts to identify a blogger's sources in exchange for the blogger's agreement to stop publishing the Web site. Apple Computer, Inc. v. Nick DePlume. No. 1-05-CV-033341 (Cal. Super. Ct. Complaint filed Jan. 18, 2005). *See also* Reporters Committee for Freedom of the Press News Media Update, *Apple strong-arms Web site into going dark,* Dec. 20, 2007, *available at* http://www.rcfp.org/newsitems/index.php?i=149 (last visited Sept. 9, 2008).

[105] Reporters Committee for Freedom of the Press News Media Update, *Anonymous bloggers protected by shield law, judge finds,* Sept. 4, 2008, *available at* http://www.rcfp.org/newsitems/index.php?i=6964 (last visited Sept. 9, 2008).

[106] NORMAN PEARLSTINE, OFF THE RECORD: THE PRESS, THE GOVERNMENT AND THE WAR OVER ANONYMOUS SOURCES 88 (2007).

[107] Walter Pincus, *Anonymous sources: Their use in a time of prosecutorial interest,* Nieman Watchdog, July 6, 2005., *available at* http://www.niemanwatchdog.org/index.cfm?fuseaction=Showcase.view&show caseid=0019 (last visited April 1, 2009).

[108] *Id.*

[109] Doug Clifton, *Jailing Reporters, Silencing the Whistleblowers,* CLEVELAND PLAIN DEALER, June 30, 2005, at B9.

CHAPTER 3

National Security Leaks and the Valerie Plame Case

But for the press, Americans might not know about the United States' "extra-legal" domestic-wiretapping program or the CIA's rendition program with "secret prisons" in foreign countries that were created as part of President George W. Bush's "War on Terror." The journalists who broke these stories won Pulitzer Prizes and were heralded as heroes of their profession. Vice President Dick Cheney called the Pulitzer honor a "disgrace," and the Bush administration and allies in Congress said the journalists might be guilty of treason or espionage, not to mention a lack of patriotism.

It is somewhat ironic, then, that Vice President Cheney was central to the leak that gave rise to one of the most significant yet peculiar journalist's privilege cases in a generation. The case focused on the leak of the identity of Valerie Plame Wilson, a CIA agent with covert status whose cover was publicly blown by journalist and conservative columnist Robert Novak. Novak got the information from two Bush administration officials, it was later revealed. The investigation into the leak resulted in the subpoenas of several journalists, and ten journalists were required to testify in the criminal trial of I. Lewis "Scooter" Libby, Cheney's chief of staff. On March 6, 2007, a Washington D.C. jury convicted Libby of five counts of obstruction of justice, making false statements and perjury.[1] The cautious, loyal and discreet Libby, described as "Cheney's Cheney," had resigned his influential government post sixteen months earlier when he became the first sitting White House official to be indicted on felony charges in 130 years.[2]

Journalists were central to the case of *The United States v. I. Lewis Libby,* the result of a long and expensive investigation into the public outing of Plame, whose identity was leaked by several Bush administration officials in an apparent attempt to undermine the credibility of Plame's husband, Joseph C. Wilson IV, a former U.S. ambassador who publicly alleged the Bush administration cherry-picked intelligence to justify the invasion of Iraq in 2003.[3]

For journalists, the Libby trial was a nightmare scenario. In trying to quash subpoenas for their testimony, journalists did not have legal precedents on their side. As a matter of ethics, journalists were split on the appropriate responses, given the aggressive nature of the special prosecutor's investigation, the presence of signed waivers from sources, and the awkward position of protecting potentially criminal wrongdoing by top executive-branch officials. As a matter of press freedom, though, the *New York Times* characterized the case as the "most serious confrontation between the government and the press since the Pentagon Papers case in 1971."[4] By the trial's end, ten journalists took to the witness stand, many of whom were forced to testify about the intricacies of their newsgathering practices.[5] Under oath, several reporters and editors seemingly violated their initial promises of confidentiality to news sources, and by doing so, helped secure Libby's conviction.

For example, Judith Miller of the *New York Times,* who spent 85 days in jail attempting to avoid having to testify, said during the trial that she agreed to deceptively identify Libby as a "former Hill staffer," walked the jury through her sketchy note-taking process imperiled during one of her interviews with Libby by a broken pen, and somewhat incredulously claimed she couldn't remember who first provided her with Plame's name, despite its presence in her notebooks as "Valerie Flame," "V.F." and "Valery.[6] Matt Cooper of *Time* magazine discussed how he peppered Libby with sensitive questions as Libby was trying to get him off the phone, prefaced with "off the record" and "on background," failed to take detailed notes of the responses, and then wrote indiscreet emails to various editors about his conversations with both Libby and Karl Rove.[7] Tim Russert, then the Washington bureau chief of NBC News, testified that Libby was lying when Libby told prosecutors and the grand jury that he first learned of Plame's identity from Russert. Russert was battered on the witness stand over his faulty memory and admitted that he, as a matter of routine, considered all conversations with top officials "off the record."

He nonetheless readily discussed his conversation with Libby when an FBI agent asked him about it, even though he and NBC subsequently decided to contest a grand jury subpoena seeking the same information that Russert had already provided to the FBI, on grounds that it would have a "chilling effect on my ability as a journalist."[8] And Bob Woodward, of Watergate fame and more recently the author of several insider accounts of the Bush administration as well as an editor for *The Washington Post*, sat in the witness chair as an audiotape was played of Woodward's interview with yet another government official who had been promised his words would remain confidential.[9]

As Max Frankel, the former executive editor of the *New York Times* whose brief on confidential sources submitted in the *Pentagon Papers* case has been widely cited by the courts and in legal scholarship, recalled in one reflection on the Libby trial:

> (T)here I sat, watching the United States government in all its majesty dragging into court the American press (in all its piety), forcing reporters to betray confidences, rifling their files and notebooks, making them swear to their confused memories and motives and burdening their bosses with hefty legal fees – all for the high-sounding purpose, yet again, of protecting our nation's secrets. Top-secret secrets! In wartime! … [Journalists'] messy relationships with officialdom were uncomfortably on display. We heard about celebrated correspondents routinely granting anonymity – better called irresponsibility – to government sources just to hear whispered propaganda and other self-serving falsehoods. We learned how our patriotic guardians of wartime secrets wantonly leak them to manipulate public opinion, protect their backsides or smear an adversary. And we learned again how clumsy are the criminal laws with which high-minded prosecutors try to discipline the politics of Washington. [10]

NATIONAL SECURITY LEAKS AND THE PRESS

The Plame affair was but one of several high-profile clashes between the press and the administration of President George W. Bush. Three newspaper disclosures about classified anti-terrorist programs highlight the role of confidential sources in journalist disclosures of government secrets. First was the disclosure of existence of secret CIA prisons in foreign countries. On Nov. 2, 2005, Dana Priest of the *Washington Post* published a story with the headline "CIA Holds Terror Suspects in Secret Prisons," that disclosed that the CIA had a secret network of prisons in foreign countries known as "black sites."[11] The story suggested the United States likely violated the laws of the host countries and argued that disclosure of the prisons' existence was in the public interest given then-recent allegations of widespread prisoner abuse by the U.S. military in Afghanistan and Iraq. The story, which publicized information classified as secret by the government, was made possible by confidential sources who were government employees who thought some measures were counterproductive to the broader "War on Terror."[12]

Government officials claimed the story damaged relations with foreign countries where the secret prisons had been held. Within days, Republican leaders of the Senate and House called for investigations into who leaked the information. Senate Majority Leader Bill Frist and House Speaker Dennis Hastert wrote in a joint statement that the "egregious disclosure could have long-term and far-reaching damaging and dangerous consequences, and will imperil our efforts to protect the American people and our homeland from terrorist attacks."[13] On the other hand, the *Washington Post* was praised for disclosing the information. "What these activities are, are the secret detention and abuse, behind dark walls, of prisoners, some of whom may be innocent. And I don't think it should be the kind of role of a U.S. newspaper in a free society like ours to be protecting the continuation of such atrocities by withholding this kind of information," said Peter Kornbluh, a senior analyst with the National Security Archive, a non-government organization that collects declassified government information.[14]

The second controversial press disclosure occurred a month later when the *New York Times* revealed the existence of a domestic wiretapping program in a story with the headline "Bush Lets U.S. Spy on Callers Without Courts."[15] The story described a secret presidential order in 2002 that authorized the National Security Agency to eavesdrop on Americans suspected of links to terrorism without court-approved warrants. The story had been in the works for more than a year, and President Bush had personally appealed to *Times* editor Bill Keller not to run the story.[16] The President, in a meeting with the newspaper's editors in the Oval Office, said the newspaper would be partially responsible if another terrorist attack occurred. The story was initially held, but later drafts of the story focused less on the specifics of technological aspects and more on questions about executive power and the possibilities of lawless action.[17] The final, published story cited "nearly a dozen current and former officials" as sources, motivated by "their concerns about the operation's legality and oversight."[18]

The third disclosure to spark outrage from the Bush administration ran on June 22, 2006, in both the *New York Times* and the *Los Angeles Times*. The newspapers reported that a secret program approved by Bush allowed counterterrorism officials to access financial records from a vast international database. The program was described as essential to tracing terrorist financing networks, but another official told reporters "the potential for abuse is enormous."[19] In the days after the initial news stories, President Bush said the "disclosure of this program is disgraceful. We're at war with a bunch of people who want to hurt the United States of America, and for people to leak that program, and for a newspaper to publish it, does great harm to the United States of America."[20] Vice President Dick Cheney was more direct: "Some in the press, in particular the *New York Times*, have made the job of defending against further terrorist attacks more difficult by insisting on publishing detailed information about vital national security programs."[21] The Republican-controlled House of Representatives voted 227-183 to "condemn" the publication of the information. A New York congressman asked the Department of Justice to investigate an espionage prosecution, and Attorney General Alberto Gonzales said the statute would likely allow for a prosecution.[22]

These disclosures, along with others about abuse at Abu Ghraib, the destruction of CIA "enhanced interrogation" videotapes, the waterboarding of prisoners and classified memos on torture, reveal longstanding tensions between the press and the state. The threats of prosecution under the Espionage Act invoked comparisons between the Bush administration and the Nixon administration. While the Bush administration said the press disclosures harmed national security by disclosing secret government programs, newspaper editors defended their reporting using the reasoning of Justice Hugo Black in the Pentagon Papers case. "Our job, especially in times like these, is to bring our readers information that will enable them to judge how well their elected leaders are fighting on their behalf, and at what price," wrote the editors of the *New York Times* and *Los Angeles Times* in a joint op-ed titled "When Do We Publish a Secret?"[23] They also discussed their practices of investigation and publication:

> How do we, as editors, reconcile the obligation to inform with the instinct to protect?
>
> Sometimes the judgments are easy. Our reporters in Iraq and Afghanistan, for example, take great care not to divulge operational intelligence in their news reports, knowing that in this wired age it could be seen and used by insurgents.
>
> Often the judgments are painfully hard. In those cases, we cool our competitive jets and begin an intensive deliberative process.
>
> The process begins with reporting. Sensitive stories do not fall into our hands. They may begin with a tip from a source who has a grievance or a guilty conscience, but those tips are just the beginning of long, painstaking work. Reporters operate without security clearances, without subpoena powers, without spy technology. They work, rather, with sources who may be scared, who may know only part of the story, who may have their own agendas that need to be discovered and taken into account. We double-check and triple-check. We seek out sources with different points of view. We challenge our sources when contradictory information emerges.
>
> Then we listen. No article on a classified program gets published until the responsible officials have been given a fair opportunity to comment. And if they want to argue that publication represents a danger to national security, we put things on hold and give them a respectful hearing. Often, we agree to participate in off-the-record conversations with officials, so they can make their case without fear of spilling more secrets onto our front pages.
>
> Finally, we weigh the merits of publishing against the risks of publishing. There is no magic formula, no neat metric for either the public's interest or the dangers of publishing sensitive information. We make our best judgment.[24]

What do the disclosures say about the editorial judgment process of journalists? Editors say they "begin an intense deliberative process" when confronted with the decision to publish sensitive information in the face of pleas not to publish. Reporters are charged with seeking alternative viewpoints and contrasting angles; government officials are invited to make the case that publication will be harmful. And then, editors make tough judgment calls. "We understand that honorable people may disagree with any of these choices – to publish or not to publish. But making those decisions is the responsibility that falls to editors, a corollary to the great gift of our independence. It is not a responsibility we take lightly. And it is not one we can surrender to the government."[25]

The public interest in the disclosures includes providing citizens with relevant facts about government programs and political decisions. How can one make sound judgments about the government's abilities in waging war without knowledge of what the government is doing? Obviously, this tension is particularly inherent to covert operations that benefit from obscurity. But the American system has largely ceded to the press the constitutional authority to shine light on these programs if they are able to learn about them. The case becomes stronger when the programs raise questions about the legality of the programs themselves. Senator Arlen Specter, chairman of the Senate Judiciary Committee at the time the banking program was disclosed, suggested the press was serving more as a check and balance for the executive branch than was Congress. "(W)hy does it take a newspaper investigation to get them to comply with the law? That's a big, important point. What else don't we know is going on until we read it in the *New York Times*?"[26] Media organizations have pointed to the public interest in these types of stories during other privilege litigation. "Stories like the recent Pulitzer Prize-winning reports exposing the black sites where the CIA detained high-value targets or the careless disregard of injured soldiers at Walter Reed Army Hospital only saw the light of day because the reporter spent years building credibility and confidence with sources," read one *amicus* brief in filed in the Steven Hatfill lawsuit.[27]

In 2008, following the disclosure of the NSA domestic spying program by the *New York Times*, Congress debated the merits of the program. Bush administration officials had tried to keep the program secret, and thus the debate was never meant to be had by Congress. In one interview, Mike McConnell, the director of national intelligence, said "Americans are going to die" because of the public nature of the debate. The enemy wasn't supposed to know about the program, he said. Steven Aftergood, who runs the Project on Government Secrecy for the Federation of American Scientists, provided this assessment of McConnell's comments: "He's basically saying that democracy is going to kill Americans."[28]

Our society has generally operated under the assumption that official secrecy is bad for democracy. The "War on Terror," however, has operated as a clandestine operation relying heavily on intelligence information that works only when conducted in secret. Disclosure of methods and information are particularly threatening to these efforts.

President Bush's administration is hardly the first or last administration to have a problem with leaks. One study by the Senate Intelligence Committee in 1987 found that 147 separate disclosures of classified information were published by eight national newspapers in a six-month period.[29] In the summer of 2010, aggressive leak investigations and prosecutions under President Barack Obama led the *New York Times* to conclude in a front-page news story that "the Obama administration is proving more aggressive than the Bush Administration in seeking to punish unauthorized leaks to the press."[30] The disclosure of hundreds of thousands of classified documents by the rogue website Wikileaks in the fall of 2010 also underscored a new environment in which the institutional press no longer served as a gatekeeper for protecting disclosure of the most sensitive types of information based on traditional journalism ethical considerations.[31]

While Wikileaks presents a paradigm-shifting example, if any story in American journalism best illustrates competing conceptions of journalistic duty to protect sources who leaked national security secrets, it is the publication of the so-called Pentagon Papers in 1971. Daniel Ellsberg, a former government employee, leaked the classified documents to *The New York Times*, which after weeks of careful deliberation began publishing the documents, as well as news stories examining their significance. President Richard Nixon ordered his administration to seek an injunction against the newspaper, resulting in one of the most important free press decisions ever issued by the Supreme Court of the United States.

In 1971, Ellsberg was a defense analyst who became convinced that the American public had been lied to and deceived about its involvement in Vietnam. After trying unsuccessfully to make the report public through several U.S. senators, Ellsberg contacted Neil Sheehan of the *New York Times*.[32] Over the course of several weeks, Ellsberg convinced Sheehan of the significance of the documents and encouraged them to be published verbatim. In his memoir, Ellsberg wrote:

> We didn't talk about protecting me as the source. I took it for granted that it would do that, up to a point, and I didn't ask for any special measures if it came to the paper's facing legal pressures. I didn't want credit either as a source or as a participant in the study, but I didn't make any requests on how the Times handled that. I assumed that the government would know, or assume, that I was the source.[33]

The *Times* began publishing excerpts and stories based on the documents on June 13, 1971, despite heated disagreement among *Times* editors and their lawyers.[34] On June 15, 1971, Attorney General John Mitchell sent the *Times* a letter asking the newspaper to suspend publication of the material and turn over the documents to the government. After the *Times* declined, the government sought and received a temporary restraining order from a federal judge. Dramatically, the case quickly made its way to the U.S. Supreme Court, and in *New York Times v. United States*, the Court sided with the newspaper's right to publish the information.[35] Justices Black, Douglas, Stewart, Brennan, White and Marshall joined in the judgment but each wrote an opinion. Justice Black, joined by Douglas, wrote a passionate defense of press freedom and concluded the First Amendment bars all prior restraints against the press. In one of the most "pro-press" statements ever written by a Supreme Court justice, Justice Black wrote:

> In the First Amendment the Founding Fathers gave the free press the protection it must have to fulfill its essential role in our democracy. The press was to serve the governed, not the governors. The Government's power to censor the press was abolished so that the press would remain forever free to censure the Government. The press was protected so that it could bare the secrets of government and inform the people. Only a free and unrestrained press can effectively expose deception in government. And paramount among the responsibilities of a free press is the duty to prevent any part of the government from deceiving the people and sending

them off to distant lands to die of foreign fevers and foreign
shot and shell. In my view, far from deserving condemnation
for their courageous reporting, the *New York Times*, the
Washington Post, and other newspapers should be
commended for serving the prupose that the Founding Fathers
saw so clearly. In revealing the workings of government that
led to the Vietnam war, the newspapers nobly did precisely
that which the Founders hoped and trusted they would do.[36]

Justices Stewart, Brennan, and White wrote the government had
the power to obtain a prior restraint against the press, but had not met
its heavy burden, and made much of the lack of congressional
authorization of such a restraint.[37] Chief Justice Burger and Justices
Harlan and Blackmun dissented. Harlan, whose opinion was joined by
the other dissenters, said the executive branch deserved great deference
in matters of foreign affairs and national security and would have
remanded the case back to lower courts.[38] Blackmun, in his own
opinion, came close to accusing the *Times* of being responsible for the
death of soldiers from the "great harm to the nation" that could come
from disclosure of the classified material.[39]

The lesser-known story about the Pentagon Papers case is what
happened to the source. Almost immediately, Ellsberg was suspected of
being the leaker, and press accounts described the search for Ellsberg
as "the largest FBI manhunt since the Lindbergh kidnapping."[40] While
the FBI couldn't find Ellsberg, CBS's Walter Cronkite did,
interviewing him on June 23 from a house in Cambridge,
Massachusetts. Ellsberg was eventually charged with twelve felonies,
carrying a maximum sentence of 115 years in prison. His trial took
place at the height of the Watergate controversy, while top-ranking
White House officials were resigning. Then, it was disclosed that the
White House had orchestrated a break-in of Ellsberg's psychoanalyst's
office, among other illegal acts committed by government agents. The
judge overseeing Ellsberg's trial granted a motion to dismiss the
indictment because of the government misconduct.[41]

In 1971, Max Frankel, then the Washington bureau chief for the
New York Times, submitted an affidavit to support the *Times'* right to
publish the so-called Pentagon Papers. In the document, Frankel
described the culture of reporting in Washington that required the use
of confidential sources. The brief is worth quoting at length, and has

been cited in several subsequent legal proceedings and scholarship on the justification for journalistic use of confidential sources:

> The Government's unprecedented challenge to *The Times* in the case of the Pentagon papers, I am convinced, cannot be understood, or decided, without an appreciation of the manner in which a small and specialized corps of reporters and a few hundred American officials regularly make use of so-called classified, secret, and top secret information and documentation. It is a cooperative, competitive, antagonistic and arcane relationship. I have learned, over the years, that it mystifies even experienced government professionals in many fields, including those with Government experience, and including the most astute politicians and attorneys.
>
> Without the use of "secrets" that I shall attempt to explain in this affidavit, there could be no adequate diplomatic, military and political reporting of the kind our people take for granted, either abroad or in Washington and there could be no mature system of communication between the Government and the people. That is one reason why the sudden complaint by one party to these regular dealings strikes us as monstrous and hypocritical – unless it is essentially perfunctory, for the purpose of retaining some discipline over the Federal bureaucracy.
>
> I know how strange all this must sound. We have been taught, particularly in the past generation of spy scares and Cold War, to think of secrets as secrets – varying in their "sensitivity" but uniformly essential to the private conduct of diplomatic and military affairs and somehow detrimental to the national interest if prematurely disclosed. By the standards of official Washington – Government and press alike – this is an antiquated, quaint and romantic view. For practically everything that our Government does, plans, thinks, hears and contemplates in the realms of foreign policy is stamped and treated as secret – and then unraveled by that same Government, by the Congress and by the press in one continuing round of professional and social contacts and cooperative and competitive exchanges of information.

The governmental, political and personal interests of the participants are inseparable in this process. Presidents make "secret" decisions only to reveal them for the purposes of frightening an adversary nation, wooing a friendly electorate, protecting their reputations. The military services conduct "secret" research in weaponry only to reveal it for the purpose of enhancing their budgets, appearing superior or inferior to a foreign army, gaining the vote of a congressman or the favor of a contractor. The Navy uses secret information to run down the weaponry of the Air Force. The Army passes on secret information to prove its superiority to the Marine Corps. High officials of the Government reveal secrets in the search for support of their policies, or to help sabotage the plans and policies of rival departments. Middle-rank officials of government reveal secrets so as to attract the attention of their superiors or to lobby against he orders of those superiors. Though not the only vehicle for this traffic in secrets – the Congress is always eager to provide a forum – the press is probably the most important.

In the field of foreign affairs, only rarely does our Government give full public information to the press for the direct purpose of simply informing the people. For the most part, the press obtains significant information bearing on foreign policy only because it has managed to make itself a party to confidential materials, and of value in transmitting these materials from government to other branches and offices of government as well as to the public at large. This is why the press has been wisely and correctly called The Fourth Branch of Government.

I remember during my first month in Washington, in 1961, how President Kennedy tried to demonstrate his "toughness" toward the Communists after they built the Berlin wall by having relayed to me some direct-quotations of his best arguments to Foreign Minister Gromyko. We were permitted to quote from this conversation and did so. Nevertheless, the record of the conversation was then, and remains today, a "secret."

I remember a year later, at the height of the Cuban missile crises, a State Department official concluding that it would surely be in the country's interest to demonstrate the perfidy of the same Mr. Gromyko as he denied any knowledge of those missiles in another talk with the President; the official returned within the hour and let me take verbatim notes of the Kennedy-Gromyko transcript – providing only that I would not use direct quotations. We printed the conversation between the President and the Foreign Minister in the third person, even though the record probably remains a "secret."

I remember President Johnson standing beside me, waist-deep in his Texas swimming pool, recounting for more than an hour his conversation the day before, in 1967, with Prime Minister Kosygin of the Soviet Union at Glassboro, N.J., for my "background" information, and subsequent though not immediate use in print, with a few special off-the-record sidelights that remain confidential ...

Similar dealings with high officials continue to this day.

We have printed stories of high officials of this Administration berating their colleagues and challenging even the President's judgment about Soviet activities in Cuba last year.

We have printed official explanations of why American intelligence gathering was delayed while the Russians moved missiles to the Suez Canal last year.

These random recollections are offered here not as a systematic collection of secrets made known to me for many, usually self-evident (and also self-serving) reasons. Respect for sources and for many of the secrets prevents a truly detailed accounting, even for this urgent purpose. But I hope I have begun to convey the very loose and special way in which "classified" information and documentation is regularly employed by our government. Its purpose is not to amuse or flatter a reporter whom many have come to trust, but variously to impress him with their stewardship of the country, to solicit specific publicity, to push out diplomatically useful information without official responsibility, and, occasionally, even to explain and illustrate a policy that can be publicly described in only the vaguest terms.

This is the coin of our business and of the officials with whom we regularly deal. In almost every case, it is secret information and much of the time, it is top secret. But the good reporter in Washington, in Saigon, or at the United Nations, gains access to such information and such sources because they wish to use him for loyal purposes of government while he wishes to use them to learn what he can in the service of his readers. Learning always to trust each other to some extent, and never to trust each other fully – for their purposes are often contradictory or downright antagonistic – the reporter and the official trespass regularly, customarily, easily, and unselfconsciously (even unconsciously) through what they both know to be official "secrets." The reporter knows always to protect his sources and is expected to protect military secrets about troop movements and the like. He also learns to cross-check his information and to nurse it until an insight or story has turned tripe. The official knows, if he wishes to preserve this valuable channel and outlet, to protect his credibility and the deeper purpose that he is trying to serve.[42]

Writing more than three decades ago, Frankel depicted the ways in which journalists' use of confidential sources aids the public's access to information. Thirty-five years after the Pentagon Papers case, Frankel sat in the courtroom during the Scooter Libby trial, involving the leak of Valerie Plame's identity as a CIA agent, and wrote afterward, "I kept thinking that the compelled testimony about reporters and their sources would end up doing more damage than even the reckless violation of a CIA agent's cover. For given the cult of secrecy that enveloped our government during the cold war and the hoarding of information that always attends the lust for power, a free unregulated and unpunished flow of leaks remains essential to the sophisticated reporting of diplomatic and military affairs, a safeguard of our democracy."[43]

THE JAILING OF JUDITH MILLER

The genesis of Judith Miller's jailing can be found in President George W. Bush's State of the Union speech on January 28, 2003, and the broader propaganda campaign to win public support for the United States' invasion of Iraq that began in March of 2003.[44] In his address to the U.S. Congress, President Bush provided three rationales for the invasion, each of which would later be undermined by evidentiary questions. Relevant to the leaking of Plame's identify were the following sixteen words: "The British government has learned that Saddam Hussein recently sought significant quantities of uranium from Africa."[45] The insertion of this allegation in the State of the Union speech surprised some intelligence experts because the CIA had several months earlier expressed to Congress its doubts about the allegation, and CIA Director George Tenet personally intervened to have the allegation removed from an important presidential speech the previous October.[46] Later, Tenet would apologize and the administration would concede that the allegation should not have been included in the speech.[47]

After the Iraq invasion, the U.S. military failed to immediately find the weapons of mass destruction that the Bush administration had claimed existed in Iraq.[48] On May 6, Nicholas Kristof of the *New York Times* published a column titled "Missing in Action: Truth," that recounted an anonymous ambassador's trip to Niger to investigate the uranium allegation and the ambassador's conclusion that there was no evidence to support it. Records would later show that the Vice President's office seized on the column as damaging to the administration's credibility, and Libby, Cheney's chief of staff, set out to learn more about this ambassador, whose identity was then unknown to senior White House officials. Later, Libby would admit to being consumed, at multiple points each day, with learning more about the former ambassador, Joseph C. Wilson IV.[49]

During his trial, Libby's notes were introduced that showed he learned from Vice President Cheney on June 11, 2003, that Wilson's wife worked in the CIA's Counterproliferation Division. Between June 10 and June 12, several government officials, including Cheney, Libby, the third-ranking State Department official, Cheney's spokeswoman, and the CIA spokesman, discussed the fact that Wilson's wife was a CIA employee, records would later show.[50] A timeline later put together by the special prosecutor showed that Wilson and Wilson's wife were matters of intense discussion within the Vice President's office in mid-June.[51]

While the Kristoff column set off an internal White House debate about Wilson and his Niger trip, Wilson became publicly identified on July 6, 2003, when he published an op-ed in the *New York Times*, appeared on "Meet the Press" and cooperated with reporters writing a profile of him in the *Washington Post*.[52] The op-ed, titled, "What I Didn't Find in Africa," made public his conclusions that the White

House ignored assessments that Iraq had in fact not been attempting to acquire uranium from Niger. Patrick Fitzgerald would later call the op-ed column a "direct attack on the credibility of the President and Vice President," and one investigative reporter said the op-ed made Cheney and Libby "preoccupied with attempting to undercut (Wilson's) allegations and discredit him personally."[53] Just days after the Wilson column's publication, the Bush administration conceded that the Niger allegation should not have been included in the State of the Union speech, an admission that prompted even greater attention to the pre-war intelligence used to justify the Iraq invasion.

One result of White House's preoccupation with Wilson was the outing of Wilson's wife as a CIA agent. The outing occurred publicly on July 14, 2003, when Robert Novak, a conservative columnist and television commentator, wrote in his syndicated column that, "Wilson never worked for the C.I.A., but his wife, Valerie Plame, is an Agency operative on weapons of mass destruction. Two senior administration officials told me his wife suggested Wilson to Niger to investigate the Italian report."[54] Two days later, on July 16, David Corn of *The Nation* crystallized the growing controversy surrounding Novak's column by asking on his blog, "Did senior Bush officials blow the cover of a U.S. intelligence officer working covertly in a field of vital importance to national security – and break the law – in order to strike at a Bush administration critic and intimidate others?" On Time.com on July 17, Matt Cooper wrote an article titled "A War on Wilson?" that quoted "some government officials" as telling *Time* of Wilson's wife's identity. Notably, the story's emphasis was on whether government officials were inappropriately leaking sensitive information to reporters.

Still, many observers saw the leak as routine interplay between journalists and politicians. "The leaks about Wilson's connection to Plame seemed typical of the conversations between reporters and government sources that had been essential to the way Washington had functioned since the founding of the republic," Norman Pearlstine of Time Inc. wrote.[55] However, the Department of Justice launched a leak investigation at the request of CIA Director George Tenet.[56] The leaks were a potential violation of the Intelligence Identities Protection Act, and articles and documents show that Plame's CIA job had been kept secret from even her closest friends, who thought she was a private energy expert, and that she had done "covert work overseas" in the previous five years.[57] But the law set a high hurdle for prosecution. For an individual with authorized access to classified information to be prosecuted to be prosecuted, the government had to prove that he or she had intentionally released the information despite knowing that the government was taking affirmative measures to conceal it.[58]

In September 2003, it became clearer that several government officials may have been involved in leaking the information after *The Washington Post* reported that "two top White House officials called at least six Washington journalists and disclosed the identity and occupation of Wilson's wife," and that the leak, in the words of one anonymous administration official, was "meant purely and simply for revenge."[59] White House spokesman Scott McClellan tried to quell calls for the appointment of a special prosecutor, saying that "there's been nothing, absolutely nothing, brought to our attention to suggest any White House involvement, and that includes the vice president's office as well."[60] McClellan would later say he himself was misled by Libby and Karl Rove.[61]

In December 2003, Attorney General John Ashcroft recused himself from the leak investigation, and his deputy appointed a special prosecutor to lead the leak investigation. The special prosecutor named to head the investigation, Patrick Fitzgerald, the U.S. Attorney in Chicago, was fiercely independent and aggressive.[62] He would also become the first special prosecutor to seek the jailing of a journalist for refusing to cooperate with his investigation.[63]

The first sign that Fitzgerald would subpoena journalists came after Fitzgerald asked White House officials to sign documents "waiving" their any promises of confidentiality they may have received from journalists. By spring 2004, Fitzgerald began contacting journalists, presenting them with the waivers and asking them for their testimony about what the sources said to the reporters about Plame. To many journalists, the waivers were meaningless on their face, having been signed by government employees who were required to do so or risk losing their jobs. The question became more difficult, however, when lawyers for the journalists considered whether it would be appropriate to contact the sources in an attempt to determine the source's true wishes. And if journalists told prosecutors they were not able to obtain personal waivers after contacting their sources, could that be used as evidence of obstruction of justice? Journalists and their lawyers plotted different paths. More pragmatic journalists were inclined to let their lawyers discuss the validity of waivers with their sources and agree to testify if the source's lawyer indicated that the waivers were legitimate. Other journalists, like Judith Miller, seemed at the outset to reject the waivers as meaningless, recognizing as well that a source's lawyer could hardly signal to the prosecutor that the waiver was sincere while signaling to the journalist's lawyers that the waiver was coercive.

For example, *Washington Post* lawyers kept both of their journalists out of legal trouble after reporters received assurances from their source's attorneys that the sources wanted the reporters to talk with prosecutors. Walter Pincus of *The Washington Post* agreed to give a deposition after his source had identified himself to the prosecutor, and Pincus's attorney confirmed with the source's attorney that the source wanted Pincus to cooperate. As part of the arrangement, the special prosecutor asked questions about his conversation with the source without ever requiring Pincus to expressly identify the source, Pincus later wrote.[64] The source was later identified in trial testimony as Ari Fleischer, the White House press secretary who passed along the information about Plame to several reporters – after learning of the information from Libby.[65] Glenn Kessler of *The Washington Post* negotiated an agreement with Fitzgerald that was limited to Kessler's conversations with Libby in early July 2003, during with Kessler said Libby never mentioned Plame.[66] At the trial, it was easy to see why Libby wanted them to testify, since Libby told neither of the reporters about Plame. Russert, too, eventually agreed to cooperate without having testify before the grand jury; instead he was interviewed under oath by Fitzgerald.[67] Russert's argument appeared to be that he had no explicitly confidential interview with Libby and was testifying as defensive tactic to correct the record and show that Russert could not have told Libby about Plame because Russert had no way of knowing the information at the time Russert was alleged to have provided it to Libby.

Unlike Pincus, Kessler and Russert, Matt Cooper of *Time* and Judith Miller of the *New York Times* contested the subpoenas in federal court, and both were held in contempt by U.S. District Court Judge Thomas Hogan.[68] Miller had not written a story about the Plame case, but the trial would later show that she had several interviews with Libby during the period in which Plame's identity was a central focus of the vice president's office.

The trial would later show that Cooper had two sources for his story about the leaking of Plame's identity – Libby and Rove. Rove was the initial source, telling Cooper in a phone call on July 11, 2003 not to "get too far out" on the Wilson story because "a number of things were going to be coming out" about Wilson. Cooper pushed Rove for more information, and Rove acknowledged that Wilson's wife, who Rove did not identify by name but said worked on weapons of mass destruction at the CIA, sent Wilson to Niger.[69] After Rove disclosed this, Rove told Cooper that he had "already said too much," according to Cooper.[70]

It was Rove's failure to initially admit this conversation to the special prosecutor that almost got him indicted for perjury and obstruction. Ironically, it was another *Time* reporter, Viveca Novak, who indiscreetly told Rove's lawyer about the Cooper-Rove conversation during cocktails at a bar, which then led Rove to contact the special prosecutor and amend his testimony. Viveca Novak (no relation to Bob Novak), had apparently learned of Cooper's interview with Rove through "water cooler" talk at *Time*, likely fueled by Cooper's numerous e-mails to editors about Rove that floated around *Time* employees. Rove's apparent explanation to the prosecutor was that he forgot about the Cooper call. In his book about *Time's* role in the case, Pearlstine wrote, "If Rove's brief interview with *Time* got him into trouble, by a strange symmetry his lawyer's conversation with *Time* helped get him out of it."[71]

Libby was Cooper's confirming source. Cooper interviewed Libby by telephone the day after he spoke with Rove. Much of the interview, conducted on the record, was about the vice president office's non-role in sending Wilson to Niger to investigate the uranium claim. But near the end Cooper said he had a few questions to ask "on background," and then asked whether he had heard that Wilson's wife was involved in Wilson's trip. Cooper testified that Libby said, "yes, I have heard that, too," or words to that effect.[72] That was all Cooper needed to report that he had two administration officials confirming the Wilson-Plame connection. Cooper had no notes from the "on background" portion of the interview.[73]

In December 2004, a three-judge panel of the U.S. Court of Appeals for the District of Columbia Circuit heard oral arguments in the Cooper and Miller subpoena case, and in February 2005 issued its decision denying the contempt appeal.[74] Cooper and Miller asserted four arguments to overturn the district court's contempt order. First, they argued that the First Amendment afforded journalists a constitutional right to conceal confidential sources. Second, they argued that the journalists had a common law, qualified privilege that had not been overcome. They also argued that the special prosecutor had violated the journalists' due process rights and had failed to comply with Department of Justice journalist-subpoena guidelines.[75]

The panel unanimously rejected each of the journalists' arguments and upheld the contempt finding, although the three judges issued separate decisions. Judge David B. Sentelle rejected all four arguments, concluding that neither a First Amendment nor federal common law privilege existed. He said the journalists failed to show how there was any material difference between their case and *Branzburg v. Hayes,* in which the Supreme Court rejected a privilege for journalists facing a grand jury subpoena. As for the common law privilege, Sentelle said *Branzburg* rejected this proposition as well, and said that because of the complexity of the issue, a privilege law was best left to the legislature. "The creation of a reporter's privilege, if it is to be done at all, looks more like a legislative than adjudicative problem," Judge Sentelle wrote.[76] Questions about who qualifies for protection and what limits there should be are policy questions that judges are ill-equipped to address, Sentelle said. Among those questions, the judge wrote, are:

> Are we then to create a privilege that protects only those reporters employed by *Time* Magazine and the *New York Times*, and other media giants, or do we extend that protection as well to the owner of a desktop printer producing a weekly newsletter to inform his neighbors, lodge brothers, co-religionists, or co-conspirators? Perhaps more to the point today, does the privilege also protect the proprietor of a web log: the stereotypical "blogger" sitting in his pajama at his personal computer posting on the World Wide Web his best product to inform whoever happens to browse his way? If not, why not? How could one draw a distinction consistent with the court's vision of a broadly granted personal right? If so, then would it not be possible for a government official wishing to engage in the sort of unlawful leaking under investigation in the present controversy to call a trusted friend or political ally, advise him to set up a web log (which I understand takes about three minutes) and then leak to him under a promise of confidentiality the information which the law forbids the official to disclose?[77]

Judge Karen L. Henderson's decision agreed with Sentelle's outcome, but she would not have decided the common-law question, and instead would have accepted for sake of argument that a common-law privilege did exist, but it had been overcome in this case. Judge David S. Tatel, meanwhile, wanted his colleagues to agree that a common-law privilege did exist and that the holding of *Branzburg* was more complicated that Judge Sentelle's reading.[78] Tatel went further by elaborating on how the common law privilege, rooted in Rule 501 of the Federal Rules of Evidence enacted by Congress, supported the judicial recognition of a qualified common-law privilege, even though Tatel too decided that the journalists should testify in the present case.

The U.S. Supreme Court, on June 27, 2005, refused to review the appeals court decisions ordering Miller and Cooper to testify. At a dramatic district court hearing on July 6, 2005, Miller unsuccessfully pleaded with the judge not to send her to jail, while Cooper surprisingly announced his agreement to testify. Cooper told the judge that when he awoke in the morning he had intended to go to jail. But "a short time ago, in somewhat dramatic fashion, I received an express, personal release from my source," Cooper told the judge. "It's with a bit of surprise and no small amount of relief that I will comply with this subpoena."[79]

Cooper had already testified about his conversations with Libby, after he said he received a direct waiver from Libby. But Cooper refused to cooperate with a second subpoena about his interview with Rove. Cooper's lawyers, Robin Bierstedt of Time Inc. and Floyd Abrams, counseled against further contact with Rove. But as Cooper was planning to go to jail along with Miller after the Supreme Court's refusal to hear the case, the *Wall Street Journal* published a story quoting Rove's lawyer, Robert Luskin, saying that Rove spoke to Cooper but had never provided Cooper with Plame's name.[80] Luskin also said Rove never sought confidential source protection from any reporter, "so if Matt Cooper is going to jail to protect a source, it's not Karl he's protecting."[81] Cooper agreed to testify after this story appeared, thus narrowly avoiding going to jail.

Miller, appearing "shaken and scared,"[82] was taken into custody by three court officers. Minutes before, she told Judge Thomas F. Hogan:

> I want to assure you I am not above the law, and do not view myself as above the law. I am here today because I believe in

the rule of law and your right to send me to prison for disobeying your ruling if you choose to do so … But I also know, again from my reporting, that the freest and fairest societies are not only those with independent judiciaries, but those with an independent press that works every day to keep government accountable by publishing what the government might not want the public to know. Journalists are not perfect, but Thomas Jefferson put it best: if he had to choose between government and newspapers, he would choose the latter, because the latter is the long-term guarantor of the former.

If journalists cannot be trusted to guarantee confidentiality, then journalists cannot function and there cannot be a free press. Your honor, I believe that a free press depends now more than ever on people willing to express their views, particularly those in government. From my experience, and the experience of investigative journalists like me, I know that many of these people in government will not talk to reporters if we cannot be trusted to protect their identity. The risks are too great; the government is too powerful; the country is too polarized …

I do not make confidentiality pledges lightly. But when I do, I must honor them. If I do not, how can I expect people to accept my assurances? When offering to protect a source, journalists seldom know in advance whether the information being provided will turn out to be insignificant, or sufficiently strong to produce a story, or of major national importance. My motive here is straightforward; a promise of confidentiality once made must be respected, or the journalist will lose all credibility and the public will, in the end, suffer. This belief is fundamental to my work and therefore who I am …

Your honor, in this case I cannot break my word just to stay out of jail. The right of civil disobedience based on personal conscience is fundamental to our system and honored throughout our history.

For four months in early 2003, I reported on soldiers in Iraq during a very sensitive and dangerous mission. I wrote about people who were truly among our nation's best and bravest – men and women willing to die for their country and its freedom. If they can do that, surely I can face prison to defend a free press.

Your honor, I do not want to go to jail, and I hope you will not send me. But I feel that I have no choice; both as a matter of personal conscience and to stand up for the many who share my views and believe truly in a vigorous and independent press.[83]

In going to jail to protect the identity of a source, Miller was "doing her job as the founders of this nation intended," said the *Times'* publisher Arthur Ochs Sulzberger Jr.[84] Bill Keller, the *Times'* executive editor, said Miller had a "choice of between betraying a trust to a confidential source or going to jail. The choice she made is a brave and principled choice, and it reflects a valuing of individual conscience that has been part of this country's tradition since its founding."[85]

The case took another bizarre twist after Miller announced that after 85 days in jail, she struck a deal with the prosecutors after a phone call with Libby convinced her that Libby wanted her to testify. Prior to her jail sentence, Miller and her attorneys refused to accept the waiver of confidentiality signed by Libby and presented to Miller by the special prosecutor as evidence that Libby wanted her to cooperate with the investigation. As her attorney Abrams wrote later, "From Miller's perspective, the signed waiver was by its nature coerced and thus not a basis for her to lay aside obligations to Libby."[86] Miller had told the judge at the sentencing hearing, "Last week, your honor, you said you could not understand a refusal to testify because the sources in this case had waived their right of confidentiality. But waivers demanded by a superior as a condition of employment are not voluntary. They are coercive. And should they become common practice, and I fear they are, they will be yet another means by wrongdoers in government to silence people who want to report facts of public import to journalists, or to express views that differ from the official orthodoxy."[87]

Abrams also recalled discussing the coercive nature of such waivers with Libby's attorney before Miller went to jail. "When I asked him if the written waiver form was by its nature coercive, Tate [Libby's lawyer] replied with startling candor. Of course the waiver form was by its nature coercive, he told me. How could it not be? If Libby had not signed it, he could not continue to work in the White House. It was as coercive, he said, as the rule that, if Libby or anyone else at the White House took the Fifth Amendment, he would be dismissed."[88] Abrams recalled several conditions for Miller's cooperation: Libby's unequivocal and uncoerced waiver, and a narrow deposition or testimony focusing only on Libby.

After several weeks in jail, Miller instructed another attorney, Robert Bennett, to again inquire as to whether Libby would contact her personally.[89] This occurred after a meeting at the jail between Miller and several of lawyers. Bennett, who had been brought into the case at a late stage, told Miller that Fitzgerald may impanel another grand jury, which would mean that Miller's jail sentence could be extended by as much as eighteen months. Bennett succeeded in getting Libby to write Miller a letter in jail, followed by a fifteen-minute phone call between Libby and Miller, while Miller was still in jail, that assured Miller that Libby in fact wanted her to testify. Soon after, Miller was released and provided testimony to the grand jury. Miller's testimony was one important piece of evidence that helped convince a jury that Libby had lied to prosecutors when he said he first learned from another journalist, NBC's Russert, that Wilson was married to a CIA agent. Miller's testimony showed that Libby indeed had knowledge of Plame earlier than he had told prosecutors. One theory is that Libby initially lied to prosecutors about how learned of Plame's identity to protect his own source, later identified during the trial as Vice President Dick Cheney, and presumed that the journalists would never testify to provide evidence to the contrary.[90]

Within weeks of Miller's cooperation with the prosecutors, Libby was indicted on five criminal counts. In announcing the indictment of Libby at a press conference carried live on national television, Fitzgerald defended his aggressive tactics against journalists.

> I was not looking for a First Amendment showdown ... I do not think that a reporter should be subpoenaed anything close to routinely. It should be an extraordinary case ... I understand why it is that newspapers want sources. And I read newspapers and I'm glad you have sources. This is different. This was a situation where the conversations between the official and the reporter may have been a crime itself ... You couldn't walk in and responsibly charge someone for lying about a conversation when there were only two witnesses to it and you talked to one. That would be insane.[91]

CONCLUSION

The Plame case was in many respects a unique situation that in legal parlance was proof that tough cases make bad law. The interests of justice, in allowing a special prosecutor to determine whether high-ranking public officials violated intelligence laws by unmasking a CIA agent to undermine a political critic, are apparent and important. If a national security crime was committed by the deliberative leak, and only two individuals know the details – the leaker and the journalist – how else is a prosecutor supposed to uncover the truth but for the testimony of the journalist? As the Miller case illustrates, it was difficult to make the case that the law was on the side of the journalists.

The consensus of media lawyers was that the judicial precedent would have bad consequences for journalists. "What has been the impact of the Fitzgerald investigation on the American press?" asked Lucy Dalglish, the executive director of the Reporters Committee for Freedom of the Press. "Prosecutors now feel empowered to go after reporters when they may have at least thought about it more carefully in the past. Now I am hearing reporters say for the first time, 'Well, maybe if our sources are manipulating us for political reasons, it is O.K. to identify them.' We haven't had this many subpoenas since the Nixon years ... My whole staff is working on this issue 24-7."[92] Miller's lawyer Floyd Abrams argued that Miller's jailing had some positive consequences, writing that Miller "will be remembered as an iconic figure in the history of American journalism. No other journalist has paid so high a price in seeking to protect her sources or done more to persuade Congress to contemplate passing, at long last, federal legislation protecting journalists who have promised confidentiality to their sources."[93]

What caused Judith Miller's about-face after 85 days in jail, and what does it say about the complex moral and ethical questions that journalists face under the prospect of indefinite incarceration? These are but a few of the many questions about journalism ethics raised by the Plame investigation and the Libby trial. At first blush, it seemed that Miller was a journalistic hero as she went to jail, fighting for an important journalistic principle. But upon Miller's release, after she decided to testify about her interviews with Libby, even Miller's own employer was questioning whether jail had been necessary all along.[94] Other journalists ensnarled in the case avoided jail after pragmatically accepting waivers of confidentiality. Miller used the same rationale to justify her decision to testify – negating the justification she used to go to jail in the first place. The jail time, and the threat of indefinite incarceration, seemed to work as a coercive tool.

The Miller case showed the practical limits of journalistic promises of confidentiality in the face of an aggressive prosecutor and unsympathetic judges – and when national security issues are at play. So-called waivers of confidentiality, viewed as legitimate in the eyes of the law, forced journalists and their editors to reconsider their promises of confidentiality. After all, did it really make sense for a journalist to go jail when a source has publicly or privately stated his wish that the reporter cooperate? When should journalists believe the source? The successful use of waivers by prosecutors is a troubling new development, with legal and ethical implications. Prosecutors argued that journalists fighting the subpoenas were doing so against the wishes of their sources, who each signed documents asking the journalists to testify. Should journalists accept these waivers as legitimate, or reject them out of hand because individuals were required to sign them as a condition of keeping their jobs? Should journalists attempt to "renegotiate" their initial promises when served with a subpoena, going back to their sources and trying to convince them to release them from earlier promises? Or were those waivers in the words of the *Times'* Bill Keller, an "insidious new menace" that put journalists and sources in impossible situations after promises of confidentiality had been given and accepted? Miller and Cooper were justified in being skeptical about the waivers, but a rigid rejection of all forms of source waivers is also problematic. In Woodward's case, for example, his source, Richard Armitage, Secretary of State Colin Powell's deputy, wanted Woodward to testify and play an audiotape of the interview to demonstrate that the leak was not a coordinated effort to discredit Wilson but the result of an indiscreet, off-hand remark.[95] Woodward would be in a peculiar spot if he refused to testify while his source was insisting that he cooperate.

The case also showed the murky ground rules that reporters and sources often agree to for interviews. What constitutes a promise of confidentiality in the first place? Matt Cooper wrote that "Rove told me the conversation was on 'deep background.' I explained to the grand jury that I take the term to mean that I can use the material but not quote it, and that I must keep the identity of my source confidential.[96] But after Matt Cooper fought for months to avoid testifying and narrowly avoided jail, Rove said, "Our ground rule was 'deep background.' I never asked to be treated as a confidential source. Everyone would have been better off if Matt had just agreed to testify about our conversation."[97] The debate over nomenclature was crucial for Norman Pearlstine, the editor-in-chief of Time Inc., who argued that Cooper should never have deemed Rove a "confidential source" in the first place, but rather an "anonymous source" that freed Cooper from legal obligations of protection. The distinction is a fine one, but it is central to new ethics guidelines established by Pearlstine after the case.

Reporting practices also came under scrutiny. The Plame case split the journalistic community on several matters. Editors and publishers turned on their own reporters in some cases. Other journalists criticized the subpoenaed journalists' reporting practices, and some reporters were accused of becoming willing participants in government propaganda campaigns.

Still others wondered what the responsibility of a journalist was when all legal appeals have been exhausted. Do they have an obligation – professionally or ethically – to go to jail? Some editors, like Time Inc.'s Pearlstine, did not think so. "I think it is detrimental to our journalistic principles to think of ourselves as above the law," Pearlstine said. Pearlstine wrote that the Plame case in particular "emboldened the Department of Justice, other prosecutors, and civil plaintiffs, leading to the biggest increase in subpoenas since the Nixon era, all seeking reporters' testimony about their confidential sources and about the information gained from them."[98]

Gabriel Schoenfeld, in his 2010 book *Necessary Secrets: National Security, the Media, and the Rule of Law*, argued that it is institutional journalists who need to reassess their moral arguments that justify disclosing classified secrets. Schoenfeld has argued that the newspapers that disclosed classified secrets should be prosecuted under the Espionage Act. "Bill Keller and Dean Baquet (the editors of *the New York Times* and *Los Angeles Times*) and journalists like them are claiming unfettered freedom of action with accountability to no one but themselves. They refuse to recognize that the law, even a law seldom or never employed as a coercive instrument, is an expression of the public's will."[99]

In the Pentagon Papers case, Daniel Ellsberg's leak of thousands of pages of classified documents ultimately resulted in a landmark Supreme Court decision upholding the press's right to publish the material, despite its secret classification. As Justice Black wrote in the court's decision, "The press was protected so that it could bare the secrets of government and inform the people." But the case was predicated in part on the ethical standards of the *New York Times*, and the care it used in vetting the material and providing necessary context and analysis. The loss of the institutional gatekeeper, especially as it relates to the disclosure of national security secrets, has raised new concerns about the limits of the privilege in both ethics and law. The posting of thousands of classified reports on the website Wikileaks in late 2010 is an example. While Daniel Ellsberg has lauded Wikileaks' founder Julian Assange, Professor Stephen J.A. Ward has called upon Wikileaks to develop a code of ethics that addresses its motivations and practices.[100] One of the fears is that the loss of journalism ethical discourse associated with new media efforts such as Wikileaks will prompt more aggressive policing and regulation of media disclosures.

These first three chapters have provided an overview of the complexities of the journalist's privilege to protect confidential sources. I have examined the general issues at stake and how journalists in particular cases have wrestled with those issues. The next four chapters look backward into American journalism and legal history and explore how the concept of journalistic duty to protect sources developed in professional practice. In examining the evolution of conceptions of duty from the colonial newspapers through the rise of journalistic professionalization to the articulation of free-press principles as positive constitutional law, we can see how the journalist's privilege has long underscored a healthy tension between government and the press, one that has eluded easy fixes in ethics as well as law.

Chapter 3 Notes

---

[1] A wealth of primary documents related to the Libby case are reprinted in MURRAY WAAS, THE UNITED STATES V. I. LEWIS LIBBY (2007). The indictment is at Waas at 11.

[2] *Id.* at 1.

[3] Judge orders Libby jailed during appeal, CNN.com, June 14, 2007, *available at* http://www.cnn.com/2007/POLITICS/06/14/libby.hearing/index.html (last visited June 1, 2009).

[4] Adam Liptak, *Reporter Jailed After Refusing to Name Source*, N.Y. TIMES, July 7, 2005.

[5] The trial transcripts are reprinted in Waas, *supra* note 1.

[6] *Id.* at 219.

[7] *Id.* at 225.

[8] *Id.* at 366.

[9] *Id.* at 404.

[10] Max Frankel, *The Washington Back Channel,* N.Y. TIMES MAGAZINE, March 25, 2007, at 42.

[11] Dana Priest, *CIA Holds Terror Suspects in Secret Prisons*, WASH. POST, Nov. 2, 2005.

[12] At least one of these leakers was later identified as an employee of the CIA's inspector general's office and was fired after failing a lie-detector test. Robert Windrem and Andrea Mitchell, *NBC: CIA officer fired after admitting leak,* MSNBC.com, Apr. 21, 2006. The employee denied the leaking. Mark Hosenball and Michael Isikoff, *Secrets of the CIA,* NEWSWEEK, April 24, 2006.

[13] Jonathan Weisman, *GOP Leaders Urge Probe in Prisons Leak,* WASH. POST, Nov. 9, 2005.

[14] On the Media, transcript, *Prison Break,* Nov. 11. 2005. available at: http://www.onthemedia.org/transcripts/2005/11/11/03 (last visited June 1, 2008.

[15] James Risen and Eric Lichtblau, *Bush Let's U.S. Spy on Callers Without Courts,* N.Y. TIMES, Dec. 16, 2005.

[16] Rachel Smolkin, *Judgment Calls,* AMERICAN JOURNALISM REVIEW, October/November 2006.

[17] *Id.*

[18] *Id.*

[19] Eric Lichtblau and James Risen, *Bank Data is Sifted by U.S. in Secret to Block Terror,* N.Y. TIMES, June 23, 2006.

[20] Smolkin, *supra* note 16.

[21] *Id.*

[22] *Id.*

[23] Dean Baquet and Bill Keller, *When Do We Publish a Secret?* N.Y. TIMES, July 1, 2006.

[24] *Id.*

[25] *Id.*

[26] ERIC LICHTBLAU, BUSH'S LAW: THE REMAKING OF AMERICAN JUSTICE 256 (2008).

[27] Brief of Amici Curiae Media Organiations in Support of Appellant Toni Locy at 3, Hatfill v. Gonzales, Civil Action No. 03-1793 (D.D.C.).

[28] Lichtblau, *supra* note 26, at 308-309.

[29] GABRIEL SCHOENFELD, NECESSARY SECRETS: NATIONAL SECURITY, THE MEDIA, AND THE RULE OF LAW (2010), at 22 (citing Mark Lawrence, *Executive Branch Leads the Leakers: Senate Staff Study Challenges Claim That Congress Is to Blame*, WASH. POST, July 28, 1987 at A13).

[30] Scott Shane, *Obama Steps Up the Prosecution of Media Leaks,* N.Y. Times, June 12, 2010, at A1.

[31] Raffi Khatchadourian, *No Secrets*, NEW YORKER, June 7, 2010, at 40.

[32] DANIEL ELLSBERG, SECRETS: A MEMOIR OF VIETNAM AND THE PENTAGON PAPERS 368 (2002).

[33] *Id.* at 373-374.

[34] SANFORD J. UNGAR, THE PAPERS & THE PAPERS: AN ACCOUNT OF THE LEGAL AND POLITICAL BATTLE OVER THE PENTAGON PAPERS 108 (1972).

[35] New York Times v. United States, 403 U.S. 713 (1971).

[36] *Id.* at 717.

[37] *Id.* at 715, 727, 724, and 730.

[38] *Id.* at 752.

[39] *Id.* at 759.

[40] Ellsberg, *supra* note 32, at 394.

[41] *Id.* at 456.

[42] Max Frankel Affidavit in Pentagon Papers Case, available at http://www.pbs.org/wgbh/pages/frontline/newswar/part1/frankel.html (last visited April 1, 2009)

[43] *Id.* at 43.

[44] *See generally* Marie Brenner, *Lies and Consequences: Sixteen Words That The World*, VANITY FAIR, April 2006, at 206.

[45] *Id.*

[46] *Id.*

[47] *Id.*

[48] *Id.*

[49] *Id.* Wilson had served as acting ambassador to Iraq before the Persian Gulf War of 1991.

[50] *Id.*

[51] *Id.*

[52] *Id.*

[53] Wass, *supra* note 1, at 2.

[54] Robert D. Novak, *Misson to Niger*, WASH. POST, July 14, 2003 at A21.

[55] NORMAN PEARLSTINE, OFF THE RECORD: THE PRESS, THE GOVERNMENT AND THE WAR OVER ANONYMOUS SOURCES 18 (2007).

[56] Douglas Jehl and David Stout, *Cover Story Kept Work for C.I.A. A Secret,* WASH. POST, Oct. 2, 2003, at 25.

[57] *Id.* and Michael Isikoff, *Plame Was Still Covert*, NEWSWEEK, Feb. 13, 2006, at 9.

[58] Pearlstine, *supra* note 55, at 28.

[59] Mike Allen and Dana Priest, *Bush Administration is Focus of Inquiry; CIA Agent's Identity was Leaked to Media,* WASH. POST, Sept. 28, 2003, at A1.

[60] *Id.*

[61] SCOTT MCCLELLAN, WHAT HAPPENED: INSIDE THE BUSH WHITE HOUSE AND WASHINGTON'S CULTURE OF DECEPTION (2008).

[62] *See* Brenner, *supra* note 44.

[63] *Id.*

[64] Walter Pincus, *Anonymous sources: Their use in a time of prosecutorial interest*, Nieman Watchdog, July 6, 2005., *available at* http://www.niemanwatchdog.org/index.cfm?fuseaction=Showcase.view&showcaseid=0019 (last visited April 1, 2009).

[65] *See* Wass, *supra* note 1, at 398 and 146.

[66] *See* Pearlstine, *supra* note 55, at 32.

[67] *Id.* at 57.

[68] *Id.* at 56.

[69] Wass at 227.

[70] *Id.*

[71] Pearlstine, *supra* note 55, at 190.

[72] Wass, *supra* note 1, at 229.

[73] In re: Grand Jury Subpoena, Miller, No. 04-3138 (2nd Cir. 2005).

[74] *Id.*

[75] *Id.*

[76] *Id.*

[77] *Id.*

[78] *Id.*

[79] Pearlstine, *supra* note 55, at 120.

[80] *Id.*

[81] *Id.*

[82] Adam Liptak, *Reporter Jailed After Refusing to Name Source*, N.Y. TIMES, July 7, 2005.

[83] Statement of Judith Miller, July 6, 2005, statement of Judith Miller to Chief U.S. District Judge Thomas F. Hogan before being jailed for contempt of court for refusing to disclose her source, available at *http://www.rcfp.org/shields_and_subpoenas/miller_statement.html* (last visited March 17, 2009).

[84] Arthur Ochs Sulzberger, Jr. and Russell T. Lewis, *The Promise of the First Amendment*, N.Y. TIMES, Oct. 10, 2004.

[85] Adam Liptak, *Reporter Jailed After Refusing to Name Source*, N.Y. TIMES, July 7, 2005.

[86] FLOYD ABRAMS, SPEAKING FREELY: TRIALS OF THE FIRST AMENDMENT 296 (2006 ed).

[87] *Id.*

[88] *Id.* at 297.

[89] *Id.*

[90] *Id.*

[91] *Transcript of Special Counsel Fitzgerald's Press Conference*, WASH. POST, Oct. 28, 2005.

[92] Marie Brenner, *Lies and Consequences: Sixteen Words That The World*, VANITY FAIR, April 2006, at 206.

[93] Abrams, *supra* note 88, at 301-302.

[94] *Id.*

[95] Waas, *supra* note 1, at 406.

[96] Matt Cooper, *What I Told the Grand Jury*, TIME, July 17, 2005.

[97] Pearlstine, *supra* note 55, at 187.

[98] *Id.*

[99] GABRIEL SCHOENFELD, NECESSARY SECRETS: NATIONAL SECURITY, THE MEDIA, AND THE RULE OF LAW (2010), at 275.

[100] Stephen J.A. Ward, *How to Reveal Secrets*, THE CANADIAN JOURNALISM PROJECT, Aug. 24, 2010 (*available at* http://www.j-source.ca/english_new/detail.php?id=5492, last visited Nov. 1, 2010).

CHAPTER 4

Early Development of Professional Duty to Protect Sources, 1721-1958

In explaining their refusal to comply with court orders seeking their testimony about confidential sources and newsgathering information, the three journalists who served record-long jail sentences between 2001 and 2007 justified their decisions on conceptions of journalistic duty. Judith Miller, the New York Times reporter who refused to reveal who told her the name of a CIA agent and spent 85 days in jail, told a federal judge that "my motive here is straightforward; a promise of confidentiality once made must be respected, or the journalist will lose all credibility and the public will, in the end, suffer." She added, "Your honor, I do not want to go to jail, and I hope you will not send me. But I feel that I have no choice; both as a matter of personal conscience and to stand up for the many who share my views and believe truly in a vigorous and independent press."[1] Blogger Josh Wolf, who served 226 days in jail, declared that a subpoena seeking his testimony before a federal grand jury was a "true assault on my code of ethics."[2] On his blog, Wolf proclaimed himself to be "longest jailed journalist in U.S. history" for "committing journalism" and "protecting his sources' confidentiality and defending the First Amendment."[3] And aspiring true-crime writer Vanessa Leggett spent 168 days in jail because, as she said, "I have a duty to uphold. I promised my sources that I would keep them confidential. And I am going to."[4]

The lack of agreement on core ethical and legal elements, examined in the last three chapters, raises questions about the historical origins and uses of the journalist's privilege. The modern claim that professional ethics and First Amendment values compel journalists to protect confidential sources, even in face of judicial coercion, is not a recent phenomenon in press law. This chapter develops the historical roots of journalistic duty to protect sources, focusing on the period of 1721 to 1958 – a period in which journalists periodically ran afoul of the law as they tried to protect confidential sources but before they explicitly advanced First Amendment arguments in the courts. While the First Amendment did not play a substantive role in early arguments of a journalist's privilege during the 19th and early 20th centuries, this chapter demonstrates that free-press values were one component of journalist's privilege ideology and legal arguments. An understanding of the development of this professional ethic is important in assessing its relevance as a constitutional argument.

Dating as far back as colonial times, expressions of duty to protect confidentiality are found in journalistic practices. Some of the first colonial newspaper editors, for example, went to jail rather than reveal the sources and authors of materials they published. As newspapers over the course of the 19th century evolved from partisan organs to independent deliverers of news to a mass audience, the increasingly importance of the occupation of a reporter led to the articulation of common values and norms. While these values were not articulated in formal codes of ethics until the 1920s, evidence of these journalistic values is found in journalistic arguments about duty to protect confidential sources in the earliest journalist's privilege cases. An examination of more than 30 legal controversies between 1848 and 1958 also shows that reporters were regularly articulating an ethical obligation to protect news sources, even in face of subpoenas and threats of judicial contempt, well before most news organizations established codes of ethics and before several key events identified by historians as turning points in the professionalization of journalism.

JOURNALISTIC DUTY IN COLONIAL TIMES

The colonial-era jailing of James Franklin and John Peter Zenger suggest that journalist's privilege arguments were part of the developing free-press theory and journalistic ideology of the first American newspaper editors. Both cases have occasionally been mentioned as journalist-privilege "firsts" in the legal and historical literature on journalist's privilege, although little scholarship has been done to extrapolate in what ways the two cases involved privilege-like claims.[5] Both newspaper publishers got themselves into trouble with colonial authorities after publishing anonymous criticisms of government officials, and both declined to name these writers when confronted with government demands. In this respect, the publishers' claims of a right to keep secret the names of writers resemble contemporary claims by journalists of a right to keep secret the names of confidential sources. In this section, I will briefly examine primary and secondary sources regarding each case and consider what each case offers to the beginnings of the ethical and legal concepts of journalistic duty to protect confidential sources.

In 1721, James Franklin began publishing the New-England Courant, only the fourth newspaper printed in colonial America and the first to publish a variety of articles that today would be commonly recognized as journalism. Franklin was a printer by trade but couldn't resist the power of the printing press to publish both his own views and those of critics of colonial authority. His newspaper was usually half of a large folio sheet, approximately 6 and ½ by 10 inches, printed in two columns on each side. Sometimes it was two pages, but when Franklin had more material, it was an entire folio sheet, folded once to make four pages.[6] On the bottom of the last page, the newspaper contained the following: "Boston: Printed and Sold by J. Franklin at his printing house in Queen Street, over against Mr. Sheaf's School, where Advertisements are taken in."[7] The newspaper appeared on Mondays, the day the mail arrived, and cost ten shillings a year, or three to four pence per edition. Circulation figures are unknown, but historians estimate that Franklin would have printed, at most, 300 copies per press run.

The content of the paper resembled many elements of modern newspapers. The first issue contained articles about the history of inoculation, a local fire that affected 150 homes, and the election of four men to the general assembly.[8] It was the first newspaper to publish election returns, which suggests an interest in promoting debate about local public affairs.[9] The second issue announced a weekly publication schedule "at the desire of several Gentlemen in town."[10] In this edition, Franklin wrote that he hoped the Courant will be of "universal use" to its readers and said he hoped that nothing published will "disparage clergy, affairs of gov't, decency, or good manners."[11] This direct dialogue with readers hadn't been seen before, and it displayed Franklin's desires for his newspaper to be a forum for a wide range of ideas, as well as active participation from readers. By the fourth issue,

Franklin printed a "Foreign Affairs" section and began to print letters from citizens. Brief book reviews appeared as did abstracts of articles from London as well as advertisements.

Franklin's newspaper was also the first to publish reports from regular "reporters." His newspaper drew articles from a cadre of local writers who often published anonymously or with pseudonyms. The paper's writers were branded the "Hell-Fire Club" by their critics, perhaps unwittingly contributing to a culture of journalistic writers unshackled to criticize authority.[12] Although they were unpaid, these writers hoped to use the forum created by the New-England Courant to establish themselves as writers and local political leaders.[13]

The Courant's content included community news and satirical and humorous pieces. In issue No. 22, Franklin published a letter from a man who claimed to be too afraid of his wife to tell her how controlling she really is. She's a regular reader of the Courant, the man wrote, so he'd rather tell her through the paper.[14] A few weeks later, the Courant published a letter from a woman saying her husband is a lazy, lying man who tricked her into marriage. He was a regular reader of the Courant, the woman wrote, and will recognize himself upon reading the letter.[15] The Feb. 26, 1722, edition contained an article that apparently identified a local prostitute in a humorous article about the immoral activities of one's neighborhood.[16] Many editions contained letters from readers, indicating the presence of a reading culture around the newspaper. The letters often refer to previous editions of the Courant and the two other daily newspapers, indicating the presence of a culture interested in public affairs. The Courant became a forum for communication in a city that had few other means of mass communication.

Franklin also published tracts regarding press freedom, including a series of essays known as Cato's Letters that originally appeared in the London Journal. The essays written by John Trenchard and Thomas Gordon are passionate defenses of freedom of conscience and thought. The articles were also critical of the church and state of 18th century England.[17] Franklin's selection of this material is revealing because it shows his support of libertarian views on press freedom, which at this time were untested in the colonies.

It was Franklin's refusal to accept as gospel the words of religious leaders that first got him into legal trouble. By 1721, inoculation for a small pox outbreak was widely debated. Inoculation was controversial, and Franklin published several items critical of religious leaders' support of inoculation. One historian noted, "The Courant was admired because Franklin said what many a reader had dreamed of saying to the stern Puritan leaders."[18] Another historian said the Courant's inoculation articles "frightened many a reader. It made them scornful of inoculation and skeptical of the Mathers."[19] The newspaper's coverage of inoculation also involved criticisms of religious leaders, including Increase and Cotton Mather, although Franklin published both pro- and anti-inoculation articles. For example, in the Nov. 13, 1721, issue, Franklin attached this editor's note to a letter: "We have receiv'd the following Letter from an unknown Hand, in favour of Inoculation, which we hope our Readers (Anti-Inoculators) will bear with, since they have been promis'd, and are well to Same Liberty of speaking their Minds in this Paper."[20] This idea of the newspaper as a marketplace for divergent ideas would appear over and over again in the New-England Courant:

> Hence, to anathematize a Printer for publishing the different Opinions of Men, is as injudicious as it is wicked. To use Curses without a Cause, is to throw them away as if they were Nothing Worth, and to rob them of their Force when there is Occasion for them.
>
> The Courant was never design'd for a Party Paper. I have once and again given out, that both Inoculators and Anti-Inoculators are welcome to speak their Minds in it; and those who have read the Courants must know, that I have not only publish'd Pieces wrote among ourselves in favour of Inoculation, but have given as full an Account of the Success of it in England, as the other Papers have done; Yet the Envy of some Men has represented me as a Tool to the Anti-Inoculators. What my own Sentiments of things are, is of no Consequence, nor any matter to any Body: I hereby invite all Men, who have Leisure, Inclination and Ability, to speak their Minds with Freedom, Sense and Moderation, and their Pieces shall be Welcome to a Place in my Paper.[21]

Franklin's first formal brush with the law came after he raised the ire of local officials after he published a pamphlet pointing to attempts to pass laws that could be used against printers.[22] He then published an article questioning whether colonial authorities were lax in dealing with pirate attacks on ships along the New England coast. Taken in total, James Franklin's newspaper had antagonized too many, too much. The Massachusetts General Court ordered Franklin jailed until he apologized. After three weeks, he relented, apologized, and was released.[23]

The direct link to privilege-related claims comes from Ben Franklin's autobiography, in which he wrote about his brother's jailing:

> One of the pieces in our newspaper on some political point, which I have now forgotten, gave offense to the Assembly. He was taken up, censured, and imprisoned for a month by the Speaker's warrant, I suppose because he would not discover the author. I, too, was taken up and examined before the Council; but though I did not give them any satisfaction, they contented themselves with admonishing me and dismissed me, considering me perhaps the apprentice who was bound to keep his master's secrets.[24]

Once out of jail, James Franklin went back on his apology and published even more strenuous defenses of printer rights. In response to calls that the Courant was too inflammatory, the newspaper published several defenses of free speech: "Without Freedom of Thought, there can be no such Thing as Wisdom and no such Thing as publick Liberty, without Freedom of Speech; which is the Right of every Man, as far as by it, he does not hurt or control the Right of another: And this is the only Check it ought to suffer, and the only Bounds it ought to Know."[25]

After James Franklin became the target of officials, he published a letter written from "your hearty Friends & Wellwishers," that listed eight rules Franklin should follow to not offend those in power, including: "be very tender of the Religion of the Country;" don't cast "injurious Reflections on the Reverend and Faithful Ministers of the Gospel;" "By no means cast any Reflections on the Civil Government;" avoid publishing "prophane and scandalous Authors:" and "Be very general in your Writing, and where you condemn any Vice, do not point out particular Persons, for that has offended many Good People, and many Occasion great disturbances in Families and Neighborhoods."[26]

James Franklin did not heed his friends' advice. In the first issue in 1723, he published an essay that proclaimed some religious leaders were "on several Accounts worse by far than those who pretend to no

Religion at all." The article was seething. About religious leaders, the author wrote, "They have the Blaze of a high Profession, when perhaps they are blacker than a Coal within."[27] Franklin was ordered by the legislature to apply for a license to continue printing but refused.[28] In the next issue, he printed a poem against oppression, saying, "My Refuge is thy Word." The General Council ordered Franklin's arrest, but the local sheriff was unable to find him for several days. However, Franklin eventually was found and arrested again.

Franklin and the Courant are routinely noted by historians as significant to American journalism's beginnings. Historian Walter Isaacson wrote the Courant "ought to be remembered on its own as America's first fiercely independent newspaper, a bold, antiestablishment journal" with an editor who was "the first great fighter for an independent press in America."[29] Historian Edwin Emery said Franklin's spirit of rebellion "helped establish the tradition of editorial independence, without which no press can be called free." Emery also speculated about Franklin's motivation. "One wonders what motivated this brash fellow. He was fully aware that independent publishers before him had suffered for their outspokenness. There was no special immunity for him. Apparently, Franklin engaged in his hazardous calling because he loved a fight. Many a career in journalism has been similarly motivated since that time, but Franklin was a pioneer of the Fourth Estate."[30]

A decade after Franklin's jailing, another colonial newspaper editor challenged the law over his right to publish anonymous writers. John Peter Zenger was indicted on a charge of seditious libel after a series of articles in 1733 and 1734 in his New-York Weekly Journal offended colonial governor William Cosby. Examples include a December 3, 1733, edition that contained stories criticizing the governor for permitting French warships to spy on defenses and allowing only his favorite members attend council meetings.[31] The thin-skinned governor had grown tired of criticism in the opposition newspaper published by Zenger and finally convinced a prosecutor to charge Zenger with seditious libel, after failed attempts at getting the colonial assembly to do so.[32] Grand juries had rejected previous attempts to indict Zenger, including one in which the grand jury rejected an indictment because of a prosecutor's failure to identify the writers of the alleged libels.[33]

The historical record of the case, derived from Zenger and his attorney Andrew Hamilton's personal accounts, makes clear that the primary legal question was whether the material was libelous, not on the question of a right to anonymous speech or a journalist's privilege. Still, Hamilton said that Zenger's protection of the identity of the governor's confidential critics are rooted in "a right of liberty of both exposing and opposing arbitrary power (in these parts of the world at least) by speaking and writing truth."[34] Hamilton argued that Zenger's publications were not false, and therefore could not be libelous, a strategy was considered a form of jury nullification since the law at the time did not allow for truth as a defense to libel claims. A jury returned a verdict of not guilty, and the case remains a central component of free-press lore for allowing popular sovereignty to trump laws suppressing truthful criticism of government. Still, while not directly a journalist's privilege case, in 1949, the New York Law Revision Commission, charged with determining whether a journalist's privilege statute should be introduced in New York, noted the Zenger case showed "that the concealment, by a journalist, of the origin of articles critical of government, was an important question in New York as early as two centuries ago."[35]

The Franklin and Zenger cases demonstrate several important things, although their relevance to contemporary privilege claims is limited. While not models of the watchdog press that would emerge later in the 19th century, the jailings of Franklin and Zenger show even the earliest American newspaper editors recognized that their societal role created ethical responsibilities and duties to challenge local authority.

Both cases also demonstrated the convergence of the developing right of anonymous speech with the development of journalism ideology that was occurring in the Revolutionary Era. Anonymous articles were commonplace in the newspapers of the American colonies, and even the writers of the Federalist Papers preferred anonymity. In his decision in the 1995 U.S. Supreme Court case McIntyre v. Ohio Elections Commission, Justice Clarence Thomas relied heavily on the colonial era's understanding of the value of anonymous political speech to rule in favor of an individual's right to distribute unsigned pamphlets regarding a local ballot initiative. For example, Justice Thomas said the Zenger case "signified at an early moment the extent to which anonymity and the freedom of the press were intertwined in the early American mind."[36] The court's majority in the McIntyre case said that:

> Under our Constitution, anonymous pamphleteering is not a pernicious fraudulent practice, but an honorable tradition of advocacy and of dissent. Anonymity is a shield from the tyranny of the majority ... The right to remain anonymous may be abused when it shields fraudulent conduct. But political speech by its nature will sometimes have unpalatable consequences, and, in general, our society accords greater weight to the value of free speech than to the dangers of its misuse.[37]

Today, the anonymous speech doctrine has continued relevance to privilege claims, especially as it concerns the rights of Internet forum posters and access to Internet Service Provider addresses.[38] As a distinct First Amendment doctrine, anonymous speech rights have become even more complicated in the Internet age. News organizations have been drawn into the legal disputes in cases arising from anonymous posters in "comments" sections, and bloggers have also tested the boundaries of legal protections. The Supreme Court has not articulated the standards for when an individual's right of anonymous speech must yield to other interests, leaving lower courts and scholars to debate the standards. Still, legal protections for anonymous speech have long been predicated on the proposition that the marketplace of ideas is enhanced when individuals have incentives to contribute to the marketplace, and anonymity is one incentive. Journalists have often been used as a vehicle for the extension of this concept.

THE RISE OF JOURNALISM AS A PROFESSION

While the colonial and Revolutionary era saw the roots of journalistic duty develop in connection with the protection of anonymous speech rights, by the second half of the 19th century journalists had fully articulated the journalist's privilege as a distinct principle in the courts. Cases involving journalists threatened with jail after failing to reveal their sources occurred periodically in the 19th and early 20th centuries, suggesting that the concept of journalistic duty to protect sources was an established and accepted journalism practice.

The evolution of journalist arguments found in the case law discussed in this chapter coincides with a number of dramatic changes in newspapers in the 19th century. Generally, historians categorize the century into three periods: the partisan press period that dominated the first three decades; the transformation of the penny press and the role of news in the Civil War between the 1830s and 1870s, and the dominance of the mass-circulation, independent newspaper by the 1880s and 1890s.

Technological inventions and developments during this century allowed for newspapers to expand in size and reach. Printing press advances lowered costs and transportation improvements allowed citizens to regularly access newspapers in ways unseen before. Paper production and railroad expansion helped lower the costs of newspaper delivery. The telegraph, created in the 1840s, allowed for faster delivery of content. The Associated Press, created in 1848, developed objectivity as a business model to sell its news to a variety of newspapers, causing some historians to argue that Associated Press was crucial to objectivity being embraced as an important value for newspapers in general.[39]

Institutionally, newspapers moved from being organs of political parties to touting independence and autonomy. The "penny press" of the 1830s established the importance of advertisers and street sales, and the content of newspapers focused on a more robust definition of "news," including political and police news at both a national and local level.[40] Social historian Michael Schudson argues that the changes in journalism in the 1830s were the result of an expanding market-based economy, growing political democracy, and the rise of an urban middle-class that emphasized political and social equality.[41]

As the technological advances and changing business models of the 19th century made newspapers more attuned to attracting readers, newspapers justified their work as being in the public interest.[42] The concept of "news" held by newspapers of the late 19th century prioritized facts and data, accumulated and synthesized quickly by reporters. Reporters were expected to be objective and impartial chroniclers of news whose work was done on behalf of the public.[43]

By the 1890s, reporters, as distinguished from editors, "constituted a self-conscious occupational group with its own myths, traditions, and clubs or other meeting places," Schudson argues. The occupation of a reporter was a social invention of the late 19th century, Schudson claims, and by the 1890s, "reporters were for the first time actors in the drama of the newspaper world."[44] Prior to this period, newspapers were generally run by editors who printed materials by correspondents, friends, and political supporters. But by 1890, newsgathering had become "a new and important calling."[45] The increase of reporters with college degrees was one cause of the improvement of newspaper writing and the rise of ethics and standards. "Reporters in the 1890s saw themselves, in part, as scientists uncovering the economic and political facts of industrial life more boldly, more clearly, and more 'realistically' than anyone had done before," Schudson argues.[46]

Other historians have identified key themes of the development of the journalism profession in the 19th century. Historian William E. Huntzicker's study of journalism between 1833 and 1865 emphasizes the "changes in technology, in social status, and in occupational roles for journalists" as causes of significant changes in the content and reach of journalism during this period.[47] Huntzicker argues that the Civil War was a turning point that cemented independence and verifiable, eyewitness reporting as an important value for journalists. Dan Schiller's work on objectivity and commercialization also examines how the changing American society in the early 19th century created a market for the penny press and the expansion of journalistic forms.[48] The new institutional role of journalism as watchdog emerged through the penny press as a necessary check on the abuses of government without subverting state authority.[49] Schiller argues that the "impartiality and independence" claimed by the penny press allowed newspaper journalists to be viewed as defenders of natural rights and the public good.[50]

There is only sparse scholarship on the development of reporting practices and journalistic professionalism in the 19th century. Writing in 2005, Professor Patrick Lee Plaisance claimed that "documentation of the evolution of how ethics came to be applied within American journalism remains sketchy."[51] Professor Hazel Dicken-Garcia has outlined the broad contours of the development of journalistic standards in the 19th century in her study of the period's press criticism.[52] The study emphasizes journalist standards and practices, as well as ideas and concepts of "right or wrong journalistic conduct" in 19th century newspapers. Over the course of the 19th century, Dicken-Garcia argues, the role of a reporter became more important to the newspaper product. At the beginning of the century, "reporters" physically worked the presses, and assembled copy from personal letters, eyewitness accounts and other newspapers. By the end of the century, reporters were actively seeking out interviews, conducting investigations and background research and developing areas of reporting specialization.[53]

Research into the history of journalism professionalization generally traces its beginnings to the early 20th century, based on the confluence of standards articulated in codes of ethics, the rise of university education, and the growing network of professional organizations and publications.[54] At the turn of the century, two trade publications emphasized journalism's professional philosophy and reflected the "press' transitional intellectual outlook from industry to quasi-profession," according to Professor Mary M. Cronin. The *Journalist* was the first regularly published trade magazine, peaking with a circulation of 7,500 in 1888.[55] *Editor & Publisher* began publication in 1901 and contained articles on professional standards and practices in almost every issue.[56] University programs were being developed to train journalists on the profession's values and norms. The first school of journalism was created in 1908 at the University of Missouri, and within four years 30 American colleges and universities were offering journalism courses.[57] In 1914, Walter Williams, the founder of the Missouri School of Journalism, published "The Journalist's Creed," a pithy statement extolling the virtuous nature of journalism and calling journalists "trustees of the public:"

> I believe in the profession of journalism. I believe that the public journal is a public trust; that all connected with it are, to the full measure of their responsibility, trustees for the public; that acceptance of a lesser service than the public service is betrayal of this trust. I believe that clear thinking and clear statement, accuracy and fairness are fundamental to good journalism. I believe that a journalist should write only what he holds in his heart to be true. I believe that suppression of the news, for any consideration other than the welfare of society, is indefensible. I believe that no one should write as a journalist what he would not say as a gentleman; that bribery by one's own pocketbook is as much to be avoided as bribery by the pocketbook of another; that individual responsibility may not be escaped by pleading another's instructions or another's dividends. I believe that advertising, news and editorial columns should alike serve the best interests of readers; that a single standard of helpful truth and cleanness

should prevail for all; that the supreme test of good journalism is the measure of its public service. I believe that the journalism which succeeds best – and best deserves success – fears God and honors Man; is stoutly independent, unmoved by pride of opinion or greed of power, constructive, tolerant but never careless, self-controlled, patient, always respectful of its readers but always unafraid, is quickly indignant at injustice; is unswayed by the appeal of privilege or the clamor of the mob; seeks to give every man a chance and, as far as law and honest wage and recognition of human brotherhood can make it so, an equal chance; is profoundly patriotic while sincerely promoting international good will and cementing world-comradeship; is a journalism of humanity, of and for today's world.[58]

By the 1920s, the existence and importance of journalism ethics was widely accepted. Journalism textbooks of this period emphasized ethical principles and decision-making. A journalist's duty to keep promises to sources was a "dominant theme" of the earliest journalism textbooks, according to one study.[59] For example, a 1904 text quoted an Associated Press reporter saying that "never betray a confidence" was a "golden rule" of journalism.[60]

Scholarly works, such as the 1925 book The Conscience of the Newspaper, by University of Kansas Professor Leon Nelson Flint, articulated the principles of ethical journalism and analyzed their practical implications for daily newspaper editors and reporters. Flint examined the journalistic allegiance to truth and the ethical questions about what is newsworthy and when is it morally right not to publish information. And in defending journalism as a profession, Flint argued that the necessity of education, the articulation of clear norms of practice and behavior, and the collective societal value of journalism show that journalism all demonstrated the professional characteristics of journalism, despite not having an enforcement mechanism. The professionalism movement even provoked lawmakers in several states to introduce legislation creating journalist licensing committees.[61]

Confidential source protection warranted only brief mention in Flint's work. In discussing the "right and wrong" of suppression, Flint emphasizes that the "trade" of "confidential news" poses several dilemmas under the heading "Don't Violate a Confidence."[62]

Journalists who disclose information that was passed in confidence sometimes are morally right to publish the information, Flint argued (without stating whether the identity of the source was relevant), but so is the publication of news based on confidential sources so long as the reporter has the support of his editor. "(R)eporters may well be cautioned against making any promises of suppression for their paper. The man higher up is the only judge in such cases," Flint wrote.[63]

Codes of ethics began to proliferate in the 1920s, although none of them explicitly dealt with the ethics of source protection. The most significant is the 1923 code of the American Society of Newspaper Editors, which listed seven "Canons of Journalism" related to responsibility; freedom of the press; independence; sincerity, truthfulness and accuracy; impartiality, fair play, and decency.[64] Historians have identified the Kansas Editorial Association's code of ethics as the first code, created in 1910.[65] By 1937, ASNE was lobbying state legislatures to pass journalist's privilege statutes.[66]

By 1940, scholars accepted the premise that journalist-source protection was a canon of journalism ethics. Writing in their book The Law of Newspapers, William R. Arthur and Ralph Crosman summarized the state of the law in regard to the journalist's privilege:

> The old and prideful newspaper tradition that a reporter will not reveal the source of information when given in confidence has no standing, in general, under the law. Newspaper codes of ethics which declare the protection of confidences to be a high principle to be faithfully observed by all engaged in the newspaper profession not only are not binding in a court of law but have been held to amount, substantially, to promises not to obey the law ... Although there is no question that a reporter has a right to withhold the source of his information for the purpose of protecting his news sources, to protect his informant, and for the ethical purpose of being a man of his word, his right ceases when a legal trial or certain investigations of interest and concern to the public are involved.[67]

The articulation of journalistic duty by 19th-century reporters, discussed next, demonstrate the early uses of norms and values as part of broader attempts by journalists to justify their work as being in the public interest. Stephen J.A. Ward argues that the revolution of newspapers in the 19th century caused a radical shift in the ethics of journalism. Journalism moved from an "ethics of persuasion" to an "ethics of popularity" during this period, Ward argues:

> The evolution of ethical norms related closely to the evolution of the mass newspaper. As journalism practice changed, it invented, reinterpreted, or gave greater stress to a number of journalistic norms. Among the most important concepts were independence, factuality, and impartiality. As newspapers' dependence on political parties declined, editors asserted their independence of opinion. As the pursuit of news led to staggering increases in circulation and advertising, newspapers trumpeted the speed, inventiveness, and factual accuracy of their reporters. They sought rhetorically to reinforce readers' confidences in the same way as the newsbook editor had tried to reduce readers' skepticism (sic). As publishers sold their papers to a wide readership of varying political views, their editors made a virtue of political neutrality and the impartiality of their reports. In this manner, the idea developed that journalists were independent professionals, who wrote impartially for the general public.[68]

Despite this period being formative in the development of the reporting occupation and the journalism professionalism movement, it is apparent from the legal cases that newspaper reporters were regularly articulating values and norms of confidential source protection in the 19th century. The cases described in the following pages show the justifications used by reporters to explain their desire to protect confidential sources, suggesting that reporters were articulating the principles of a journalist's privilege that viewed the reporter as an important watchdog of government.

The three dozen cases of actual or threatened jailing of journalists between 1848 and 1957 are drawn from an examination of this period's court decisions, legislative reports, law reviews, and journalism histories. The analysis of these cases identified to the extent possible the arguments that journalists advanced to keep secret their sources and newsgathering information.

This research is valuable in examining the evolution of journalists' legal arguments, although the research is limited by a problem of sources. One legal historian writing in 1970 noted that many cases went unreported in court reports in the prior to the mid 20th century: "(S)ince most courts impose only minimal penalties on recalcitrant newsmen, a newsman adjudged in contempt may not bother to demand a hearing; hence, many incidents may have gone unreported."[69] Another problem existed in identifying and examining the cases in which journalists cooperated with investigations seeking the identity of their sources. Donald A. Ritchie recounted a few of these examples in his history of the Washington press corps, and Leigh Gregg discussed many more cases in her Ph.D. dissertation about journalists and congressional contempt power in the 19th century.[70]

This research found several errors exist in the historical literature. For example, the two most comprehensive secondary sources make several important omissions. Both Maurice Van Gerpen and the Virginia Law Review identify the first privilege case in 1857, overlooked the jailing of journalist John Nugent a decade earlier. And David Gordon, in his own revisionist history correcting the record about the first state to pass a journalist's shield bill, claims that the case at the center of his study, the 1886 jailing of John T. Morris of the Baltimore Sun, was the "first widely reported newsmen's privilege case."[71] This research suggests that several cases exist before 1886 that could be considered better candidates.

JOURNALISTS AND CONGRESSIONAL SUBPOENAS: HOSTILITY, THEN SYMPATHY

The first significant battleground for compelled testimony from journalists came by way of congressional subpoenas with which journalists refused to comply. These cases established that journalists would not readily obey legislative demands and that the limited punishment failed to coerce journalists to testify after being held in contempt. They also demonstrate that journalists used various arguments to justify their refusal to cooperate with government subpoenas, including freedom of the press claims, even if these weren't formal assertions of constitutional rights. Evidence is also found to suggest that over time, lawmakers grew sensitive to journalist claims of ethical duty to protect sources as being in the public interest. Finally, the journalist cases also helped establish the legal parameters for congressional coercion more generally.[72]

Several histories contend that the first journalist privilege claim in the 19th century came in 1857 when the New York Daily Times reported allegations of inappropriate lobbying and bribery in Congress.[73] But more recent scholarship has identified the first case as the 1848 jailing of New York Herald reporter John Nugent. The first four cases of journalists refusing to identify confidential sources noted identified in this research all involve subpoenas to journalists by Congressional committees.

In 1848, Nugent was imprisoned in one of the U.S. Senate's committee rooms for one month after he refused to disclose the source who leaked a secret treaty ending the U.S. war with Mexico, while the treaty was under debate by the Senate in executive session.[74] Nugent's publication of the secret treaty was the final straw for several senators concerned about violations of secrecy rules, and they suspected the president or the secretary of state as the source. In turn, the administration blamed the leak on an unidentified senator. The District of Columbia Circuit Court upheld the Senate's contempt order, focusing primarily on the rights of the Senate to hold recalcitrant witnesses in contempt.[75]

Jailed for a month, Nugent "passed his captivity in comfort" and was even able to send stories to be published in the Herald with the dateline "Custody of the Sergeant-at-Arms."[76] The Herald doubled Nugent's pay while he was being held in the committee room and also published the names of senators who had previously leaked information to the paper. Nugent was released for "health reasons," which historian Don Ritchie claims was the Senate's way of saving face and disposing of the matter.[77] The case shows that newspapers of the mid-19th-century had already developed a habit of publishing government leaks. As Ritchie recounts:

> (Herald editor) James Gordon Bennett condemned the Senate's 'mean and contemptible' actions toward his correspondent and he demonstrated its hypocrisy by publishing a list of senators who regularly slipped secrets to Washington letter writers. The Herald claimed that Daniel Webster divulged the secret sessions to Charles W. March of the New York Tribune; Senator John M. Clayton leaked to James E. Harvey of the Philadelphia North American; and Senator Lewis Cass kept Felix Grund of the Philadelphia

Public Ledger well informed. The Democratic Herald commended the Whig North American for printing "the best reports of those secret debates" and proclaimed Whig senators as "the most comprehensive leakers." The Herald thus exposed – for a fleeting moment – the mutually beneficial relationship between congressional leaders and the press.[78]

The first reported case in the 19th century had all the hallmarks of privilege cases of a later era: a journalist receiving an "illegal leak" publishes a story of great public interest, is jailed for refusing to reveal a source, and becomes a martyr among his colleagues while holding fast to his promises of confidentiality.

In the histories that overlooked the Nugent case, the 1857 case involving James W. Simonton of the New York Daily Times was identified as the first journalist's privilege case in the 19th century. Simonton reported that a group of land speculators was successfully bribing several members in the House with $1,000 a vote.[79] A House committee launched an investigation into the newspaper's source and ordered Simonton jailed after he refused to identify the source.[80] Simonton was heralded by his peers in the press as a "lion" whose "able and manly impromptu defense of his rights, and of the liberty and independence of the Press" was reported to be admired by "intelligent men," showing the existence of professional collegiality surrounding ethical claims.[81] Simonton spent 19 days in jail before the House freed him, deciding that jail would not compel his testimony, nor was it essential to their investigation after several House members involved in the bribery scandal resigned.[82] In her Ph.D. dissertation about the case, Leigh Gregg discussed the role of the Contempt Statute of 1857 in giving Congress explicit authority to hold recalcitrant witnesses in contempt, and categorized Simonton's defenses as procedural, evidentiary, constitutional and "press functional," which included arguments that his accusations were a duty to the public good and that journalistic ethics prohibited breaches of confidence.[83] In recounting the Times' editorial coverage of the case, Gregg noted that the newspaper viewed journalism as a "young, evolving profession, unorganized, and needing to eliminate its partisanship to fulfill its duty of denouncing wrongs in the public arena."[84] This recognized the problems of partisanship in justifying journalism's watchdog role, which were complicated in the case because Simonton himself had admitted to prior lobbying activities.[85]

Subsequent cases signaled even stronger professional support for journalists refusing congressional subpoenas. In 1871, reporters Zeb L. White and Hiram J. Ramsdell of the New York Tribune published a version of a diplomatic treaty that the executive branch released but was deemed classified by the Senate. The journalists refused to reveal their source, citing "professional honor," and their editor announced in an editorial that he was doubling their salaries for the duration of the jail sentence.[86] This sparked a Wisconsin senator to remark that the newspaper's action was criminal, as it was aiding and abetting a crime.[87] Other senators were more sympathetic to press-rights concerns. Senator Shurz of Missouri spoke of the case's "grave conflicts of duty perplexing to the conscience of any man ... and it is extremely difficult for the most conscientious man to decide in which direction the voice of honor or the voice of duty calls him."[88] The journalists apparently spent nine days in incarceration until the Senate's session adjourned.[89]

In 1894, several newspapers published allegations that certain unnamed senators had been bribed for their votes favorable to the sugar industry. A committee subpoenaed reporter Elisha J. Edwards of the Philadelphia Press, and John S. Shriver of the New York Mail and the Express, who both refused to reveal their sources. The Senate then sought to hold the journalists in contempt, and the case then moved to the District of Columbia courts.[90] The journalists argued that public policy should provide for a journalist's privilege.[91] A judge rejected the argument, saying that privileging journalists would encourage more libelous, untruthful and scandalous publications.[92] A federal judge hearing the case ruled that until Congress acted legislatively, the courts cannot "distinguish the public duty of the newsgatherer from that of other individuals," but noted that he did not believe the names sought by the Senate were relevant to its investigation.[93]

Journalists facing subpoenas or other inquiries from Congress in the 19th century lost their legal arguments, although as the cases recounted above show, several journalists maintained their promises of confidentiality even after being jailed and justified their actions by referring to the duty of newsmen. Perhaps the growing defiance by journalists contributed to the increasing sympathy shown by Congress when journalists invoked claims of duty to protect sources. By 1943, Congress appeared more deferential to a journalist whose sources it sought. During World War II, the Akron Beacon-Journal published a story that reported union seamen had refused to unload important cargo on a Sunday because of union rules, and the article received widespread attention.[94] City editor Charles C. Miller was called before a House committee to reveal his paper's sources and declined, while Navy officials said no event ever occurred.[95] The committee did not jail Miller after his refusal to comply with its request and said that while it would have been "helpful" to its inquiry if the journalist cooperated, it understood the "customary practice of newspapers in not revealing the sources of such stories."[96] One historian called this case the "first official body that recognized" the right of the journalist's privilege.[97]

In 1945, Albert Deutsch, a reporter for PM, a leftist daily newspaper published in New York City in the 1940s, was subpoenaed for the sources of stories he wrote critical of the medical coverage for military veterans.[98] The New York Times, which published several stories about the case, said "the action may put the House on record for the first time on the question whether a reporter may be published for refusing to violate a confidence placed in him by a news source."[99] Deutsch refused to testify on the grounds of his "own personal integrity and professional ethics," as well as "freedom of the press."[100] Deutsch argued that his stories were "constructive," although one lawmaker said it was the House Veterans Committee that "is supposed to be investigating veterans' facilities and not newspaper men."[101] Deutsch was cited for contempt by the committee, although the full House declined to take up the matter, and the veterans committee rescinded its contempt charge after public criticism of its actions.[102]

Seven years later, reporter Edward Milne of the Providence Journal and Bulletin was subpoenaed by a House committee investigating charges against Wisconsin Senator Joseph McCarthy. Milne refused to turn over his notes and testify about his sources, and the House committee "expressed its understanding of the newsman's obligation to his sources."[103]

This exploration of the case law of attempts by Congress at compelling testimony from journalists shows that as early as 1848, journalists were advancing privilege claims based on professional ethics. By the mid-20th century, Congress was more willing to defer to journalists, who had more directly tied their professional ethics to free-press concepts.

Cases involving state Legislatures and local governmental units have also appeared in the legal-history literature. In 1897, the California Supreme Court ruled that two reporters for the San Francisco

Examiner, A.M. Lawrence and L.L. Levings, did not have a legal privilege to avoid contempt charges from the state Legislature after they refused to reveal the sources of stories that alleged state lawmakers were taking bribes. The court said the evidence sought from the journalists was relevant and important to the legislative inquiry. The court also said, "It cannot be successfully contended, and has not been seriously argued, that the witnesses were justified in refusing to give these names upon the ground that the communications were privileged."[104]

In 1911, Thomas Hamilton, a reporter for the Augusta (Georgia) Herald, declined to reveal his police sources for a story about a local homicide when subpoenaed by the city's board of police commissioners. Hamilton was convicted of contempt and sentenced to a $50 fine and not more than five days in jail, which was upheld by the Georgia Supreme Court. Hamilton argued that compelled testimony of a journalist was akin to a claim of "forfeiture of estate" in that it would cause him to lose his job because a reporter must be able to keep the confidence of his sources.[105] The journalist said, "It would ruin me in my business. It would cause me to lose my position as a newspaper reporter for the Augusta Herald, and would prevent my ever engaging in the occupation of a newspaper reporter again."[106] He told the investigating committee that he had promised his source confidentiality, a promise the journalist considered sacred.[107] The courts rejected Hamilton's arguments. The state Supreme Court ruled that "to sustain such a doctrine would render courts impotent, and the effort to administer justice oftentimes a mockery."[108]

One other case appears in the legal-history literature regarding state legislative actions. In 1934, L. Vance Armentrout, the acting editor of the Louisville Courier-Journal, refused to cooperate with a state legislative inquiry into which an anonymous state legislator wrote a satirical account of legislative activities that was published in the paper. The editor apparently was jailed for one hour before he was freed, without having cooperated.[109]

GRAND JURIES AND THE PUBLIC INTEREST

A grand jury is a unique creation of law that is intended to investigate whether charges ought to be filed in a particular case. Two types of privilege cases arise regarding grand juries. One involves subpoenas issued to journalists for their testimony or notes while the grand jury conducts an investigation. Another is the attempt to determine the source of leaks to journalists regarding grand jury activity, which is supposed to remain secret.

The first reported case involving a journalist receiving a subpoena from a grand jury is the 1873 case involving New York Tribune city editor William G. Shanks. Shanks refused to identify the author of an article that was alleged to contain libelous statements, telling the grand jury, "I decline to answer the question, because I am instructed, as one of the editors of the paper, not to give the name of writers of articles published in it. It is one of the office regulations, and on the principle that the paper, and not the editor, is responsible."[110] Shanks was committed to the county jail indefinitely, although his commitment was overturned by a judge because of its indefinite duration. On appeal, a judge ruled that "no court could possibly hold that a witness could legally refuse to give the name of the author of an alleged libel, for the reason that the rules of a public journal forbade it," and said that "(i)f, for reasons of public policy, it shall be deemed wise to hold only the editor or publisher of a paper liable for its contents, then the legislature alone can so declare by express enactment, for the contrary doctrine has become too firmly and fixedly imbedded in the common law by the lapse of ages, to be ever altered or disturbed by the courts."[111]

In 1913, a reporter for the Jersey Journal, Julius Grunow, was held in contempt after he refused to testify before a grand jury about sources for a story he wrote about potential graft among village trustees. Grunow told the court, "I declined to give the sources of my information or the names of any person or persons who gave me any information about it and gave as my reason for such refusal that I was a newspaper reporter and therefore could not give up my sources of information." The New Jersey Supreme Court upheld the contempt order, writing that a privilege finds "no countenance in the law. Such an immunity, as claimed by the defendant, would be far reaching in its effect and detrimental to the due administration of law. To admit of any such privilege would be to shield the real transgressor and permit him to go unwhipped of justice."

Also in 1913, George Burdick, the city editor of the New York Tribune, was called before a grand jury and asked to reveal who in the Treasury Department leaked information about customs frauds. As reported by the New York Times, when the fraud was being investigated, "the ship news reporter of The Tribune learned that something was afoot. He conferred with his city editor and the story was printed. When hauled to court and questioned as to their sources of news the two newspaper men refused to answer. A law was cited forbidding customs agents from giving out news of their doings, and the newspaper men said that if they testified they might incriminate themselves."[112] Strangely, the journalist then received a pardon from President Wilson as a means to compel his testimony. Burdick refused to cooperate, and a district court judge held him in contempt. The U.S. Supreme Court overturned the contempt order on the grounds that Burdick did not have to accept the pardon. The New York Times editorialized: "The decision did not go into the right of newspaper men to receive confidential information and protect their informants, but it had the effect of settling that question, since in the future any newspaper man interrogated concerning the source of his information may not only plead his constitutional immunity, but refuse a pardon."[113] In Government and Mass Communications, Zechariah Chafee noted, "(T)he fact remains that the city editor did not talk. He got all the practical advantage of a special newspaper privilege by dressing himself up in the United States Constitution. The prosecution would have been just as well off and saved much trouble for many persons if Burdick had been quietly dismissed from the stand as soon as he declined to betray a confidence."[114]

A number of other cases occurred in which journalists claimed constitutional rights in refusing to testify before grand juries or about grand jury leaks. In 1917 a reporter for the St. Louis Republic, Robert E. Holliway, refused to identify the source of a story regarding the details of a secret grand jury indictment. His contempt sentence was upheld by the Missouri Supreme Court, which refused to recognize a self-incrimination claim. The court said it was irrelevant that the illegal disclosure of the grand jury information was made to "someone desiring to 'scoop' his competitor in the business and printing of so-called news."[115] In 1919, the Colorado Supreme Court upheld a lower court's finding of criminal contempt against the editor of the Colorado Springs Labor News after the editor refused to reveal his sources for a story that alleged a grand jury investigating local corruption was stacked with individuals politically opposed to the political party in power.[116]

Subsequent cases in the 1930s have garnered notice in the legal-history literature. In 1931, the editor of the Hopwell (Va.) News was

sentenced to 30 days in jail for contempt after he refused to provide a
grand jury with the name of a letter writer who had criticized a court
proceeding.[117] The editor, J.W. Mapoles, spent seven days in jail before
a judge released him, saying the sentence was sufficient.[118] In 1933, a
reporter for the San Diego Union, William G. Cayce, faced contempt
charges for refusing to testify before a grand jury investigating a
murder. His attorneys won a dismissal of the case after the grand jury
served an indictment without Cayce's testimony.[119]   In   1934,   A.L.
Sloan of the Chicago American also had contempt charges dropped
after he refused to a tell a grand jury where he received information
about a bribery case, although a judge admonished the reporter for
invoking a right against self-incrimination.[120]

One of the 1930s cases shows how journalists articulated their
ethical and legal arguments. In 1935, Martin Mooney, a reporter for the
New York American, wrote a series of articles about a gambling
network. Mooney was subpoenaed by a grand jury for the names of the
gamblers he interviewed, but he refused to provide them.[121] After being
cited for contempt, Mooney told the judge:

> I believe that a newspaperman is only valuable in his
> profession while he holds in secret confidence information
> given to him on any story and particularly a story of this kind.
> While I first came before the Grand Jury, the purpose of that
> visit was to give the 21 members assembled a general picture
> of conditions. I have readily cooperated to that extent and then
> found out that they were pressing for names and addresses,
> and questions that I could not answer because I wanted to
> work in New York next month. By answering these questions
> I would be branded as a heel, not only in my profession but
> among the people who gave me this information.[122]

The transcript of this unreported decision, reprinted in a state
legislative document years later, shows several discussions between the
judge and the journalist. The judge stressed that the common law had
not extended a privilege to newspapermen in the same way it did to
attorneys and doctors, and that the source of such a privilege would
have to come from the higher courts or from the legislature. The judge,
in drawing comparisons to historical impetus for the attorney and
doctor privileges, said:

I am not prepared to say what the future may hold for newspapermen, or what the policy of the state should be, but the ground urged by this witness is something more or less that was urged at the commencement of the historical development of the privilege which culminated into the existence of recognized privileges between client and attorney, doctor and patient, and those which the law recognizes at common law and which has been embodied in our statute.[123]

Mooney said it was "a great injustice that an innocent newspaperman should be the great prize corralled by the grand jury during its long investigation."[124] The journalist was given a $250 fine and sentenced to 30 days in jail, which was upheld on appeal. The appeals court's decision made clear that the common law did not provide for a journalist's privilege similar to doctors and lawyers, and the source of such a privilege would have to come from the legislature.[125] During oral arguments, Mooney's attorney argued that confidential sources "have been largely instrumental in the exposure of crime and bring about reform" and that requiring compelled disclosure of journalists would "destroy the efficacy of this great instrument for the public welfare."[126] The Mooney case was noted in several law review articles in the 1930s, and in the decade following the case, several shield bills were introduced in the New York state legislature as a result of the decision.

In 1948, an editor and a reporter for the Newburgh News, Douglas Clarke and Charles Leonard, were fined $100 each and sentenced to 10 days in jail for refusing to tell a grand jury the source of copies of lottery tickets published in the newspaper. [127] The journalists argued that their publication was in the public's interest and was intended to inform authorities of criminal activity.[128] They told a judge who held them in contempt: "The code of ethics of the newspaper profession, without any statutory authority, stipulates without compromise that violation of a confidence is the gravest ethical omission of which a newspaper man can stand accused. We feel that we are bound to comply with this principle and to make any sacrifice to perpetuate the lofty ideas of the newspaper profession."[129] The journalists wrote stories from their jail cells and received numerous "congratulatory messages and presents." Their case also sparked the introduction of shield law legislation in New York.[130]

Also in 1948, reporter Nat Caldwell refused to comply with a grand jury subpoena seeking testimony about a story he wrote in the Tennessean about alleged protection bootleggers were receiving from the Tennessee Highway Patrol. In an reported decision, a judge dismissed the subpoena, saying it was "worthless for establishing the commission of any crime."[131] Notably, the judge added: "The press must get its information thru others, of necessity much is given in confidence, and I am unable to hold the witness in contempt in this matter. It's true it is hard to have serious charges made against a public official on hearsay evidence but at times much good has been done in that way."[132]

In 1950, the Florida Supreme Court upheld the contempt conviction and 30-day jail sentence of Miami Life editor Reuben J. Clein, who had refused to tell a prosecutor who provided him with information about a grand jury investigation into local corruption. The editor testified:

> I have printed every thing that I am at liberty to disclose. If I was to reveal the source of my information I may as well go out of business. That has been a moot question for years and years – as to whether or a newspaper man – when he does not do any wrong, don't obstruct justice – has been generally granted that privilege. If I was obstructing justice or done something wrong or hurt something, or hurt some investigation that someone was carrying on, it would be a different matter. Of if I had lied; if I hadn't told the truth. Newspaper men have more or less taken it for granted through the years that they would be accorded that courtesy. It is more or less of an unwritten law.[133]

The Florida Supreme Court quoted approvingly of another state's lower court ruling that suggested a qualified privilege be applied in the common law: "Though there is a canon of journalistic ethics forbidding the disclosure of a newspaper's source of information – a cannon worthy of respect and undoubtedly well founded, it is subject to a qualification – it must yield when in conflict with the interests of justice – the private interest involved must yield to the interests of the public."[134]

Grand jury investigations, and investigations of grand jury leaks, continue to this day to be problematic for journalists when subpoenaed as part of either of type of case. This research suggests this is a longstanding problem and shows the role grand jury related-subpoenas played in the articulation of the early journalist's privilege principle.

Somewhat surprisingly, the legal literature recounts only three cases involving subpoenas at a trial level during this period. One reason may be because of deficiencies in legal reporting, not the absence of cases. In the cases identified, the civil court cases involved journalists subpoenaed as part of a libel case, where the source of the information is often crucial to resolving the legal dispute. In 1886, the Georgia Supreme Court refused to allow a newspaper editor to invoke a privilege against testifying about the source of an alleged libel, holding that the editor would be considered the author himself if he did not reveal the source of the defamation.[135] A similar ruling by an Ohio court in 1901 rejected the availability of a journalist's privilege in a libel case.[136]

The first of the two criminal trial cases involved the 1935 subpoena to T. Norman Palmer of the Brooklyn Eagle in New York City. During a trial involving a "rifle gang," prosecutors subpoenaed the reporter to bolster their case. But the judge ruled that the reporter did not have to testify. "This court recognizes the right of a newspaperman to refrain from divulging sources of his information. If you feel that in doing this [taking the stand], it may interfere with this right you are at liberty to not take the stand at this time."[137] A second case appearing in the legal literature involved a subpoena to a reporter during the prosecution of Ethel and Julius Rosenberg for espionage. The judge in the case ruled the information was not relevant to the proceedings.

RECOGNITION OF JOURNALISTIC DUTY IN EARLY STATE AND FEDERAL LEGISLATION

While judges were generally unwilling to create a legal privilege for journalists to avoid subpoenas and compelled testimony, legislatures began to recognize the public policy implications by the turn of the century. In 1896, Maryland became the first state to pass a journalist's privilege statute, prodded in part by the jailing of Baltimore Sun reporter John Morris a decade earlier. Three decades would pass until legislative activity would be spurred by another high-profile case, this involving the jailing of three reporters for the Washington Times whose investigative reporting uncovered the existence of dozens of illegal bars in the capital city. Members of Congress introduced federal shield legislation for the first time in 1929, and seven additional states passed shield laws in the 1930s. By 1950, 12 states had passed statutory shield laws. The legislative activity suggests that the journalistic articulation of duty to protect sources became a matter of public policy for which journalists found increasing popular support. The rhetorical value of journalistic articulation of duty was an important component in sparking legislative attention.

The Maryland debates were partly prompted by the case of John Morris.[138] On December 10, 1886, Morris a reporter for the Baltimore Sun, was summoned before a grand jury and asked to explain his sources for a story that reported about the secret grand jury indictment against a local sheriff.[139] He told a judge that he "promised his informant not to reveal his name, and that he considered himself bound by that promise."[140] In a subsequent letter to the judge, Morris said "it is to be regretted" that he received information that "ought not to have been communicated to" him, but said that the information "seemed to be actual truth" and that "as a member of an honorable profession" he must "refuse to violate the confidence reposed in him."[141] The judge said Morris should not have ever made such a promise of confidentiality, although the judge seemed reticent to jail Morris in part because he was a popular journalist and recent president of the Baltimore Journalists' Club.[142] The case, covered daily in the Baltimore Sun, took a strange turn when the indictment against the sheriff was dropped and a key witness was charged with perjury. Morris continued to refuse to identify the source of the leak about the original, and now rescinded, indictment, and was sentenced to jail. He served 17 days, until the grand jury's term expired.[143] His lawyers argued that only a fine could be used as punishment and emphasized that Morris's action "was thoroughly honorable and conscientious."[144] The Baltimore Sun editorialized:

> (T)o the detriment of no one and in the line of his vocation, (Morris) refused to betray the source of his information, preferring to accept the consequences in his own person, whatever they might be. There is no honorable man, in or out of journalism, who will not commend Mr. Morris' course. For ourselves, while we can but regret the occurrence, we desire to

say that we appreciate the manly sense of honor which has prompted him throughout.[145]

A decade after the jailing, the Maryland Legislature passed the first shield statute in the United States. David Gordon's history of the bill suggests that lobbying by the Baltimore Journalists' Club was influential in getting the bill introduced.[146] The International League of Press Clubs, at its fifth annual meeting in 1895, had also discussed making the issue a priority for other state legislatures.[147] The law, signed by the governor on April 2, 1896, was labeled as "an act to protect reporters and other newspaper men from being compelled to disclose the source of any news or information procured for publication in any legal or legislative proceedings in the state of Maryland."[148] In addition to the Morris jailing, the lobbying by the Baltimore Journalists' Club and the high esteem in which Maryland journalists were generally held at the time, Gordon hypothesized that the Maryland law was also the result of the lobbying by journalists who regularly covered the Maryland legislature.[149]

The passage of the Maryland statute prompted introduction of similar legislation during the first legislative term of the new state of Utah in 1896, with the help of the International League of Press Clubs, whose conference was attended by a Utah legislator. The bill passed a committee vote, but the bill was called unnecessary by at least two Utah newspapers, and failed to win approval.[150]

It would be another three decades before another high-profile case re-energized legislative interest in the journalist's privilege problem. In 1929, grand jury subpoenas to three reporters for the Washington Times, Gorman M. Hendricks, Linton Burkett, and Jack E. Nevin Jr., prompted widespread attention and sparked lawmakers in several states, and in the U.S. Congress, to introduce journalist privilege legislation.[151] The reporters had participated in an investigation by the newspaper into illegal bars, or speakeasies, during the Prohibition era. The reporters visited 49 illegal establishments and reported on the prices and procedures of the bootlegging operations, without naming their exact locations. The subpoenas sought the names and addresses of particular bootleggers, but the reporters said disclosure of the names would violate "newspaper ethics."[152] "Their purpose, they told the jury, was solely to develop a news story of crime in Washington as an aid to the very cause for which a grand jury session is called," reported Editor & Publisher.[153]

The journalists were initially jailed after their refusal to cooperate, although a different judge ordered their release after "the end of a full day in jail, during which they reported that they had been accorded splendid treatment," the New York Times reported. "Other reporters calling to interview them found one in the jail barber shop and another finishing a second helping of breakfast."[154] Their release was short-lived, and they were back in jail within a few days to serve their 45-day sentence.[155] The Washington Times' editor, William Randolph Hearst, called the jailing an "outrage," and doubled the reporters' salary while in jail.[156] Hearst also presented each reporter with a gold watch, a check for $1,000 and ordered a public reception to be held in the reporters' honor.[157] Ralph W. Benton, the Times' managing editor, said:

> Too much cannot be said of the fine journalistic spirit shown by the three loyal reporters who of their own volition and counter to the advice of counsel elect to go to jail rather than betray newspaper confidences. It is certainly a proud era in the history of any newspaper when it can tell the wide world that any confidences given its representatives are sacred and that rather than violate these confidences its reporters will serve time behind bars ...
>
> The Washington Times, convinced that the police were corrupt and that the district attorney's office was inefficient, began serial publication more than a week ago of a reporter on the Washington rum traffic. This result was the result of an investigation conducted two years ago at the direction of a high state official of national prominence, whose statement at a dinner that Washington was wet was challenged by a cabinet member. This report listed 62 speakeasies and bootleggers. It had been kept secret until the Times obtained a copy of it and began publication. The purpose of the publication was to show that there has been continuous violation of the prohibition law and laxity on the part of enforcement officers.[158]

The jailing prompted Sen. Arthur Capper of Kansas and Rep. Fiorello H. LaGuardia of New York to introduce a bill in the U.S. Congress that gave reporters "immunity from prosecution for refusal to reveal sources of news information, except in cases involving acts of treason."[159] Capper, a publisher of several important daily and weekly newspapers in Kansas, said:

> I feel that the protection of newspaper men in their refusal to divulge sources of information given them in confidence is a subject that ought to have attention. My bill will at least serve the purpose of promoting thought and discussion on the subject. If a newspaper man is given information under his promise not to divulge the source, I'm in entire sympathy with him in his keeping that pledge and I do not believe he should be forced to divulge the source under penalty of being jailed for contempt. Just how far we can go in a law seeking this protection, I do not know. I am aware that it is a controversial question as to whether or not a newspaper reporter should have immunity in such cases. It may be that this immunity should be withheld in the event that in obtaining the information the reporter himself participated in or abetted the breaking of a law. Those are questions that must be discussed and decided in the light of acceptable legal practice.[160]

Editor & Publisher editorialized in favor of the federal law, saying the Washington Times journalists had been treated as criminals, "though the object of their enterprise plainly was to serve the public weal."[161] The editorial criticized the district attorney for seeking "to make these reporters serve as prosecuting witnesses, though he must well know that the function of the newspaper is to inform, not prosecute, certainly not assume vicarious responsibility of the dry enforcement agents."[162] The New York Times reported that "the movement here to provide a law to give judicial sanction to the journalistic ethics which forbids the disclosure of news sources grew out of the recent imprisonment for contempt of three reporters of The Washington Times."[163] Rep. Louis Ludlow of Indiana, who was identified in the Times as a former Washington correspondent for 30 years, was quoted as saying, "A free, alert and courageous press is the nation's strongest safeguard. There can be no free press in this republic if newspaper reporters are to live in terror of grand jury inquisitions and jail sentences."[164] Neither house of Congress voted on the bills, the first of more than one hundred similar proposals introduced periodically in the future.

CONCLUSION

This chapter examined the following research questions: What types of legal claims did journalists make between 1721 and 1958 that resemble contemporary journalist's privilege claims? What types of stories and sources generated subpoenas, and in what types of legal proceedings were these most common? How successful were journalists in avoiding testimony or having to turn over newsgathering material? What ethical and legal arguments did journalists make in these cases?

It is clear that from the very beginning, newspaper editors and reporters were asked to disclose the identity of sources of information published in their newspapers. Stories critical of government officials and those involving secret hearings and documents were common types of stories that provoked attempts to ascertain journalist sources. Journalists relied on a variety of arguments in their claims of a privilege. First among them was that a newsman's code of ethics dictated that a reporter not reveal a source. This concept gained further traction after codes of ethics began to proliferate, but it was asserted well before codes were codified. Connected to this argument was a similar argument that journalists would violate newsroom policies or rules, often unwritten, if they testified. Second, journalists in several cases argued that compelled disclosure was a forfeiture of estate that they had a right to protect, asserting that they would lose their job or livelihood because testifying would mean the reporter would no longer be able to cultivate sources necessary for him to be successful as a journalist. Third, journalists argued a Fifth Amendment right against testifying, often arguing that they might be implicated in a crime or investigation. Notably, it was this theory that the U.S. Supreme Court used in the Burdick case. Journalists also argued in some cases that the subpoena was not relevant or that information could have been obtained elsewhere. Finally, journalists from the very first cases often argued that the public benefit of their reporting outweighed the costs of compelled disclosure.

In several ways, these arguments resemble modern arguments, including those put forward by recently jailed journalists Judith Miller, Josh Wolf and Vanessa Leggett. Journalists were more likely than not to lose their legal arguments in the 19th and early 20th century, although over time legislatures and judges appeared more sympathetic to journalistic claims.

Research into the 19th-century development of the journalist's privilege presents a number of constraints. The reported cases in the law reports provide one window into disputes, but what is equally important is what the law reports do not contain. Judicial orders by the lower courts would not always make their way into law reporters. Cases in which journalists cooperated with authorities would often not produce a written legal record. Informal arrangements between journalists and prosecutors or legislatures are not recorded.

Still, this research is important for the following reasons. This research establishes that the concept of duty to protect news sources, and the ideology of the journalist's privilege more generally, has roots in the colonial era and was a central component of journalist legal arguments throughout the 19th century. The 1848 Nugent case provides early evidence that journalists valued confidential sources enough to go to jail to protect their identity and to support broader principles of watchdog journalism. The jailing of James W. Simonton in 1857 showed that the support for journalists seeking to protect sources extended beyond the parochial interests of competition, as journalists of competing newspapers supported him. The willingness of journalists to be jailed, and their release without revealing the source, established the likelihood that jail sentences were futile as a coercive tool. And the action by state legislatures shows that public support for the journalist's privilege principle was important in establishing legal protections.

The early legal cases show that journalists claimed that confidential sources were crucial to their ability to report the news and expose corruption and misconduct. The next chapter examines how these arguments justifying journalistic behavior morphed into First Amendment arguments.

Chapter 4 Notes

---

[1] Statement of Judith Miller, July 6, 2005, statement of Judith Miller to Chief U.S. District Judge Thomas F. Hogan before being jailed for contempt of court for refusing to disclose her source, available at *http://www.rcfp.org/shields_and_subpoenas/miller_statement.html* (last visited March 17, 2009).

[2] *Statement of Josh Wolf, Journalist, On His Freedom From Jail*, Center for Media and Democracy, April 3, 2007, available at http://www.prwatch.org/node/5922 (last visited March 3, 2009).

[3] The statement was featured on his Web site, *available at* http://www.joshwolf.net/freejosh/ (last visited Sept. 6, 2008).

[4] Guillermo X. Garcia, *The Vanessa Leggett Saga*, AMERICAN JOURNALISM REVIEW, March 2002.

[5] JEFFERY A. SMITH, PRINTERS AND PRESS FREEDOM: THE IDEOLOGY OF EARLY AMERICAN JOURNALISM (1988) and ROBERT W.T. MARTIN, THE FREE AND OPEN PRESS: THE FOUNDING OF AMERICAN DEMOCRATIC PRESS LIBERTY, 1640-1800 (2001).

[6] LEO J.A. LEMAY, THE LIFE OF BENJAMIN FRANKLIN, VOLUME 1: JOURNALIST, 1706-1730, *109 (2006)*.

[7] *New-England Courant,* Aug. 7, 1721.

[8] *New-England Courant, Aug. 7, 1721.*

[9] Jeffery Smith, "James Franklin," in DICTIONARY OF LITERARY BIOGRAPHY, VOLUME 43: AMERICAN NEWSPAPER JOURNALISTS, 1690-1872, 125 (1985).

[10] For the purposes of this paper, I will use the capitalization and punctuation that appears in the *Courant*. The only textual change made is to use the standard letter "s," which often appeared as an "f" in the *Courant*.

[11] *New-England Courant, Aug. 7 – Aug. 14, 1721.*

[12] *See* Smith, *supra* note 5, at 212.

[13] *See* Lemay, *supra* note 6, at 87. Benjamin Franklin's annotated copies of the *New-England Courant* identified the real identities of article authors.

[14] *New-England Courant, Dec. 25 – Jan. 1, 1721/2.*

[15] *New-England Courant, Jan. 22 – Jan. 29, 1722.*

[16] *New-England Courant, Feb. 2 – Mar. 5, 1722.*

[17] ERIC BURNS, INFAMOUS SCRIBBLERS: THE FOUNDING FATHERS AND THE ROWDY BEGINNINGS OF AMERICAN JOURNALISM (2006)

[18] EDWIN EMERY, THE PRESS AND AMERICA 52 (1954 ed.).

[19] *See* Burns, *supra* note 17, at 58.

[20] *New England Courant, Nov. 13 – Nov. 20, 1721.*

[21] *New-England Courant, Nov. 27 – Dec 4, 1721.*

[22] *See* Smith, *supra* note 5, at 215.

[23] *See* Burns, *supra* note 17, at 63.

[24] New York Law Revision Commission, Leg. Doc. No. 65 (A), (1949) at 48, quoting from THE AUTOBIOGRAPHY OF BENJAMIN FRANKLIN 23-24 (1936).

[25] *New England Courant, July 2 – July 9, 1722.*

[26] *New England Courant, Jan. 21 – Jan. 28, 1722.*

[27] *New England Courant, Jan. 7 – Jan. 14, 1723.*

[28] Smith, *supra* note 5, at 217.

[29] WALTER ISAACSON, BENJAMIN FRANKLIN: AN AMERICAN LIFE, 22, 34 (2003).

[30] EDWIN EMERY, THE PRESS AND AMERICA at 50-51 (1954).

[31] *Id.* at 75.

[32] *Id.* at 76.

[33] Doug Linder, *The Zenger Trial: An Account, available at* http://www.law.umkc.edu/faculty/projects/ftrials/zenger/zengeraccount.html (last visited March 3, 2009).

[34] *Id.*

[35] New York Law Revision Commission, Leg. Doc. No. 65 (A), at 16 (1949) [hereafter referred to as NYLRC].

[36] McIntyre v. Ohio Elections Commission, 514 U.S. 334 (1995).

[37] *Id.* at 357.

[38] *See, for example,* Aaron C. Davis, *Media Need Not Reveal Web Posters' Identities,* WASH POST, Feb. 28, 2009 at B08; Nathaniel Gleicher, *John Doe Subpoenas: Toward a Consistent Legal Standard,* 118 YALE L.J. 320 (2008) and Ryan Martin, *Freezing the Net: Rejecting a One-Size Fits-All Standard for Unmaking Anonymous Internet Speakers in Defamation Lawsuits,* 75 U. CIN. L. REV. 1217 (2007). See also Justice Thomas's opinion in McIntyre v. Ohio Elections Commission, 514 U.S. 334 (1995).

[39] MICHAEL SCHUDSON, DISCOVERING THE NEWS 4 (1978).

[40] *Id.* at 22.

[41] *Id.* at 30-31.

[42] *Id.* at 88.

[43] *Id.*

[44] *Id.* at 162.

[45] *Id.* at 163.

[46] *Id.* at 167.

[47] WILLIAM HUNTZICKER, THE POPULAR PRESS, 1833-1865 1 (1999).

[48] DAN SCHILLER, OBJECTIVITY AND THE NEWS: THE PUBLIC AND THE RISE OF COMMERCIAL JOURNALISM (1981).

[49] *Id.* at 55.

[50] *Id.* at 75.

[51] Patrick Lee Plaisance, *A Gang of Pecksniffs Grows Up: The evolution of journalism ethics discourse in The Journalist and Editor and Publisher*, 6 JOURNALISM STUDIES 479, 480 (2005).

[52] HAZEL DICKEN-GARCIA, JOURNALISTIC STANDARDS IN NINETEENTH CENTURY-AMERICA (1989).

[53] *Id.* at 19.

[54] Stephen Banning, *Truth is Our Ultimate Goal: A Mid-19th Century Concern for Journalism Ethics,* AMERICAN JOURNALISM, Winter 1999, at 19.

[55] Mary M. Cronin, *Trade Press Roles in Promoting Journalistic Professionalism, 1884-1917,* 8 JOURNAL OF MASS MEDIA ETHICS, 227, 232 (1993).

[56] *Id.* at 233.

[57] STEPHEN J.A. WARD, THE INVENTION OF JOURNALISM ETHICS: THE PATH TO OBJECTIVITY AND BEYOND, 209 (2004).

[58] *See* RONALD T. FARRAR, A CREED FOR MY PROFESSION: WALTER WILLIAMS, JOURNALIST TO THE WORLD 203 (1998).

[59] Joseph A. Mirando, *Lessons on Ethics in News Reporting Textbooks, 1867-1997,* 13 JOURNAL OF MASS MEDIA ETHICS 26.

[60] *Id.* at 28.

[61] LEON NELSON FLINT, THE CONSCIENCE OF THE NEWSPAPER 396-406 (1925).

[62] *Id.* at 91.

[63] *Id.* at 92.

[64] Republished at *Id.* at 427.

[65] Reprinted at *Id.* at 429.

[66] ALICE PITTS, READ ALL ABOUT IT! 50 YEARS OF ASNE 54 (1974).

[67] WILLIAM R. ARTHUR AND RALPH L. CROSMAN, THE LAW OF NEWSPAPERS 257 (1940).

[68] STEPHEN J.A. WARD, THE INVENTION OF JOURNALISM ETHICS: THE PATH TO OBJECTIVITY AND BEYOND 190-191 (2004).

[69] Margaret Sherwood, *The Newsman's Privilege: Government Investigations, Criminal Prosecutions and Private Litigation,* 58 CAL. L. REV. 1198, 1201 (1970).

[70] DONALD A. RITCHIE, PRESS GALLERY: CONGRESS AND THE WASHINGTON CORRESPONDENTS (1991) and Leigh F. Gregg, The First Amendment in the 19th Century: Journalists' Privilege and Congressional Investigation (Ph.D. dissertation, University of Wisconsin, 1984).

71 David A. Gordon, The 1896 Maryland Shield Law: The American Roots of Evidentiary Privilege for Newsmen, 22 Journalism Monographs 1 (1972).

72 See Watkins v. United States, 354 U.S. 178 (1957).

73 Two important sources made this mistake. See Maurice Van Gerpen, Privileged Communication and the Press: The Citizen's Right to Know Versus the Law's Right to Confidential News Source Evidence 6 (1979) and B.K.K., The Right of a Newsman to Refrain from Divulging the Sources of His Information, 36 Vir. L.R. 61 (1950) [hereafter referred to as BKK].

74 David A. Gordon, Protection of News Sources: The History and Legal Status of the Newsman's Privilege 186 (Ph.D. dissertation, University of Wisconsin, 1971).

75 Id. at 187-188.

[76] Ritchie, supra note 70, at 27.

[77] *Id.* at 27-30.

[78] *Id.* at 29.

[79] BKK, *supra* note 73, at 76.

[80] Van Gerpen, *supra* note 73, at 7.

[81] *New York Daily Times*, Jan. 23, 1857.

[82] Van *Gerpen, supra note 73*, at 7.

[83] Gregg, *supra* note 70, at 566.

[84] *Id.* at 574.

[85] *Id.*

[86] Van Gerpen *supra* note 73, at 7.

[87] BKK *supra* note 73, at 78.

[88] *Id.*

[89] *Id.*

[90] Gordon, *supra* note 74, at 192.

[91] BKK, *supra* note 73, at 79.

[92] *Id.* at 80.

[93] Gordon, *supra* note 74, at 194.

[94] BKK, *supra* note 73, at 80.

[95] *Id.* at 81.

[96] *Id.* at 80.

[97] *Id.*

[98] *See* BKK, *supra* note 73, at 81, and *Hearings before the House Commission on World War Veterans' Legislation Part 1*, 79th Cong. 1st Sess. Pp. 165-342 (1945). A fascinating biography of the reporter appears at http://bms.brown.edu/HistoryofPsychiatry/deutsch.html (last visited Mar. 1, 2009).

[99] N.Y. Times, May 19, 1945, at p. 8.

[100] *Id.*

[101] *Id.*

[102] N.Y. Times, May 23, 1945, at p. 20 and May 30, 1945, at p. 17.

[103] Van Gerpen, *supra* note 73, at 9.

[104] Ex parte Lawrence and Levings, 116 Cal. 298, 200 (Cal. 1897).

[105] Plunkett v. Hamilton, 136 Ga. 72 (Ga. 1911).

[106] Gordon, *supra* note 74, at 201.

[107] *Id.*

[108] *Id.* at 202.

[109] BKK, *supra* note 73, at 72, *See also* Editor & Publisher, Mar. 17, 1934, at p. 5-6 and N.Y. Times, March 10, 1934, at p. 2.

[110] NYLRC, *supra* note 35, at 17.

[111] *Id.* at 17.

[112] N.Y. Times, Jan. 26, 1915, at p. 6.

[113] N.Y. Times, Jan. 27, 1915, at p. 8.

[114] ZECHARIAH CHAFEE, GOVERNMENT AND MASS COMMUNICATIONS: A REPORT FROM THE COMMISSION ON THE FREEDOM OF THE PRESS 498 (1947).

[115] Ex Parte Holliway, 272 Mo. 108, 117.

[116] Joslyn v. The People, 67 Colo. 297.

[117] N.Y. Times, Jan. 1, 1932, at p. 1 and N.Y. Times, Jan 3, 1932, at p. 20.

[118] N.Y. Times, Jan. 5, 1932, at p. 18 and Editor and Publisher, Jan. 9, 1932, at p. 7.

[119] L.A. Times, Aug. 13, 1933, at p. C10 and Editor and Publisher, Aug. 19, 1933, at p. 20.

[120] *Editor and Publisher*, Aug. 11, 1934, at p. 10.

[121] NYLRC, *supra* note 35, at 18.

[122] *Id.* at 18-19.

[123] Gordon, *supra* note 74, at 238.

[124] NYLRC, *supra* note 35, at 21.

[125] *Id.* at 23-24.

[126] Gordon, *supra* note 74, at 242.

[127] BKK, *supra* note 73, at 74, NYLTC at 27. See also 79 N.Y.S. 2d 413 and N.Y. Times Feb. 28, 1948, Feb 9. 1948, March 2, 1948, and March 30, 1948.

[128] Gordon, *supra* note 74, at 256.

[129] NYLRC, *supra* note 35, at 28.

[130] *Id.* at 28.

[131] *Id.* at 63.

[132] *Id.* at 64.

[133] In Clein v. State, 52 So. 2d 117, 118-119 (Fla. 1950).

[134] *Id.* at 120.

[135] Pledger v. State of Georgia, 77 Ga. 242 (Ga. 1887).

[136] Clinton v. Commercial Tribune Co., 11 Ohio Dec. 603 (1901).

[137] BKK, *supra* note 73, at 70, citing Editor & Publisher, Aug .24, 1935, at p. 6.

[138] *See* Gordon, *supra* note 71, for an interesting revisionist history of the case in which he corrects a number of historical inaccuracies.

[139] *Id.* at 11-12.

[140] *Id.* at 12.

[141] *Id.* at 13.

[142] *Id.* at 13 and 7.

[143] *Id.* at 21.

[144] *Id.* at 15.

[145] *Id.* at 20-21, citing the Baltimore Sun, Dec. 23, 1886, at p. 2.

[146] *Id.* at 24.

[147] N.Y. Times, June 12, 1895.

[148] Gordon, *supra* note 71, at 6-7.

[149] *Id.* at 36-37.

[150] *Id.* at 479.

[151] NYLRC, *supra* note 35, at 17.

[152] N.Y. Times, Oct. 31, 1929 at p. 14.

[153] George H. Manning, *Three Washington Reporters Sent to Jail for Refusing to Reveal Source of News,* Editor & Publisher, Nov. 2, 1929, p. 5.

[154] N.Y. Times, Nov. 1, 1929, at p. 14.

[155] N.Y. Times, Nov. 6, 1929, at p. 57.

[156] Editor & Publisher, Nov. 2, 1929.

[157] George H. Manning, *Reporters Go Back to Jail, Refusing Confidential Data to Grand Jury,* Editor & Publisher, Nov. 9, 1929, at p. 6.

[158] *Id.*

[159] NYT, Nov. 19, 1929, at p. 23.

[160] George H. Manning, *Capper Author of Bill Protecting News Men in Contempt Cases,* Editor & Publisher, Nov. 16, 1929, at p. 8.

[161] *Id.*

[162] *Id.*

[163] *Id.*

[164] *Id.*

The First Amendment and Newsgathering Rights in the *Branzburg* Era

The legal arguments that journalists advanced in the 19th and early 20th centuries were rooted primarily in claims that emphasized journalism's functional roles as public watchdogs and agents of public information. The profession agreed about the importance of confidential sources in fulfilling its social and political roles. Other legal arguments included the claim that reporters would lose their livelihoods if they were forced to betray confidences because they would be unable to convince sources to trust them. Reporters relied on this professional tradition of source protection as a justification for special legal consideration on the rare occasion in which they were called upon to divulge sources, acknowledging the lack of a formal legal basis for the recognition of their claim. They used journalism ethics and professional standards to justify their practices to authorities, win the support of their readers, and convince politicians, lawyers and judges of their virtue in the defiance of attempts at compelled disclosure.

While principles of press freedom and journalistic independence were clearly raised by journalists in early privilege cases, the First Amendment did not explicitly enter the lexicon of privilege claims until 1957, when the New York Herald Tribune claimed the First Amendment protected one of its reporters from revealing the identity of a confidential source.[1] Four years later, the Hawaii Supreme Court rigorously assessed the accumulating press-clause precedents of the

U.S. Supreme Court in deciding that First Amendment values were at stake in a journalist's privilege case.[2] And then, in 1972, after federal appellate decisions split on the First Amendment application to the journalist's privilege, the Supreme Court addressed the question in Branzburg v. Hayes.[3] The decision has been the only attempt by the Supreme Court to apply the First Amendment to the journalist's privilege, and its interpretations over the years by the lower courts has continued to shape the development of the privilege as both a legal and ethical concept.[4]

The evolution of the privilege from professional ethic to First Amendment right came in the context of broader efforts by the institutional press to secure special consideration as a matter of constitutional right. Implicit in the First Amendment-based privilege argument is that journalism is a special category of "press" that deserves its own considerations because of its structural role in American democracy.[5] There is significant evidence to support this argument in the First Amendment rhetoric of U.S. Supreme Court decisions. For example, the Court has described the press as an "information-gathering agent of the public"[6] and as a "mighty catalyst in awaking public interest in government affairs, exposing corruption among public officers and employees and generally informing the citizenry of public events and occurrences."[7] The history of the Supreme Court's press clause rulings also present the apparent contradictions that go to the heart of the issue: while "the press" is recognized as a fundamentally important institution of American democracy, it may be too difficult to define and comprise too many disparate elements to mean anything more than an individual's right to disseminate information.[8]

The history of the Supreme Court's modern interpretation of the press clause begins in the 1930s, when the court heard several cases over state regulations of the press, following the "incorporation" of the Bill of Rights that occurred with the 1925 case Gitlow v. New York, which held that the Fourteenth Amendment's due process clause applied the First Amendment to actions of the states as well as the federal government.[9] A second pivotal period occurred in the 1970s, when several cases required the court to answer whether the press was entitled to "special rights" based on its structural and institutional roles.10 The cases in each era involved important questions about democracy and journalism: When can the government stop a newspaper from publishing? Can newspapers be taxed at higher levels than other businesses? Should the press be given special access to court proceedings or prisons in its role in informing the public about public affairs? Do newspapers have the editorial freedom to decide against publishing statements by political candidates who have been attacked in its pages? In deciding these cases, justices routinely wrestled with a profound question: What about the press makes it special as a matter of constitutional law?

This chapter adopts a chronological organization in sketching the First Amendment relevance to the journalist's privilege. First, it explores the intellectual and doctrinal developments of the modern First Amendment in the 1910s and 1920s and then examines the foundational press cases of the 1930s and 1940s. Second, the chapter offers a descriptive analysis of the first major legal decisions in which First Amendment-based journalists' privilege arguments were made, and rejected, by state and federal courts, in the 1950s and 1960s. Next, the chapter analyses the arguments and interpretations stemming from the 1972 Supreme Court's decision in Branzburg v. Hayes, which remains to date the most important legal decision on the question of a journalist's privilege. Then, the chapter briefly discusses how the courts handled other newsgathering rights claims in the 1970s, demonstrating the complexity of providing special legal status to particular visions of journalism and newsgathering. Finally, the chapter summarizes some key points of theoretical debate that remain today.

THE BIRTH OF THE MODERN FIRST AMENDMENT

Journalists ensnarled in the courts of the 19th century did not rely on First Amendment rights because the nature of First Amendment jurisprudence dramatically changed in the first decades of the 20th century. It wasn't until after pivotal Supreme Court decisions between 1917 and 1927 that lawyers, scholars and judges crafted coherent theories about press rights rooted in the First Amendment. The birth of the "modern" First Amendment, at least as a matter of positive, legal doctrine, with relevance to average Americans, can be traced to the 1920s. Before this, the First Amendment was generally not considered a limitation on government action of local and state officials.[11]

To be sure, the history of the First Amendment has a philosophic genesis predating its textual birth in the Bill of Rights, dating back to 1644 with John Milton's defenses of unlicensed printing, the virtues of a life of uncensored ideas found in books and the grappling of truth and falsity.[12] Historians Jeffery A. Smith and Robert W.T. Martin have found the intellectual seeds of the First Amendment in the ideology and practice of colonial newspaper editors in the 18th century, including the newspapers of James Franklin and John Peter Zenger, the tracts of John Trenchard and Thomas Gordon in *Cato's Letters*, and the passionate pamphlets of revolutionaries like Thomas Paine.[13] The original intent of the First Amendment has been studied through the debates over the language of the First Amendment and James Madison's political philosophy, as well as the lessons learned from President Thomas Jefferson's repudiation of the Sedition Act of 1798.[14] Further evidence of the "meaning" of the First Amendment can be found in its integration into the belief systems of average Americans in the 19th century, as explored by historians David Rabban, Donna Lee Dickerson and Michael Kent Curtis.[15]

None of these starting points would lead one astray from the central principles of the modern First Amendment.[16] But as a matter of positive, articulated constitutional principle, the birth of the modern First Amendment is most concretely found in the decade between 1917 and 1927. It was in this decade that the foursome of Learned Hand, Oliver Wendell Holmes, Louis Brandeis and Zechariah Chafee provided the judicial and scholarly impetus for dramatic shifts in law that provided the framework for some of the Supreme Court's most important 20th century First Amendment doctrines, such as the "breathing space" for criticism of government officials in *New York Times v. Sullivan*,[17] the repugnance toward prior restraints in the *Pentagon Papers* case,[18] or the speech-protective illegal-advocacy test in *Brandenburg v. Ohio*.[19] The precedents in both doctrine and theory for these pivotal decisions stem from the judicial and intellectual activity of the decade between 1917 and 1927.

It is instructive to briefly sketch the historical context of this formative period in the First Amendment. Historian Robert K. Murray outlined the "national hysteria" that accompanied America's involvement in World War I, resulting in congressional passage of the Espionage Act of 1917 and the Sedition Act of 1918 that authorized widespread suppression of radical thought and dissenting views.[20] These statutes were the first since 1798 in which Congress explicitly sanctioned speech critical of the government. Such suppression might seem shocking by today's standards, but one example is the conviction and 10-year prison sentence, upheld by the U.S. Supreme Court, of

Eugene Debs, the Socialist Party's candidate for president who gave a speech denouncing conscription and the war.

The first challenge to the Espionage Act to reach the federal courts came in 1917. Federal district judge Learned Hand was assigned the case, in which a revolutionary journal called the *Masses* was excluded from the U.S. mail based on its political content.[21] Judge Hand, appointed as a district court judge in New York in 1909, is thought to be perhaps the most brilliant and influential American judge not to have been appointed to the U.S. Supreme Court. In the *Masses* case, Hand enjoined the government from excluding the Masses from the mail and rejected the view that speech could be punished based on its "bad tendency" – the predominant constitutional test of the day for speech suppression.[22] Instead, Hand articulated a legal test that focused on the "nature of the utterance itself" and allowed for punishment only where the speech was intended to incite illegal activity.[23] In his analysis of Hand's personal letters for a biography, Professor Gerald Gunther concluded Hand's approach in the *Masses* case "was indeed a distinctive, carefully considered alternative to the prevalent analyses of free speech issues."[24] As a matter of immediate law, Hand's decision had little effect, and its ruling was quickly overturned by the Second Circuit Court of Appeals. But the case sparked Hand's interest in the First Amendment, which subsequently led to an important and consequential exchange of letters with Justice Oliver Wendell Holmes, Jr.[25]

Holmes stands as a peculiar hero in First Amendment history, in part because his sweeping rhetoric of the value of free speech and press was delivered in cases in which he upheld prosecutions of political dissenters whose speech arguably failed to meet the standards he was articulating. In the spring of 1919, Holmes voted in favor of the suppression of speech in three cases, *Schenck v. U.S.*, *Debs v. U.S.*, and *Frohwerk v. U.S.*[26] *Schenck* remains a foundational case in virtually all law-school textbooks on the First Amendment. In it, Holmes upheld the conviction of Schenck, the general secretary of the Philadelphia Socialist party, based on leaflets opposing the draft the organization mailed. (*Frohwerk* upheld the conviction of a German-language newspaper that published anti-war articles, and *Debs* upheld the conviction of the Socialist Party's presidential candidate.) Holmes's *Schenck* opinion was the first significant Supreme Court decision to interpret the scope and limits of First Amendment protections. The court unanimously upheld Schenck's conviction, and Justice Holmes' opinion stressed the necessity of the state to conduct war free from internal sabotage by dissent.

By the fall of 1919 Holmes' views evolved. In *Abrams v. U.S.*, Holmes in fact made something of a shift.[27] The case involved the prosecution of several men who dumped leaflets that criticized the war effort from a New York City rooftop. Justice Holmes, joined by Justice Brandeis, dissented when the majority upheld the conviction, although Holmes peculiarly noted that his dissent did not suggest he had changed his mind about the appropriateness of conviction in the three earlier cases. Still, Holmes went on to make an eloquent defense of the value of free speech for its truth-seeking potential. His dissent invoked skepticism about the certainty of opinions and acknowledged that because "time has upset many fighting faiths," the "best test of truth is the power of thought to get itself accepted in the competition of the market."

Between 1919 and 1927, the Supreme Court continued to uphold convictions of individuals based on their radical and dissenting speech, affording Justices Holmes and Brandeis a number of opportunities to hone their logic of free expression in dissents and concurrences. The Red Scare that followed World War I invoked heightened fears of radicalism but also furthered provoked growing attention civil liberties claims. The Supreme Court's attention to free speech claims intensified, even if the outcomes generally still favored the state over the claims of radicals. Justice Louis Brandeis' eloquent concurrence in *Whitney v. California* is perhaps the most important single opinion on the First Amendment in the court's history, in part because it articulates multiple rationales for the First Amendment that later informed a number of disparate First Amendment doctrines and theories. Brandeis, who served on the Supreme Court from 1916 to 1939, had signed onto Holmes' dissent in *Abrams*, and Holmes did the same to Brandeis' opinion in *Whitney*. In the opinion, Brandeis recognized that freedom of speech and press were important for individual autonomy and self-fulfillment, central to the concept of self-government and citizen sovereignty, and necessary for the search for truth in a marketplace of ideas.[28]

Zechariah Chafee, Jr., then a Harvard Law School professor, also heavily influenced the intellectual development of the First Amendment during this pivotal period. Chafee's work as a scholar more broadly influenced thinking about the First Amendment. Chafee developed his philosophy first in a series of articles, and then in 1920 in *Freedom of Speech*, revised by him in 1941 as *Freedom of Speech in the United States*. To this day, he is described as the preeminent scholar in the modern defense of the First Amendment. Writing in the *Reviews in American History,* John Wertheimer in 1994 said Chafee's *Freedom of Speech* "is arguably the century's most important on the subject" and that Chafee "was a seminal figure – some say *the* seminal figure – in the development of modern constitutional notions about free speech."[29] Some scholars, like Mark A. Graber, criticize Chafee for ignoring historical evidence and even "deliberately manipulating history and theory" by stressing consequentialist values of the First Amendment at the expense of a more general individual liberty right.[30] By emphasizing the social value of free speech to democracy, Chafee's conception, later refined by Alexander Meiklejohn, invoked a different rationale than his 19th-century forebearers such as Theodore Schroeder.[31] Chafee dismissed the Blackstone concept that freedom of the press meant simply freedom from prior restraints and argued that protection from subsequent prosecution was essential if individuals were to be free to discuss public affairs. It is from these theoretical roots that the journalist's privilege emerged as a First Amendment argument.

THE FOUNDATIONAL PRESS CASES OF THE 1930S AND 1940S

Three cases in the 1930s prompted Supreme Court justices to probe the original intent of the press clause, leading them to cement the importance of several Revolutionary-era libertarian thinkers as forefathers of First Amendment thought. The landmark 1931 decision in *Near v. Minnesota* struck down a law allowing the state to shut down a newspaper deemed to be a public nuisance through "malicious, scandalous and defamatory" reporting.[32] In establishing that liberty of the press "has meant, principally although not exclusively, immunity from previous restraints or censorship,"[33] the court set a high bar for when a prior restraint may be appropriate. The *Near* decision used several historical references to explain how the First Amendment's press clause was intended to support principles of truth-seeking and checking government power and set forth a powerful precedent and was hailed immediately by journalists as a landmark court decision.[34]

Similar historical references came in the 1936 case of *Grosjean v. American Press Co.*,[35] where the court struck down a law that required the largest nine newspaper publishers in Louisiana to pay a two-percent licensing tax. In the decision, Justice George Sutherland noted the historical struggles of the press in the one hundred years prior to the adoption of the First Amendment, citing John Milton's "Appeal for the Liberty of Unlicensed Printing" and the colonial anger against Britain's tax on newspapers in 1765.[36] Justice Sutherland also drew on the historical role of the press as serving as an institutional check on government. The court noted the newspaper tax at issue was not an ordinary tax applied to all businesses, but one "with a long history of hostile misuse against the freedom of the press." And in bringing together the historical nature of the press with the checking value, the court said:

> The newspapers, magazines, and other journals of the country, it is safe to say, have shed and continue to shed, more light on the public and business affairs of the nation than any other instrumentality of publicity; and since informed public opinion is the most potent of all restraints upon misgovernment, the suppression or abridgement of the publicity afforded by a free press cannot be regarded otherwise than with grave concern ... A free press stands as one of the great interpreters between the government and the people. To allow it to be fettered is to fetter ourselves.[37]

If the *Grosjean* case embraced the importance of the institutional press, the court two years later suggested a different interpretation of the press clause. In *Lovell v. City of Griffin*, the court struck down a statute requiring people distributing leaflets to first get a permit from the city.[38] The court said that the "liberty of the press is not confined to newspapers and periodicals. It necessarily embraces pamphlets and leaflets ... The press in its historic connotation comprehends every sort of publication which affords a vehicle of information and opinion."[39] *Lovell* supported the proposition that freedom of the press was not to be viewed as an institutional right but an individual right.

In rejecting bans on prior restraints for even the most obnoxious newspaper, taxes on a subset of newspapers, and requirements to register before distributing pamphlets, the court attempted to justify its decisions with the original intent of the First Amendment and the historical events that led colonists to revolt against Britain. The 1930s decisions in *Near*, *Grosjean* and *Lovell* foreshadowed the paradox that would follow in subsequent cases. Their holdings created a strong presumption of freedom for the institutional press based on their functions and principles, while at the same time ruling that press rights are about individual liberty.

By the 1940s, several press cases involved claims pitting free-press principles against other constitutional rights and interests, requiring the court to engage in rights balancing. Here, cases involved claims that had to be balanced against the interests of the judicial system, a clash that would periodically test press freedom through the 1980s. In 1946, the Court in *Pennekamp v. State of Florida* struck down a contempt conviction against an editor of *The Miami Herald* who was found guilty of unlawfully criticizing a circuit court judge.[40] The Court found that while the *Herald's* editorials omitted the "full truth" and "did not state objectively the attitude of the judges," the newspaper was nonetheless within its First Amendment rights to criticize government officials, including judges. The case's concurring opinion by Justice Felix Frankfurter is particularly colored with language that both emboldens the ideals of a free press but chastened it with responsibility.

> Without a free press there can be no free society. Freedom of the press, however, is not an end in itself but a means to the end of a free society ... A free press is vital to a democratic society because its freedom gives it power. Power in a democracy implies responsibility in its exercise. No institution in a democracy, either governmental or private, can have absolute power. Nor can the limits of power which enforce responsibility be finally determined by the limited power itself ... In plain English, freedom carries with it responsibility even for the press; freedom of the press is not a freedom from responsibility for its exercise.[41]

In a second case pitting freedom of the press and the constitutional right to a fair trial against one another, *Craig v. Harney,* a divided court overturned the criminal contempt convictions of journalists who criticized a judge for not accepting a jury verdict in a civil case.[42] Justice Frank Murphy, in his concurrence, noted that judges need to be prepared for criticism in part because of the power they wield in the criminal justice system. Punishing journalists for criticizing government actions is particularly egregious, the justice wrote.[43] By the 1950s, the meanings of the press clause were taking shape, at least as expressed by the Supreme Court, but they still remained malleable.

THE FIRST AMENDMENT-BASED PRIVILEGE ARGUMENT EMERGES IN THE COURTS

The first case in which journalists explicitly turned to the First Amendment as a legal shield against compelled disclosure of confidential sources came in *Garland v. Torre*.[44] In January 1957, Marie Torre, a television and radio columnist for the *New York Herald Tribune*, published a story about problems CBS was having in getting singer Judy Garland to commit to the format and date for the first of several television shows Garland was under contract to do.[45] The story quoted an anonymous CBS television executive discussing contract negotiation problems, who speculated, "I don't know, but I wouldn't be surprised if it's because she thinks she's terribly fat."[46] Torre quoted Garland's agent as denying that the show's problems were Garland's fault. Garland filed a lawsuit against CBS for breach of contract and libel, seeking $1.4 million in damages. In depositions, several executives rumored to be Torre's sources denied talking to the reporter.[47] Torre testified in a deposition that the comments in her story were the "exact words" of a CBS informant, but she refused to identify the source any further.[48]

Inside the *Herald Tribune,* lawyers argued that Torre had no legal right to avoid complying with a trial judge's order to reveal her source, and Torre herself was worried that her editors would not pay for costly legal bills to fight a subpoena.[49] Given the rather trivial substance of the story and that the subpoena was issued in the context of a libel lawsuit, this was not the ideal case to litigate the privilege principle in hopes of establishing broader common-law protections, lawyers argued. Still, Torre told her editors that her source "had done me a favor, given me information I was after, and now I couldn't repay his kindness and helpfulness by revealing information that would probably get him fired – I just wasn't going to do that."[50] For Torre, it was a matter of personal integrity as well as professional principle.

After the trial judge held Torre in criminal contempt for failing to disclose her source, the *Herald Tribune* appealed to the Second Circuit Court of Appeals.[51] One of the newspaper's lawyers later recalled that they advanced First Amendment arguments at the insistence of the newspaper's editor, Brown Reid. "Brown Reid's sincerity in this belief 'was almost palpable,'" one of the lawyers, Sheldon Oliensis, recalled in a book about the *Herald Tribune's* history.[52]

> "My reporters are not going to disclose their sources," (Reid) said. It didn't matter to him whether the case was about a missing dog or a fat entertainer. Defending the principle involved was more important to him than winning. Reid himself, having been apprised that the paper's case would have been more promising and heroic if it had involved, say, corruption in high places or a comparable instance in which the public's need to know could have been invoked, recalled: "I took the position that you can't always choose the ground on which to fight."[53]

The decision by the Second Circuit Court of Appeals, written by Judge Potter Stewart before he was appointed to the U.S. Supreme Court, rejected Torre's arguments. Judge Stewart wrote that although "we accept at the outset the hypothesis that compulsory disclosure of a journalist's confidential sources of information entail an abridgment of press freedom by imposing some limitation upon the availability of news,"[54] the First Amendment interests must be balanced the societal interests in the functioning of the courts. Stewart wrote that the "concept that it is the duty of a witness to testify in courts of law has roots fully as deep in our history as does the guarantee of a free press."[55] The identity of Torre's source "went to the heart" of Garland's lawsuit and the judicial order seeking the identity was narrowly tailored to the case at hand.[56] Stewart said the subpoena also was appropriate because Garland made other reasonable attempts to identify the source.[57] The standards would later serve as models for the test Stewart would put forth 14 years later when he, as a Supreme Court justice, dissented in *Branzburg v. Hayes*.

The U.S. Supreme Court declined to hear the case, and Torre was sentenced to 10 days in jail. In its appeal to the high court, the *Herald Tribune's* lawyers claimed the Second Circuit's decision would have an immediate chilling effect "on the willingness of news sources to transmit news in confidence to reporters and the news media. It will lend aid to any forces seeking to choke off the flow of information ...

The First Amendment mandates against restraints at any stage of the flow of news to the public."[58] When Torre appeared before the trial judge after the Supreme Court declined to take the appeal, he "blew up" at her, telling the newspaper's lawyers, "Make this girl talk! I don't want to send her to jail."[59] Torre was given a few days to prepare for her jail sentence and worried that judge might again sentence her to further jail time after the initial 10-day sentence. A "leading Wall Street lawyer" assured her that the judge was unlikely to "risk public censure" by being viewed as persecuting a journalist.[60] Torre regretted telling her city editor who her source was just before she was to begin her jail sentence. The editor promptly called the source in an attempt to convince him to come forward and thwart Torre's imminent jailing, to no avail.[61] Asked nearly 25 years later to name her source for a history of the *Herald Tribune*, Torre declined.[62]

Garland v. Torre was the first case in which journalists explicitly asked judges to find a First Amendment right to avoid providing compelled disclosure of news sources. Three years later, the Supreme Court of Hawaii turned to the *Garland* case but expanded upon the First Amendment analysis in the case of *In Re Appeal of Alan L. Goodfader.*[63] The case involved a wrongful termination lawsuit brought by a former personnel director, Nesta M. Gallas, against a city and county commission. Goodfader, a reporter for a daily newspaper, had attended a meeting in which Gallas' firing was discussed, and Gallas sought the reporter's testimony in an attempt to prove the illegality of the firing. The reporter testified that "about a week and a half before Mrs. Gallas was fired, I received confidential information that an attempt to fire her was being considered."[64] Asked to identify the source, Goodfader said, "It would be a very grievous breach of my professional ethics for me to say anything which might lead back to my source."[65]

Goodfader's First Amendment argument drew from the rhetoric of several U.S. Supreme Court decisions, discussed earlier in this chapter, which the Hawaii court emphasized in concluding that "forced disclosure of a reporter's confidential source of information, may, to some extent, constitute an impairment of freedom of the press."[66]

The state high court emphasized the importance of the press' public-education and watchdog functions that several U.S. Supreme Court decisions had heralded as important aspects of the First Amendment. "(O)ne of the primary purposes of the freedom-of-the-press clause of the First Amendment is to preserve the right of the

American people to full information concerning the doings or misdoings of public officials in order to guard against maladministration in government," the court wrote.[67] The court cited several U.S. Supreme Court cases as evidence of constitutional recognition of this free-press value: "A free press stands as one of the great interpreters between the government and the people. To allow it to be fettered is to fetter ourselves," (*Grosjean v. American Press Co.*);[68] Liberty of the press "was especially cherished for the immunity it afforded from previous restraint of the publication of censure of public officers and charges of official misconduct," (*Near v. Minnesota*);[69] The First Amendment "rests on the assumption that the widest possible dissemination of information diverse and antagonistic sources is essential to the welfare of the public, that a free press is a condition of a free society," (*Associated Press v. United States*);[70] among others.[71]

The journalist's First Amendment argument was summarized as the following: (1) freedom to gather news is inseparable from freedom to print news; (2) compelled disclosure of confidential sources is a restraint on gathering news; and (3) therefore compelled disclosure is infringement on the free-press clause. The court found no previous precedent supporting these propositions:

> We readily perceive the disadvantages to a news reporter where his desire to remain silent under a pledge of confidentiality is not accommodated, but we are unable to find, in any of the many decisions touching on the First Amendment that we have been referred to and have considered, any basis for concluding that the denial of a claim under the newsman's code constitutes an impairment of constitutional rights.[72]

The court spoke favorably of the public-policy rationales for a privilege and accepted the argument "that forced disclosure of a reporter's confidential source of information may, to some extent, constitute impairment of freedom of the press."[73] Still, the Court rejected the creation of a First Amendment-based privilege. Instead, it focused on whether the subpoena was of "enough importance to her case and appeared sufficiently likely to be productive" in obtaining admissible evidence.[74] After concluding that the subpoena sought to establish evidence of collusion among committee members in firing the public official, the court upheld the compelled disclosure order.[75]

A dissenting opinion said that "news gathering and news dissemination are inseparable aspects of a single publishing process and should not be separable in law, if we are to give to liberty of the press 'the broadest scope that could be countenanced in an orderly society.'" The dissent cited as examples U.S. Supreme Court decisions protecting the anonymous speech rights of individuals who distributed handbills and booklets,[76] and the compelled disclosure of individuals' identities "at the last stop of the news dissemination process – the purchaser of the books."[77] The dissent supported a balancing test of competing interests.

The *Garland* and *Goodfader* decisions demonstrate the morphing of journalism ethics arguments into First Amendment arguments. Principles of journalism ethics were increasingly used to justify constitutional-based rights claims by journalists, relying on the public-information and "watchdog" functions of the press. These First Amendment-based journalist's privilege claims appeared to make some headway in state and the lower federal courts,[78] and a split in the federal appellate courts prompted the Supreme Court to consolidate four cases in *Branzburg v. Hayes.*

BRANZBURG V. HAYES: THE SUPREME COURT CONSIDERS THE JOURNALIST'S PRIVILEGE

The ethical and legal landscape of the journalist's privilege was dramatically reshaped in 1972, when the Supreme Court issued its decision in Branzburg v. Hayes.[79] While the Court ruled, 5-4, that journalists did not have a First Amendment right to avoid subpoenas from grand juries, various interpretations of the holdings have been offered in the ensuing years, thanks in part to a concurring opinion by Justice Lewis Powell.[80]

The *Branzburg* decision was the result of four appellate cases that were consolidated, each involving a reporter's potential first-hand evidence of criminal activity.[81] In each of the cases, the journalists argued that their ethical duty to protect sources should be recognized as a matter of law, and in these particular cases as a constitutional right emanating from the First Amendment's press clause.

Paul Branzburg, a reporter for the Louisville, Ky., *Courier-Journal*, wrote several stories about marijuana use at a time when there was public debate about drug legalization. His stories covered many facets of drug use and abuse, including how marijuana was manufactured and sold, how school officials seemed ignorant to the drug use among students, and how public officials only superficially debated the policy issues of regulation and enforcement.[82] Two separate grand juries investigating illegal drug activity subpoenaed Branzburg to testify. Branzburg declined to name his confidential sources, citing the Kentucky shield statute, the Kentucky constitution, and the First Amendment.[83] In both cases, the Kentucky courts ruled that the shield statute did not protect from Branzburg from refusing to "disclose the identity of persons seen by him in the perpetuation of a crime,"[84] although the court did allow Branzburg to avoid revealing any other "confidential associations, sources or information."[85]

The third case involved a television news reporter and photographer for a New Bedford, Mass., television station. During a period of civil unrest in New Bedford that involved "fires and other turmoil,"[86] Paul Pappas was assigned to cover a press conference with members of the Black Panthers. He asked for, and was granted, permission to come back later in the evening to film an expected police raid on the Black Panther's headquarters in a boarded-up store.[87] Pappas agreed not to disclose anything he saw and heard, other than to photograph and report on the police raid. No raid occurred, and Pappas did not broadcast a story about the night. Still, he was subpoenaed by a county grand jury investigating the Black Panthers. The Massachusetts high court said it assumed the grand jury's investigation into the Panthers, linked to possible "serious civil disorders" including "gunfire in certain streets," was serious enough to justify the reporter's testimony.[88]

The fourth case involved a federal grand jury subpoena issued to Earl Caldwell, a reporter for the *New York Times* who was assigned to cover black militant groups, including the Black Panther Party. Caldwell, who is African-American, had been sent by the paper to cover the movement in part because of his race; a white reporter had been unsuccessful at getting good stories.[89] His stories were based on several months of interviews and detailed the history of the party, the content of its program, and the nature of its support among both blacks and whites.[90] One of the stories quoted a statement by a Panther leader advocating the violent overthrow of the government. A federal grand jury in the Northern District of California investigating the Panthers subpoenaed Caldwell's testimony concerning the Panthers' "aims, purposes, and activities."[91] Caldwell and the *New York Times* argued that Caldwell's testimony would destroy his ability to report on the Black Panthers and "suppress vital First Amendment freedoms ... by driving a wedge of distrust and silence between the news media and the militants."[92] The journalists argued that "so drastic an incursion upon First Amendment freedoms" should not be undertaken "in the absence of a compelling government interest – not shown here."[93]

While Branzburg and Pappas lost their legal arguments in the state courts, Caldwell won his case before the Ninth Circuit Court of Appeals, which ruled that the First Amendment did in fact provide a qualified privilege for journalists. The Supreme Court of the United States likely took the four cases, in part, to resolve the disparate holdings.

Notably, there was a crucial factual trap in the Court's deciding *Branzburg* along with *Pappas* and *Caldwell* cases. The *Pappas* and *Caldwell* cases did not involve direct observation of a commission of crime, while *Branzburg* involved a reporter's refusal to give a state grand jury evidence about first-hand observations of drug use. Asking a judge to allow a journalist to avoid testifying about first-hand observations of criminal activity made the case a difficult one for the privilege principle.

The journalists' First Amendment arguments were based on the following claims: (1) journalists sometimes need to make promises of confidentiality to gather news; (2) compelled disclosure of confidential sources will deter sources from cooperating with journalists in gathering news; (3) and this will harm the free flow of information protected by the First Amendment.[94] The journalists did not argue for an absolute First Amendment privilege, but rather sought a qualified privilege that could only be overcome when the information the reporter has is unavailable from other sources and the need for the information is "sufficiently compelling" to override the harm to First Amendment interests.

The split among the justices highlighted clearly the competing constitutional interests of protecting freedom of the press and the interests of the criminal justice system. Justice Byron White and the majority framed the issue as this: "The sole issue before us is the obligation of reporters to respond to grand jury subpoenas as other citizens do and to answer questions relevant to an investigation into the commission of crime."[95] A grand jury proceeding, White said, has two functions: to determine if probable cause exists to believe a crime has been committed, and to protect citizens from unfounded criminal prosecutions. Its investigative powers are necessarily broad, and the grand jury plays an important, constitutional role that outweighs any burden on newsgathering that might come from the occasional subpoena to reporters. Grand juries only concern themselves with alleged crimes, and the vast majority of source-reporter relations have nothing to do with criminal activity, White said. White said that while grand jury subpoenas to journalists might be considered an "incidental burden" on freedom of the press, it has generally been held that the First Amendment does not guarantee the press a constitutional right of special access to information not available to the public generally.[96] "Only where news sources themselves are implicated in crime or possess information relevant to the grand jury's task need they or the reporter be concerned about grand jury subpoenas," he wrote.[97]

White acknowledged that sources may in fact be deterred from talking to journalists if their identities may later be disclosed – the argument of a chilling effect for news sources. But he concluded that the "evidence fails to demonstrate that there would be a significant construction of the flow of news to the public."[98] Then, White criticized the journalists who argued for a qualified constitutional privilege as opposed to an absolute one, saying support for a qualified privilege undermines the journalists' arguments. "If newsmen's confidential sources are as sensitive as they are claimed to be, the prospect of being unmasked whenever a judge determines the situation justifies it is hardly a satisfactory solution to the problem," White wrote.[99]

Still, White said that newsgathering as a practice did implicate the First Amendment, although he failed to elaborate. "We do not question the significance of free speech, press or assembly to the country's welfare. Nor is it suggested that news gathering does not qualify for First Amendment protection; without some protection for seeking out the news, freedom of the press could be eviscerated."[100]

In addition to prioritizing the grand jury's investigative role over the free-press interests, White said several problems existed with the journalist's privilege as a constitutional principle. Among them was the problem of who qualifies for protection, an issue that in the first decade of the 21st century would again be an important issue of litigation with the rise of bloggers:

The administration of a constitutional newsman's privilege would present practical and conceptual difficulties of a high order. Sooner or later, it would be necessary to define those categories of newsmen who qualified for a privilege, a questionable procedure in light of the traditional doctrine that liberty of the press is the right of the lonely pamphleteer who uses carbon paper or a mimeograph just as much as the large metropolitan publisher who utilizes the latest photocomposition methods.101

Later, Justice Stewart would look back on the *Branzburg* case and describe the vote as "four and a half to four and a half" because of Justice Powell's concurrence that he wrote to emphasize "the limited nature of the Court's holding."[102] In his two-paragraph concurrence that seems at odds with some of the majority's holding, Powell wrote that journalists facing subpoenas "will have access to the court on a motion to quash." Judges should apply a "case-by-case" balancing by "the striking of a proper balance between freedom of the press and the obligation of all citizens to give relevant testimony with respect to criminal conduct," Powell wrote.[103]

In dissent, Justice William Douglas supported an absolute privilege and emphasized the chilling effects of the decision on journalists and their sources.[104] Douglas' passionate decision said anything less than an absolute privilege would be based on "timid, watered-down emasculated versions of the First Amendment," and criticized the lawyers for the journalists for advocating a qualified privilege, a pragmatic strategy adopted by the lawyers for their arguments before the Supreme Court.[105] Douglas drew from the work of First Amendment philosopher Alexander Meiklejohn, who emphasized the value of unfettered information to citizens engaged in democratic processes. Douglas wrote:

Today's decision will impede the wide-open and robust dissemination of ideas and counterthought which a free press both fosters and protects and which is essential to the success of intelligent self-government. Forcing a reporter before a grand jury will have two retarding effects upon the ear and the pen of the press. Fear of exposure will cause dissidents to communicate less openly to trusted reporters. And, fear of accountability will cause editors and critics to write with more restrained pens ... The press has a preferred position in our constitutional scheme, not to enable it to make money, not to set newsmen apart as a favored class, but to bring fulfillment to the public's right to know. The right to know is crucial to the governing powers of the people, to paraphrase Alexander Meiklejohn. Knowledge is essential to informed decisions.[106]

Justice Stewart's dissent, which was joined by Justices William Brennan and Thurgood Marshall, supported a qualified privilege that he defined with a three-part test.[107] Stewart's test would require an individual subpoenaing a journalist to demonstrate (1) the journalist has information that is clearly relevant to violation of law; (2) the information sought cannot be obtained by alternative means less destructive of the First Amendment; and (3) a compelling and overriding interest in the information.[108] Stewart said the "reporter's constitutional right to a confidential relationship with his source stems from the broad societal interest in a full and free flow of information to the public."[109] Stewart's test was adopted almost verbatim from the *amicus* brief of Professor Alexander Bickel of Yale Law School.[110]

As a matter of purely historical speculation, the *Branzburg* case also reached the Supreme Court just after the retirement of Justice Hugo Black, who in the *Pentagon Papers* case months earlier had written one of the strongest defenses of freedom of the press in the history of the Court.[111] Black, it has been speculated, almost certainly would have supported a privilege.[112] However, Powell, Black's replacement, provided the crucial fifth vote in the case to reject a First Amendment privilege. At a congressional hearing in 1972, Irwin Karp, counsel for the Authors League of America, called the *Branzburg* decision "an accident of history" given the conventional wisdom that its outcome would have been different had it arrived at the Court the term before.[113]

If a Supreme Court decision is supposed to provide clarity for lower courts, the *Branzburg* decision can be categorized as a stunning failure. Several federal appellate courts have characterized the majority's decision as a "plurality,"[114] using the logic that the holding of a divided Supreme Court is best ascribed to the "narrowest grounds" of agreement among the justices.[115] Many lawyers successfully convinced judges to look at Justice Powell's concurrence as the controlling decision, and the concurrence has been the cause of significant analysis and speculation over the years.[116] In their behind-the-scenes insider book *The Brethren: Inside the Supreme Court*, Bob Woodward and Scott Armstrong claimed that Powell, then new to the court, gave his vote to the majority "after much hesitation," and wrote his concurrence explicitly to narrow its holding.[117] In a 2007 academic-journal article drawing from Powell's archival files and interviews with his clerks, Professor Michelle Kimball concluded that Powell supported a qualified privilege, based on his notes and his discussions with his clerks, but was hesitant to conclude its basis was in constitutional law.[118]

The *Branzburg* decisions showed different approaches to evaluating the First Amendment interests raised by the journalist's privilege. The majority's decision, perhaps unfairly, seemed to require greater empirical proof of the chilling effects that could occur with compelled disclosure of journalists' sources. Over time, however, the decision was not a fatal blow to the journalist's privilege as a constitutional construct, and in fact, the decision unexpectedly was a mixed victory for press advocates, as its interpretations over the years created a qualified privilege in some circumstances. The Powell concurrence is one reason *Branzburg* did not completely close the door to a judicially recognized constitutional privilege. The majority's focus on the substantial interests of the grand jury also left the door open to a qualified privilege in other circumstances, an opening that was later seized upon by journalists in privilege cases.

Notably, the journalists in the *Branzburg* case never revealed their sources despite the decision of the Supreme Court. In the *Caldwell* and *Pappas* cases, the grand juries were never reconvened, while Branzburg was held in contempt *in absentia* in Kentucky, and Michigan officials did not arrest and extradite him.[119]

NEWSGATHERING AS A FIRST AMENDMENT RIGHT

In the decade following *Branzburg*, the Supreme Court's press clause decisions reflected deep disagreement about the actual meaning of the press clause. By the end of 1970s, two distinct doctrinal approaches to the press clause emerged. One approach, embodied by Chief Justice Warren Burger and others, viewed the press clause as complementary to the speech clause as an individual right afforded to every citizen. The second approach, embodied by Justice Stewart and others, was that the press clause is better viewed as granting institutional protections to practitioners of "the press" because of their special, structural role in informing the public of public affairs and in serving as watchdogs of government. Perhaps the most forceful articulation of this view came in a 1974 speech by Justice Stewart, in which he analyzed the constitutional history of the First Amendment's free press clause and concluded that its "primary purpose" was to "create a fourth institution outside the Government as an additional check on the three official branches."[120]

Doctrinally, one could view the press clause holdings as largely distinguished by Isaiah Berlin's "negative" and "positive" liberty dichotomy.[121] That is, the press clause establishes "negative" rights for individuals to be free from legal constraints on publication. In fact, the most important free press decisions in American constitutional history have created a legal doctrine that dictates the press to be free from pre-publication prior restraints and post-publication damages, with some important and nuanced exceptions. However, this expansive constitutional protection rarely extends to notions of positive liberty, or the right of the press to gather or access information.

The doctrinal lines of cases involving prior restraints and newsgathering rights claims generally illustrate the negative/positive rights distinction. Today, the idea that the state can justly prohibit publication of information is anathema to established constitutional principles. Unless the publisher violates clearly articulated legal rules regarding things such as libel, obscenity, copyright violations, or invasions of privacy, the publisher is rarely liable for post-publication damages. Supreme Court decisions creating this wall around the press have comprised the heart of free-press law in the twentieth century largely on negative liberty grounds.

The first substantive Supreme Court ruling on freedom of the press, in *Patterson v. Colorado*, seemed to embrace the Blackstonian view that the absence of prior restraints was the fundamental meaning of freedom of the press.[122] The repugnance toward prior restraints was the central theme in the landmark *Near* and *Pentagon Papers* decisions as well.

The limits on post-publication damages have also been framed using negative rights approaches, although they have positive liberty aspects as well. Practically speaking, the most important development has come in the area of libel. In *New York Times v. Sullivan*, the Supreme Court proclaimed the need for "breathing space" for criticism of public officials and determined that some false statements of fact were inevitable in robust public debate and therefore cannot be punished absent knowing falsity or reckless disregard for the truth.[123] Government desires to keep secrets is another common thread throughout these cases, and the Court has ruled that states cannot criminally sanction the publication of truthful information, such as the publication of confidential judicial information. Protection from post-publication damages based on the First Amendment has also been extended to various tort actions, including such things as a First Amendment defense to claims of intentional infliction of emotional distress, borne out of *Hustler v. Falwell,* the case involving a lawsuit brought by the Rev. Jerry Falwell against *Hustler* magazine's advertisement parody that depicted Falwell discussing his first sexual encounter with his mother in an outhouse. The press has also won a number of privacy lawsuits in which individuals suing the press over disclosure of information where courts have deemed the matters to be appropriate matters of public concern, invoking First Amendment defenses in the publication of the material.[124] The view that government is limited from censoring or punishing the press is what Lee Bollinger aptly calls "the central meaning of freedom of the press,"[125] and to a large degree, these press-friendly precedents adopt a "negative liberty" view of press freedom.

Press claims were viewed more skeptically by the Supreme Court when they were viewed as claims of positive liberty. Two years after *Branzburg*, in 1974, the Court ruled in *Pell v. Procunier* that a state law prohibiting journalists from interviewing prison inmates did violate the First Amendment's press clause.[126] The Court prioritized the interests of the prison's administration and the diminished rights of prisoners while dismissing almost uniformly any suggestion that members of the press had any "rights" associated with conducting interviews of prisoners. "The First and Fourteenth Amendments bar government from interfering in any way with a free press. The Constitution does not, however, require government accord the press special access to information not shared by members of the public generally," the Court wrote.[127] The Court ruled the same way in a similar case the same year.[128] While the majorities found that the First Amendment did not grant special rights to the press, Justice Powell in *Saxbe v. Washington Post Co.* argued that giving journalists so-called special rights was required if they were to fulfill their constitutional duties under the press clause of the First Amendment.[129]

At some point official restraints on access to news sources, even though not directed solely at the press, may so undermine the function of the First Amendment that it is both appropriate and necessary to require the government to justify such regulations in terms more compelling than discretionary authority and administrative convenience. It is worth repeating our admonition in *Branzburg* that "without some protection for seeking out the news, freedom of the press could be eviscerated" ... In seeking out the news the press therefore acts as an agent of the public at large. It is the means by which the people receive that free flow of information and ideas essential to intelligent self-government. By enabling the public to assert meaningful control over the political process, the press performs a crucial function in effecting the societal purpose of the First Amendment. That function is recognized by specific reference to the press in the text of the Amendment and by the precedents of this court.[130]

Four years later, in *Houchins v. KQED*, the Court upheld a similar rule prohibiting journalists from interviewing inmates at a county jail. In this case, the Court recognized the public interests served by journalists: "They can be a powerful and constructive force, contributing to remedial action in the conduct of public business. They have served that function since the beginning of the Republic."[131] Collectively, the prison access cases and the privilege and search cases demonstrate the Court's reluctance to embrace newsgathering and access claims in part because it would require the Court to articulate rules in which members of the press would be treated differently than other citizens as a matter of constitutional rights.

By 1978, the contradictions and dilemmas of the press cases gained specific acknowledgement in court decisions. In *First National Bank of Boston v. Bellotti,* the court overturned a state court ruling that prohibited banks and corporations from lobbying the public on referendum issues unrelated to their business interests.[132] In its First Amendment analysis, the court paid particular attention to the freedom of the press to criticize and influence government. Chief Justice Burger, in his concurring opinion, focused on this distinction between media and non-media companies His opinion detailed the controversy of the press clause like no other opinion.[133] "The Court has not yet squarely resolved whether the Press Clause confers upon the 'institutional press' any freedom from government restraint not enjoyed by all others."[134] Burger quoted extensively from historian Leonard Levy, and he wrote that those who favor institutional press protections must find evidence "on the part of the Framers for which no supporting evidence is available." Burger essentially made Levy's argument part of constitutional law, at least to the extent that a concurring opinion can be read as such. Burger wrote, "The liberty encompassed by the Press Clause, although complementary to and a natural extension of the Speech Clause liberty, merited special mention simply because it had been more often the object of official restraints."[135] Levy's history was Burger's first reason to reject institutional rights for the press; the second reason was practical. "The very task of including some entities within the 'institutional press' while excluding others, whether undertaken by legislature, court, or administrative agency, is reminiscent of the abhorred licensing system of Tudor and Stuart England – a system the First Amendment was intended to ban from this country."[136]

If by the late 1970s Justice Burger embodied the approach that the press is not special as a matter of constitutional doctrine, Justice Stewart represented a powerful voice for the institution of the press. In three decisions in 1978, Stewart passionately defended the institutional press. In his concurring opinion in *Houchins v. KQED*, the prison-access case discussed earlier, Stewart attacked Burger's position in *Bellotti*. "That the First Amendment speaks separately of freedom of speech and freedom of the press is no constitutional accident, but an acknowledgement of the critical role played by the press in American society. The Constitution requires sensitivity to that role, and to the special needs of the press in performing it effectively."[137] Stewart also pointed out it was important to study the reasons why journalists sought access to jails. "When on assignment, a journalist does not tour a jail simply for his own edification. He is there to gather information to be passed on to others, and his mission is protected by the Constitution for very specific reasons."[138] In *Landmark Communications, Inc., v. Virginia,* the court reversed a state court's ruling against a newspaper publisher who violated a state law by revealing details of an investigation into misconduct by a judge.[139] In his concurring opinion, Stewart noted it was permissible to punish the leaker of confidential materials but not the newspaper.

If the constitutional protection of a free press means anything, it means that government cannot take it upon itself to decide what a newspaper may or may not publish. Though government may deny access to information and punish its theft, government may not prohibit or punish the publication of that information once it falls into the hands of the press, unless the need for secrecy is manifestly overwhelming.[140]

Finally, in *Zurcher v. Stanford Daily,* the court upheld the exercise of a search warrant at the *Stanford Daily* college newsroom in which police sought unpublished photographs of a protest.[141] "It seems to me self-evident that police searches of newspaper offices burden the freedom of the press," Stewart wrote. "The knowledge that police officers can make an unannounced raid on a newsroom is thus bound to have a deterrent effect on the availability of confidential news sources. The end result, wholly inimical to the First Amendment, will be a diminishing flow of potentially important information to the public."[142]

The role of the press in both the *Houchins* and *Zurcher* cases needs emphasis in a discussion about special rights for the press. Both reveal an important reality about the press as being different. Journalists seeking access to prisons do so not for personal reasons, but as representatives of the public. And when journalists seek protections from searches of their newsrooms, it is not simply for personal privacy reasons. Because their work invariably informs the public, broader societal interests are raised than in searches of private citizens.[143]

Summarizing the state of interpretation of the press clause in 1977, Professor Margaret A. Blanchard reduced the Supreme Court's evolving rule regarding press rights to a simple question: What can the public do in a like situation?[144] If the public has a right to attend trials or obtain documents, so too do members of the press. But the result of the press-rights cases was clear to Blanchard in 1977: If the public must be required to provide testimony, comply with search warrants, and be restricted by administrative rules in obtaining documents, so too must members of the press. "In the 1977 Term the Justices took greater pains then ever before to tell the press that it has no special First Amendment protections beyond that granted to the individual," Blanchard wrote that year in the *Supreme Court Review.*[145]

Cases involving press clause interpretation dropped precipitously after this period, leaving the implications to be debated among scholars and the lower courts. One case that limited the fears of access advocates is *Richmond Newspapers v. Virginia,* a case that Justice John Paul Stevens called a "watershed case" because it established a public right to newsworthy information.[146] *Richmond Newspapers* established the precedent that criminal trials were required to be public absent "an overriding interest articulated in findings."[147] The Court has also extended this concept to jury voir dire and preliminary hearings. But importantly, *Richmond Newspapers* was decided not as a press case but one involving First and Sixth Amendment claims more generally, noting, for example, "the right of access to places traditionally open to the public."[148]

To summarize, newsgathering and access claims rooted in conceptions of freedom of the press have failed to generate much traction in Supreme Court rule-making, in contrast to prior restraint and post-publication damages claims, which explains in part why journalists do not have an explicit First Amendment right to protect confidential sources. This is largely based on the "either-or" logic of the press clause as being an individual or institutional right and relying on the negative/positive liberty dichotomy. Is "freedom of the press" an individual liberty that primarily concerns itself with the individual right to disseminate information, or is it better viewed as a collective right bestowed on an institution of professional watchdogs, or perhaps more aptly a right of anyone serving the "functions" of the press? An individual-rights view has no conceptual problem with prior restraint or post-publication damage claims because they generally can apply to anyone who publishes information. Newsgathering claims ostensibly require rights to be applied to discreet classes of individual (i.e., newsgatherers), and this becomes problematic.

The failure to develop a strong conceptual framework for future newsgathering and access claims is troublesome from the perspective of journalistic autonomy. As Robert D. Sack argued three decades ago, one need not get lost in the theoretical morass of the debate over individual versus institutional rights. Sack argues that free-press protections are better thought of in functional terms. "What it should protect is not the institution, but the role of the press," he wrote. A functional analysis allows one to get past the definitional problems of "who" is the press and allows one to think about the questions in broader terms.

Ultimately, questions of newsgathering and access are best framed when they are rooted in the history and traditions of the press, and the support of those concepts in the free-press decisions of the Supreme Court. This would require the development of a press theory that prioritizes what today we define as "journalism," something that should remain a potential line of theoretical development for mass communication scholars.

CONCLUSION

The articulation of a journalist's privilege that emerged during the late 19th and early 20th century was a result of journalism professionalization and the increasing discourse of journalism ethics that emphasized journalism's broader social and political functions. In the rare occasions when journalists were called upon to reveal confidential sources, they relied on a myriad of arguments to justify their refusal to cooperate with authorities. It wasn't until the mid-20th century that the journalist's privilege became a concept of constitutional law, when journalists drew upon the Supreme Court's evolving free-press doctrine to justify a privilege based on the First Amendment. The 1972 *Branzburg* decision was the result of a decade of lower court rulings in which judges wrestled with how to apply the evolving free-press doctrine to journalist claims of a constitutional privilege.

The failure of the Supreme Court to embrace substantive newsgathering rights in *Branzburg* as part of its First Amendment jurisprudence highlights several unresolved problems in free-press theory. The libertarian, negative-rights based approach remains a central tenet of free-press theory. This approach is also central to Supreme Court's free-press doctrine that emphasizes repugnance toward prior restraints and publication damages, with some important exceptions, while remaining skeptical toward newsgathering and access rights. A coherent theory that supports some newsgathering and access claims as matters of constitutional law, perhaps one that sets minimum standards required by First Amendment values, has yet to be adopted by the courts.

Of course, the First Amendment as an element of the Constitution suggests we think about it strictly in terms of constitutional doctrine, or the fruit of Supreme Court decision-making. In this sense, future development of a newsgathering doctrine requires a coherent theoretical framework that finds support in history and practice, and one that can adequately address the concerns and fears of scholarly skeptics. Harry Kalven once said that constitutional and common law development is a process of making the law "pure." Purity, though, is forever shifting. The legal dogma of a century ago has in profound ways been rejected, reformed and remade. The law is always evolving, and the challenge for free-press theorists who support newsgathering rights is to develop a coherent theoretical framework that will support the evolution of law in a way that enhances free press values.

But the First Amendment is also an important political principle whose strength relies in part upon public opinion. Courts are generally predisposed against advancing doctrine too noxious to popular sentiment or to established precedent. Media law theorists might well explore the relationship between contemporary practice, public opinion, and the political sphere of public law as a way to nurture constitutional principles. If, as media attorney Bruce Sanford fears, [149] the press should worry much more about public opinion than the courts for its future vitality, more attention to statutory solutions might be beneficial, akin to the model of open meetings and open records laws that are incredibly important to the press and find their genesis legislatively, not from judicial and constitutional doctrine. That is the focus of the next chapter, which examines newsgathering rights and journalism ethics in the context of legislative debates over the journalist's privilege.

Chapter 5 Notes

---

[1] Garland v. Torre, 259 F.2d 545 (2nd Cir. 1958).

[2] In Re Appeal of Alan L. Goodfader From Order Compelling Him to Answer Questions on Deposition, 45 Haw. 317 (Haw. 1961).

[3] Branzburg v. Hayes, 408 U.S. 665 (1972).

[4] *See* chapter seven for a discussion about post-*Branzburg* privilege cases in the lower courts.

[5] See generally Erwin Chemerinsky, *Protect the Press: A First Amendment Standard for Safeguarding Aggressive Newsgathering.* 33 UNIVERSITY OF RICHMOND LAW REVIEW 1143 (1999-2000).

[6] Cox v. Broadcasting Corp. v. Cohn, 420 U.S. 594 at 609 (1975).

[7] Estes v. Texas, 381 U.S. 532, 539 (1965).

[8] *See generally* Erik Ugland, *Demarcating the Right to Gather News: A Sequential Interpretation of the First Amendment*, 3 DUKE J. CONST. L & PUB. POL'Y 113 (2008).

[9] Gitlow v. New York, 268 US 652 (1925).

[10] Margaret Blanchard, *The Institutional Press and Its First Amendment Privileges,* 1978 SUPREME COURT REVIEW 225 (1978).

[11] *See generally* LEONARD LEVY. EMERGENCE OF A FREE PRESS (1985).

[12] JOHN MILTON, AREOPAGITICA: A SPEECH FOR THE LIBERTY OF UNLICENSED PRINTING (1644), in VINCENT BLASI, IDEAS OF THE FIRST AMENDMENT 56 (2006).

[13] JEFFERY A. SMITH, PRINTERS AND PRESS FREEDOM: THE IDEOLOGY OF EARLY AMERICAN JOURNALISM (1988) and ROBERT W.T. MARTIN, THE FREE AND OPEN PRESS: THE FOUNDING OF AMERICAN DEMOCRATIC PRESS LIBERTY, 1640-1800 (2001).

[14] JAMES MORTON SMITH, FREEDOM'S FETTERS: THE ALIEN AND SEDITION LAWS AND AMERICAN CIVIL LIBERTIES (1956).

[15] DAVID RABBAN, FREE SPEECH IN ITS FORGOTTEN YEARS (1997), DONNA LEE DICKERSON, THE COURSE OF TOLERANCE: FREEDOM OF THE PRESS IN NINETEENTH-CENTURY AMERICA (1990) and MICHAEL KENT CURTIS, FREE SPEECH, 'THE PEOPLE'S DARLING PRIVILEGE': STRUGGLES FOR FREEDOM OF EXPRESSION IN AMERICAN HISTORY (2000).

[16] *Id.*

[17] New York Times v. Sullivan, 376 U.S. 254 (1964).

[18] New York Times v. United States, 403 U.S. 713 (1971).

[19] Brandenburg v. Ohio, 395 U.S. 444 (1969).

[20] ROBERT K. MURRAY, RED SCARE: A STUDY IN NATIONAL HYSTERIA, 1919-1920 (1955).

[21] Masses Pub. Co. v. Patten, 244 Fed. 535 (1917).

[22] *Id.*

[23] *Id.*

[24] Gerald Gunther, *Learned Hand and the Origins of Modern First Amendment Doctrine: Some Fragments of History,* 27 STAN. L.R. 719 (1975).

[25] *Id.,* and Fred Ragan, *Justice Oliver Wendell Holmes Jr., Zechariah Chafee Jr., and the Clear and Present Danger Test for Free Speech: The First Year, 1919,* 58 JOURNAL OF AMERICAN HISTORY 24 (June 1971).

[26] Schenck v. United States, 249 U.S. 47 (1919), Debs v. United States, 249 U.S. 211 (1919), and Frohwerk v. United States, 249 U.S. 204 (1919).

[27] Abrams v. U.S., 250 U.S. 616 (1919).

[28] Whitney v. California, 274 U.S. 357 (1927).

[29] John Wertheimer, *Freedom of Speech: Zechariah Chafee and Free-Speech History,* 22 REVIEWS IN AMERICAN HISTORY 365 (1994).

[30] Mark A. Graber, *Transforming Free Speech: The Ambiguous Legacy of Civil Libertarianism* (1991).

[31] *Id.*

[32] Near v. Minnesota, 283 U.S. 697 (1931).

[33] *Id.* at 716.

[34] The decision cited several historical documents, including a letter sent by the Congressional Congress on October 26, 1774, to the inhabitants of Quebec discussing the "five great rights," and the writings of James Madison, The court also quoted James Madison's passionate defense of the press during ratification of state Constitutions. Madison noted the press's importance in "canvassing the merits and measures of public men" and said some abuse by the press is required to protect the greater freedom, "and can the wisdom of this policy be doubted by any who reflect that to the press alone, chequered as it is with abuses, the world is indebted for all the triumphs which have been gained by reason and humanity over error and oppression." *Id.* at 718.

[35] Grosjean v. American Press Co., 297 U.S. 233 (1936).

[36] *Id.* at 246.

[37] *Id.* at 250.

[38] Lovell v. City of Griffin, 303 U.S. 444, (1938).

[39] *Id.* at 453.

[40] Pennekamp v. State of Florida, 328 U.S. 331, (1946).

[41] *Id.* at 354-355.

[42] Craig v. Harney, 331 U.S. 367, (1947).

[43] *Id.* at 383.

[44] Garland v. Torre, 259 F.2d 545 (2nd Cir. 1958).

[45] *Id.*

[46] RICHARD KLUGER, THE PAPER: THE LIFE AND DEATH OF THE NEW YORK HERALD TRIBUNE at 537 (1986).

[47] *Id.*

[48] *Id.*

[49] *Id.*

[50] *Id.* at 537.

[51] Garland v. Torre, 259 F.2d at 547.

[52] Kluger, *supra* note 46, 561.

[53] *Id.* at 561.

[54] Garland v. Torre, 259 F.2d at 548.

[55] *Id.* at 548.

[56] *Id.* at 549.

[57] *Id.* at 551.

[58] Kluger, *supra* note 46, at 561.

[59] *Id.* at 562.

[60] *Id.*

[61] *Id.*

[62] *Id.* at 563.

[63] In Re Appeal of Alan L. Goodfader From Order Compelling Him to Answer Questions on Deposition, 45 Haw. 317 (Haw. 1961).

[64] *Id.* at 319.

[65] *Id.* at 319.

[66] *Id.* at 480.

[67] *Id.*

[68] Grosjean v. American Press Co., 297 U.S. 233, 250 ("The predominant purpose of the grant of immunity here invoked was to preserve an untrammeled press as a votal source of public information. The newspapers, magazines, and other journalis of the country, it is safe to say, have shed and continue to shed, more light on the public and business affairs of the nation than any other instrumentality of publicity, and since informed public opinion is the most potent of all restraints upon misgovernment, the suppression or abridgment of the publicity afforded by a free press cannot be regarded otherwise than with grave concern … A free press stands as one of the great interpreters between the government and the people. To allow it to be fettered is to fetter ourselves."

[69] Goodfader, 45 Haw. at 323.

[70] *Id.* at 323-324.

[71] The court also quoted press friendly rhetoric from Bridges v. California, 314 US 252 (1941).

[72] Goodfader, 45 Haw. at 327-328.

[73] *Id.* at 329.

[74] *Id.* 337-338.

[75] *Id.* 344.

[76] Talley vs. California, 362 U.S. 60.

[77] Rumely v. United States, 197 F. 2d 166, *aff'd on other grounds*, 345 U.S. 41.

[78] See e.g., State v. Knops, 49 Wis. 2d 647 (1971); Alioto v. Cowles Communications, Inc. C.A. No. 52150 (N.D. Cal. 1969); In re Grand Jury Witnesses, 322 F. Supp. 573 (N.D. Cal. 1970); People v. Dorhn, Crim. No. 69-3808 (Cook County, Ill., Cir. Ct. 1970).

[79] Branzburg v. Hayes, 408 U.S. 665 (1972).

[80] *Id.*

[81] *Id.*

[82] Donna M. Murasky, *The Journalist's Privilege: Branzburg and Its Aftermath,* 52 TEX. L.R. 829, 832 (1974).

[83] The Kentucky shield statute, Ky. Rev. Stat. Ann. § 421.100 (1972), states: No person shall be compelled to disclose in any legal proceeding ... or before any grand or petit jury ... or before any ... legislative body, or any committee thereof, or elsewhere, the source of any information procured or obtained by him, and published in a newspaper ... by which he is engaged or employed, or with which he is connected.

[84] Branzburg v. Pound, 461 S.W.2d 345 (Ky. 1970).

[85] Branzburg v. Hayes, 408 U.S. 665 at 670 (1972).

[86] *Id.* at 671.

[87] *Id.* at 672.

[88] *Id.* at 674.

[89] James C. Goodale, *Branzburg v. Hayes and the Developing Qualified Privilege for Newsmen,* 26 HASTINGS L.J. 709, 711 (1974-1975).

[90] Murasky, *supra* note 83, at 833.

[91] Branzburg at 675.

[92] *Id.* at 676.

[93] *Id.* at 676.

[94] *Id.* at 680.

[95] *Id.* at 682.

[96] *Id.* at 682-683.

[97] *Id.* at 691.

[98] *Id.* at 693.

[99] *Id.* at 702.

[100] *Id.* at 681.

[101] *Id.* at 703-704.

[102] Potter Stewart, *Or of the Press*, 26 HASTINGS L.J. 631 (1974-1975).

[103] Branzburg at 710.

[104] *Id.* at 711.

[105] *Id.* at 713.

[106] *Id.* at 720-721.

[107] *Id.* at 725.

[108] *Id.* at 743.

[109] Id. at 726.

[110] Goodale, *supra* note 90, at 714.

[111] New York Times Co. v. United States, 403 U.S. 713, 715 (1971) ("The press was protected so that it could bare the secrets of government and inform the people.").

[112] *See* David A. Gordon, *Had Black Ruled in Branzburg, in* HUGO BLACK AND THE FIRST AMENDMENT (Everett Dennis ed. 1978); Sean W. Kelly, *Black and White and Read All Over: Press Protections After Branzburg,* 57 DUKE L.J. 199 (2007).

[113] *Newsmen's Privilege, Hearings Before Subcommittee No. 3 of the House Committee on the Judiciary,* 92d Cong., 2d Session (1972) (hearings on Sept. 21, 27, 28 and Oct. 4 & 5, 1972) at 114.

[114] In re Grand Jury Matter, Gronowicz, 764 F.2d. 983, 900 (3d Cir. 1985), United States v. Model Magazine Distribs., Inc., 955 F.2d 229, 234 (4th Cir. 1992); United States v. Smith, 135 F.3d. 963, 968 (5th Cir. 1998); Farr v. Pitchess, 522 F.2d 464, 467 (9th Cir. 1975).

[115] See Sonja R. West, *Concurring in Part and Concurring in the Confusion,* 10 MICH. L. REV. 1951, 1953 (2006).

[116] *See* Michele B. Kimball, *The Intent Behind the Cryptic Concurrence that Provided a Reporter's Privilege,* 13 COMM. L. & POL'Y 379 (2008); Sonja R. West, *Concurring in Part and Concurring in the Confusion,* 104 MICH. L. REV. 1951 (2006).

[117] BOB WOODWARD AND SCOTT ARMSTONG, THE BRETHREN: INSIDE THE SUPREME COURT, 223 (1979).

[118] Michele B. Kimball, *The Intent Behind the Cryptic Concurrence that Provided a Reporter's Privilege*, 13 COMM. L. & POL'Y 379 (2008);

[119] James Goodale, *Branzburg v. Hayes and the Development Qualified Privilege for Newsmen*, 26 HASTINGS L.J. 709, 719 (1974-1975).

[120] Potter Stewart, *Or of the Press,* 26 HASTINGS L.J. 631, 636 (1974)

[121] ISAIAH BERLIN, FOUR ESSAYS ON LIBERTY (1969).

[122] LUCAS A. POWE, THE FOURTH ESTATE AND THE CONSTITUTION: FREEDOM OF THE PRESS IN AMERICA 2-8 (1991).

[123] New York Times v. Sullivan, 376 U.S. 254 (1964).

[124] *See, for example,* Cox Broadcasting Corp. v. Cohn, 420 U.S. 469 (1975) and Florida Star v. B.J.F., 491 U.S. 524, 541 (1989).

[125] LEE C. BOLLINGER, IMAGES OF A FREE PRESS 1 (1991).

[126] Pell v. Procunier, 417 US 817 (1974).

[127] *Id.*

[128] Saxbe v. Washington Post Co., 417 U.S. 843, (1974).

[129] *Id.*

[130] *Id.* at 860.

[131] Houchins v. KQED, 438 U.S. 1, 8 (1978).

[132] First National Bank of Boston v. Bellotti, 435 U.S. 765 (1978).

[133] *Id.*

[134] *Id.* at 798.

[135] *Id.* at 800.

[136] *Id.* at 801.

[137] *Id.* at 17.

[138] *Id.*

[139] Landmark Communications, Inc. v. Virginia, 435 U.S. 829, (1978).

[140] *Id.* at 849.

[141] Zurcher v. Stanford Daily, 436 U.S. 547 (1978).

[142] *Id.* at 573.

[143] Floyd Abrams, *The Press Is Different: Reflections on Justice Stewart and the Autonomous Press,* 7 HOFSTRA L. REV. 564, at 585 (1978-1979).

[144] Blanchard, *supra* note 10, at 228.

[145] Blanchard, *supra* note 10, at 229.

[146] Richmond Newspapers v. Viriginia, 448 U.S. 555, 581 (1980).

[147] *Id.*

[148] *Id.*

[149] BRUCE SANFORD, DON'T SHOOT THE MESSENGER, HOW OUR GROWING HATRED OF THE MEDIA THREATENS FREE SPEECH FOR ALL OF US (1999).

After the First Amendment Fails: The Journalist's Privilege as Legislative Public Policy, 1972-1975

After the Supreme Court of the United States rejected a First Amendment rights-based journalist's privilege in 1972, journalists feared that they would become seriously handicapped in their ability to serve as independent watchdogs. While the Supreme Court had taken a skeptical tone toward newsgathering rights as a matter of constitutional law, journalists turned elsewhere in their attempts to create a legal right for their ethical concept of duty to protect sources. After *Branzburg v. Hayes,* the battle for legal recognition intensified in legislatures and in courtrooms. The next two chapters focus on two pivotal fronts: the congressional debates in the 1970s, heretofore not dissected in the academic scholarship, and in the federal judiciary. The legislative debates analyzed in this chapter suggest that lawmakers can be attuned to First Amendment values in ways that many media scholars overlook or minimize. The evolution of the common law, meanwhile, discussed in the following chapter, shows that judges have interpreted *Branzburg* in different ways, and have found alternative means to provide journalists some judge-made legal protections. The chapters explain how the journalist's privilege as an ethic translated into positive law despite the Supreme Court's refusal to embrace newsgathering as a First Amendment right.

OVERVIEW OF CONGRESSIONAL HEARINGS, 1972-1975

Between 1972 and 1975, Wisconsin Congressman Robert W. Kastenmeier presided over the most extensive hearings in congressional history on a journalist's shield law, or what was then called a "newsmen's privilege." Many journalists and press advocates had presumed the First Amendment's guarantee of freedom of the press conferred to them this right,[1] but after losing their arguments before the Supreme Court in 1972, they turned to Congress for legal protection. Over the next three congressional terms, Kastenmeier's Subcommittee No. 3 of the House Judiciary Committee convened seventeen hearings, reviewed eighty-six newsmen's privilege bills and heard testimony from sixty-nine witnesses.[2] Although historical scholarship on the federal journalist's privilege occasionally notes Senator Sam J. Ervin's subcommittee hearings when discussing the aftermath of *Branzburg*,[3] Kastenmeier's House hearings have been largely ignored in the literature.[4]

The House hearings began during the end of the 92nd Congress, when Kastenmeier's judiciary subcommittee of nine members convened on September 21, 1972, to discuss twenty-six newsmen's privilege bills that had been authored and cosponsored by more than sixty lawmakers in the weeks after the Supreme Court issued its *Branzburg* decision.[5] While the First Amendment provided no testimonial privilege, Justice Byron White for the *Branzburg* majority wrote that Congress and state legislatures had the authority to create statutory privileges:

> At the federal level, Congress has the freedom to determine whether a statutory newsman's privilege is necessary and desirable and to fashion standards and rules as narrow or broad as deemed necessary to address the evil discerned and, equally important, to refashion those rules as experience from time to time may dictate. There is also merit in leaving state legislatures free, within First Amendment limits, to fashion their own standards in light of the conditions and problems with respect to the relations between law enforcement officials and press in their own areas.[6]

At the time, the *Branzburg* case was the latest in a string of showdowns between the press and the Nixon administration. The year before, President Richard Nixon sought a prior restraint, ultimately unsuccessfully, against the *New York Times* and the *Washington Post* to stop publication of a series of articles on based on the so-called Pentagon Papers.[7] One Nixon scholar said the president had an "instinctive, visceral hatred of the news media" that fed "an unprecedented, transparent assault on the media and individual reporters,"[8] and historians have documented his administration's covert and overt attacks on reporters and press credibility.[9] Journalists also offered data documenting the increase in subpoenas from the government seeking information from their newsgathering. For example, the *Chicago Sun-Times* and the *Daily News* received thirty subpoenas in the first two years of the Nixon administration, including eleven subpoenas to one reporter. During one thirty-month period, NBC and CBS received one hundred and twenty-four subpoenas.[10]

The sting of the *Branzburg* ruling was exacerbated by several immediate cases in which journalists were threatened with jail, and press advocates pointed to them as evidence of the need for congressional action. The congressional record demonstrates that lawmakers were disturbed by the headlines of journalists going to jail.[11] Peter Bridge of the *Newark News* in New Jersey was the first reporter jailed after the *Branzburg* decision, spending twenty days in county jail for a May 2, 1972, story in which he quoted a commissioner of the Newark Housing Authority as saying she had been offered a bribe for a vote on hiring an executive director. Bridge had been found in contempt for refusing to answer questions, and he lost appeals to both the New Jersey and U.S. supreme courts. He was released when the grand jury term expired.[12] In November 1972, William T. Farr was jailed on contempt charges stemming for a story he wrote two years earlier for the *Los Angeles Herald-Examiner* in which he reported details from a prosecution witness's pretrial statement about the Charles Manson case.[13] Also in 1972, Joseph Weiler, a reporter from the Memphis *Commercial Appeal*, was under threat of contempt of court for his failure to disclose to a state senate committee who told him about abuse at a state hospital.[14] And John Lawrence of the *Los Angeles Times* served several hours in jail for refusing to turn over confidential tapes in what David Halberstam proclaimed was "perhaps the most important Watergate story so far."[15]

Because of the *Branzburg* ruling and the high-profile cases on September 15, 1972, Kastenmeier, a Wisconsin Democrat who had come to the national press's defense in the *Pentagon Papers* case,[16] issued a press release saying the newsmen's privilege "urgently needs Congressional action."[17] The first congressional hearings in the fall of 1972 occurred as lawmakers were running for re-election and President Nixon was campaigning for what would be a landslide re-election victory. Kastenmeier said the some two dozen proposals reflected the tension "between two principles that are vital to our democratic institutions."[18] The first was the "well-established rule that government is entitled, to, and must be able to secure, the testimony of its citizens."[19] The second "equally urgent proposition," was the public's right to receive information from journalists who sometimes must rely on confidential sources and information.[20]

During five hearings in September and October 1972, the committee heard from twenty-five witnesses, representing journalists, executive branch officials and lawmakers whose proposals varied significantly. By the end of the 92nd Congress, the essential arguments had already emerged. The Department of Justice argued the legislation was unnecessary because prosecutors were already sensitive to First Amendment concerns and subpoenaed journalists only when absolutely necessary, limited by voluntary guidelines that required the attorney general himself to approve subpoenas and created narrow circumstances in which subpoenas could be issued.[21] Journalists advocated absolutist proposals, while lawmakers proposed varying levels of protection.[22] Many proposals called for a federal bill to pre-empt state statutes and apply to state officials and courts.[23] Questions were also raised about who should qualify for protection,[24] and whether that protection should extend to both confidential and non-confidential newsgathering information.[25]

As the 93rd Congress convened in early 1973, there appeared to be broad support among House members to pass a bill, and hearings scheduled in the Senate signaled the bill's importance in that chamber of Congress as well.[26] At the first of ten hearings in February and March of that year, the chairman of the House Judiciary Committee, Rep. Peter W. Rodino, a New Jersey Democrat, appeared before the subcommittee and said legislation was urgently needed that would "guarantee ... freedom of the press."[27] Kastenmeier remarked optimistically "that during the month of March we ought to be able to resolve the question."[28] Kastenmeier said twenty-eight bills had been introduced so far in the 93rd Congress, and "the number rises almost daily."[29] He laid forth his charge to the subcommittee: "Shall Congress enact a newsmen's privilege? If a privilege is to be enacted, shall it be absolute or qualified and if qualified in what respect? And should its application be confined to federal proceedings or should it also bind the states? And who shall be eligible for the privilege?"[30]

Ultimately, one hundred and forty-three members of the House would introduce or co-sponsor fifty-five bills in the 93rd Congress.[31] Following the February and March hearings in which the nuances of these proposals were debated, Kastenmeier ushered a compromise bill through his subcommittee during several markup sessions. On June 14, 1973, the subcommittee voted to send to the full Judiciary Committee an amended version of H.R. 5928, originally drafted by Rep. William Cohen, then a freshman Republican from Maine and later Secretary of Defense under President Bill Clinton.[32] The bill created a two-tiered privilege, developed in part by University of Michigan Law School Professor Vince Blasi, that provided absolute protection against investigative subpoenas and qualified protections in adjudicative proceedings. The bill also applied to state court proceedings and provided a broad functional definition of those who qualified for protection.[33] Kastenmeier's files indicate that on March 26, 1974, the full Judiciary Committee discussed the bill, and "[T]here was stiff opposition from both those groups who feel the bill goes too far and those who think it does not go far enough."[34] In his remarks to the full committee, Kastenmeier said the bill, as amended, "reflects the view held by the Subcommittee majority that a broad privilege is needed but must be consistent with the orderly functioning of the judicial system."[35] He also noted that the "trend on the part of media in the direction of absolute as distinguished from qualified privilege" had since subsided. "The media, originally badly split, are now very substantially united behind this bill."[36]

The bill languished in committee, according to Kastenmeier's notes, because of more pressing matters.[37] First it was the vice-presidential confirmation proceedings of Gerald Ford after the resignation of Vice President Spiro Agnew. Also, ironically enough, the Watergate scandal had the effect of putting the privilege debates on the back burner, as looming large was the possibility of presidential impeachment, which fell under the purview of the committee.[38] The 93rd Congress adjourned without the bill's further advancement.

After President Nixon's resignation and the start of the 94th Congress in 1975, Kastenmeier hadn't given up on a newsmen's privilege. Kastenmeier's subcommittee, now named the Subcommittee on Courts, Civil Liberties and the Administration of Justice, held two hearings on H.R. 215, the successor to H.R. 5928, and the four other bills introduced.[39] H.R. 215, called the "News Source and Information Protection Act of 1975," drafted by Reps. Kastenmeier, Cohen and Tom Railsback, an Illinois Republican, was described as the "distillation of several years of considered information gathering."[40] But opposition from both the press and government officials immediately surfaced, and the bill did not advance past the sub-committee level.

ELEMENTS OF THE CONGRESSIONAL DEBATE: THE BASIC ARGUMENTS

Journalists argued that a free press was a necessary component of American democracy, and that to adequately gather news and inform the public, journalists need to go beyond reporting what "official" sources say, and sometimes needs to receive information from confidential sources. These confidential sources range from government officials to members of dissident groups. If journalists are forced to reveal the identities of these sources, the sources will dry up, to the detriment of an informed citizenry. Journalists may also lose their independence by becoming agents for government information.

A.M. Rosenthal, managing editor of *The New York Times* in 1973, told lawmakers that the public learns information about its government through two channels: the official one and the unofficial one.[41] Both are important to journalists trying to make sense of the world. It is the unofficial channel of information dissemination that is threatened when journalists can be forced to reveal confidential sources. "These sources are as varied as the news itself," Rosenthal said. "Every single day in the year the public, through the press, gets some of its most important information" from confidential sources.[42] Rosenthal explained that sources seek confidentiality for a variety of reasons, some noble and some not. Many people face formal and informal punishment if they're identified as talking to journalists, whether or not they are providing sensitive information. Some think important facts should be made public, while others want journalists to better understand complexities.[43]

During the first hearings in 1972, journalists were the loudest advocates for a privilege. Robert G. Fichenberg, the chairman of the Freedom of Information Committee of the American Society of Newspaper Editors, called the *Branzburg* decision "a direct blow at the right of people to be fully informed without hindrance by the government" and claimed that few sources would reveal sensitive information to reporters if they knew their identities would be revealed.[44] John Finnegan, chairman of the Freedom of Information Committee of the Associated Press Managing Editors Association, described a history of press refusals to identify sources of information dating back to the eighteenth century and John Peter Zenger's refusal to identify contributors to his colonial newspaper.[45] "If it was essential in the early history of our country for a journalist to keep sources confidential, it is even more essential for that right to be maintained today in our complex society," Finnegan said.[46] Among those complexities, Finnegan said, are "bureaucratic ineptitude," "corruption" and political dissident groups.[47] "A newsman who is attempting to uncover governmental corruption or stupidity or malfeasance or who is attempting to explain to his readers about drug abuse, crime or organizations which may be in confrontation with our society's accepted norms is acting in the public interest," Finnegan said.[48] At times, this public interest can best be served when a journalist obtains information after a promise of confidentiality, he argued.[49] Guy Ryan, president of Sigma Delta Chi, then the nation's largest professional journalism society with more than 24,000 members,[50] gave an impassioned plea about the role of reporters in gaining sources trust to inform the public about public affairs: "It boils down to this – when a door is slammed in a reporter's face, the door actually is being slammed in the face of the public."[51]

Several arguments were advanced in opposition to a journalist's privilege. At the first hearing in 1972, Roger Cramton, the assistant attorney general for the Office of Legal Counsel in the Department of Justice, said the Department of Justice opposed an absolute privilege, but "does not oppose in principle the creation of a qualified privilege."[52] Still, Cramton presented several arguments against creating any privilege. Cramton said any bill is problematic in defining who and what qualifies for a privilege.[53] He also claimed such a law would unduly slow down government investigations by burdening federal courts and grand jury procedures with determining whether compelled disclosure requirements had been met under the qualified bills.[54]

Finally, Cramton argued that "it is doubtful" that a qualified privilege would have any additional practical effect not accomplished by attorney general guidelines regarding journalist subpoenas. Cramton said these guidelines, created, by Attorney General John Mitchell in August 1970, rendered a statute unnecessary.[55] Before federal prosecutors could subpoena a member of the press, the guidelines require that "all reasonable attempts" be made to obtain information from non-press sources. They require negotiations to be attempted with the press before subpoenas are issued and require a "willingness to respond to particular problems" raised by the news media in those negotiations.[56] And no federal prosecutor can request a press subpoena without specific approval by the attorney general. Cramton said the guidelines provide "significant safeguards against any use of the subpoena power which would endanger First Amendment rights or interfere with a vigorous and effective press."[57] He provided data showing fewer than fifteen requests for subpoenas had been approved between 1970 and 1972 under the guidelines. "This is not a serious problem that needs legislation at this time," Cramton told the committee.[58]

Kastenmeier expressed his suspicion about relying on executive branch promises of restraint. "Given recent history," Kastenmeier said, "the press in America is apprehensive about its relationship to the federal government, particularly to an ever more powerful executive branch."[59] Why, Kastenmeier asked, should the attorney general's guidelines, which can be changed at any time, assure the press they will not be targeted indiscriminately? "The press is not totally incapable of protecting itself," Cramton replied. "The press is highly vocal; it makes itself heard, and its views known. If changes did occur, I am sure that the Congress and this subcommittee would be prepared to step in and attempt to correct any abuses with very prompt enactment of legislation."[60] Journalists could seek redresses in federal courts, Cramton also said, if they feel targeted by undue government pressures, and those courts could determine whether subpoenas are unreasonable, thus allowing "the First Amendment aspect to be vindicated."[61]

The assistant attorney general's statement is significant for two reasons: first, it invited congressional action when subpoena abuses can be demonstrated, and second, it invited federal judges to weigh the First Amendment interests on a case-by-case basis, despite *Branzburg's* majority opinion.

By the 1975 hearings, the Justice Department took a more skeptical view of even the most qualified of proposals. Antonin Scalia, the future Supreme Court justice who was then the assistant attorney general for the Office of Legal Counsel in the Department of Justice, presented the committee with a number of hypothetical situations in which law enforcement would be hampered by the refusal of journalists to cooperate with ongoing police investigations. Journalists might use the privilege statute to refuse to turn over to police letters from a kidnapper or person planning a "series of bombings," or refuse to turn over videotapes of an the attempted assassination of a prominent political figure or a political protest involving allegations of police misconduct. [62] The freedom of the press is important, Scalia said, but "I think the balancing can best be achieved by wise exercise of administrative discretion under the constant guidance and prodding, if necessary, of legislative inquiries such as this."[63]

Kastenmeier, in response, criticized Scalia's assurances that decisions about journalist subpoenas are best left to the executive branch. "Why should the people of this country, why should the news community, Congress, people of this country, as well as law enforcement officials, feel that only law enforcement officers should set rules and regulations?" Kastenmeier asked Scalia. "They can be changed at any time. John Mitchell [who as President Richard Nixon's attorney general had been convicted in the Watergate cover-up case months earlier] can devise them for us all, and they are subject to change. But why should we just rely on executive fiat here? Why is there so much more wisdom in that than there is in Congress passing a law?"[64]

One committee member called Scalia "much too defensive" and another said the Department of Justice "seems to be regressing" based on Scalia's staunch opposition to any privilege bill.[65]

EXTENT OF PROTECTION: ABSOLUTE OR QUALIFIED

The eighty-six bills introduced between 1972 and 1975 generally fell
into three categories: absolute, strictly qualified, or qualified.

Bills creating an absolute privilege immunized journalists from any
subpoena seeking information collected during newsgathering. Bills
establishing a strictly qualified privilege called for a strong privilege
that could be overcome "where there is substantial evidence that
disclosure of privileged information is required to prevent a threat to
human life, espionage, or of foreign aggression.[66] Bills offering a
qualified privilege generally followed some version of Justice Stewart's
dissent in *Branzburg* that gave journalists a privilege that could be
overcome by demonstration that the information sought was clearly
relevant to a law violation, the information was unavailable by other
means, and there was a compelling and overriding interest in the
information.[67] Much of the debate in the latter hearings involved the
nature of the limits of the privilege.

The twenty-six bills introduced in the 92nd Congress included
several that were identical to others, and seven bills can be considered
as representative of the total. [68] The testimony from the authors of
many of these bills demonstrated the motivations for the range of
protections.

Three of the seven primary bills were absolutist. Rep. Jerome
Waldie of Ohio, Rep. Bella Abzug of New York, and Rep. Dan
Kuykendall of Tennessee were the leading sponsors of absolutist bills
in the House. Rep. Waldie's and Rep. Abzug's bills read: "That a
person connected with or employed by the news media or press cannot
be required by a court, the legislature, or any administrative body, to
disclose before the Congress of any other Federal court or agency, any
information or the source of any information procured for publication,
or broadcast."[69]

A companion absolutist bill was introduced in the Senate by
Senator Alan Cranston, Democrat of California.[70] Cranston, a former
reporter for the International News Service before World War II,
argued:

> The press need and should have maximum legal protection,
> which our bill would provide, to meet their responsibilities in
> a free and open society. The First Amendment is not a piece of

special interest legislation for the news and publishing industries; it is a governmental guarantee to a free people without which they could not remain free for long.[71]

Cranston quoted several award-winning journalists whose work was based on confidential sources and described the types of stories these reporters broke with the aid of confidential sources.[72] And he ended with a defense of absolutism that he said was embraced in Justice Douglas's dissent in *Branzburg*. "No exception, no limit, no qualification should be placed on a total and absolute privilege of press confidentiality," Cranston said.[73]

Most absolutists believed that any qualifications would water down a privilege and provide chilling effects for news sources. Cranston said other privileges, such as the attorney-client and priest-penitent privileges, are absolute, and said several scholars, including Harvard Law Professor Paul Freund, concluded that "any qualification creates loopholes which will destroy the privilege."[74] Cranston provided several hypothetical examples. What about the quality of meat being sold to the public? Is that a threat to human life that could meet the requisite threshold under the language of some qualified bills to compel a journalist's testimony about sources in the food-packaging industry?[75]

Committee members were clearly drawn to the absolutist argument that Cranston advanced. Kastenmeier called Cranston's testimony a "powerful, compelling statement."[76] Committee member Rep. Robert Drinan of Massachusetts said it was "the strongest and most logical statement that I think the committee has heard for the absolute privilege."[77] Another committee member, Rep. Edward Mezvinsky, later wrote that he thought a qualified bill would result "in sabotaging the First Amendment guarantee of freedom of the press" and said such a bill would do more harm than good.[78]

Bills creating a qualified privilege generally protected journalists from subpoenas unless a judge determined that the information was relevant to a law violation, the information was unavailable by other means, and there was a compelling and overriding national interest in the information. H.R. 16527, titled the "Free Flow of Information Act," introduced by Rep. Charles Whalen, Republican of Ohio, provided for a qualified privilege modeled closely after Stewart's three-part test and had drawn more cosponsors than any other. Whalen, a former economics professor, would go on to publish a book arguing the value of a newmen's privilege in American democracy.[79] In his remarks before Kastenmeier's committee, Whalen advanced two principal arguments: A privilege law provides the public with a free flow of information, and legal protections ensure press independence:

> The most reliable indicator of whether a society strives to be free or totalitarian is the extent to which the press is free: free to investigate, free to criticize, free to publish what it deems. An absolute requirement for a free society is a free press. The press can be neither free nor effective unless it is totally free from government influence and coercion.[80]

Rep. William S. Moorhead of Pennsylvania testified in support of Whalen's H.R. 16527, which was identical to his H.R. 16638. Moorhead called this "the most workable compromise between groups that wanted total and absolute protection under all circumstances and those who believed that the limitation should be quite substantial. This is a compromise between those two extremes."[81] Rep. Edward I. Koch of New York, a future mayor of New York City, testified about his two bills, H.R. 837 and H.R. 16542, which would have created a qualified privilege, but he said he was open to changing them based on the committee's recommendations. Kastenmeier called Koch "the father of all legislation in this field" given his early interest in drafting a law.[82]

The so-called "strictly qualified" proposal was introduced by Rep. Ogden Reid of New York. It provided for compelled disclosure only after a judge found "substantial evidence that disclosure of the information is required to prevent threat to human life, over espionage or of foreign aggression."[83] Reid was elected in 1962 as a Republican, but became a Democrat in 1972 in part because of his opposition to President Nixon. Reid's family had owned the *New York Herald Tribune*, and he was the newspaper's editor when columnist Marie Torre went to jail after being sued by Judy Garland over the identity of a source Torre used in a column that said Garland was hesitant to do a series of television specials because "she thinks she's fat."[84] He knew firsthand the difficulties journalists faced when they decided to disobey a court order and go to jail to protect a source. "None of these men or women has anything to gain personally by going to jail," Reid testified:

They do not do it for their own good. They pay – or are fully prepared to pay – the heavy price of their freedom because they are professional journalists who know from their years of experience that the future flow of important news to the public will be materially diminished if the confidentiality of news sources is betrayed.[85]

Reid said after the *Branzburg* case "it is absolutely essential" for Congress to pass legislation.[86]

Disagreement among journalists and press advocates over the extent of protection began immediately. During the 1972 hearings, Robert G. Fichenberg, the chairman of the Freedom of Information Committee of the American Society of Newspaper Editors, said editors were open to various proposals, but he gave early pragmatic support to Whalen's qualified proposal. "This provides a reasonable safeguard against frivolous or vindictive uses of subpoenas" while still allowing for extraordinary circumstances where the government meets high burdens for compelled disclosure, Fichenberg said.[87] Stanford Smith, president of the American Newspaper Publishers Association, presented a comparative analysis of various bills and said his member newspapers were being asked which ones they could support.[88] "My present assessment is that the majority feel that absolute privilege is neither attainable nor necessarily in the public interest," Smith said. "Some have reluctantly come to the conclusion, however, that absolute is the only one that will do the job. So here is the problem."[89]

But others worried that qualifications would not provide adequate protections for journalists. Victor Navasky of the American Civil Liberties Union, and later editor of *The Nation,* objected to reliance on the attorney general guidelines, suggesting that the recent disclosure of wire-tapping of the telephone of Martin Luther King Jr. under national security laws "is one of the dramatic instances of how an Attorney General comes to fool himself in defining that national interest."[90] The ACLU also suggested that some of the qualifications in some bills, including those that provided an exception in cases of possible espionage, could have been used to prevent the publication of the Pentagon Papers.[91]

Others evaluated the various bills in an attempt to find the right balancing of interests. By the spring of 1973, a study by the Association of the Bar of the City of New York concluded that a newsmen's privilege "would advance the fundamental values inherent in freedom of the press without unduly hampering the legitimate interest of law enforcement."[92] Representing the New York bar, Professor Benno C. Schmidt Jr. of Columbia Law School, who would later become president of Yale University, advocated a privilege that would apply to state proceedings and that could be invoked only by professional journalists. The bar also favored limiting the privilege to "the identification of confidential sources or of any information that is received by a reporter in confidence."[93] Schmidt said lawyers disagreed about the nature of the qualified privilege, but said the committee should define "particularly those kinds of investigative needs that should overcome a protection of a reporter's confidential sources."[94] One exception widely agreed upon was for civil libel lawsuits where a reporter's reliance on a confidential source affects the assessment of truth or carelessness in reporting. A threat to a specific human life and the clandestine transmission of espionage-related information also deserve different treatment, Schmidt argued.[95] As for information and sources about past crimes, Schmidt said the standard should be whether the case involved the loss of life. And Schmidt would allow for the privilege to be overcome in criminal trials so long as a criminal defense attorney or prosecutor "can demonstrate to the judge that a reporter has information, received in confidence, which bears on evidence that is not available from any alternative means."[96]

Paradoxically, Schmidt cautioned the committee in going too far in widening the exceptions. He said victimless crimes and crimes involving governmental corruption should be immune from compelled disclosure.[97] "You get to the point," Kastenmeier interjected, "where the exceptions are so many that it becomes difficult to administer and it seems to hold less promise for those who seek a meaningful privilege."[98] Press organizations would make the same argument with greater force and frequency.

Professor Vince Blasi, the leading scholar on the issue, testified February 5, 1973, and cautioned the subcommittee to resist an "all or nothing" attitude that was beginning to emerge. He said the goal of a statute should be to minimize the number of subpoenas and "the indiscriminateness with which they are thrown around."[99] Blasi had also recently published an important study, called *The Newsman's Privilege: An Empirical Study*, that drew from forty-seven interviews and a mail survey of one thousand reporters and found that investigative journalists regularly use promises of confidentiality to obtain information and believe in the importance of these confidential relationships.[100] Blasi's model qualified privilege statute distinguished between investigative and adjudicative subpoenas, with a shield law prohibiting absolutely the former and allowing some types of the latter. Investigative subpoenas are generally broader in focus and often more damaging to confidentiality, he said. Blasi also proposed limiting protection to those who swear under oath that they are breaking a promise of confidentiality which was necessary to gain the information in the first place, or that serious harm to an ongoing source relationship would occur upon disclosure.[101] "This is not for amateurs. This is for professionals," Blasi testified.[102] Blasi would have required anyone seeking a subpoena of a journalist to demonstrate with rigorous specificity the need for and importance of the information sought. Committee member Rep. Thomas Railsback, in particular, liked Blasi's distinctions and said they were better than any bill thus far introduced.[103]

The 1973 hearings revealed widespread disagreement over the extent of protection a law should afford journalists – a division that would later contribute to the failure of a bill becoming law. Kastenmeier's notes show that he and his committee's general counsel attempted to count committee votes on various bills. Three members were likely to favor absolutist bills, and two supported qualified bills, with three others were listed as undecided, but not likely to support absolutist bills. Notably, no one on the committee was marked as opposing outright any kind of privilege. [104]

During the 1973 hearings, the committee heard from fourteen lawmakers who authored various bills. Rep. Whalen's H.R. 2230, called the "Free Flow of Information Act" and offering a qualified privilege, drew seventy cosponsors.[105] Still, absolutists were advancing their proposals with greater strength. Rep. William Hudnut of Indiana testified that his discussions with journalists had convinced him that Whalen's qualified privilege did not go far enough. His bill, H.R. 4383, was absolute, and identical to the absolute bills introduced in the previous Congress.[106] Rep. Reid, the New York congressman and former newspaper editor who in the previous Congress proposed a qualified law, testified about his change of heart after seeing judges three states with shield statutes "emasculate these laws and ... strip away the protection which they were intended to confer on newsmen."[107] He specifically cited the jailings of Edwin A. Goodman in New York, Peter Bridge in New Jersey, and William Farr in California.[108] Rep. Reid, too, now favored an absolute privilege. Rep. Lawrence Coughlin of Pennsylvania testified in support of is H.R. 3369, called the "News Media Source Protection Act." His bill established absolute protection for investigative subpoenas, and a qualified privilege for adjudicative proceedings, similar to Professor Blasi's proposal.[109]

Still, the range of coverage and the scope of the privilege left many confused. Gov. Thomas J. Meskill of Connecticut testified that he was sent twenty-one different bills in preparation of his testimony. "I am sorry to tell you that I am not completely sold on any of them," he said. "With few exceptions, the sponsors of the measures being proposed seem to be engaged in a race to see who can offer the most complete shield."[110] Less than two weeks later, one congressman noted that half of thirty-eight bills introduced by that point called for absolute protection, and many called for state-law preemption.[111]

While several journalists and press organizations initially supported a qualified bill, more were speaking out in favor of an absolute law. On January 31, 1973, the Joint Media Committee, a consortium of news organizations created to draft a bill, withdrew its support of a qualified privilege in favor of an absolute privilege.[112] Earl Caldwell, the *New York Times* reporter whose coverage of the Black Panther movement resulted in a subpoena fight that became one of the four cases consolidated in *Branzburg*, and Peter Bridge, the first journalist jailed after the *Branzburg* case, testified in support of an absolute privilege.[113] A.M. Rosenthal, the managing editor of the *New York Times*, declared: "I do believe that absolute legislation is terribly important. I am afraid of qualifications, however well intended, however well designed. One man's qualification is another man's restriction. I do fear the precedent of writing qualifications in the First Amendment."[114]

And Jack C. Landau, on behalf of the Reporters Committee for Freedom of the Press, also supported an absolute privilege:

We believe that the absolute privilege is necessary in order to counteract the increasing trend of censorship, to repair the previous damage done to the First Amendment and to reaffirm, in the public's mind, the determination of the media to continue to inform the public fully while honoring all pledges of confidentiality.[115]

The Reporters Committee had been founded in 1970 after a group of about forty journalists met at Georgetown University to discuss the implications of Earl Caldwell's subpoenas, and between 1970 and 1976 documented five hundred incidents of subpoenas being served on journalists.[116]

WHO QUALIFIES? DEFINITIONAL PROBLEMS

Defining who would qualify for a newsmen's privilege also raised questions about the First Amendment and policy line-drawing. To define who qualifies for protection, it is necessary to say the law protects some people and not others. This raised issues of whether the press clause of the First Amendment applies to the mainstream media as members of a profession, or whether it applies to every citizen's right to publish. Justice White in *Branzburg* relied heavily on this problem in his rationale for rejecting a privilege.[117] Today, those concerns are heightened by the explosion of bloggers.[118] In the 1970s, lawmakers wondered whether academic researchers, lecturers, book authors, photographers and cameramen for example, should be covered by legislation.

At the first hearing in 1972, Kastenmeier asked Roger Cramton, the deputy attorney general, "Would it, in fact, not be better to try to clear up ambiguities and uncertainties by an attempted statutory definition to leave people somewhat more certain as to how the law affects them?"[119] Not really, Cramton said. A broad definition "is the only way you carry out the objective and purpose advancing the interest of free speech as well as that of the commercial press," Cramton said. "But the broader the objective in purpose, the more you run into problems of litigation in terms of the definition."[120] Kastenmeier asked whether that boundary-setting was within the purview of Congress to decide. The problem, Cramton said, is that the media are changing. More people are doing interpretive and opinionated commentary, he said, and researchers and scholars do many of the same things journalists do. These people all believe that confidential sources are important and could dry up without legal protections. Kastenmeier finished questioning Cramton on an optimistic note for passage of a bill: "Well, it seems to me we have to be able, at some point, to define what we are talking about when we talk about freedom of the press and the application of the First Amendment to the press."[121]

Professor Benno Schmidt said that while definitional problems were significant to the constitutional issue that the Supreme Court confronted, Congress was free to create a statute as it saw fit. First-time freelance reporters, for example, might not be able to establish appropriate status as professional journalists and might not qualify under a statute, depending on the language. Schmidt said under-inclusion might be a "cost worth paying in order to have a statute whose application is reasonably clear so that people can understand who is covered and who is not."[122] His standard would require a reporter to demonstrate an "employment relationship with a news medium" or alternatively a "record of past publication that will make it clear that he is a journalist."[123]

Stanford Smith, president of the American Newspaper Publishers Association, said the question was a difficult one:

> Some of us, myself included, are concerned about what might appear on the surface to be easy, but is really very difficult. What is a newsman? If a citizen turns to his trusty typewriter and writes a tract and then has a letter shop print it and maybe he takes it around to everybody in his community, is he or is he not a newsman? Many of us are concerned about dividing up the First Amendment. It is intended to apply equally to everybody.[124]

Irwin Karp, counsel for the Authors League of America, testified in support of ensuring that book authors receive equal protection under a shield law, saying "some of the greatest investigative reporting has been done by authors writing for publication in book form."[125] Many book authors do the same things as traditional reporters, and thus deserve the same protections as those employed by newspapers and television news stations, he argued. Dan Lacy, senior vice president of McGraw-Hill Publications Co., said the heart of the protection should stem to "investigative reporters" regardless of medium or form.[126]

The text of bills submitted highlighted the degree to which lawmakers were willing to extend the protection beyond traditional journalists. Some were narrowly crafted to apply only to professional journalists and would not apply to freelancers, book authors, historians, lecturers or academics – all categories of "information disseminators" raised during the committee hearings as potentially warranting privilege protection in some circumstances.[127] Others applied only to "a person connected with or employed by the news media or press."[128] Attempts to fashion a more functional definition include bills that applied to "those who gather, write or edit information for the public or disseminate information to the public."[129] Ultimately, Kastenmeier and his colleagues synthesized the definitional problems into their H.R. 215 in the 94th Congress, defining "newsman" as "any man or woman who is a reporter, photographer, editor, commentator, journalist, correspondent, announcer or other individual ... engaged in obtaining, writing, reviewing, editing or otherwise preparing information in any form for any medium of communication to the public."[130] Kastenmeier's proposal struck a balance between those wanting a narrow privilege only for professional journalists and those seeking to expand the protection to a wide range of individuals who might communicate to the public.

CONFIDENTIAL VS. NON-CONFIDENTIAL INFORMATION

Should the privilege only apply to the identity of sources to whom journalists promised confidentiality, or should the privilege extend to a wider range of newsgathering material, including non-confidential, unpublished information such as interview transcripts and notes, and video and audio outtakes?

While confidential sources in investigative reporting garnered the most focus, several journalists, particularly in television, argued that a privilege should protect journalists from disclosing non-confidential information. Chet Casselman, president of the Radio and Television News Directors Association, argued that "entire streams of information will become shallow and polluted" if journalists were required to turnover unaired newsgathering information in response to subpoenas.[131] Richard W. Jencks, vice president of CBS News, also argued that subpoenas for unpublished material would undermine the credibility and independence of news organizations.[132] A number of witnesses argued that compelled testimony of information not necessarily obtained with a direct promise of confidentiality could also have a chilling effect on people's willingness to talk with journalists.

Victor S. Navasky of the ACLU used Earl Caldwell's case as an example in which a reporter's credibility is undermined if sources know the reporter might be forced to testify before a grand jury:[133]

> [M]erely appearing before the grand jury would spoil his credibility in the black community because they couldn't know what he would be saying behind closed doors. There is a lot of suspicion about reporters from establishment publications anyway. I think confidentiality is important, but there are other instances where protecting nonconfidentiality is equally important if what we are after is to serve the public's right to know.[134]

Of the nineteen legal cases involving journalist's privilege claims being monitored in 1973 by the Reporters Committee for Freedom of the Press, only two dealt with privilege claims for non-confidential information.[135] A local television reporter and cameraman from Buffalo appealed a court order requiring their testimony about what they saw during a riot on a visit to a prison and argued that inmates wouldn't have talked to them if they thought the journalists would testify before a grand jury.[136] Peter Bridge of the *Newark News* was jailed for three weeks after he refused to release unpublished details of an interview he conducted with a government whistleblower who he named in his story.[137]

Over time, Kastenmeier's committee saw a greater need to protect confidential source information than all newsgathering information. While subpoenas for non-confidential information raised concerns that the press would be unnecessarily used as an investigative arm as government, which has its own potential chilling effects on individuals' willingness to cooperate with the press, the disclosure of confidential sources was viewed as a greater threat to newsgathering. Professor Benno Schmidt argued that investigative needs of eyewitness reporter testimony outweigh the potential newsgathering harm a reporter may face for disclosing non-confidential information, but such harm is greater when a reporter is forced to break a confidential promise. "[T]he heart of a statutory privilege ought to be protection of the identification of confidential sources or of any information that is received by a reporter in confidence," Schmidt told Kastenmeier's committee.[138]

APPLICATION OF THE PRIVILEGE TO THE STATES

By November 1972, eighteen states had journalist's privilege statutes that governed state law enforcement and court proceedings.[139] A general consensus among journalists and policy makers emerged that subpoenas at the state level were a greater problem for most journalists than federal subpoenas, in part, Professor Benno Schmidt said, because the Attorney General guidelines, issued after negative reaction to the Caldwell subpoenas, had apparently eliminated prosecutorial abuse at the federal level. [140] "In Congressional hearings last fall none of the spokesmen for privilege legislation could point to a single instance of subpoena abuse by the Justice Department since the guidelines," Schmidt said in the spring of 1973.[141] James Cornwell, president of the National Newspaper Association, argued that federal law would be meaningful only to big city newspapers whose staffs regularly cover the federal government. Subpoena threats in state government proceedings were more important to most newspapers, Cornwell said. Whether a bill should pre-empt state laws became another central point of debate.

Preemption raised several policy and constitutional issues. Opponents of pre-emption argued that it "would be terribly unwise as a matter of policy" and a perversion of federalism by allowing the national legislature to dictate the state legislative and judicial matters.[142] Several state legislatures recently had adopted shield laws, and a model state statute was under development by Professor Vince Blasi. What would become of these state laws? Constitutionally, most experts agreed that pre-emption was within the power of Congress, but they wondered whether it was wise as a matter of policy. By 1975, lawmakers agreed that pre-emption would set the bar for state subpoenas, but state legislatures were free to expand protections if they saw fit. The primary concern among privilege advocates was that the subpoena threat was most pervasive at the state level. Jack Landau of the Reporters Committee for Freedom of the Press, said, "The danger exists at the state and local level as well as with the federal government. We think it would be pyrrhic victory for the Congress to pass a shield law which covered only 1 of the 51 jurisdictions where newsmen may be subpoenaed."[143]

LESSONS OF FAILURE

The failure to enact a shield law in the 1970s was not a result of a lack of effort, as evidenced by the dogged attention of Robert Kastenmeier.[144] In addition to the length and number of hearings on the matter – more so than any other committee in congressional history on the issue of a journalist's privilege – Kastenmeier's personal records suggest he possessed a deep philosophical curiosity about the role of the press, likely furthered by his other concerns about government abuse of power. Kastenmeier's files contains correspondence with a number of media scholars, as well as a copy of Justice Stewart's famous remarks on November 2, 1974, at the Yale Law School Sesquicentennial Convocation, later reprinted in the *Hastings Law Journal* under the title "Or of the Press."[145]

Additionally, Kastenmeier's comments and questions during committee meetings demonstrated a broad belief in the importance of press freedom and the public value of investigative reporting. For example, he drew from his personal observations in lamenting the loss of press freedom in the Philippines, where he served as a member of the U.S. Army in the 1940s.[146] His experiences of witnessing improper government abuses against the press during the Nixon era also cemented his skepticism about the intentions of government officials, as evidenced by his comments during several of his hearings, notably his exchanges with Antonin Scalia.[147] And he regularly emphasized protecting the process of investigative reporting should be at the core of any bill's protections.

These principles were among those that Anthony Lewis,[148] who published a book in 2007 that he called a "biography" of the First Amendment,[149] admired in Kastenmeier when Lewis gave the Robert W. Kastenmeier Lecture at the University of Wisconsin Law School about civil liberties in the wake of the September 11, 2001, terrorist attacks: "To deliver a lecture named after Bob Kastenmeier is an honor I greatly prize. He was one of the truly outstanding members of the House of Representatives, who fought for all of us against constant pressures to shortcut the fair procedures that protect our freedom."[150] His pivotal role in the 1976 revision of the Copyright Act, in particular, won Kastenmeier lasting praise as a thoughtful legislator. One scholar writing for a 1992 symposium dedicated to Kastenmeier's legacy wrote: "[B]y eschewing dogma and philosophy and by virtue of his thoughtful, deliberate nature and devotion to the greater public interest, Kastenmeier put together compromises that enabled controversial legislation to pass."[151]

In the immediate aftermath of the *Branzburg* decision, widespread bi-partisan support in Congress suggested a privilege bill was imminent, and Kastenmeier was optimistic, even stating in March 1973 that he hoped to have a bill negotiated within months. The final bill hammered out in the 94th Congress, H.R. 215, was the culmination of three years of intensive debate and was offered as the best compromise. The qualified privilege adhered closely to Justice Stewart's three-part test in his *Branzburg* dissent,[152] would have applied to state proceedings,[153] would have covered only information journalists received in "express or implied" confidence,[154] and provided a broad functional definition of who qualified for protection.[155]

The bill's failure to become law can be explained by several factors. First, opposition from both journalist groups and executive-branch officials left lawmakers unable to satisfy either side. Representing the executive branch, assistant attorney general Antonin Scalia said the bill "would make a mockery of the criminal justice process."[156] Journalism advocacy groups were important to lawmakers developing their opinions on various provisions of bills. The Newspaper Guild called an earlier draft of H.R. 215 "so shot with defects, even as a qualified privilege measure, that it is an open invitation for widespread abridgement of the very First Amendment rights it ostensibly would protect."[157] The Reporters Committee for Freedom of Press also opposed the bill. "We appreciate the interest of this subcommittee, and its chairman, in the problems of journalists in the wake of *Branzburg*," said spokesman Jack Nelson of the *Los Angeles Times*. "But we feel that a qualified shield law might make the situation worse, and so we oppose H.R. 215."[158] Fred Graham of CBS summarized four reasons journalists oppose a qualified law: the theoretical position that a qualified bill violates the First Amendment because of its limits of press freedom; a hesitancy to rely on congressional action because what Congress gives, it can take away; disappointment in qualified privilege laws at the state level; and fear that any qualified bill, no matter how narrow the qualifications, could be watered down on the floor of Congress just prior to passage.[159]

Journalists also pleaded directly to Kastenmeier to kill the bill, according to records in his files. Miles McMillin, the editor of The

Capital Times from Kastenmeier's home district of Madison, Wisconsin, wrote that he was "persuaded that no legislation at all is preferable to a 'qualified' shield law" because it would add to the diluting of freedom of the press.[160] In an interview several years later, Kastenmeier said the failure to pass a law was due in large part because of this dissension among the press.[161]

In addition to the opposition by both journalist groups and the executive branch, there was a growing sense that *Branzburg* just might protect journalists after all. James Goodale, the lawyer who represented reporter Earl Caldwell in the case, published an influential law review article in 1975 arguing that his analysis of the *Branzburg* decisions supported a constitutional qualified privilege, which had started to emerge in lower courts despite *Branzburg's* central holding.[162] Goodale argued the lower court cases "do seem to be developing a qualified newsman's privilege similar to the one newsmen themselves proposed to the Supreme Court in *Branzburg,* a test substantially adopted by Stewart in his dissent."[163] Other scholars tracing these post-*Branzburg* legal developments gave journalists hope that appealing to lower courts for First Amendment protection would be better for them than relying on Congress for statutory protection.[164] Indeed, in one of the first privilege cases to reach an appeals court after *Branzburg*, the United States Court of Appeals for the Ninth Circuit declared that the *Branzburg* holding "seems to require that the claimed First Amendment privilege and the opposing need for disclosure be judicially" balanced.[165] On April 23, 1975, Kastenmeier said there was "less of a sense of urgency" on the matter after time revealed that *Branzburg* didn't open the flood gates for press subpoenas.[166]

While privilege bills were introduced sporadically after 1976,[167] including after the Supreme Court's 1978 *Zurcher v. The Stanford Daily* decision regarding police searches of newsrooms,[168] Congress did not again seriously consider a privilege bill until 2004, when a consensus arose among journalists and media lawyers that federal common law protections seemed to be in retreat.[169] The next chapter examines the rise and fall of the common law protections.

CONCLUSION

In 1974, Rep. Kastenmeier asked, "Should Congress provide newsmen with the right to refuse to testify about their confidential news sources and information? This is one of the most perplexing Constitutional issues of our day."[170] Thirty-five years later, the courts, Congress, and the press are wrestling with the same perplexities.

In part, this chapter illustrates the elusiveness of the journalist's privilege in constitutional theory, judicial doctrine and public policy. The evolution of policy resolutions in eighty-six journalist shield bills debated during the House hearings of the 1970s show that Rep. Kastenmeier and his congressional colleagues studiously tried to reconcile the competing public interests in their attempt to create a compromise bill that would win enough support. Ultimately, the bill's failure to become law can be ascribed to two primary reasons: widespread opposition by journalist groups and executive branch officials, and a diminished sense of urgency because of the development of common-law protections in the courts.

This chapter also offers a window into the policy questions raised by a federal shield statute. The evolution of the policy resolutions in eighty-six bills over three years demonstrates various resolutions to the most contentious elements of the journalist's privilege. A comparison of press arguments in the 1970s and the hearings between 2004 and 2008 shows a number of key policy concessions press advocates have made over time. The vast majority of news organizations no longer advocate for absolutist proposals, and lawmakers and journalists have largely given up on the concept of pre-emption, in part because of the increase in protections at the state level.[171] The nature of qualifications and the definitions of who is a journalist continue to be the primary sources of disagreement for the 111th Congress.[172]

Finally, this history shows that advocacy work by journalist organizations and academic scholarship played an important role in the development of privilege legislation. Lawmakers valued the insights offered by press organizations and studied closely the positions taken by different press groups, including consortiums created for privilege advocacy, like the Joint Media Committee,[173] and the newly formed Reporters Committee for Freedom of the Press.[174] Scholars such as Vince Blasi, Benno Schmidt and Paul Freund were also looked to as experts who helped lawmakers understand the implications of various provisions and proposals. The importance of advocacy groups and the deference to scholars in the 1970s debates suggest their continued relevance to lawmaking today.

Chapter 6 Notes

---

[1] *See, for example,* Letter from Miles McMillin, editor and publisher of
The Capital Times (May 9, 1975), (Robert Kastenmeier Papers, Wisconsin
Historical Society, M91-025, Box 164) (recounting a subpoena received by his
newspaper after it published details misconduct by county government
officials. "I was confident that the First Amendment would keep me out of jail
if I protected our sources.").

[2] *Newsmen's Privilege, Hearings Before Subcommittee No. 3 of the House
Committee on the Judiciary,* 92d Cong., 2d Session (1972) (hearings on Sept.
21, 27, 28 and Oct. 4 & 5, 1972) [hearinafter 1972 Hearings]; *Newsmen's
Privilege, Hearings Before Subcommittee No. 3 of the House Committee on the
Judiciary,* 93rd Cong., 1st Session (1973) (hearings on Feb. 5, 7, 8, 26 & Mar.
1, 5, 7, 12, 14 & 20, 1973) [hearinafter 1973 Hearings]; *Newsmen's Privilege,
Hearings Before the Subcommittee on Courts, Civil Liberties, and the
Administration of Justice of the Committee on the Judiciary,* 94th Cong., 1st
Session (1975) (hearings on Apr. 23 & 24, 1975) [hearinafter 1975 Hearings].

[3] This is partly because Ervin himself wrote a law review article on the
issue and his hearings. *See* Sam J. Ervin Jr., *In Pursuit of a Press Privilege,* 11
HARV. J. ON LEGIS. 233 (1974); *Newsmen's Privilege, Hearings Before the
Subcommittee on Constitutional Rights of the Senate Committee on the
Judiciary,* 93rd Cong., 1st Session (1973) (hearings on Feb. 20, 21, 22, 27 &
Mar. 13 & 14, 1973).

[4] Exceptions include MAURICE VAN GERPEN, PRIVILEGED COMMUNICATION
AND THE PRESS: THE CITIZEN'S RIGHT TO KNOW VERSUS THE LAW'S RIGHT TO
CONFIDENTIAL NEWS SOURCE EVIDENCE 147-70 (1979) (discussing some
elements of the House bills, 147-170, and placing the increase in subpoenas in
the 1960s and 1970s in the context of social changes); William E. Lee, *The
Priestly Class: Reflections on a Journalist's Privilege,* 23 CARDOZO ARTS &
ENT. L.J. 635, 662 (2006) (noting the failure of Congress to pass a shield law in
the immediate aftermath of *Branzburg).* A search on Oct. 1, 2008, of "Robert
Kastenmeier" and "newsmen's privilege" or "reporter's privilege" found no
articles in the law review database of LexisNexis and the ProQuest Research
Library of scholarly journals. A search of the JSTOR database turned up four
hits, but each was irrelevant to Kastenmeier's newsmen's privilege hearings.

[5] 1972 Hearings, *supra* note 2, at 1. The precise nomenclature itself was
quickly challenged, both on grounds that "newsmen" was sexist and that
"privilege" implied special rights to reporters. Later bills had titles such as the

News Source and Information Protection Act, H.R. 215, 94th Cong., 1st Sess., (1975).

[6] *Id.* at 706.

[7] New York Times v. United States, 403 U.S. 713 (1971).

[8] STANLEY I. KUTLER, THE WARS OF WATERGATE 161 (1990). CBS News correspondent Daniel Schorr was the subject of an FBI background investigation that made its way to the White House; CBS News' John Hart was investigated by the IRS after the White House became furious over his reports.

[9] JEFFERY SMITH, WAR AND PRESS FREEDOM 187 (1999). The Nixon administration used the Internal Revenue Service and Federal Bureau of Investigation to intimidate reporters, aggressively investigated news leaks and cut the budget of the Corporation for Public Broadcasting after allegations of liberal bias. *See also* Lance Murrow, *Naysayer to the Nattering Nabobs*, TIME, Sept. 30, 1996, *available at* http://www.time.com/time/magazine/article/0,9171,985217-1,00.html (last visited April 1, 2009); and CORYDON B. DUNHAM, FIGHTING FOR THE FIRST AMENDMENT: STANTON OF CBS V. CONGRESS AND THE NIXON WHITE HOUSE XI-XII (1997) (The press was also on edge over a congressional investigation into the Feb. 23, 1971 broadcast of a CBS News documentary titled "The Selling of the Pentagon," which reported on the Pentagon's use of propaganda. A congressional committee subsequently subpoenaed CBS's president for outtakes of the program, and after he refused, a committee voted to hold him in contempt of Congress.).

[10] 1972 Hearings, *supra* note 2, at 246.

[11] *Id.* at 194 (Rep. Dan Kuykendall of Tennessee lamented the jail threat to reporter Joseph Weiler of the Memphis *Commercial Appeal.*).

[12] 1973 Hearings, *supra* note 2, at 69-75.

[13] *Id.* at 66 and 334.

[14] 1972 Hearings, *supra* note 2, at 195.

[15] DAVID HALBERSTAM, THE POWERS THAT BE 640 (1979).

[16] Letter from Robert Kastenmeier et al., "Dear Colleague" (June 16, 1971) (Robert Kastenmeier Papers, Wisconsin Historical Society, M91-025, Box 26) (Kastenmeier and eight other members of the House of Representatives asked their colleagues to support an *amicus curiae* brief on the *Times'* behalf. Their letter said the *Times'* reporting was "invaluable because the articles clearly demonstrate the history of this tragic mistake by showing the trail we left as four presidents led us into the quicksand of Vietnam.").

[17] Press Release (Sept. 15, 1972) (Robert Kastenmeier Papers, Wisconsin Historical Society, M91-025, Box 26).

[18] 1972 Hearings, *supra* note 2, at 1.

[19] *Id.*

[20] *Id.*

[21] *Id.* at 22-29.

[22] See *infra* text accompanying notes 104-155.

[23] See *infra* text accompanying notes 177-182.

[24] See *infra* text accompanying notes 156-169.

[25] See *infra* text accompanying notes 170-177.

[26] *See generally* Ervin, *supra* note 5. Ervin Jr.'s subcommittee in the Senate held six hearings on the matter, and after failing to reach consensus seemed content to let the House wrestle with the growing difficulties. Ervin noted "[T]he year-long push for shield legislation which followed the *Branzburg* decision was, for a number of reasons, beginning to fizzle in the summer of 1973." *Id.* at 274.

[27] 1973 Hearings, *supra* note 2, at 4.

[28] *Id.* at 6.

[29] *Id.* at 2.

[30] *Id.*

[31] H.R. 717, 93d Cong. (1st Sess. 1973); H.R. 1263, 93d Cong. (1st Sess. 1973); H.R. 1735, 93d Cong. (1st Sess. 1973); H.R. 1794, 93d Cong. (1st Sess. 1973); H.R. 1813, 93d Cong. (1st Sess. 1973); H.R. 1818, 93d Cong. (1st Sess. 1973); H.R. 1819, 93d Cong. (1st Sess. 1973); H.R. 1985, 93d Cong. (1st Sess. 1973); H.R. 2002, 93d Cong. (1st Sess. 1973); H.R. 2015, 93d Cong. (1st Sess. 1973); H.R. 2101, 93d Cong. (1st Sess. 1973); H.R. 2187, 93d Cong. (1st Sess. 1973); H.R. 2200, 93d Cong. (1st Sess. 1973); H.R. 2230, 93d Cong. (1st Sess. 1973); H.R. 2231, 93d Cong. (1st Sess. 1973); H.R. 2232, 93d Cong. (1st Sess. 1973); H.R. 2233, 93d Cong. (1st Sess. 1973); H.R. 2234, 93d Cong. (1st Sess. 1973); H.R. 2433, 93d Cong. (1st Sess. 1973); H.R. 2563, 93d Cong. (1st Sess. 1973); H.R. 2584, 93d Cong. (1st Sess. 1973); H.R. 2651, 93d Cong. (1st Sess. 1973); H.R. 3143, 93d Cong. (1st Sess. 1973); H.R. 3181, 93d Cong. (1st Sess. 1973); H.R. 3369, 93d Cong. (1st Sess. 1973); H.R. 3460, 93d Cong. (1st Sess. 1973); H.R. 3482, 93d Cong. (1st Sess. 1973); H.R. 3520, 93d Cong. (1st Sess. 1973); H.R. 3595, 93d Cong. (1st Sess. 1973); H.R. 3725, 93d Cong. (1st Sess. 1973); H.R. 3741, 93d Cong. (1st Sess. 1973); H.R. 3811, 93d Cong. (1st Sess. 1973); H.R. 3964, 93d Cong. (1st Sess. 1973); H.R. 3975, 93d Cong. (1st Sess.

1973); H.R. 4020, 93d Cong. (1st Sess. 1973); H.R. 4035, 93d Cong. (1st Sess. 1973); H.R. 4135, 93d Cong. (1st Sess. 1973); H.R. 4275, 93d Cong. (1st Sess. 1973); H.R. 4383, 93d Cong. (1st Sess. 1973); H.R. 4423, 93d Cong. (1st Sess. 1973); H.R. 4456, 93d Cong. (1st Sess. 1973); H.R. 4749, 93d Cong. (1st Sess. 1973); H.R. 5060, 93d Cong. (1st Sess. 1973); H.R. 5167, 93d Cong. (1st Sess. 1973); H.R. 5194, 93d Cong. (1st Sess. 1973); H.R. 5198, 93d Cong. (1st Sess. 1973); H.R. 5227, 93d Cong. (1st Sess. 1973); H.R. 5317, 93d Cong. (1st Sess. 1973); H.R. 5322, 93d Cong. (1st Sess. 1973); H.R. 5908, 93d Cong. (1st Sess. 1973); H.R. 5928, 93d Cong. (1st Sess. 1973); H.R. 6133, 93d Cong. (1st Sess. 1973); H.R. 6138, 93d Cong. (1st Sess. 1973); H.R. 6739, 93d Cong. (1st Sess. 1973); H.R. 7330, 93d Cong. (1st Sess. 1973). The text of these bills are included in 1973 Hearings, *supra* note 2, at 588-754. A list of the sponsors of the bills is at 1973 Hearings, *id.* at 585-87.

[32] Remarks of the Honorable Robert W. Kastenmeier Reporting H.R. 5928, as Amended, to the Full Committee, (Undated) (Robert Kastenmeier Papers, Wisconsin Historical Society, M91-025, Box 26).

[33] *Id.* ("The term 'newsman' means any man or woman who is a reporter, photographer, editor, commentator, journalist, correspondent, announcer, or other individual (including partnership, corporation, association, or other legal entity existing under or authorized by the laws of the United States or any state) engaged in obtaining, writing, reviewing, editing, or otherwise preparing information in any form for any medium of communication to the public.").

[34] Letter to Thomas E. Bolger from Robert Kastenmeier (Apr. 5, 1974) (Robert Kastenmeier Papers, Wisconsin Historical Society, Box 185).

[35] Remarks of the Honorable Robert W. Kastenmeier Reporting H.R. 5928, as Amended, to the Full Committee, (Undated) (Robert Kastenmeier Papers, Wisconsin Historical Society, M91-025, Box 26).

[36] *Id.*

[37] *Id.*

[38] James Kilpatrick, *Press, Media Should Say no to Congress' Shield Law Offer,* THE OREGONIAN, Mar. 29, 1974, at 41. Kilpatrick, a syndicated conservative columnist, wrote in a column: "If the full committee can stop hassling over impeachment for a few days, in order to consider this matter, [Kastenmeier's] bill may even be sent to the floor. It has taken 18 months of hard work to reach this stage. Scores of witnesses have been heard; a dozen drafts of proposed bills have been reviewed and discarded; if any bill at all is to be passed, it will be the Kastenmeier bill or something close to it," *Id.*

[39] The five bills discussed by the subcommittee during the 94th Congress were H.R. 215, 94th Cong. (1st Sess. 1975), H.R. 172, 94th Cong. (1st Sess. 1975), H.R. 562, 94th Cong. (1st Sess. 1975) , H.R. 6213, 94th Cong. (1st Sess. 1975), and H.R. 6228, 94th Cong. (1st Sess. 1975).

[40] 1975 Hearings, *supra* note 2, at 104.

[41] 1973 Hearings, *supra* note 2, at 238.

[42] *Id.*

[43] 1973 Hearings, *supra* note 2, at 239.

[44] 1972 Hearings, *supra* note 2, at 43.

[45] *Id.* at 55. *See also* Charles D. Tobin, *From John Peter Zenger to Paul Branzburg: The Early Development of Journalist's Privilege,* MEDIA L. RESOURCE CTR. BULL. 28 (2004).

[46] *Id.*

[47] *Id.*

[48] *Id.*

[49] *Id.*

[50] *Id.* at 63.

[51] *Id.* at 66.

[52] *Id.* at 21.

[53] *Id.* at 26. Most of the bills provided the privilege to those employed by traditional press entities like newspapers, broadcast networks and magazines. Cramton said he it was "troublesome" that academic researchers, novelists, lecturers and dramatists "who may rely on confidential sources of information and who contribute to a vigorous exchange of opinion and information" would be excluded from protection. He noted that Justice White raised similar concerns in rejecting a First Amendment-based privilege. *Id.* at 26.

[54] *Id.* at 26-27.

[55] *Id.* at 28.

[56] *Id.*

[57] *Id.* at 23.

[58] *Id.* at 32.

[59] *Id.* at 34.

[60] *Id.* at 35.

[61] *Id.*

[62] 1975 Hearings, *supra* note 2, at 7.

[63] *Id.* at 14.

[64] *Id.* at 21-22.

[65] *Id.* at 26, 27.

[66] These strictly qualified privilege bills were H.R. 837 (introduced Jan. 22, 1971, by Rep. Koch) and H.R. 1084 (introduced Jan. 22, 1971, by Rep. Reid).

[67] These qualified privilege bills were H.R. 16527 (introduced by Rep. Charles Whalen Jr.) and H.R. 16542 (introduced Sept. 6, 1972 by Rep. Koch)

[68] H.R. 837, 92d Cong. (1st Sess. 1971); H.R. 16542, 92d Cong. (2d Sess. 1972); H.R. 16527, 92d Cong. (2d Sess. 1972); H.R. 15972, 92d Cong. (2d Sess. 1972); H.R. 1084, 92d Cong. (2d Sess. 1972); H.R. 15891, 92d Cong. (2d Sess. 1972); H.R. 16713, 92d Cong. (2d Sess. 1972); H.R. 2584, 92d Cong. (1st Sess. 1972); H.R. 3301, 92d Cong. (1st Sess. 1972); H.R. 4271, 92d Cong. (1st Sess. 1972); H.R. 4272, 92d Cong. (1st Sess. 1972); H.R. 5328, 92d Cong. (1st Sess. 1972); H.R. 5653, 92d Cong. (1st Sess. 1972); H.R. 6902, 92d Cong. (1st Sess. 1972); H.R. 8098, 92d Cong. (1st Sess. 1972); H.R. 8118, 92d Cong. (1st Sess. 1972); H.R. 8519, 92d Cong. (1st Sess. 1972); H.R. 10563, 92d Cong. (1st Sess. 1972); H.R. 14334, 92d Cong. (2d Sess. 1972); H.R. 16001, 92d Cong. (2d Sess. 1972); H.R. 17024, 92d Cong. (2d Sess. 1972); H.R. 16236, 92d Cong. (2d Sess. 1972); H.R. 16196, 92d Cong. (2d Sess. 1972); H.R. 17105, 92d Cong. (2d Sess. 1972); H.R. 16638, 92d Cong. (2d Sess. 1972); H.R. 17173, 92d Cong. (2d Sess. 1972).

[69] H.R. 15891, 92d Cong. (2d Sess. 1972) (introduced July 17, 1972, by Rep. Abzug) & H.R. 15972, 92d Cong. (2d Sess. 1972) (introduced July 20, 1972, by Rep. Waldie). H.R. 16713, 92d Cong. (2d Sess. 1972) (introduced Sept. 19, 1972, by Rep. Kuykendall). Kuykendall's bill inserted "or who is independently engaged in gathering information for publication or broadcast" as part of the definition, but was otherwise identical to Abzug and Waldie's bills.

[70] Days after the *Branzburg* decision, Cranston introduced S. 3786, the companion bill to H.R. 15972, introduced by Rep. Jerome Waldie, also a California Democrat. The bill comprised a single sentence: "A person connected with or employed by the news media or press cannot be required by a court, a legislature, or any administrative body to disclose before Congress or any federal court or agency any information or the source of any information procured for publication or broadcast."

[71] 1972 Hearings, *supra* note 2, at 176.

[72] *Id.* at 176-80.

[73] *Id.* at 179.

[74] *Id.* at 180.

[75] *Id.*

[76] *Id.* at 185.

[77] *Id.* at 187.

[78] Letter from Rep. Edward Mezvinsky (Mar. 26, 1974) (Robert Kastenmeier Papers, Wisconsin Historical Society, M91-025, Box 26).

[79] CHARLES W. WHALEN JR., YOUR RIGHT TO KNOW (1973).

[80] 1972 Hearings, *supra* note 2, at 142-43.

[81] *Id.* at 166.

[82] *Id.* at 167. Koch introduced the first bill in the 92d Congress, before the *Branzburg* decision was issued by the Supreme Court. H.R. 837, 92d Cong. (1st Sess. 1971).

[83] H.R. 1084, 92d Cong. (1st Sess. 1971).

[84] 1972 Hearings, *supra* note 2, at 154. The case is *Garland v. Torre*, 259 F.2d 545 (2d Cir., 1958).

[85] *Id.* at 156.

[86] *Id.*

[87] *Id.* at 44.

[88] *Id.* at 78 -100.

[89] *Id.* at 75.

[90] *Id.* at 226.

[91] *Id.* at 234.

[92] 1973 Hearings, *supra*note 2, at 9.

[93] *Id.* at 14.

[94] *Id.* at 14.

[95] *Id.* at 15.

[96] *Id.*

[97] *Id.*

[98] *Id.* at 16.

[99] *Id.* at 129.

[100] Vince Blasi, *The Newsman's Privilege: An Empirical Study*, 70 MICH. L. REV. 229 (1971-1972).

[101] 1973 Hearings, *supra* note 2, 129.

[102] *Id.* at 135.

[103] *Id.* at 137.

[104] Memo from Herb Fuchs to Robert Kastenmeier, "Guesstimate of Subcommittee Votes on Newsman's Privilege," (Feb. 27, 1973) (Robert

Kastenmeier Papers, Wisconsin Historical Society, M91-025, Box 26).
Absolutists included Reps. Drinan, Wayne Owen and Edward Mezinsky. Reps.
Danielson and Railsback supported a qualified bill. The three others, Reps.
Smith, Sandman and Cohen, were listed as supporting a "qualified privilege at
most."

[105] 1973 Hearings, *supra* note 2, at 167 ("(1) [T]here is probable cause to
believe that the person from whom the information is sought has information
which is clearly relevant to a specific probable violation of law; (2) the
information sought cannot be obtained by alternative means; and (3) there is a
compelling and overriding national interest in the information.").

[106] *Id.* at 178.

[107] *Id.* at 412.

[108] *Id.* at 413.

[109] *Id.* at 379.

[110] *Id.* at 195-96.

[111] *Id.* at 395.

[112] *Id.* at 167. The Joint Media Committee consisted of the Associated
Press Managing Editors Association, the American Society of Newspaper
Editors, Sigma Delta Chi, the Radio and Television News Directors
Association, and the National Press Photographers Association.

[113] *Id.* at 73, 219.

[114] *Id.* at 243.

[115] *Id.* at 52.

[116] *See* McKay, *supra* note 26, at 108, 112.

[117] Branzburg, 408 U.S. 665, 704 (1972) (A reporter's privilege would
inevitably give rise to "practical and conceptual difficulties of the highest
order" because "sooner or later, it would be necessary to define those
categories of newsmen who qualified for the privilege").

[118] O'Grady v. Superior Court, 44 Cal. Rptr. 3d 72 (Cal. Ct. App. 2006),
overturning Apple Computer, Inc. v. Doe, No. 1-04-CV-032178 (Cal. Super.
Ct., Mar. 1, 2005) (ruling that bloggers who regularly cover the computer
industry could invoke the California shield law for journalistic protection). *See
also* Laurence B. Alexander, *Looking Out for the Watchdogs: A Legislative
Proposal Limiting the Newsgathering Privilege to Journalists in the Greatest
Need of Protection for Sources and Information,* 20 YALE L. & POL'Y REV. 97
(2002); Kraig L. Baker, *Are Oliver Stone and Tom Clancy Journalists?
Determining Who Has Standing to Claim the Journalist's Privilege,* 69 WASH.

L. REV. 739 (1994); Linda L. Berger, *Shielding the Unmedia: Using the Process of Journalism to Protect the Journalist's Privilege in an Infinite Universe of Publication,* 39 HOUS. L. REV. 1371 (2003); Clay Calvert, *And You Call Yourself a Journalist? Wrestling With a Definition of "Journalist" in the Law,* 103 DICK. L. REV. 411, (1999); Stephanie J. Frazee, *Bloggers as Reporters: An Effect-Based Approach to First Amendment Protections in a New Age of Information Dissemination,* 8 VAN. J. ENT. & TECH. L. 609 (2005); Scott Neinas, *A Skinny Shield is Better: Why Congress Should Propose a Federal Reporters' Shield Statute That Narrowly Defines Journalists,* 40 U. TOL. L. REV. 225 (2008); Mary Rose Papandrea, *Citizen Journalism and the Reporter's Privilege,* 91 MINN. L. REV. 515 (2006); Joseph S. Alonzo, *Restoring the Ideal Marketplace: How Recognizing Bloggers as Journalists Can Save the Press,* 9 N.Y.U. J. LEGIS. PUB. POL. 751 (2006); Daniel A. Swartwout, *In Re Madden: The Threat to New Journalism,* 60 OHIO ST. L.J. 1589 (1999).

[119] 1972 Hearings, *supra* note 2, at 35.

[120] *Id.* at 35-36.

[121] *Id.* at 36.

[122] 1973 Hearings, *supra* note 2, at 17.

[123] *Id.* at 17.

[124] 1972 Hearings, *supra* note 2, at 75.

[125] *Id.* at 113. Karp specifically cited as examples Ida Tarbell's *History of the Standard Oil Company,* Seymour Hersh's *My Lai 4,* and Alfred W. McCoy's *The Politics of Heroin in Southeast Asia.*

[126] 1973 Hearings, *supra* note 2, at 103.

[127] H.R. 837 in the 92d Congress applied to "a reporter, editor, commentator, journalist, writer, correspondent, announcer, or other person directly engaged in the gathering or presentation of news for any newspaper, periodical, press association, newspaper syndicate, wire service, or radio or television station."

[128] HR 1263, 93rd Cong. (1973).

[129] HR 2187, 93rd Cong. (1973).

[130] H.R. 215, 94th Cong. (1975).

[131] 1972 Hearings, *supra* note 2, at 62.

[132] *Id.* at 202.

[133] *Id.* at 226.

[134] *Id.* at 234.

[135] 1973 Hearings, *supra* note 2, at 66.

[136] *Id.*

[137] *Id.*

[138] *Id.* at 14.

[139] Arkansas, ARK. STAT. ANN. § 43-917 (1964); Alabama, ALA. CODE RECOMPILED, TIT. 7, § 370 (1960); Alaska, ALASKA STAT. § 09.25.150-220 (1967); Arizona, ARIZ. REV. STAT. ANN. § 12-2237 (1969); California, CAL. EVID. CODE ANN. § 1070 (1971); Illinois, PUBLIC ACT 77-1623 (1971); Indiana, IND. ANN. STAT. § 2-1733 (1968); Kentucky, KY. REV. STAT. § 421.100 (1969); Louisiana, LA. REV. STAT. § 45:1451-54 (1970); Maryland, MD. ANN. CODE ART. 35 §2 (1971); Michigan, MICH. STAT. ANN. § 28.945 (1) (1954); Montana, MONT. REV. CODES ANN. TIT. 93, CH. 601-2 (1964); Nevada, NEV. REV. STAT. § 49.275, 49.385 (1971); New Jersey, N.J. STAT. ANN. TIT. 2A, CH. 84A, § 21, 29 (1969); New Mexico, N.M. STAT. ANN. § 20-1-12.1 (1953); New York, N.Y. CIV. RIGHTS LAW § 79-H (1970); Ohio, OHIO REV. CODE ANN. § 2739.12 (1953); Pennsylvania, PA. STAT. ANN. TIT. 28, 330 (1969). The texts of these statutes are listed in 1973 Hearings, *supra* note 2, at 282-90.

[140] 1973 Hearings, *supra* note 2, at 12

[141] *Id.* at 25.

[142] *Id.* at 89.

[143] *Id.* at 53.

[144] Kastenmeier represented Wisconsin's Second Congressional District in the House of Representatives, encompassing the state capital of Madison, from 1959 to 1991, when, ironically enough, he was defeated for re-election by a local television anchor.

[145] Stewart, *supra* note 33, at 633 (arguing that the First Amendment's press clause is not a textual redundancy but a proclamation that the organized press are to receive constitutional protection in their role as a de facto fourth branch of government).

[146] 1972 Hearings, *supra* note 2, at 158.

[147] 1975 Hearings, *supra* note 2, at 20-22.

[148] Anthony Lewis's career includes two Pulitzer Prizes at the *New York Times* and the James Madison Visiting Professorship at Columbia University, where he teaches about the First Amendment.

[149] ANTHONY LEWIS, FREEDOM FOR THE THOUGHT THAT WE HATE: A BIOGRAPHY OF THE FIRST AMENDMENT (2007).

[150] Anthony Lewis, *Civil Liberties in a Time of Terror*, 2003 WIS. L. REV. 257 (2003).

[151] Ralph Oman, *Bob Kastenmeier and the Legislative Process: Sui Generis and Proud of It,* 55 LAW & CONTEMP. PROBS. 241, 241-42 (1992) (The Spring 1992 edition of *Law and Contemporary Problems* was devoted to Kastenmeier and his role in copyright legislation).

[152] H.R. 215, Sec. 4, (2), 94th Cong., 1st Sess., (1975) (information could be obtained after the party seeking the information demonstrated "(A) that disclosure of such identity or information is indispensable to the establishment of the offense charged, the cause of the action pleaded, or the defense interposed in such action; (B) that such identity or information cannot be obtained by alternative means; and (C) that there is compelling and overriding public interest in requiring disclosure of the identity or the information."

[153] H.R. 215, Sec. 3, 94th Cong., 1st Sess., (1975).

[154] H.R. 215, Sec. 4 (1), 94th Cong., 1st Sess., (1975).

[155] H.R. 215, Sec. 2 (1), 94th Cong., 1st Sess., (1975) ("[T]he term 'newsman' means any man or woman who is a reporter, photographer, editor, commentator, journalist, correspondent, announcer, or other individual (including partnership, corporation, association, or other legal entity existing under or authorized by the laws of the United States or any State) engaged in obtaining, writing, reviewing, editing, or otherwise preparing information in any form for any medium of communication to the public.").

[156] 1975 Hearings, *supra* note 2, at 7.

[157] Statement on H.R. 5928, "The Newsman's Privilege Act" By the International Executive Board of The Newspaper Guild, Adopted May 2, 1974, (Robert Kastenmeier Papers, Wisconsin Historical Society, Box 185).

[158] 1975 Hearings, *supra* note 2, at 95.

[159] *Id.* at 96.

[160] Letter from Miles McMillin, editor and publisher of *The Capital Times* (May 9, 1975), (Robert Kastenmeier Papers, Wisconsin Historical Society, M91-025, Box 164).

[161] Jonathan Friendly, *Prosecutors Increase Efforts to Make Press Name Sources,* N.Y.TIMES, Nov. 26, 1983, at A1.

[162] James C. Goodale, *Branzburg v. Hayes and the Developing Qualified Privilege for Newsmen,* 26 HASTINGS L.J. 709 (1974-1975).

[163] *Id.* at 743.

[164] Donna M. Murasky, *"The Journalist's Privilege: Branzburg and Its Aftermath,* 52 TEX. L.R. 829 (1974).

[165] Farr v. Pitchess, 522 F. 2d 464, 468 (9th Cir. 1975).

[166] 1975 Hearings, *supra* note 2, at 13 (Scalia said that between March 1973 and March 1975, the Department of Justice issued forty-six subpoenas, compared to thirteen in the prior thirty months).

[167] Some shield bills introduced after this point include: H.R. 14029, 95th Cong., (2d Sess. 1978); H.R. 14309, 95th Cong. (1978); H.R. 368, 96th Cong. (1979). *See also The History of Shield Legislation*, NEWS MEDIA AND THE L., Winter 2007, *available at* http://www.rcfp.org/news/mag/31-1/cov-thehisto.html (last visited April 22, 2007) (mentioning bills introduced in 1979 by Rep. Bill Green, in 1981 by Rep. Philip Crane and 1987 by Sen. Harry Reid).

[168] 436 U.S. 547 (1978).

[169] *See* Lucy A. Dalglish & Casey Murray, *Déjà vu All Over Again: How a Generation of Gains in Federal Reporter's Privilege Law is Being Reversed,* 29 U. ARK. LITTLE RICK L. REV. 13 (2006); Elizabeth A. Graham, *Uncertainty Leads to Jail Time: The Status of the Common-Law Reporter's Privilege,* 56 DEPAUL L. REV. 723 (2007); Kara A. Larsen, *The Demise of the First Amendment-Based Reporter's Privilege: Why This Current Trend Should Not Surprise the Media,* 37 CONN. L. REV. 1235 (2005); Erik W. Laursen, *Putting Journalists on Thin Ice: McKevitt v. Pallasch,* 73 U. CIN. L. REV. 293 (2004); Will E. Messer, *Open Season on the Journalist's Privilege: Do Recent Rulings Represent a Trend Against Assertions of the Privilege or Proper Applications of Existing Law?* 94 KY. L.J. 421 (2005).

Committee on Communications & Media Law, *The Federal Common Law of Journalists' Privilege: A Position Paper,* 60 THE RECORD, 2005, at 214.

[170] Robert W. Kastenmeier, *The Case for a Media Shield Law,* WASH. POST, Mar. 25, 1974, at A20.

[171] For a history of state protections, *see generally* Laurence B. Alexander & Ellen M. Bush, *Shield Laws on Trial: State Court Interpretation of the Journalist's Statutory Privilege.* 23 J. LEGIS. 215 (1997); Anthony L. Fargo, *Analyzing Federal Shield Law Proposals: What Congress Can Learn from the States,* 11 COMM. L. & POL'Y 35 (2006).

[172] *See* Declan McCullagh, *Senator: Bloggers Will "Probably Not" be Deemed Journalists,* CNET NEWS.COM, Oct. 10, 2005.

[173] 1973 Hearings, *supra* note 2, at 167. The Joint Media Committee consisted of the Associated Press Managing Editors Association, the American Society of Newspaper Editors, Sigma Delta Chi, the Radio and Television News Directors Association, and the National Press Photographers Association.

---

[174] Floyd J. McKay, *First Amendment Guerillas: Formative Years of the Reporters Committee for Freedom of the Press*, JOURNALISM AND MASS COMM. MONOGRAPHS 107 (2004).

CHAPTER 7

The Rise and Fall of Federal Judicial Protections, 1972-2003

While the U.S. Supreme Court in its 1972 *Branzburg v. Hayes* decision appeared to reject a judicially created journalist's privilege and Congress between 1972 and 1975 failed to pass a shield law, journalists did not stop using confidential sources, and media lawyers did not stop litigating cases in which confidential sources were sought from journalists. As discussed in the previous chapter, one of the reasons media organizations retreated from their support of a federal shield law by 1975 was because of the emerging protections in the lower federal courts, both despite and because of the *Branzburg* ruling. This chapter describes how the journalist's privilege developed in the federal courts between 1972 and 2003, a period of time when nearly every federal appellate circuit upheld some type of qualified privilege for journalists. The legal basis for the privilege was initially rooted in the First Amendment and thus considered a qualified constitutional right. Many lower court judges adopted a version of the three-part test articulated by Justice Potter Stewart in the *Branzburg* dissent, creating judicial standards based on relevance, exhaustion of alternative sources and compelling state interests. Over the years, the judicial reasoning and precedents of these cases on the constitutional question provided additional support for a common-law privilege rooted in federal rules of evidence.

By 2003, however, the tide appeared to turn away from journalist protections. The jailing of Vanessa Leggett in 2001 garnered significant attention, but it was a 2003 decision by Judge Richard Posner of the Seventh Circuit Court of Appeals that solidified the shift away from the developing qualified privilege. Posner's decision in *McKevitt v. Pallasch* was interpreted as eliminating a privilege in the Seventh Circuit, comprising Illinois, Wisconsin and Indiana, and quickly became cited by courts in other circuits not bound by its precedent but nonetheless drawn to it.[1] Posner himself has cited his decision as holding that no federal qualified reporter privilege exists – interpreting an already broad ruling even more broadly.[2]

Almost universally, media lawyers and scholars who have studied the evolution of the federal common law journalist's privilege cite the *McKevitt* case as perhaps the single most important cause of the confluence of legal losses in post-2003 cases involving journalists being jailed or threatened with jail. In assessing the judicial landscape following the cases examined in part one of this book,[3] Lee Levine, a media lawyer in Washington D.C., and adjunct professor at Georgetown University Law Center, said, "The intellectual godfather of what's happened is Judge Posner and his decision in the *McKevitt* case. It seems to have raised questions that although not entirely unprecedented were rarely raised, and certainly not raised by anyone as influential as he. He sort of lit the fire and these cases were the kindling that sparked the flame."[4]

POST-BRANZBURG FIRST AMENDMENT-BASED QUALIFIED PRIVILEGE

The Posner decision was peculiar in part because of its dramatic departure from decades of federal appellate precedents.

Following the *Branzburg* decision, James Goodale, the general counsel for the *New York Times* during the *Pentagon Papers* case and Earl Caldwell's lawyer in the *Branzburg* case, developed a new strategy for journalists' source protection. In a 2009 interview, Goodale was not shy in crediting his 1975 law review article, *Branzburg v. Hayes and the Developing Qualified Privilege for Newsmen*,[5] for the creation of the privilege in the lower courts. "I created it," Goodale said.[6]

Goodale's strategy in the months and years following *Branzburg* was to argue that Justice Byron White's majority decision in *Branzburg* was actually a plurality decision, and he consistently labeled it as a plurality in his seminal law review article. Therefore, Goodale argued that the central holding of *Branzburg* was to be found in Powell's concurrence. Reflecting decades later on his process of thinking about the case, Goodale said,

> You have to start with what the hell does Powell mean? Did he write something for nothing? No. He meant something ...So you have to construct some sort of theory that would support what he said. When you start thinking about it, it seemed to me that he was saying that this is not an absolute right of the government, and once you conclude that it's not the absolute right of the government, it follows that it's a qualified right of the government, and you turn it around and it's a qualified right of the reporter.[7]

By 1974, several lower courts, mostly at the district level, had adopted some sort of balancing test to use when journalists contested subpoenas. Goodale cited these cases in his law review article as evidence that *Branzburg's* holding did not preclude recognition of a qualified privilege.[8]

One of the first significant appellate decisions finding a qualified privilege came the same year of *Branzburg*, when the Second Circuit Court of Appeals in 1972 ruled in *Baker v. F & F Investment* that a journalist did not have to reveal his source in the context of a civil lawsuit. In finding that the plaintiffs had not exhausted other available sources of information, the appellate court wrote, "The Court in *Branzburg*, as the Court of Appeals had done in *Garland*, applied traditional First Amendment doctrine, which teaches that constitutional rights secured by the First Amendment cannot be infringed absent a 'compelling' or 'paramount' state interest ... and found such an overriding interest in the investigation of crime by the grand jury."[9] The narrow interpretation of *Branzburg*, the recognition of First Amendment interests, and the adoption of a form of Stewart's three-part test in his *Branzburg* dissent, was characteristic of later court rulings.

Subsequently, dozens of federal court decisions began to embrace some version of a qualified privilege rooted in the First Amendment.[10] In 1975, the Ninth Circuit Court of Appeals in *Farr v. Pitchess* said that it was "clear that *Branzburg* recognizes some First Amendment protections of news sources."[11] The case involved a judge's attempt to discover who leaked a purported confession in the Charles Manson murder case to reporter William T. Farr of the *Los Angeles Herald Examiner*. Farr spent 46 days in jail in 1972 after he refused to name his source. When he went to work for the Los Angeles District Attorney's Office two years later, a judge once again sought the identity of Farr's source. The court held that while Farr had legitimate First Amendment defenses to a subpoena seeking the identity of a source who impermissibly leaked him court records, those interests were outweighed by the judiciary's need to protect defendants' rights in criminal trials.[12]

By 1981, in *Zerilli v. Smith*, the District of Columbia Court of Appeals wrote that the privilege should prevail in "all but the most exceptional cases."[13] The case involved a civil lawsuit over government disclosure of sealed information. Newsgathering protections were essential for journalists to fulfill the mission of a free press, the court wrote:

> The press was protected so that it could bare the secrets of government and inform the people. Without an unfettered press, citizens would be far less able to make informed political, social and economic choices. But the press' function as a vital source of information is weakened whenever the ability of journalists to gather news is impaired.[14]

The variety of cases reviewed by the federal courts created different views on the scope of protection and standards to use for different types of cases. Grand jury subpoenas were the most difficult for journalists to challenge, given the clarity of the *Branzburg* decision on this question. Generally, the privilege that developed was stronger in cases involving confidential sources, although judges did in some cases extend the privilege to cover non-confidential information, such as broadcast outtakes, or notes from on-the-record interviews.[15] Judges have also been less willing to extend the privilege to cover eyewitness observations.[16] Civil litigants generally had to meet higher burdens than prosecutors, with criminal defendants in between on a spectrum of burden.[17]

Generally, federal judges applied some version of Justice Stewart's three-part test from *Branzburg*, using the following standards, often referred to as the relevance, materiality and exhaustion requirements:

To overcome the privilege and obtain compelled disclosure, a litigant must make a clear and specific showing that the information sought is 1) highly material and relevant to the underlying claim, 2) necessary or critical to the maintenance of the claim, and 3) unavailable from alternative sources.[18]

There were many cases that provided limits to a broad privilege. For example, in the 1979 case of *Herbert v. Lando* the Supreme Court ruled that that a privilege did not prevent a public-figure libel plaintiff from inquiring into newsroom deliberations in his attempt to meet the high burden plaintiffs face in proving that defendants acted with actual malice.[19] And journalists almost universally lost in cases in which grand juries sought information about criminal activities. By the late 1990s, it was generally presumed that journalists did in fact have some level of qualified privilege in most federal circuits in a non-grand jury context. The growing body of case law also helped judges assess difficult questions about the nature and scope of the privilege. Some research has focused on various components of the evolving judicial standards and found widespread disparities among circuits. For example, Kristin M. Simonetti documented the wide variety of approaches judges have taken in determining the exhaustion prong, arguing that the approaches reveal a general ad hoc balancing that is often at the heart of privilege decisions.[20] Professor Anthony Fargo has documented the different treatment by federal circuits regarding non-confidential information, such as unaired video outtakes, including apparent retreats in a trend of extending protections to such information.[21]

RECOGNITION UNDER THE COMMON LAW: THE *JAFFEE* TEST

As a strict matter of law, the privilege in many of the cases discussed thus far was rooted in the First Amendment and constitutional law. Over time, judges also found a basis for the privilege in the common law.

One basis for the common law journalist's privilege is found in the Federal Rules of Evidence passed by Congress in 1975 and an interpretation of the rules by the U.S. Supreme Court in *Jaffee v. Redmond*, a 1996 case involving the recognition of a psychotherapist-patient privilege.[22] Rule 501 of the federal rules allows for the courts to develop privileges in light of "reason and experience."[23] In *Jaffee,* the Court used three considerations: 1) the significant public and private interests to be served by a privilege, 2) balancing the interests of the privilege against the burden on information seeking, and 3) "reason and experience."[24] Based on this, the Court in *Jaffee* ruled that a legal privilege for psychotherapists and patients "promotes sufficiently important interests to outweigh the need for probative evidence."[25] The court emphasized that the psychotherapist-patient privilege was "rooted in the imperative need for confidence and trust,"[26] and that threat of disclosure would "impede development of the confidential relationship necessary for successful treatment."[27]

The "reason and experience" standard for creating common-law privileges easily supports a journalist's privilege, and several scholars and judges have argued that the journalist's privilege should be recognized as a privilege under the Rules of Evidence based on the *Jaffee* decision and the Supreme Court's balancing of interests.[28] In one of the earliest common-law privilege decisions, the Third Circuit in the 1979 case *Riley v. City of Chester* held that the "strong public policy which supports the unfettered communication to the public of information, comment and opinion and the Constitutional dimension of that policy, expressly recognized in *Branzburg v. Hayes,* lead us to conclude that journalists have a federal common law privilege, albeit qualified, to refuse to divulge their sources."[29] In the case, the Third Circuit tossed out a subpoena to a journalist whose testimony was sought in a civil suit between a police officer and incumbent mayor, in which the cop alleged the mayor violated his privacy during the cop's bid to replace the mayor. The appeals court said:

> Because of the importance to the public of the underlying rights protected by the federal common law news writer's privilege and because of the "fundamental and necessary interdependence of the Court and the press" … trial courts should be cautious to avoid an unnecessary confrontation between the courts and the press. Although there may be cases in which the confrontation is inevitable, this was clearly not one of them.[30]

The *Jaffee* framework provided yet another legal mechanism for journalists to receive legal protections under the common law. But it leaves unanswered one of the most critical questions: Who should receive the privilege?

WHO IS A JOURNALIST?

One of the most important questions today is whether bloggers qualify as journalists for privilege protection. A survey of federal court cases assessing the strength of the qualified privilege in federal common and constitutional law shows that a number of so-called "information disseminators" have claimed to be journalists for the purpose of the privilege. Courts have been asked to extend the privilege to freelance writers,[31] professors and academic researchers,[32] book authors,[33] student-newspaper reporters,[34] a professional wrestling commentator,[35] employees of specialized trade publications,[36] political advocacy groups,[37] a television news helicopter pilot,[38] a radio station owner,[39] a public relations firm,[40] and a film producer.[41] Four federal appellate decisions in particular articulated a common approach to cases involving non-traditional journalists. In general, the test that emerged from these cases required that a person be engaged in activities traditionally associated with newsgathering, and that the person had the intent at the beginning of a newsgathering process to disseminate the information to the public.

The first appellate case to deal extensively with the definitional question, the 1977 case of *Silkwood v. Kerr-McGee*, involved a documentary filmmaker seeking to avoid providing testimony and documents in a civil action.[42] Arthur "Buzz" Hirsch had produced a documentary film about the death of Karen Silkwood, who was investigating alleged misconduct by the Kerr-McGee Corporation. As part of a lawsuit filed by the Silkwood family against Kerr-McGee, Kerr-McGee issued a subpoena for Hirsch's notes and testimony. Hirsch answered some questions, but refused to testify or provide documents about information he obtained with promises of confidentiality.[43] The Tenth Circuit Court of Appeals concluded Hirsch was sufficiently like a newspaper reporter to be able to invoke the privilege, even though he was not a "regular newsman."[44] The court noted Hirsch's previous work experience as a freelance reporter and concluded: "His mission in this case was to carry out investigative reporting;" he spent "considerable time and effort in obtaining facts and information;" and he had planned "to make use of this in preparation of the film."[45] Once the court determined that Hirsch could invoke the privilege, it declined to order his testimony after applying a test articulated in *Garland v. Torre*,[46] and put forth by Justice Stewart in his *Branzburg* dissent, requiring that the party seeking the information attempt to obtain the information elsewhere, that the information goes to the heart of the matter and that the information be of certain relevance.[47]

Using a similar approach of comparing the methods and values of non-traditional privilege claimants to newspaper reporters, the Ninth Circuit Court of Appeals in 1993 ruled that an investigative book author could invoke the privilege. In *Shoen v. Shoen*,[48] the court ruled in favor of Ronald Watkins, an author of two previous investigative books. Watkins was subpoenaed to testify in a civil defamation case about interviews for a book he was working on about the conflicts among members of the Shoen family who were battling for control of the U-Haul moving-van company.[49] An Arizona state appeals court ruled that the state reporter's shield statute explicitly excluded investigative book authors such as Watkins,[50] so Watkins sought protection under the qualified First Amendment privilege in federal law.

The federal appeals court ruled that the "journalist's privilege is designed to protect investigative reporting, regardless of the medium used to report the news to the public."[51] The court mentioned the famous investigative reporter Bob Woodward, noting that it would "unthinkable" to say as a matter of law that Woodward would be allowed to invoke the privilege in his capacity as a newspaper reporter but not as a book author. The court said investigative book authors have historically played a vital role in bringing to light "newsworthy facts on topical and controversial matters of great public importance."[52] The court saw "no principled basis" for excluding Watkins from protection, noting, "What makes journalism journalism is not its format but its content."[53] The court said the key question was whether an individual is "gathering news for dissemination to the public."[54] The appropriate test, the court said, was the one first articulated by the Second Circuit Court of Appeals in *von Bulow v. von Bulow* (discussed below), requiring that an individual have an intent to disseminate information prior to a newsgathering process. The court interestingly stressed that the privilege was intended to protect the dissemination of "news," and the court acknowledged it was leaving unanswered the question of whether authors of history would be covered under its definition, since a historian's intent is not the dissemination of "news."[55]

The *Silkwood* and *Shoen* decisions show that documentary film-makers and investigative book authors used sufficiently similar methods and had similar purposes to traditional newspaper reporters so as to be eligible for a journalist's privilege. What about professors, graduate student researchers and student journalists? Four courts have issued disparate rulings.

In 1998, the First Circuit Court of Appeals in *Cusumano v. Microsoft* ruled that two professors working on a book about the Internet browser wars between Microsoft and Netscape were entitled to journalist-privilege protection.[56] Microsoft subpoenaed two professors from Massachusetts Institute of Technology and Harvard Business School for details of their research in the context of an anti-trust case. The court found the research process for the professors was indistinguishable from that of traditional reporters. In concluding that "academics engaged in pre-publication research should be accorded protection commensurate to that which the law provides to journalists," the court determined that academic researchers would face the same "chilling effects" of compelled disclosure as traditional journalists, and therefore there would be corresponding damage to the First Amendment value of free flow of information to the public from expert researchers.[57] The court wrote:

> As with reporters, a drying-up of sources would sharply curtail the information available to academic researchers and thus would restrict their output. Just as a journalist, stripped of sources, would write fewer, less incisive articles, an academician, stripped of sources, would be able to provide fewer, less cogent analyses. Such similarities of concern and function militate in favor of a similar level of protections for journalists and academic researchers.[58]

Two cases involving Ph.D. students resulted in different rulings. In 1984, a federal judge in New York ruled that a Ph.D. student did not have to turn over a journal in which he kept notes for his dissertation when those notes were sought in the context of a police investigation into a fire at a restaurant the student was observing.[59] The judge concluded that the public policy reasons for a journalist's privilege cannot be distinguished from those of scholars who collect data for subsequent publication and that "serious scholars are entitled to no less protection than journalists."[60] The judge briefly discussed academic freedom and the importance of field notes to scholars, particularly social scientists. Concluding that scholars are entitled to invoke a qualified privilege developed in the common law, the judge said the government had made "no showing of any substantial government need" for the journal and therefore dismissed the subpoena.[61] The Ninth Circuit Court of Appeals in 1993, however, ruled in *Scarce v. U.S.* that a Ph.D. student was required to provide testimony to a federal grand jury despite invoking a journalist's privilege.[62] The student, who studied and participated in the animal rights movement, had a personal relationship with a suspect in the vandalism of an animal research facility, and his testimony was sought about his knowledge of the crime. In mostly skirting the definitional questions, the appeals court ruled that even if a journalist's privilege was present in common law, it did not apply to federal grand juries given the *Branzburg* holding.[63]

In 1993, a federal judge in New York allowed a college student to invoke the privilege under federal law even though the state statute protected only "professional journalists."[64] The case involved a student journalist at the State University of New York at Buffalo who was subpoenaed to provide a tape recording of an interview with an associate dean conducted in connection with a story the student wrote in the college newspaper. The dean was being sued by a former professor over a job dispute. The judge analyzed the student's actions and concluded they were sufficiently similar to those of traditional journalists to warrant the privilege.[65]

Additional district court cases demonstrate that judges have used broad definitions of "newsgathering," the "press" and "journalism" when considering the journalist's privilege. Three district court cases involved privilege claims by individuals reporting on the financial industry. In 1992, a federal judge in Pennsylvania determined that a credit-reporting agency was entitled to invoke a privilege because its publications had "all the attributes" that the Supreme Court has said are "indicative of the press:" a regular circulation to a general population, a history of creating its own editorial analysis, and independent control over form and content.[66] The subpoena came in the context of a class-action suit alleging securities fraud against a paper-manufacturing company, and the plaintiffs were seeking information that the company executives provided about its finances to Standard & Poor's Corporation. The central question, the judge said, was whether "a journalist's privilege" extended to S&P. The judge said he could make no content distinction between publishers of corporate financial information and publishers of other types of news.[67] The judge ruled that S&P could invoke a qualified privilege and found that the plaintiffs had not met the threshold burden necessary for disclosure.

A financial analyst could invoke the privilege, a federal judge in Massachusetts ruled in 1992, because he was "engaged in the dissemination of investigative information to the investing business community" on matters of public concern.[68] The analyst had written a report questioning a medical-laser system based in part on anonymous sources and distributed the report to potential investors. A medical-supply company claimed to have suffered financial losses because of the report and wanted the identity of the sources for a civil lawsuit.[69] The court ruled that the analysts' need for confidential sources to do his job as an independent analyst outweighed the company's need for the information.[70] Important to the judge's analysis was the analyst's claim that confidential sources were crucial to his job and that current and future sources would likely dry up if he was forced to reveal their identities, to the detriment of the public good to be had from his research.

On the other hand, a federal judge in New York ruled in 1993 that both federal and state law precluded a financial newsletter from invoking the privilege.[71] The case involved a dispute between Marriott Corporation and its shareholders, and Marriott sought the deposition of individuals working for a small newsletter called *Daily Insights*. The judge ruled that the information sought was central to the dispute and the plaintiffs had overcome a qualified privilege had one existed. However, the judge ruled that the newsletter did not qualify for protection and said the newsletter "has not born its burden of demonstrating" that its employees are 'professional journalists.'"[72] In ruling that the newsletter was not "journalistic," the judge said the newsletter had limited distribution, a small subscriber base of "far less" than 100 people, and no staff member designated as a reporter, editor, or journalist.[73]

The financial-publication cases suggest that a standard may indeed be hard to articulate for which public communicators should and should not receive protection. However, other cases in which judges have excluded privilege-protection provide evidence that journalistic values and practices are an important component in the analysis.

In *von Bulow v. von Bulow*, a 1987 case before the Second Circuit of Appeals, the court provides some key elements of the limits of privilege application to claimants. [74] The case involved a civil action filed by the children of Martha von Bulow against her husband Claus von Bulow, the underlying allegation being that Claus von Bulow had poisoned their mother, leaving her in a permanent coma. Andrea Reynolds, whom the court described as an "intimate friend" and "steady companion" of Claus von Bulow, was ordered to turn over investigative reports she commissioned on the lifestyles of the von Bulow children, notes she took during the criminal trial of von Bulow, and a manuscript of a book she had written about the von Bulow prosecution. She argued that these documents were protected by a journalist's privilege. [75]

In rejecting Reynolds' claim, the Second Circuit Court of Appeals articulated "certain principles" to govern definitional questions of the journalist's privilege. These included the importance of "the process of newsgathering" as a First Amendment value. In determining who qualifies for protection, courts should ask "whether the person, at the inception of the investigatory process, had the intent to disseminate to the public the information obtained through the investigation." [76] The person must be "involved in activities traditionally associated with the gathering and dissemination of news." [77] Courts must conduct an intent-based factual inquiry into assertions of the privilege and cannot simply rule out non-traditional newsgatherers. The burden, however, is on the person seeking the privilege. [78] Reynolds failed to meet these standards, the court ruled, despite having written an unpublished manuscript and having received press passes from several news organizations in the past, in part because she admittedly sought the information "for my own peace of mind" and that her primary motivation in compiling her information was for the vindication of Claus von Bulow. [79] Her promises of confidentiality, the court concluded, were not given out of "journalistic necessity." [80]

The court's determination that Reynolds was not engaged in traditional newsgathering was based on the same rationale used by the First Circuit Court of Appeals in the 1988 case *In re Jeffrey Steinberg*. [81] The court refused to allow campaign workers to invoke a journalist's privilege to keep secret notebooks they created during the campaign, ruling that they made no showing that the material was part of a "journalistic endeavor."[82] The notebooks were wanted in the context of a grand jury probe into fundraising fraud.

Other cases involving material of political organizations have provoked more complex considerations. Two district courts have also found that political organizations and advocacy groups could invoke the privilege. In *Builders Association of Greater Chicago v. County of Cook*,[83] a judge allowed the Chicago Urban League to withhold details of a confidential survey under the privilege because it was information gathered with the intent to disseminate to the public. The judge noted it would be content-based discrimination to exclude the group simply because it was political in purpose.[84] A federal judge in Colorado used a different approach to arrive at the same conclusion in *Quigley v. Rosenthal*,[85] a case in which the Anti-Defamation League was subpoenaed to reveal confidential information in a defamation suit. Because the organization "publishes numerous periodicals, books and pamphlets and regularly engages in newsgathering activities," it qualifies as a "newsperson" under the law and thus was able to invoke the privilege.[86]

While the standards adopted by several circuits over the years provide wider latitude for non-traditional journalists, the case of *In re: Madden* (*Titan Sports v. Turner Broadcasting*) provides additional guidance as to where courts may draw lines.[87] Mark Madden, an employee of World Championship Wrestling (WCW), a professional wrestling and entertainment company, recorded commentaries for a 900-number hotline in which he made allegedly false and misleading statements about wrestlers from the World Wrestling Federation (WWF), a competing organization. In a lawsuit between the WWF and WCW, the WWF subpoenaed Madden to reveal the sources of his information. Madden invoked a journalist's privilege under Pennsylvania law and federal common law. A federal district court ruled Madden was a "journalist" because he intended to disseminate information to the public.[88] But the Third Circuit Court of Appeals overturned the lower court decision, saying it did not correctly analyze the content of the information being disseminated. The person claiming the privilege, the appeals court said, "must be engaged in the process of 'investigative reporting' or 'news gathering.'"[89]

The court said its decision in *Madden* was rooted in the *von Bulow* and *Shoen* analyses. "This test does not grant status to any person with a manuscript, a web page or a film, but requires an intent at the inception of the newsgathering process to disseminate investigative news to the public. As we see it, the privilege is only available to persons whose purposes are those traditionally inherent to the press; persons gathering news for publication."[90] Madden, the court argued, was simply passing along information from his employer with a "primary goal" of "advertisement and entertainment – not to gather news or disseminate information."[91] The court went on,

> (A)s an author of entertaining fiction, he lacked the intent at the beginning of the research process to disseminate information to the public. He, like other creators of fictional works, intends at the beginning of the process to create a piece of art or entertainment. Fiction or entertainment writers are permitted to view facts selectively, change the emphasis or chronology of events or even fill factual gaps with fictitious events – license a journalist does not have. Because Madden is not a journalist, it follows that he cannot conceal his information with the shadow of the journalist's privilege.[92]

This review of relevant federal case law offers guidance for determining who qualifies for the privilege in federal law, beginning with the tests articulated in *Silkwood* and *von Bulow* and expanded in detail in *Shoen* and *Madden*. The tests aim to protect those people traditionally associated with journalism who set out at the beginning of a process to collect information and then present it to the public, regardless of whether the person is employed by a newspaper or a similar "traditional" media company.

This review also suggests that journalistic ethics and values have been relevant to judicial decision-making, albeit implicitly. In rejecting Madden's claims, for example, the Third Circuit Court of Appeals emphasized Madden's failure to be ethically bound by traditional newsgathering conventions and a pursuit of the truth. In rejecting Andrea Reynolds' claims, the Second Circuit Court of Appeals emphasized her personal relationships with the principal actors and her lack of intent to publicly disseminate as important factors. On the other hand, judges extending the privilege to non-traditional journalists have emphasized an individual's mission of disseminating news in the public interest, the importance of investigative reporting and seeking facts, the significance of editorial judgment and independence, and the value in "activities traditionally associated with the gathering and dissemination of news."[93]

Many cases arising in state courts differ significantly from their federal counterparts because state statutes often include clauses that define who qualifies for the privilege, and therefore state judicial decisions are often simply a matter of statutory interpretation. Many states specifically confine the privilege to traditional journalists or news organizations. Thirty-nine states have statutory protections.[94] Ten other states have some constitutional or common-law protection. Only Wyoming has no recognized protection.[95]

Some statutes provide broad definitions for privilege application. The District of Columbia's shield law defines "news media" as "newspapers, magazines, journals, press associations, news agencies, wire services, radio, television, or any printed, photographic, mechanical, or electronic means of disseminating news and information to the public."[96] Maryland's law lists eight types of media protected, and adds as a ninth, "any printed, photographed, mechanical, or electronic means of disseminating news and information to the public."[97] Nebraska's law, similar to New Jersey's, covers those engaged in "gathering, receiving, or processing of information for any medium of communication to the public," and states that a "medium of communication shall include, but not be limited to, any newspaper, magazine, other periodical, book, pamphlet, news service, wire service, news or feature syndicate, broadcast station or network, or cable television system."[98] Oregon protects anyone "connected with, employed by or engaged in any medium of communication."[99]

Other states have narrower or more specific laws. Georgia's law covers only those whose material is disseminated "through a newspaper, book, magazine, or radio or television broadcast."[100] Illinois requires a newspaper or periodical, including electronic, to have a general circulation and be published at regular intervals.[101] Kentucky protects only those employed by or connected to a newspaper, radio, or television station.[102] Oklahoma's law protects only those "regularly engaged" in gathering and preparing news "for any newspaper, periodical, press association, newspaper syndicate, wire service, radio or television station, or other news service."[103]

Especially in states with more narrow definitions that emphasize the status, rather than the function, of the class of people qualifying for protection, statutes are sometimes construed strictly to deny the privilege to news gatherers. In 1986, a district court in New York ruled that student journalists working on the student newspaper at Hofstra University could not invoke the privilege because the New York shield law is "limited to protecting the class of professional journalists, who, for gain or livelihood are engaged in preparing or editing news for a newspaper."[104] The court also cited case law defining a newspaper as having a "paid circulation" and "entered at the United States post office as a Second Class matter."[105] In 1987, the Sixth Circuit Court of Appeals upheld lower court rulings in both state and federal courts that ruled that a television reporter was not eligible to invoke Michigan journalist's privilege because it covered only "reporters of newspapers or other publications."[106]

The Arizona statutory privilege could not be invoked by an investigative book author, the Arizona court of appeals court ruled in 1992 in *Matera v. Superior Court,* because Arizona's statute, adopted in 1937, is "limited to persons engaged in the gathering and dissemination of news to the public on a regular basis."[107] The law was intended only to apply to those who gather news on an ongoing basis as "part of the organized, traditional, mass media."[108] The court observed that "the statute was not designed to protect the information gathered, but rather was designed to aid a specific class of persons – members of the media – in performing their jobs free from the inconvenience of being used as surrogate investigators."[109] A book author was not part of the organized, traditional media as defined by the legislature, the court ruled.

A fourth example of narrow statutory interpretation is found in *Price v. Time*, a case involving a libel lawsuit filed by an Alabama football coach against *Sports Illustrated* and reporter Don Yaeger.[110] In 2005, the Eleventh Circuit Court of Appeals upheld a determination by a district judge that the Alabama statutory privilege did not cover a magazine reporter because the Alabama statute covered only employees of "any newspaper, radio broadcasting station or television station."[111] The court ruled that the plain language of the statute and the legislature's intent excluded magazines from protection. While hewing to narrow statutory interpretation, the appeals court ruled that the reporter had a qualified First Amendment privilege and required that the coach overcome the federal common law's three-prong test, based on Justice Stewart's *Branzburg* dissent, before ordering the reporter's disclosure of confidential sources.[112] The two parties settled the lawsuit without the public disclosure of the confidential sources.[113]

In one unusual case, the Colorado Supreme Court held that a news helicopter pilot could invoke the privilege and refuse to give testimony in a pre-trial criminal proceeding.[114] The news station had entered into an agreement with the police that allowed the police to use the news helicopter to conduct a search of a suspected drug dealer with the understanding that the television station could later report on it. While it was questionable whether the news station inappropriately became an agent of the police, the court ruled that the helicopter operator was acting in his capacity as a journalist at the time, and thus could be prevented from testifying.[115] The state statute in question defined "newsperson" as any member of the mass media or any employee who is employed to "gather, receive, observe, process, prepare, write, or edit news information."[116]

Other cases show even more unusual entities attempting to invoke the privilege. In a 1995 New Jersey case, a public relations company attempted to invoke the privilege to avoid providing testimony and documents about a client it represented.[117] The firm was subpoenaed in a civil lawsuit between two companies to provide documents it created when developing a strategy to respond to an explosion at a chemical plant. The firm argued that because it "regularly disseminates information to the public regarding newsworthy events," and because the information it obtained was provided after promises of confidentiality, it should be able to invoke the privilege.[118] The New Jersey statute broadly defines news media to include "printed ... means of disseminating information to the general public." However, the court rejected the argument, saying public relations firms are "neither part of the traditional or nontraditional news media."[119] The court said the firm was more "part of the news" rather than a member of the news media reporting news.[120]

The state cases show that judicial decisions use widely different standards in evaluating non-traditional cases based on whether the state statute defines a covered individual using based on status or functional tests.

MCKEVITT V. PALLASCH: THE TIDE TURNS

The general consensus among media lawyers is that the expansion of protections for journalists that occurred in the 1970s, 1980s and 1990s began to retreat in the early part of the first decade of the 21ˢᵗ century. The most significant cause of this retreat was the peculiar case of *McKevitt v. Pallasch*.[121]

Judge Richard Posner, of the Seventh Circuit Court of Appeals based in Chicago, did not need to issue a lengthy written opinion in the case of *McKevitt v. Pallasch*. The three Chicago journalists under subpoena had already turned over audiotapes at the heart of the legal dispute, so the legal claim was moot by the time Judge Posner circulated an opinion to two other judges for their approval.[122] Perhaps he was just being diligent with his delayed explanation of the panel's refusal to stay an order from a district judge requiring the journalists to turn over the tapes. But perhaps also Judge Posner, a prolific writer considered one of America's most influential legal minds, saw the case as an opportunity to influence a legal doctrine that had evolved for 30 years and was in the early stages of new tumult. In addition to serving on the Seventh Circuit Court of Appeals, Posner teaches at the University of Chicago Law School and is the author of 2,200 legal decisions, 40 books and more than 300 articles. He is also the jurist most frequently cited in scholarly articles, earning more citations than the next two highest, Ronald Dworkin and Oliver Wendell Holmes, combined.[123] A legal "pragmatist" who has advocated for economic models of analysis in First Amendment law, Posner had also written critically of the institutional press.[124] Whatever the motivation, Posner penned a brief decision – five pages in the federal reporter, only half of which dealt with journalist's privilege issues – that seven years later is arguably the most significant turning point in federal law governing protections for journalistic sources since the Supreme Court's decision in *Branzburg v. Hayes*.[125]

The *McKevitt* case is rooted in an unusual set of facts. The subpoenas to reporters Abdon Pallasch and Robert Herguth of the *Chicago Sun-Times* and Flynn McRoberts of the *Chicago Tribune* came from defense attorneys in Ireland who were in the midst of a terrorism trial and looking for evidence to impeach the credibility of a prosecution witness.[126] In the summer of 2003, Michael McKevitt was facing charges of leading a terrorism organization, based on his role in a violent group blamed for a 1998 bombing in Omagh, Ireland, that killed 29 people. A witness in the Ireland trial was David Rupert, a "mole" who under direction of the FBI and British intelligence had initially infiltrated a group of Irish-American activists in Chicago and later met with McKevitt.[127] Just before the trial was set to begin, McKevitt's attorneys learned that Rupert had given interviews to the Chicago journalists in hopes of convincing them to write a book about his life as an FBI informer. In 2001, after McKevitt's arrest, the Chicago journalists had written three newspaper stories about Rupert's connections to McKevitt and the Chicago Irish-American activists.[128] A book agent hired by Rupert contacted McRoberts, who in turn invited Pallasch to collaborate, based on his prior reporting on Rupert's role in the FBI investigation. When McRoberts left the project, Hergurth replaced him.[129]

The journalists taped hours of interviews with Rupert as preliminary work for a book that was intended to be part autobiography of an FBI mole, and part contemporary history of the FBI and its involvement in Northern Ireland. Rupert, a 6-foot 6-inch tall former Midwestern truck driver who today is reportedly in the witness protection program, said he discussed in the interviews everything from his childhood through his involvement with McKevitt and McKevitt's radical organization called the "Real IRA."[130] Rupert convinced the journalists to agree to split any profits with him, which Rupert said he intended to use to support his family because he feared his FBI payments would soon stop. One FBI report included in the case file at the National Archives in Chicago quoted Thomas J. Kneir, the special agent in charge of the Chicago FBI office as saying, "Quite frankly, he was afraid that the American and British governments would abandon him after he was no longer needed."[131]

The FBI was not happy to learn, on around June 5, 2003, that Rupert had been shopping around a book about his work for the FBI. They warned him of a confidentiality agreement he had signed with the FBI – including Rupert's agreement not to disclose, among other things, "information which benefits from the practical obscurity from the public eye."[132] It appears the FBI, therefore, had as much to gain from reviewing the journalists' tapes as did McKevitt – perhaps explaining why the FBI demanded to first review and transcribe the tapes after McKevitt's subpoenas were issued on June 20, 2003. The FBI first sought access directly from the journalists. "I said no,"

Pallasch said later. "We have a First Amendment."[133] Then, the FBI intervened in the court case. U.S. Attorney Patrick Fitzgerald, the same man who would later send *New York Times* reporter Judith Miller to jail, filed a "Statement of Interest of the United States" that argued, "There is a substantial likelihood that these materials include information that directly relates to a national security investigation conducted by the Federal Bureau of Investigation (FBI), in conjunction with the British Security Service, concerning the activities of the Irish terrorist group the 'Real IRA.'"[134]

The Chicago journalists initially made a pact to fight the subpoenas, and agreed to go to jail if necessary. On July 3, 2003, Pallasch tried to explain to his two sons, ages seven and nine, that he might be going to jail.[135] In court, the journalists argued that McKevitt's lawyers were on a fishing expedition and had three years to find evidence to impeach the witness.

Judge Ronald Guzman of the District Court of Northern Illinois dismissed these concerns, and gave Pallasch and the two other journalists 24 hours to turn over audiotapes.[136] Just days before the U.S. judge's ruling, Rupert was asked on the witness stand in Ireland whether he objected to the release of the tapes. He said no, something McKevitt's American lawyers seized on to weaken the journalist's privilege claims by arguing that the material in question was not confidential. Notably, the judge in the McKevitt trial declined to declare whether the tapes were relevant to trial. Still, Judge Guzman in Chicago ordered the tapes be turned over to the FBI, which were then to be provided to McKevitt's attorney. The judge rejected claims that a First Amendment or federal common law privilege applied in the case, saying that any interest in a privilege was outweighed by the "possible use of this material in a serious criminal trial of an alleged terrorist and the general public interest in fair, thorough, and effective investigations and trials of criminal terrorist activities."[137] The judge even alluded to the Sept. 11, 2001, terrorist attacks, saying that "recent events have made clear we have a substantial interest in investigating and prosecuting terrorism both here and abroad."[138]

The journalists immediately sought a stay of the district court order. Pallasch, a graduate of Northwestern University's journalism school and a former reporter at the *Chicago Tribune* and *Chicago Lawyer* magazine, later said he was confident that the judicial system's checks and balances would ultimately vindicate his journalist's privilege claim. "I always imagined that when the fateful day came, I would march off to jail, smiling," Pallasch later wrote.[139] "Public pressure would mount, and an appellate court would overturn the order, releasing me."[140] Instead, the appeals court swiftly rejected a motion to stay the district court order while it considered an appeal. The request was filed at 9 a.m. on July 3. At 10:30 a.m., the Seventh Circuit issued a one-page unsigned order rejecting the stay. "Herguth, McRoberts and I agreed we were going to jail," Pallasch later wrote.[141] The denial of a stay did not provide much hope that the Seventh Circuit Court of Appeals would be open to an appeal on the merits, and the journalists' lawyers urged the journalists to turn over the tapes. "They warned us that by going further, we would likely do more harm than good," Pallasch said. "Cut off the process now and [it's a] non-precedential, one-time bad decision."[142] The journalists, grudgingly, agreed and turned over the tapes. The tapes played no major role in the trial, and McKevitt was convicted in Ireland on the terrorism charges.[143]

The lawyers' advice to the Chicago journalists was well intentioned given the uncertainties of the federal common law journalist's privilege. While dozens of lower court decisions had limited *Branzburg's* holding to grand jury subpoenas and interpreted Powell's concurrence to support a qualified privilege in other contexts, the lack of comparative precedents and the swift rejection of a request for a stay did not bode well for the journalists. The journalists also had another disadvantage: while a consensus of district court decisions in the Seventh Circuit clearly established a qualified journalist's privilege, the qualified privilege had only been tacitly approved at the appeals level, and therefore the privilege was less articulated and robustly defended than in many other circuits.

Five weeks after the tapes were turned over and the issue was moot, Judge Richard Posner of the Seventh Circuit issued his opinion in the *McKevitt* case. Posner's disposal of the journalist's privilege began with a peculiar tease, noting that Justice Powell's concurrence in *Branzburg* supported a case-by-case balancing of freedom of the press against the obligation to assist in criminal proceedings. Posner wrote, "(M)aybe [Powell's] opinion should be taken to state the view of the majority of the Justices – though this is uncertain, because Justice Powell purported to join Justice White's 'majority' opinion" which rejected a First Amendment-based privilege.[144] Then, Posner cited nine appellate decisions between 1986 and 1998 which he said are representative of a "large number of cases" that "conclude, rather surprisingly in light of *Branzburg*, that there is a reporter's privilege."[145] How this was surprising to Posner is unclear, given his own explication of Powell's concurrence mere sentences before. In discussing these precedents, he wrote that some courts "essentially ignore *Branzburg*" while others "audaciously declare that *Branzburg* actually created a reporter's privilege."[146] Posner concluded: "The approaches that these decisions take to the issue of privilege can certainly be questioned."[147] Posner, though, didn't question these approaches so much as summarily dismiss them without any further intellectual exercise. He also rejected the application of Illinois's journalist's privilege statute, first contending that it was "not applicable" in the federal case, contradicting an earlier Seventh Circuit Court of Appeals decision, and secondly concluding that if did apply, the journalists failed to properly make the claim, thus waiving their reliance on it.[148]

Posner briefly noted the competing interests in the case at hand, saying that the federal interest in cooperating in foreign criminal proceedings "is obvious" but conceded that newsgathering is "inhibited" by the inability of reporters to assure source confidentiality.[149] Posner relied heavily on Rupert's statement from the witness stand that he did not oppose the motion to compel the Chicago journalists to turn over the tapes, concluding, "There is no conceivable interest in confidentiality in the present case."[150] Dozens of courts have in fact recognized a privilege for non-confidential information, and Posner cited six appellate decisions that did so.[151] Posner asserted that the rationales for journalistic protections for non-confidential information – including "concern with harassment, burden, using the press as an investigative arm of government, and so forth" – "were rejected by *Branzburg* even in the context of a confidential source."[152] Therefore, Posner concluded, "these courts may be skating on thin ice."[153]

Journalists, Posner concluded, should be treated like any other subject of a subpoena. "It seems to us that rather than speaking of privilege, courts should simply make sure that a subpoena duces tecum directed to the media, like all other subpoenas duces tecum, is reasonable in the circumstances, which is the general criterion for judicial review of subpoenas," Posner wrote.[154] "We do not see why there need to be special criteria merely because the possessor of the documents or other evidence sought is a journalist." Posner claimed this approach "has support in *Branzburg* itself."[155]

Posner also questioned the motives of the Chicago journalists, saying their real motivation was to maximize profits from a tell-all book whose marketability would be lessened by public disclosure of the tapes. Posner claimed that Rupert's lack of objection to the tapes' disclosure put the journalists in the position of advocating for secrecy. "If anything, the parties to this case are reversed from the perspective of freedom of the press, which seeks to encourage publication rather than secrecy. Rupert *wants* the information disclosed; it is the reporters, paradoxically, who want it secreted (emphasis in original)."[156] He opined as to the motivation by saying, "The reason they want it secreted is that the biography of him that they are planning to write will be less marketable the more information in it that has already been made public."[157]

Finally, the *McKevitt* decision is peculiar because it began and ended with a notation that the case is moot. At the outset, Posner noted that the turning over of the tapes had "mooted the appeal" but asserted in his introduction that "there is no irregularity in a court's explaining the ground a decision after the decision itself has been made ending the case."[158] Posner again alluded in his final sentence to the irrelevance of his ruling to the case at hand: "The appeal is dismissed as moot."[159]

Almost immediately, media lawyers recognized the decision's significance for two reasons. First, Posner himself is among the nation's most influential legal minds, and his decisions therefore carry great intellectual authority. "When I saw Judge Posner's decision I shuddered," said Robin Bierstedt, deputy general counsel for Time Inc.[160] "He's extremely intelligent and highly regarded. Once Posner, one of the brightest lights on the bench ever, read *Branzburg* and said, 'What's going on here?', that allowed lawyers and judges to reconsider what had become the conventional reading of the case that really relied on the concurring opinion of Justice Powell."[161]

Second, the decision's practical effect was seen as eliminating a privilege inside the Seventh Circuit and influencing other circuits as supportive precedent in future cases. For this reason, 26 media organizations filed an *amicus curiae* brief that argued Posner's opinion "conflicts with decisions from ten out of eleven Circuits that have recognized the existence of some form of the reporter's privilege."[162] The groups asked for one of four alternatives: for the full Seventh

Circuit to rehear the case; for a modification of Posner's decision to recognize the existence of a journalist's privilege; for the opinion to be withdrawn as improvidently issued; or for the opinion to be modified in a way that limits its reach to the particular set of facts.[163] The media organizations claimed that Posner's "broad assertion" that subpoenas to journalists should be evaluated by the same criteria as any other subpoena "challenges the fundamental notion that a qualified privilege against compelled disclosure of newsgathering exists under federal law."[164] Both the media organizations and lawyers for the Chicago journalists also argued that the sweeping precedent needed review, because Posner issued his opinion without following well-established norms of judicial decision-making. "(W)ithout adversarial briefing, argument, or (apparently) circulation of the opinion to the entire court … the panel issued a published opinion effectively denying the existence of a First Amendment privilege, placing this Circuit in conflict with other Courts of Appeal save one."[165] On October 14, 2003, the Seventh Circuit Court of Appeals issued an order denying the appeal for rehearing. The order stated that the three judges on the original panel all voted to deny the petition, while none of the active judges requested a vote on the petition for a rehearing.[166]

Afterward, Posner explained his reasoning in an interview with the *Columbia Journalism Review*, saying, "There was this terrible misunderstanding by the lower middle courts of *Branzburg*. There's no privilege. The Supreme Court said there's no privilege."[167] Still, Posner's approach sparked immediate negative reaction. "What I personally found offensive was that the decision came out of nowhere – no briefing, no oral arguments," said lawyer Victor Kovner, who wrote the *amicus* brief. "Posner, unfortunately, read *Branzburg* broadly – overbroadly, in our opinion, and rejected a host of post-*Branzburg* jurisprudence – without the benefit of a briefing, without the benefit of hearing from the press."[168]

THE EFFECTS OF THE MCKEVITT DECISION

The *McKevitt* decision had important and near immediate effects, both inside and outside of the Seventh Circuit.

As a matter of federal law in the Seventh Circuit, journalists in Wisconsin, Illinois and Indiana never had as explicit privilege protection as journalists in many other circuits. Prior to *McKevitt*, the qualified journalist's privilege in the Seventh Circuit was the product of eleven district court decisions and two appellate decisions, and significantly, neither appellate opinion was rooted in robust support for a qualified privilege, as is the case in a number of other circuits.[169]

The most thorough treatment of the privilege issue in the Seventh Circuit has come from the district court in the Northern District of Illinois, which encompasses Chicago. District court judges, beginning in 1978, consistently found that the First Amendment and the federal common law provide journalists with a qualified journalist's privilege, even in light of *Branzburg,* if not because of it. In *Gulliver's Periodicals v. Chas. Levy Circulating Company*, the first reported case involving a journalist's privilege claim in the Seventh Circuit, a district judge dismissed subpoenas against two reporters of the weekly *Chicago Reader* who wrote a story about disputes between two periodical-distribution companies that subsequently resulted in litigation.[170] As part of the legal dispute, the journalists received third-party deposition notices, which they moved to quash, citing the First Amendment and the Illinois Reporter's Privilege Statute.[171] Chas. Levy, the company that served the subpoenas, argued that the First Amendment provided no protection to journalists, based on the *Branzburg* ruling, and that the state statute was inapplicable to federal proceedings. The district court said the state statute was relevant in cases where federal statutes are silent, but said the state statute was not dispositive. Instead, the district court concluded that the First Amendment required a balancing of interests to avoid "unnecessary impediments" to newsgathering.[172] "The case law in this area is somewhat ambiguous," the judge wrote, but began the analysis with *Branzburg*, noting that its holding was limited to subpoenas to journalists from grand juries and that Justice Powell's concurrence required a case-by-case balancing by the courts.[173] "The *Branzburg* case, as well as others, suggests a proposition that this court readily embraces: that the newsgathering process qualifies for First Amendment protection."[174] The district court concluded that compelled disclosure of a news source "implicates and involves an infringement on freedom of the press" that can only be overcome by consideration of the relevance and materiality of the information sought, whether the information is crucial to the legal dispute, and whether the party seeking the information has exhausted other means of obtaining it.[175] Citing a Tenth Circuit case, the district judge said: "Disclosure in the course of a 'fishing expedition' is ruled out in a First Amendment case."[176] The judge ruled that the journalist subpoenas would "not provide a source of crucial information going to the heart" of the claim, and quashed the subpoenas. The court suggested the privilege applied to all newsgathering material, whether or not it is confidential. While not precedential, the district court decision unambiguously embraced the early development of the federal common law journalist's privilege, rooted in part, and to varying degrees, in the First Amendment.

The *Gulliver's Periodicals* case laid the foundation for at least eight subsequent district court rulings that supported a qualified journalist's privilege in the Seventh Circuit, at least at a trial level.[177] The trial courts broadly acknowledged and embraced the federal common law privilege that had become legal consensus in the decades after *Branzburg*.[178]

While the record is less voluminous at the appeals court level, the Seventh Circuit Court of Appeals twice upheld lower court decisions that quashed or limited subpoenas to journalists. The most substantial treatment of the issue by the appeals court came in 1992 in *Desai v. Hersh*, a case involving a libel lawsuit filed by Morarji Desai, a former prime minister of India, against journalist Seymour Hersh.[179] In his book, *The Price of Power: Kissinger in the Nixon White House*, Hersh reported about the CIA's reliance on a "reliable source" for information regarding the 1971 India-Pakistan War and concluded that the source was "undoubtedly Moraji Desai," who Hersh asserted was a paid informer to the CIA. Desai denied these allegations, and sought the identity of Hersh's sources in the context of his libel lawsuit against Hersh. A district court relied on Illinois's journalist's privilege statute in deciding that Hersh could testify about the reliability of his sources without identifying them. Hersh testified that he had six confidential sources – "two were out of government, one was in the CIA, one was in the world of the NSA ... and two were in the White House."[180] A jury sided with Hersh, and on appeal, Desai contested the district court's ruling to allow Hersh to testify without revealing his sources. First, Desai argued that Hersh as a book author wasn't allowed to invoke the privilege, an argument the court rejected by noting Hersh's previous work as an investigative journalist. Second, the Seventh Circuit Court of Appeals said there "is no doubt" that the state law was correctly applied to the federal case.[181]

In 1995, the Seventh Circuit upheld a district court decision quashing a subpoena to a *Chicago Tribune* reporter, whose testimony was sought by a defense attorney attempting to undermine the credibility of a witness in a criminal trial – precisely the same context as the *McKevitt* case.[182] In this case, *U.S. v. Lloyd*, the appeals court did not discuss the journalist's privilege directly but merely found the district court did not violate its discretion by throwing out the subpoena.[183]

The *McKevitt* ruling rejected the logic of those cases, and has been interpreted by scholars and lawyers – not to mention the judge who wrote the decision – as eliminating a privilege altogether. However, an analysis of case law in the Seventh Circuit since 2003 suggests that judges wishing to provide journalists with some protection may be able to limit and distinguish the *McKevitt* holding. Fourteen cases in the Seventh Circuit cited *McKevitt* between 2003 and 2007, but only six cases involved privilege issues directly, and several of them had outcomes favorable to journalists.[184]

As a matter of precedent, *McKevitt v. Pallasch* is not binding on federal courts outside of Wisconsin, Illinois and Indiana. However, as evidence of Posner's influence, the decision has been cited in a number of court decisions ruling against journalists, including cases involving journalists James Taricani and Judith Miller, as well as decisions in the Wen Ho Lee privacy lawsuit and the subpoena for phone records of the *New York Times* in connection to an investigation into an Islamic charity. While legal norms explain why *McKevitt* citations populated decisions in the Seventh Circuit, what made this case significant elsewhere, especially given its inherent overreaching?

One of the first signs of *McKevitt's* importance was the adoption of Posner's reasoning by the First Circuit Court of Appeals in its decision to hold in civil contempt James Taricani, the Rhode Island television reporter who was leaked a videotape purporting to show evidence of a bribery scheme involving a local mayor.[185] The First Circuit adopted Posner's approach almost in its entirety, rejecting arguments by Taricani that the First Amendment and a federal common law privilege provided him with a legal right to avoid revealing the identity of the person who leaked the videotape in violation of a court order. Chief Judge Michael Boudin said Taricani's First Amendment argument "is an uphill one in light of *Branzburg*" and then rejected the contention that the holding in *Branzburg* was limited to grand jury subpoenas.

Rather, *Branzburg* only allowed for First Amendment arguments in cases involving "a showing of bad faith purpose to harass" the press.[186] "One distinguished judge has questioned whether *Branzburg* now offers protection beyond what ordinary relevance and reasonableness requirements would demand," Judge Boudin wrote, citing Posner's decision in *McKevitt*.[187] In embracing Posner's pejorative phrasing, Boudin labeled one First Circuit appellate decision finding a common-law privilege "elderly," and questioned its holding that *Branzburg* was limited to grand jury subpoenas – despite Justice White's description in *Branzburg* that "the sole issue before us is the obligation of reporters to respond to grand jury subpoenas as other citizens do and to answer questions relevant to an investigation into the commission of crime."[188] Taricani was sentenced to six months' home confinement despite a special prosecutor's independent discovery of the source of the leak after the leaker publicly identified himself.

McKevitt also was cited by a district court in the Sixth Circuit in a case in which a journalist was required to identify who leaked to him records related to the discipline of a police officer who fired his gun into a car filled with teenagers. In *Lentz v. City of Cleveland*, a subpoena was issued by the police officer in the context of litigation with the city of Cleveland. Citing a litany of cases that created a qualified federal privilege, the judge then cited *McKevitt* as the sole contrary ruling outside the Sixth Circuit, summarizing its holding as "declining to adopt a federal privilege for news reporters."[189] The Sixth Circuit had been one of the only circuits to previously hold that a qualified privilege did not exist. The judge used the *McKevitt* precedent in the Seventh Circuit to find new support for the Sixth Circuit's rejection of the existence of a privilege and ruled that the subpoena was reasonable under the circumstances.[190]

It may be understandable for courts in circuits with no or limited recognition of a federal journalist's privilege to be drawn to *McKevitt* as helpful precedent, as was the case in the First and Sixth Circuit cases discussed above.

McKevitt was also cited in two cases in the District of Columbia Circuit, where a privilege had been robustly established. The first was the lawsuit filed by Wen Ho Lee against the federal government, accusing it of violating privacy laws after government employees leaked information about a criminal investigation focused on Lee. A judge cited the *McKevitt* decision, along with a Sixth Circuit decision, as examples of circuits denying the existence of a privilege.[191] And in the Valerie Plame leak investigation, special prosecutor Patrick Fitzgerald cited *McKevitt* as an example of a source waiving the privilege, in his attempt to persuade the District of Columbia Court of Appeals that the written waivers he obtained from Bush administration officials undermined Judith Miller's claim to a qualified privilege.[192] As D.C. Court of Appeals Judge David S. Tatel pointed out in a concurrence in which he ruled that a federal qualified privilege existed based on widespread precedent across most circuits, the cases were hardly analogous, but Fitzgerald's reliance on Posner's reasoning demonstrates yet another facet of *McKevitt's* significance.

In an unusual twist, a district judge from the Southern District of New York even cited to *McKevitt* as evidence that Justice Powell's concurrence should be viewed as the controlling decision in *Branzburg*. This case involved Fitzgerald's attempt to obtain phone records of the *New York Times* in his investigation into an Islamic charity linked to terrorist organizations.[193] Without acknowledging Posner's holding or central argument, the district judge wrote of *McKevitt*: "(A)t least one court has acknowledged at least the possibility that 'since the [four] dissenting Justices would have gone further than Justice Powell in recognition of the reporter's privilege, and preferred his position to that of the majority opinion ... maybe his opinion should be taken to state the view of the majority of justices."[194] The district court failed to note that Posner explicitly disavowed this proposition. The district court ruled for the *Times* and dismissed the subpoena, but the Second Circuit overruled the district court, ruling that a qualified privilege, if it exists, would have been overcome in the case.[195]

Media law experts started noticing *McKevitt's* potential significance within months of the decision. In the spring of 2004, Heather Stamp concluded in the *DePaul University Journal of Art and Entertainment Law* that "journalists in the Seventh Circuit are caught in a state of confusion, disbelief and concern," and that *McKevitt* failed to reconcile its outcome with the "volumes of decisions" to the contrary.[196] Erik W. Laursen writing in the *University of Cincinnati Law Review* accused Posner of failing to consider the "bigger picture" in dismissing the dozens of contrary court opinions.[197] And by 2005, Professor Anthony Fargo wrote that *McKevitt's* importance was multi-faceted: rejecting a privilege in the Seventh Circuit for non-confidential information, at a minimum, and in providing ammunition to other circuits looking to narrow the privilege in their jurisdictions.[198]

CONCLUSION

This chapter has described the rise and the fall of the journalist's privilege as articulated by federal judges between 1972 and 2003, a period in which media lawyers seemed to turn the *Branzburg* precedent on its head and convince judges of the supremacy of their interpretations. To a large degree, James Goodale and other media lawyers succeeded in reinterpreting a Supreme Court decision from a stunning loss into a remarkable victory. The successes in legal strategy were muted in 2003 with Judge Richard Posner's decision in *McKevitt v. Pallasch*, a decision that had remarkable influence given the peculiarities of the facts. Judge Posner's decision is more important than any single high-profile privilege decision because it not only resulted in negative effects for the journalists in the case but because it audaciously declared that three decades of common law development of the journalist's privilege principle was either in error or non-existent.

The legacy of the decision is undermined by its own failures of internal persuasiveness, and the opinion itself is ripe for dissection. Posner made several dubious assumptions about the facts. The "waiver" of confidentiality in the context of trial cross-examination is less significant when one considers the coercive nature of the waiver. At a minimum, one can question the assumption that the tapes in question were not confidential, therefore undermining a critical component of Posner's rationale. Secondly, Posner rejected well-established principles from decades of common law development in a manner that can best be described as an edict, rather than by any novel or rigorous intellectual exercise. Posner said he simply re-read the *Branzburg* decision and came up with a contrary conclusion. This renders the decision ultimately unsatisfying. Third, the authority of the *McKevitt* case as precedent is undermined by the case's flawed judicial decision-making process, since Posner chose to issue his sweeping opinion without adversarial briefing or argument on the issues.

Not surprisingly, James Goodale's take on Posner is blunt. "Posner is a flaming right wing nut," Goodale said in a 2009 interview, explaining the decision in liberal-conservative terms. The lawyer who has been described in a headline as "The Father of the Reporter's

Privilege"[199] argued that the *McKevitt* decision would not have lasting impact. He said in an interview:

> The reporter's privilege is like any civil right. When you have conservatives in power, they want the power to go to the government, which means the power is taken away from the civil litigants; and therefore the right in the balancing process becomes diminished and discounted by the temper of the times. I think that's what we've seen with the reporter's privilege. You've had a lot of conservative judges who don't want to support a privilege that tangles up the government with respect to the government's actions. And when the tide turns, as it's going to, you'll see, I am sure, that there will be a tilt the other way.[200]

While the federal constitutional and common law development muted the need for a statutory privilege following the *Branzburg* decision, the retreat that began with *McKevitt* and continued through the Bush administration shows the continuing fragility of the privilege as a matter of positive law. In the post-*McKevitt* landscape, journalists used the same practices and arguments in their use and protection of confidential sources, but the law seemed to be turning against them. The next and final chapter assesses roads forward for journalists.

Chapter 7 Notes

<hr>

[1] These cases are explored later in this chapter.

[2] *United States Department of Education v. National Collegiate Athletic Association*, 481 F.3d 936 at 938 (7th Cir. 2007), citing *McKevitt v. Pallasch*, 339 F.3d 530 (7th Cir. 2003).

[3] In the Taricani case, *See* In re Special Proceedings, Misc. No. 01-47T (D.R.I., October 2, 2003), In re Special Proceedings, 291 F. Supp. 2d 46 (D.R.I., December 2003), and In re: Special Proceedings, No. 03-2052 and 04-1383 (1st Cir., June 21, 2004); In the Plame case, *See* In re: Grand Jury Subpoena, Judith Miller, No. 04-3138, (D.C. Cir., Decided Feb. 15, 2005; Reissued June 29, 2007); in the BALCO case, *See* In Re Grand Jury Subpoenas to Mark Fainaru-Wada and Lance Williams, No. CR 06-90225 (D.N.Cal., August 15, 2006); In the Wen Ho Lee case, *See* Wen Ho Lee v. DOJ, No. 99-3380 (D.D.C., Oct. 9, 2003), Wen Ho Lee v. DOJ, No. 99-3380 (D.D.C., Aug. 18, 2004), Wen Ho Lee v. DOJ, No. 04-5301 (D.C. Cir., June 28, 2005), Wen Ho Lee v. DOJ, No. 04-5301 (D.C. Circ., Nov. 3, 2005); In the Hatfill case, *See* Steven J. Hatfill v. Alberto Gonzales, No. 03-1793 (Dist. Ct. of D.C., Aug. 13, 2007); In the Wolf case, *See* In re: Grand Jury Investigation dated Feb. 1, 2006, (U.S. v. Wolf), Order Denying Joshua Wolf's Motion to Quash Subpoena, No. CR 06-90064 MISC MMC (MEJ) (N. Dist. Of Cal., April 5, 2006), In re: Grand Jury Subpoena (Wolf v. U.S.), No. 06-16403, (9th Cir., Sept. 8, 2006) (unpublished decision); and in the Islamic charities case, *See* New York Times v. Alberto Gonzales, 04 CV 7677, (S.D.N.Y., Feb. 24, 2005).

[4] Interview with author, Nov. 12, 2007.

[5] James C. Goodale, *Branzburg v. Hayes and the Developing Qualified Privilege for Newsmen,* 26 HASTINGS L.J. 709 (1974).

[6] Personal interview.

[7] *Id.*

[8] Goodale, supra note 5, at 720.

[9] Baker v. F & F Investment, 470 F.2d. 778, 781 (2d Cir. 1972)

[10] Some early federal appellate decisions by circuit, for example, are Bruno & Stillman, Inc. v. Globe Newspaper Corp., 633 F.2d 583 (1st Cir. 1980); United States v. Burke, 700 F.2d 70 (2d Cir. 1983); United States v. Cuthbertson, 630 F.2d 139 (3d Cir. 1980); LaRouche v. NBC, 780 F.2d 1134 (4th Cir. 1986); Miller v. Transamerican Press, 621 F.2d 721 (5th Cir. 1980); Cervantes v. Time, Inc., 646 F.2d 986 (8th Cir. 1972); Farr v. Pitchess, 522 F.2d

464 (9th Cir. 1975); Silkwood v. Kerr-McGee Corp., 563 F.2d 433 (10th Cir. 1977); Zerilli v. Smith, 656 F.2d 705 (D.C. Cir. 1981).

[11] Farr v. Pitchess, 522 F.2d 464, 467 (9th Cir. 1975).

[12] *Id.*

[13] Zerilli v. Smith, 656 F.2d 705, 712 (D.C. Cir. 1981).

[14] *Id.* at 710-711, quoting New York Times v. United States, 403 U.S. 713, 717 (1971).

[15] *See, for example*, Shoen v. Shoen, 5 F.3d 1289 (9th Cir. 1993); U.S. v. La Rouche, 841 F.2d 1176 (1st Cir. 1988); Von Bulow v. Von Bulow, 811 F.2d 136 (2d Cir. 1987); and U.S. v. Cuthbertson, 630 F.2d 139 (3d Cir. 1980).

[16] *See, for example,* U.S. v. Criden, 633 F.2d 346 (3rd Cir. 1980).

[17] *See* Karl Schmid, *Journalist's Privilege in Criminal Proceedings: An Analysis of United States Courts of Appeals' Decisions from 1973 to 1999*, 39 AM. CRIM. L. REV. 1441 (2002).

[18] This specific articulation is from REPORTER'S PRIVILEGE, published by Debevoise & Plimpton, Media & Communications Group, 28 (1996).

[19] Herbert v. Lando, 441 U.S. 153 (1979).

[20] Kristin M. Simonetti, *First Amendment Reporter's Privilege: Interpretation and Application of the Exhaustion Requirement in the Federal Circuit Courts of Appeals*, Paper Presented to the AEJMC Law Division, 2008 Southeast Colloquium, Auburn University, Auburn, Ala., March 14, 2008 (on file with author).

[21] Anthony L. Fargo, *Reconsidering the Federal Journalist's Privilege for Non-Confidential Information: Gonzales v. NBC*, 19 CARDOZO ARTS & ENT. L.J. 355 (2001) and Anthony L. Fargo, *Is Protection From Subpoenas Slipping? An Analysis of Three Recent Cases Involving Broadcast News Outtakes*, 47 J. BROAD. & ELEC. MEDIA 455 (2003).

[22] Jaffee v. Redmond, 518 U.S. 1, (1996).

[23] For a history of Rule 501, *see generally The Federal Common Law of Journalists' Privilege: A Positon Paper,* 50 THE RECORD 214 at 219 (2005).

[24] *Id* at 220.

[25] Jaffee, 518 U.S. at 9.

[26] *Id.* at 10.

[27] *Id.*

[28] *See generally* Anthony L. Fargo, *Common Law or Shield Law? How Rule 501 Could Solve the Journalist's Privilege Problem,* 33 WM. MITCHELL L. REV. 1347 (2007).

[29] Riley v. City of Chester, 612 F.2d 708 (3rd Cir. 1979).

[30] *Id.* at 718.

[31] Playboy Enterprises v. Los Angeles County, 154 Cal. App. 3d 14, (C.A. Ct. App. 1984); People v. Von Villas, 10 Cal. App. 4th 201, (C.A. Ct. App. 1992); Northside Sanitary Landfill, Inc. v. Bradley, 462 N.E.2d 1321, (Ind. App. Ct. 1984).

[32] U.S. v. Doe (In the matter of Richard Falk) 332 F. Supp. 938 (D. Mass. 1971); Wright v. Jeep Corp, 547 F. Supp. 871 (E.D. Mich. 1982); In re: Grand Jury Subpoena, 583 F. Supp. 991 (E.D.N.Y. 1984); In re: Grand Jury Proceedings (Scarce v. U.S.), 5 F.3d 397 (9th Cir. 1993); Cusumano v. Microsoft, 162 F.3d 708 (1st Cir. 1998).

[33] Shoen v. Shoen, 5 F.3d 1289 (9th Cir. 1993); Florida v. Trepal, 24 Med. L. Rptr 2595 (Fla. Cir. Ct. 1996); People v. Le Grand, 67 A.D.2d 446 (N.Y. App. Ct. 1979); Matera v. Superior Court, 825 P.2d 971 (Ariz. App. Ct. 1992).

[34] Blum v. Schlegel, 150 F.R.D. 42 (W.D.N.Y. 1993); New York v. Hennessey, 13 Med. L. Rptr 1109 (N.Y. Dist. Ct. 1986).

[35] In re: Madden (Titan Sports v. Turner Broadcasting), 151 F.3d 125 (3rd Cir. 1998).

[36] Apicella v. McNeil Laboratories, Inc., 66 F.R.D. 78 (E.D.N.Y. 1975); In Re: Scott Paper, 145 F.R.D. 366 (E.D. Penn. 1992); Summit Tech., Inc. v. Healthcare Capitol Group Inc., 141 F.R.D. 381 (D. Mass. 1992); PPM America v. Marriot Corp., 152 F.R.D. 32 (S.D.N.Y. 1993); Commodity Futures Trading Commission v. The McGraw-Hill Companies, 390 F. Supp. 2d 27 (D. D.C. 2005); In the Matter of the Petition of Burnett, 269 N.J. Super. 493 (N.J. Super. Ct. 1993); Cukier v. American Medical Association, 259 Ill. App. 3d 159 (Ill. App. Ct. 1994).

[37] Builders Assoc. of Greater Chicago v. County of Cook, 1998 U.S. Dist. LEXIS 2991 (N.D. Ill. 1998); Quigley v. Rosenthal, 43 F. Supp. 2d 1163 (D. Col. 1999); Anti-Defamation League v. San Francisco 67 Cal. App. 4th 1072 (Cal. Ct. App. 1998).

[38] Henderson v. Colorado, 879 P.2d 383 (Col. 1994).

[39] In re: Gordon v. Boyles, 9 P.3d 1106 (Col. 2000).

[40] In re Napp Technologies, Inc., 338 N.J. Super. 176 (N.J. Super. Ct. 2000).

[41] Silkwood v. Kerr-McGee, 563 F.2d 433 (10th Cir. 1977).

[42] *Id.*

[43] *Id.* at 434.

[44] *Id.* at 436.

[45] *Id.* at 436-437.

[46] Garland v. Torre, 259 F.2d 545 (2ⁿᵈ Cir. 1958).

[47] Silkwood, 563 F.2d at 438.

[48] Shoen v. Shoen. 5 F.3d 1289 (9ᵗʰ Cir. 1993).

[49] *Id.* at 1290.

[50] Matera v. Superior Court, 170 Ariz. 446 (Ariz. Ct. App. 1992).

[51] Shoen, 5 F. 3d at 1293.

[52] *Id.*

[53] *Id.*

[54] *Id.*

[55] *Id.* at 1294.

[56] Cusumano v. Microsoft, 162 F.3d 708 (1ˢᵗ Cir. 1998).

[57] *Id.* at 714.

[58] Id. at 714.

[59] In re Grand Jury Subpoena, 583 F. Supp. 991 (E.D. N.Y. 1984)

[60] *Id.* at 993.

[61] *Id.* at 995.

[62] In re Grand Jury Proceedings, Scarce v. U.S., 5 F.3d 397 (9ᵗʰ Cir. 1993).

[63] *Id.*

[64] Blum, 150 F.R.D. at 43.

[65] *Id.* at 45.

[66] In re: Scott Paper, 145 F.R.D. at 369.

[67] *Id.* at 368-369.

[68] Summit, 141 F.R.D. at 384.

[69] *Id.* at 383.

[70] *Id.* at 385.

[71] PPM America v. Marriott Corp., 152 F.R.D. 32 (S.D.N.Y. 1993).

[72] *Id.* at 35.

[73] *Id.*

[74] Von Bulow v. Von Bulow, 811 F.2d 136 (2ⁿᵈ Cir. 1987).

[75] *Id.* at 138-139.

[76] *Id.* at 143.

[77] *Id.* at 142.

[78] *Id.* at 144.

[79] *Id.* at 145.

[80] *Id.* at 146.

[81] In Re Jeffrey Steinberg, 837 F.2d 527 (1ˢᵗ Cir. 1988).

[82] *Id.* at 528.

[83] Builders Association of Greater Chicago v. County of Cook, 1998 U.S. Dist. LEXIS 2991 (N.D. Ill. 1998).

[84] *Id.* at 16.

[85] Quigley v. Rosenthal, 43 F. Supp. 2d 1163, (D.C. Col. 1999).

[86] *Id.* at 1173.

[87] In re: Madden (Titan Sports v. Turner Broadcasting), 151 F.3d 125 (3rd Cir. 1998).

[88] *Id.* at 127.

[89] *Id.* at 130.

[90] *Id.* at 129-130.

[91] *Id.* at 130.

[92] *Id.* at 130.

[93] Von Bulow, 811 F.2d at 147.

[94] REPORTERS COMMITTEE FOR FREEDOM OF THE PRESS. THE REPORTER'S PRIVILEGE, *available at* http://www.rcfp.org/privilege/index.html.

[95] *See* Anthony L. Fargo, *Analyzing Federal Shield Law Proposals: What Congress Can Learn from the States,* 11 COMM. L. & POL'Y 35 (2006).

[96] D.C. Code §16-4701.

[97] Md. Cts & Jud. Proc. Code Ann. §9-112.

[98] Neb. Rev. Stat. § 20-144; N.J. Stat. Ann. Tit. 2A, ch. 84A, 21a.

[99] Or. Rev. Stat. § 44.620, 44.510.

[100] Ga. Code Ann. § 24-9-30.

[101] 735 Ill. Comp. Stat. Ann 5/8-901.

[102] Ky. Rev. Stat. Ann. § 421.100.

[103] Okla. Stat. tit. 12, § 2506.

[104] New York v. Hennessey, 13 Med. L. Rptr 1109 (N.Y. Dist. Ct. 1986).

[105] *Id.* at 1110.

[106] In re Grand Jury Proceedings, Storer Communications, Inc. v Wayne County, 810 F. 3d 580 (6th Cir., 1987).

[107] Matera v. Superior Court. 170 Ariz. 446 (Ariz. App. Ct.1992).

[108] *Id.* at 448.

[109] *Id.*

[110] Price v. Time, 416 F. 3d 1327 (11th Cir. 2005).

[111] Alabama Code 12-21-142 (1975).

[112] Price v. Time, 416 F.3d at 1334-35.

[113] Alicia A. Caldwell, *Publisher settles defamation suit by ex-WSU coach Price*, THE (SPOKANE) SPOKESMAN-REVIEW, Oct. 10, 2005.

[114] Henderson v. Colorado, 879 P.2d 383 (Col. 1994).

[115] *Id.*

[116] *Id.* at 393.

[117] In re Napp Technologies, 338 N.J. Super. 176 (N.J. Sup. Ct. 2000).

[118] *Id.* at 181-182.

[119] *Id.* at 187.

[120] *Id.* at 187.

[121] McKevitt v. Pallasch, et al., 339 F.3d 530 (7th Cir. 2003).

[122] See *Amici Curiae* Brief of ABC. Inc., Advance Publications, Inc., The Associated Press, Bloomberg L.P., CBS Broadcasting Inc., Gannet Company, Inc., The Heart Corporation, The McClatchy Company, the McGraw-Hill Companies, National Broadcasting Company, NYP Holdings, Inc., Newsweek, Inc., The New York Times Co., Seattle Times Company, Time Inc., Tribune Company, Turner Broadcasting Systems, Inc. (CNN), The Washington Post, Reed Elsevier Inc., American Society of Newspaper Editors, Association of American Publishers, the National Association of Broadcasters, National Public Radio, the Radio-Television News Directors Association, Reporters Committee for Freedom of the Press, Silha Center for the Study of Media Ethics and Law, Society of Professional Journalists for Leave to File Brief of *Amici Curiae,* filed Aug. 29, 2003, in McKevitt v. Pallasch, et al., 339 F.3d 530 (7th Cir. 2003).

[123] *See Who Are the Top 20 Legal Thinkers in America?* LEGAL AFFAIRS, available at http://www.legalaffairs.org/poll/ (last visited March 30, 2008). *See also* Larissa MacFarquhar, *The Bench Burner,* THE NEW YORKER, Dec. 10, 2001, and John Giuffo, *Judging Richard,* COLUMBIA JOURNALISM REVIEW, November/December 2005.

[124] *See* Anthony Fargo, *Pragmatism, Posner and the Press: Judicial Philosophy in Action* (Conference Paper, International Communication Association, Oct. 5, 2006). On Posner and the First Amendment, *See, e.g.,* Richard Posner, *Free Speech in an Economic Perspective,* 20 SUFFOLK U. L. REV. 1 (1986), and a response by Peter J. Hammer, *Free Speech and the 'Acid Bath': An Evaluation and Critique of Judge Richard Posner's Economic Interpretation of the First Amendment,* 87 MICH. L. REV. 499 (1988-1989); Jed Rubenfeld, *The First Amendment's Purpose,* 53 STAN. L. REV. 767 (2001), and a response by Richard Posner, *Pragmatism Versus Purposivism in First*

Amendment Analysis, 54 STAN. L. REV. 737 (2002), and a response by Jed Rubenfeld, *A Reply to Posner*, 54 STAN. L. REV. 753 (2001-2002); Calvin TerBeek, *Pragmatism in Practice: An Evaluation of Posner's Pragmatic Adjudication in First Amendment and Fourth Amendment Cases*, 48 S. Tex. L. Rev. 471 (Winter 2006), and Richard Posner, *Legal Reasoning from the Top Down and from the Bottom Up: The Question of Unenumerated Constitutional Rights*, 59 U. Chi. L. Rev. 433 (1992). On Posner's views on the press, *See e.g.,* Richard Posner, *Bad News*, N.Y. TIMES, July 31, 2005.

[125] *Branzburg v. Hayes*, 408 U.S. 665 (1972).

[126] *McKevitt* at 531.

[127] Abdon Pallasch, *The Tapes*, MEDILL, Fall/Winter 2003.

[128] Robert C. Herguth, *Mole may have fooled Irish group in Chicago*, CHICAGO SUN-TIMES, Apr. 22, 2001; Abdon M. Pallasch, *Sting that began here snares IRA renegades*, CHICAGO SUN-TIMES, May 12, 2002; Abdon M. Pallasch, *Irish rebel backers gather at Pub*, CHICAGO SUN-TIMES, May 20, 2001.

[129] Pallasch, *supra* note 127.

[130] Transcript of Testimony from "The Special Criminal Court Green Street, Dublin, DPP v. Michael McKevitt," Day 6, June 26, 2003, in original case file, *McKevitt v. Pallasch.*

[131] Brief in Opposition of Abdon M. Pallasch and Flynn McRoberts to Request Pursuant to 28 U.S.C. 1782 For An Order Requiring the Production of Documents and Things for Use in a Proceeding in a Foreign Tribunal, Case No. O3 C 4218 U.S. District Court for Northern District of Illinois, Eastern Division.

[132] Memo of Mark Lundgren, "To: Chicago, From: Chicago," Oct. 10, 2001, in original case file, *McKevitt v. Pallasch.*

[133] Pallasch, *supra* note 127.

[134] Statement of Interest of the United States, June 30, 2003, in original case file, *McKevitt v. Pallasch.*

[135] Pallasch, *supra* note 127.

[136] Order of Judge Richard A. Guzman, July 2, 2003, No. 03 C 4218, in original case file, *McKevitt v. Pallasch.*

[137] *Id.*

[138] *Id.*

[139] Pallasch, *supra* note 127.

[140] *Id.*

[141] *Id.*

[142] *Id.*

[143] *Id.*

[144] *McKevitt* at 531-532.

[145] These are In re Madden, 151 F.3d 125, (3d Cir. 1998); United States v. Smith, 135 F.3d 963, (5th Cir. 1998); Shoen v. Shoen, 5 F.3d 1289, (9th Cir. 1993); In re Shain, 978 F.2d 850, (4th Cir. 1992); United States v. LaRouche Campaign, 841 F.2d 1176, (1st Cir. 1988); von Bulow v. von Bulow, 811 F.2d 136, (2d Cir. 1987); and United States v. Caporale, 806 F.2d 1487, (11th Cir. 1986).

[146] *McKevitt* at 532.

[147] *Id.*

[148] *McKevitt* at 533. *Contra* Desai v. Hersh, 954 F.2d 1408 (7th Cir. 1992).

[149] *McKevitt* at 532.

[150] *Id.*

[151] In re Madden, 151 F.3d 125 (3d Cir. 1998), Shoen v. Shoen, 5 F.3d 1289, (9th Cir. 1993); United States v. LaRouche Campaign, 841 F.2d 1176, (1st Cir. 1988); Gonzales v. National Broadcasting Co., 194 F.3d 29, (2d Cir. 1999); United States v. Burke, 700 F.2d 70, (2d Cir. 1983); United States v. Cuthbertson, 630 F.2d 139 (2d Cir. 1980); *But see* United States v. Smith, 135 F.3d 963 (5th Cir. 1998) and In re Grand Jury Proceedings, 810 F.2d 580 (6th Cir. 1987).

[152] *McKevitt* at 533.

[153] *Id.*

[154] *Id.*

[155] *Id.*

[156] *Id.*

[157] *Id.*

[158] *Id.* at 531.

[159] *Id.* at 535.

[160] Interview with author, Nov. 13, 2007.

[161] *Id.*

[162] *Amicus* brief, *supra* note 122.

[163] *Id.*

[164] *Id.*

---

[165] "Petition of Defendants-Appellants Abdon Pallasch, Robert C. Herguth and Flynn McRoberts for Rehearing En Banc, filed Aug. 22, 2003, Doc # 1654870, No. 03-2753, No. 03-2754.

[166] Order, McKevitt v. Pallasch, 2003 U.S. App. LEXIS 21058 (7th Cir. Oct. 16, 2003).

[167] John Giuffo, *Judging Richard*, COLUMBIA JOURNALISM REVIEW, November/December 2005.

[168] *Id.*

[169] The pre-*McKevitt* district court cases are *Gulliver's Periodicals v. Chas. Levy Circulating Co.*, 455 F. Supp. 1197 (N.D. Ill 1978), *Alexander v. Chicago Park District*, 548 F. Supp. 277 (N.D. Ill. 1982), *U.S. v. Lopez* 1987 WL 26051, 14 Med. L. Rptr. 2203 (N.D. Ill. 1987), *May v. Collins*, 125 F.R.D. 535 (S.D. Ind. 1988), *U.S. v. Bingham*, 765 F. Supp. 954 (N.D. Ill. 1991), *Liebhard v. Square D Company*, 1992 U.S. Dist. LEXIS 11971 (N.D. Ill. 1992), *Neal v. Harvey*, 173 F.R.D. 231 (N.D. Ill. 1997), *Builders Assn of Greater Chicago v. County of Cook*, 1998 WL 111702 (ND Ill 1998), *Warzon v. Drew*, 155 F.R.D. 183 (E.D. Wis. 1994), *Warnell v. Ford Motor Company*, 183 F.R.D. 624 (N.D. Ill. 1998); *U.S. v. Jennings*, 1999 WL 438984 (N.D. Ill. 1999). The appellate cases are *Desai v. Hersh*, 954 F.2d 1408 (7th Cir. 1992) and *U.S. v. Lloyd*, 71 F.3d. 1256 (7th Cir. 1995). A third appellate case, *FMC Corp. v. Capital Cities/ABC Inc.*, 915 F.2d 300 (7th Cir. 1990) briefly discussed the constitutional and state statutory privilege but found both were irrelevant to the facts. The case involved FMC's attempt to require ABC to turn over documents that were missing from its files but did not involve subpoenas for confidential sources.

[170] Gulliver's Periodicals, LTD. v. Chas. Levy Circulating Company, 455 F. Supp. 1197 (N.D. Ill 1978).

[171] Reporter's Privilege, 735 I.L.C.S. 5/8-901 to 909.

[172] Gulliver's Periodicals, 455 F. Supp. at 1202.

[173] *Id.*

[174] *Id.*

[175] *Id.*

[176] *Id.* at 1203.

[177] *See, for example*, Alexander v. Chicago Park District, 548 F. Supp. 277 (N.D. Ill. 1982) (recognizing in the district a qualified privilege from the First Amendment protecting journalists from compelled disclosure of "sources and source material," although the judge ruled against the journalists regarding

first-person observations); U.S. v. Lopez 1987 WL 26051 (N.D. Ill. 1987) (concluding that *Gulliver's* holding was "at least in civil cases, (the privilege) extends to all underlying, unpublished material gathered in preparation for a news story or broadcast regardless of whether the source of the material is confidential … Since *Branzburg*, federal courts have with near uniformity recognized a qualified privilege for the protection of reporters' notes and other source materials.") May v. Collins, 125 F.R.D. 535 (S.D. Ind. 1988) (district judge cited more than a dozen cases finding a qualified privilege, and quashed subpoenas issued to two reporters for testimony about unpublished details related to stories about conditions at a local jail. "This Court acknowledges that compelling testimony of newspaper reporters runs afoul of an important societal interest in protecting the free flow of information to the public," Judge Brooks wrote*)*; Warzon v. Drew, 155 F.R.D. 183 (E.D. Wis. 1994) (a district court discussed privilege precedents in ten other circuits that had found a privilege, and concluded that a qualified privilege protected a *Milwaukee Journal* reporter from testifying in connection to a civil suit filed against the state of Wisconsin by a former state employee). Neal v. Harvey, 173 F.R.D. 231 (N.D. Ill. 1997) (district judge quashed a subpoena to Sylvia Gomez, an investigative reporter with WBBM-TV in Chicago, whose testimony was sought in a civil lawsuit, ruling that "facts acquired by a journalist in the course of newsgathering enjoy a qualified privilege against compelled disclosure"); Builders Assn of Greater Chicago v. County of Cook, 1998 WL 111702 (ND Ill 1998) (district court ruled that a qualified reporter's privilege could be invoked by the Chicago Urban League, whose records were sought in the context of a lawsuit over business contracts for minority owned companies. The Urban League argued that it was an "information gatherer" able to invoke the privilege, and that the documents sought contained sensitive information that was provided by individuals after promises of confidentiality); U.S. v. Jennings, 1999 WL 438984 (N.D. Ill. 1999) (district judge concluded that *Branzburg* does "support some First Amendment protection of the press from harassment to disclose confidential sources" based on the judge's review of case law in other circuits, but the judge declined to expand the protection to non-confidential information. The judge refused to quash the subpoena, noting the absence of any confidential information because the interview was conducted on the record. "(I)n a criminal case, the First Amendment does not protect journalists from disclosure of nonconfidential, relevant information that is sought in good faith").

[178] Only one reported district court decision questioned the existence of a privilege altogether, and that case involved a dispute unrelated to newsgathering. In *NLRB v. Evansville Courier*, a magistrate judge refused to quash a subpoena to a newspaper issued by an administrative agency, which sought to identify who placed a job advertisement that allegedly discriminated against union applicants. NLRB v. Evansville Courier, 937 F.Supp. 804 (S.D. Ind. 1996).

[179] Desai v. Hersh, 954 F.2d 1408 (7th Cir. 1992).

[180] *Id.* at 1410.

[181] *Id.*

[182] U.S. v. Lloyd, 71 F.3d. 1256 (7th Cir. 1995).

[183] *Id.*

[184] Hare v. Zitek, 2006 U.S. Dist. LEXIS 50269 (N.D. Ill. July 24, 2006) (a former police officer suing officials in the Village of Stickney, Ill., for retaliation, sought to stop the defendants from subpoenaing a local reporter to testify about articles she wrote about the case. Citing *McKevitt*, the judge wrote: "(T)he Seventh Circuit has declined to recognize a reporter's privilege. Having said this, the Court is mindful that there are necessarily concerns about forcing a reporter to disclose her sources; it is not something the Court would do lightly." Then, two sentences after saying no privilege exists, the court nonetheless created one by stating that the reporter would only be compelled to testify "if the defendants can establish, via proffer at trial, that they have a real need for the information and that the information is not available from another source"); Solaia Tech. v. Rockwell Automation Inc., 2003 U.S. Dist. LEXIS 20196 (N.D. Ill. Nov. 10, 2003) (district court ordered a magazine to turn over audio tapes of an interview of a person involved in litigation on the grounds that they were not confidential, but ruled that an anonymous letter the magazine received related to the case was "confidential" and therefore protected by a federal common-law privilege. The court said this analysis was consistent with Posner's *McKevitt* decision based on the confidentiality distinction); Hobley v. Burge, 223 F.R.D. 499 (N.D. Ill. 2004) (district court judge dismissed a subpoena for a journalist's notes in the context of a lawsuit brought by Madison Hobley, a Chicago man who allegedly was tortured by police. The subpoena was issued to John Conroy, a reporter for the weekly *Chicago Reader* who had spent more than a decade reporting on allegations of police brutality, coerced confessions and wrongful convictions in Chicago. This, the court noted, was "specifically rejected" in *McKevitt*, at least in the context of non-confidential

information. "The Movants argue that the decision in *McKevitt* was wrongly
decided, and ask the court to look to the reasoning" in *Neal* and *Gulliver's
Periodicals*, which the court declined to do, noting, "the decision in *McKevitt* is
the law in this Circuit, which this court is bound to follow."[184] The judge then
distinguished the facts from *McKevitt*, after extensively summarizing Judge
Posner's ruling, and determined that the key distinction was whether the
material sought was confidential. The court used this framework to analyze
"the interests protected by the First Amendment" to conclude that letters
written by Hobley to Conroy must be turned over to the police officials, but
notes from interviews are protected. The notes would require Conroy to testify
in order to decipher them, "multiplying the burden" put on newsgathering. The
district court quoted from Conroy's affidavit about the possible chilling effects
of becoming an arm of law enforcement, and the inability of future confidential
sources to come forward because of his inability to protect their identities.
"Nothing in *McKevitt* suggests that a reporter's notes are discoverable in civil
litigation simply because the reporter interviewed a party to that litigation."[184]
The subpoena for reporter's notes "is the classic fishing expedition for
something that might be helpful."); Patterson v. Burge, 2005 U.S. Dist. LEXIS
1331 (N.D. Ill. Jan. 5, 2005) (judge said that *McKevitt* had ruled out a common
law privilege, but using the reasonableness standard, the judge quashed the
subpoena. Plaintiff made a "weak showing" of the materiality of the
information sought to the case, there was a "lack of any compelling public
interest in disclosure such as was present in McKevitt," and there was a
"significant burden on important private and public interests compelled
production in this case would involve"); Bond v. Utreras, 2006 U.S. Dist.
LEXIS 46279 (N.D. Ill. June 27, 2006) (writer and blogger named Jamie
Kalven asserted that a subpoena served on him in connection with his reporting
of the alleged abuse would place an undue burden on him as a journalist. "Mr.
Kalven is not relying on any claim of privilege – and wisely so; the Seventh
Circuit has rejected the notion of a federal reporter's privilege," the judge
wrote, citing *McKevitt*. Applying "*McKevitt's* reasonableness standard," the
judge ruled that the defendants in the lawsuit had not established that Kalven
had any information unavailable to them, and limited the subpoena to questions
only about the woman claiming to have been sexually, physically and mentally
abused by police officers, rather than interviews and documents related to 23
other named individuals); United States v. Hale, 2004 U.S. Dist. LEXIS 8905
(N.D. Ind. Apr. 6, 2004 (The only reported district court decision citing

McKevitt that gave a wholly unfavorable outcome to journalists is *U.S. v. Hale.* CNN reporter Jeff Flock filed a motion to quash a subpoena served on him by federal prosecutors, who sought his testimony for a trial of a man Flock interviewed. The prosecutors wanted Flock's testimony about the defendant's demeanor during and after the interview, arguing that the testimony was crucial to their case. The district judge ruled that there was no issue of confidentiality involved, and using the *McKevitt* reasonableness standard, the judge said "the mere fact that Flock is a reporter does not automatically render the subpoena unreasonable." Given that there was no evidence that the government sought Flock's testimony about non confidential information for "any improper purpose," the subpoena was reasonable under the circumstances, the judge ruled.)

[185] In re: Special Proceedings, No. 03-2052 and 04-1383 (1ˢᵗ Cir., June 21, 2004).

[186] *Id.*

[187] *Id.*

[188] *Id.,* referencing Farr v. Pitchess, 522 F.2d 464 (9ᵗʰ Cir. 1975). Justice White, writing for the Branzburg majority, at Branzburg v. Hayes, 408 U.S. 665 at 682.

[189] Lentz v. City of Cleveland, 410 F. Supp. 2d 673 at 701 (N.D. Ohio 2006)

[190] *Id.*

[191] Wen Ho Lee v. DOJ, 368 U.S. App. D.C. 220 at 301 (D.C. Cir. 2005).

[192] In re: Grand Jury Subpoena, Judith Miller, 365 U.S. App. D.C. 13 at 110 (D.C. Cir., Feb. 15, 2005).

[193] New York Times Co. v. Gonzales, 382 F. Supp. 2d 457, (S.D.N.Y. 2005).

[194] *Id.*

[195] New York Times v. Gonzalez, 459 F.3d 160.

[196] Heather Stamp, *McKevitt v. Pallasch: How the Ghosts of the Branzburg Decision Are Haunting Journalists in the Seventh Circuit,* 14 DePaul-LCA J. Art & Ent. L. 363 (Spring 2004).

[197] Erik W. Laursen, *Putting Journalists on Thin Ice: McKevitt v. Pallasch,* 73 U. Cin. L. Rev. 293 (Fall 2004).

[198] Anthony L. Fargo, *The Year of Leaking Dangerously: Shadowy Sources, Jailed Journalists and the Uncertain Future of the Federal Journalist's Privilege,* 14 Wm. & Mary Bill Rts. J. 1063 (2005-2006).

[199] Nikki Scwab, *The Father of the Reporter's Privilege*, U.S. NEWS AND WORLD REPORT, Oct. 25, 2007, *available at* http://www.usnews.com/articles/news/national/2007/10/25/qa-the-father-of-the-reporters-privilege.html?PageNr=2 (last visited July 1, 2009).

[200] Personal interview.

CHAPTER 8

The Future of Journalism Ethics in Journalist's Privilege Law

In 2010, institutions of journalism were in the midst of significant transformation.[1] Declining circulation, decreasing advertising revenue worsened by a severe economic recession, competition from the Web and downsizing all raised profound problems for the sustainability of many newspapers.[2] Between 2001 and 2010, American newspapers shed 25 percent of their newsroom employees, including 13,500 jobs in 2008 and 2009 alone, according to the American Society of News Editors.[3] Boston and San Francisco, two of the country's most vibrant big cities, were said to face the prospect of being no-newspaper towns.[4] As Walter Isaacson, the former chairman and CEO of CNN and managing editor of *Time* magazine, wrote in February 2009, "During the past few months, the crisis in journalism has reached meltdown proportions. It is now possible to contemplate a time when some major cities will no longer have a newspaper and when magazines and network-news operations will employ no more than a handful of reporters."[5]

The "death" of newspapers is matched with the rise of so-called social networking media that largely eliminate the market need for professional moderators of content.[6] Bloggers have proliferated on the Internet, with a wide range of purposes, standards and expertise. On television, serious journalism faces near-extinction by entertainment and partisan-slanted opinion shows whose purpose is to not to inform but rather to persuade and reinforce political ideologies. The traditional journalism platforms of print, radio and television have struggled to remain relevant to audiences, while the Web has become the latest frontier for new forms of information dissemination.[7] The gatekeeper function of the mass media is changing, and traditional journalism is struggling for economic viability in the new media environment. Scott Gant's book about the transformation of press law in the Internet age, provocatively titled, *We're All Journalists Now,* emphasizes the democratic-enhancing possibilities of the elimination of mainstream media's filter on information dissemination.[8] Yet, in reality, we are not all journalists now. The challenge for the field of journalism ethics is to chart the standards and purposes of journalism in this new Internet era that are rooted in the values and standards that have come to define journalism and its social and political functions, at the same time the support system of professionalization is eroded by shrinking audiences, credibility and organizational size.[9]

This chapter argues that some of the modern problems with the journalist's privilege as a legal rule can be resolved by taking into consideration journalism ethical principles and standards, especially in three areas: the nature of qualifications and limits to protection, judicial "public-interest balancing" and qualification of an individual as a journalist for legal protections. If journalism ethics is largely a system of thinking about the idealistic views of journalism's social and political functions, then a sense of the past is important. Journalistic ideals, values, standards and practices have not developed in a vacuum, and the case studies and history of journalist-source relationships discussed in this book have revealed the core journalistic principles at the heart of the source-protection ethic, the range of competing values and interests at play, and the ethical and legal problems that are found in journalistic practices.

Journalism ethical discourse is important to the continued strength of the journalist's privilege as a legal and ethical principle. This concluding chapter synthesizes the relationship between ethics and law in the context of journalist's privilege by discussing different approaches to some of the modern problems and controversies. Issues relating to confidential sources remain ripe controversies in newsrooms and courtrooms, and scholarship can continue to search for solutions. Additionally, working journalists who rely on confidential sources need an understanding of the ethical and legal issues that can arise in practice to make informed decisions and minimize legal vulnerabilities.

This research set out to explore the following questions: (1) How did it come to be that journalists believe they are morally and ethically justified to go to jail to protect the identity of confidential sources? (2) How did this professional duty develop in American journalism? (3) How have journalists' arguments changed over time? and (4) Why is confidential-source protection a continuing problem in journalism practice, ethics, and law?

The central thesis of this book is that journalistic protection of confidential sources has developed as an important ethical norm through the process of professionalization that has occurred in the journalism profession and that the ethical norms have to varying degrees become legal principles in statutory, constitutional and common law. As I've explored in earlier chapters, the roots of the journalist's privilege can be found in the developing journalistic ideology and free-press theory of the colonial era. Printers James Franklin and John Peter Zenger were jailed for their refusal to identify the names of writers and the sources of information in their newspapers, using the language of free-press values in the defense. Franklin in particular spoke of the "liberty" of individuals to anonymously reach the marketplace of ideas through his newspaper and relished being in the position of challenging centers of power, both in government and in religion.[10]

The tradition of source protection as an established professional practice began in earnest in the mid-19th century. Newspapers underwent dramatic changes during this century, generally transforming from organs of political parties at the beginning of the century to independent, commercial, mass-market driven news organizations by the end of the century. The rise of the "penny press" in the 1830s prompted newspapers to adopt independence and impartiality as values, characteristics that would increasingly define journalism. During the course of this transformation, the distinct occupation of "reporter" became increasingly important, and clear professional standards and practices developed. By the end of the 19th century, journalism had its own values that were closely linked to its ideals of serving the public interest by seeking and disseminating news.

It was in this context that journalists first thwarted attempts by the government to learn the identity of news sources. The cases examined in chapter four show that newspaper reporters regularly challenged subpoenas and other requests for confidential source information despite having no basis in law for doing so. It was a matter of professional ethics to defy such requests. As early as 1848, news leaks were viewed as being mutually beneficial to politicians and journalists, and by extension a contribution to the public interest.[11] In 1857, journalists appeared to have developed a professional consensus of source protection when they defended one their competitors as a "lion" for defending the "liberty and independence of the press" in his refusal to provide the identity of a confidential source to a committee of the House of Representatives.[12] Journalists regularly argued that the public interest in protecting news sources was the basis for the professional ethic of rigid source protection. The ethic was canonized in the earliest journalism textbooks, including a 1904 text stating that "never betray a confidence" was a "golden rule" of journalism.[13] In 1940, one of the first press-law textbooks called the journalist's privilege "an old and prideful newspaper tradition."[14]

Chapters five, six and seven explained how journalists in the 20th century have been successful in codifying in law this professional ethic. This occurred in several distinct realms. Journalists have been remarkably successful in codifying the ethic through legislation, at least at the state level. The first state to pass a statute was Maryland, in 1896. (In 2010, Wisconsin and Kansas became the latest states – there are 39 in all – to enact shield legislation.) Often, state legislatures became interested in the privilege after a particular controversy. The jailing of three journalists for the *Washington Times* in 1929 prompted several states to pass legislation protecting journalists, and it also prompted the first congressional consideration of a federal shield law.[15] Chapter six examined in detail the congressional hearings of the 1970s in which legislators attempted to reconcile the public policy disputes following the U.S. Supreme Court's rejection of a First-Amendment based journalists' privilege. The historical research into the congressional debates of the 1970s showed that legislators were convinced of the public interest in the journalist's privilege, despite being unable to reconcile competing proposals. As a matter of constitutional right, the privilege has emerged as a key context for debate over the meaning of the press clause of the First Amendment. Beginning with the 1957 case of *Garland v. Torre*, journalists expressly argued that the First Amendment created a journalist's privilege, based on journalism's functional role as a watchdog of government and in keeping the public informed of news. Chapter five examined why this argument failed to become embraced as a matter of Supreme Court doctrine, although chapter seven showed the journalist's privilege remained a viable matter of positive law in the lower courts.

The historical research supports the hypothesis that journalism ethics and standards can play a role in better understanding, and perhaps finding solutions to, these legal uncertainties. History suggests that the development of professional standards and the ethical discourse surrounding them sparked legal protections in the first place. The public policy arguments that have been successful in obtaining statutory protections draw from utilitarian justifications for journalism and its importance to democratic values. And when journalists challenge and occasionally violate court orders, they justify their civil disobedience as rooted in journalism and free-press principles.

Articulating the public interest in using confidential sources should remain an important component in journalism ethics discourse. Key questions debated in legal analysis are directly influenced by ethical issues: What are the purposes of confidentiality, and how do journalists evaluate its limits? What does a promise of confidentiality require of journalists and their employers?   What is expected of journalists, as a matter of professional ethics, when the law compels them to provide testimony? Are all confidential source promises the same, or should journalists make distinctions based on the content of the leaked material or the motives of leakers? Should journalists be more willing to break promises if the leak itself was a potential crime? How should journalists balance the potential legal vulnerabilities with the duty to publish important stories?

Any type of privilege should strongly protect journalists' use of confidential sources where the disclosure can be justified in public interest and utilitarian terms, and should only be able to be overcome in cases where the government has an overwhelmingly compelling interest in the information. This is rooted in ethical principles as well. An absolutist privilege has never been a tenet of the ethical doctrine, and the next section highlights a recent example that demonstrates that journalists sometimes do break promises of confidentiality for particularly compelling reasons.

Still, privilege law that comports with ethical principles needs to recognize the general public interest in the privilege principle and protect some abuses. The federal shield statute passed by the House of Representatives in the 110th and 111th Congresses, as well as Judge

Tatel's common-law proposal in the Miller case, are two strong models of a qualified privilege.

The central components of a model qualified privilege need to set high burdens on the government or plaintiffs seeking a journalist's sources, similar to Justice Stewart's three-prong test in *Branzburg*. The compromise statute that emerged from Rep. Robert Kastenmeier's hearings in 1975 refined these prongs as follows. A journalist could be compelled to reveal the information if: "(A) that disclosure of such identity or information is indispensable to the establishment of the offense charged, the cause of the action pleaded, or the defense interposed in such action; (B) that such identity or information cannot be obtained by alternative means; and (C) that there is compelling and overriding public interest in requiring disclosure of the identity or the information."[16]

Thirty-five years later, the Congressional bills adopted similar three-part tests requiring certain threshold burdens be met, and then adding an additional layer of analysis that would require a judge to balance "the public interest" in compelled disclosure against the "public interest in gathering or disseminating news or information." Under the proposed federal statute, the balancing would occur in cases in which a confidential source's identity was sought, and could only be compelled in cases involving terrorism, to prevent imminent death or significant bodily harm, to identity someone had disclosed a trade secret, personally identifiable health information, or "nonpublic personal information" or to identity a leaker of information that "has caused or will cause significant and articulable harm to the national security."[17] While some categories are troublingly broad, such as "nonpublic personal information" and "terrorism," the inclusion of the public-interest balancing, which will be discussed further below, allows journalists another layer of defense.

A law needs to include a functional definition of who is a journalist to prohibit the law from protecting only "official" journalists employed by news organizations. I offer a "comprehensive functional analysis" later in this chapter that provides a solution for the definitional problem.

PASSING A FEDERAL SHIELD LAW

More than 80 years ago, three Washington, D.C. journalists published a piece of undercover reporting that shined light on 49 speakeasies that were thriving in the capital city under the noses of politicians and the police. For upholding their professional code of ethics despite the fact that the law was not on their side, the journalists' publisher, William Randolph Hearst, doubled the reporters' salaries, bought each a gold watch, and held a public reception in their honor. Today, journalists don't usually get the same treatment. As part one of this book documented, journalists in recent time have faced more subpoenas and more aggressive legal tactics to get them to comply, while cash-strapped news organizations have paid millions in legal fees defending First Amendment values. After the actual jailing of the *New York Times'* Judith Miller, Rhode Island television reporter James Taricani, and San Francisco blogger Josh Wolf, and after the threatened jailings of several others, including the *San Francisco Chronicle's* Mark Fainaru-Wada and Lance Williams, Congress once again attempted to pass a federal shield law.

In early 2010, the 111th Congress appeared poised to pass journalist's shield law legislation after the House of Representatives passed the Free Flow of Information Act.[18] The bill was identical to the bill passed by the House in 2008 on a vote of 389-21.[19] That bill, H.R. 2102, failed to become law in the 110th Congress after it died in the Senate without a vote and was under threat of a veto by President George W. Bush.[20] Journalists had been optimistic when the 111th Congress convened in 2009. The bill's loudest supporters also ranged the political spectrum, from conservative Republican Mike Pence of Indiana in the House to liberal Democrat Charles Schumer of New York. Shield bill supporters for the first time had a Department of Justice and a president who were on record supporting a shield law – removing a significant impediment that was in place in both the 1970s and the 2005-08 debates.[21] In both of those periods of legislative debate on a shield bill, Justice Department lawyers opposed legislation and raised both reasonable and hyperbolic claims about the consequences of giving journalists a qualified privilege to avoid subpoenas for newsgathering information.

The election of President Barack Obama provided shield law advocates a unique opportunity to press their case in the 111th

Congress without executive-branch opposition.[22] The stars appeared to align for journalists when the House overwhelmingly passed the Free Flow of Information Act, and for the first time a White House and Justice Department were on record in support. However, a handful of senators balked over a number of provisions in the House bill and its Senate counterpart and worked to hammer out compromises. The compromises in the summer of 2010 centered on the creation of a "terrorism" exception and in the language of who qualifies as a journalist for protection. Wikileaks' disclosure of 75,000 classified documents related to the Afghanistan war prompted a number of senators to revise the bill, and include a record of legislative history to show their intent to explicitly exclude Wikileaks from protection. "Wikileaks should not be spared in any way from the fullest prosecution possible under the law," said New York Sen. Chuck Schumer, a leading sponsor of the bill. "Our bill already includes safeguards when a leak impacts national security, and it would never grant protection to a website like this one, but we will take this extra step to remove even a scintilla of doubt."[23]

Who qualifies for the privilege was one of the primary points of debate. An analysis of congressional bills shows that the definitional provisions have generally narrowed over time. The first bills were problematically broad, which contributed to concerns that almost anyone could qualify for protection. For example, a leading House bill in 2005 defined a covered person as "any entity that disseminates information by print, broadcast, cable, mechanical, photography, electronic or other means."[24] Revised bills continued to narrow the definitional provision. Senator Richard Lugar, R-Ind., a leading author of a Senate bill, saying bloggers will "probably not" be deemed journalists under the law and Senator John Cornyn, R-Tex., as saying, "The relative anonymity afforded to bloggers, coupled with a certain lack of accountability, as they are not your traditional brick-and-mortar reporters who answer to an editor or publisher, also has the risk of creating a certain irresponsibility when it comes to accurately reporting information."[25]

By 2007, bills were limited to an individual "engaged in journalism … who regularly gathers … or publishes news … for a substantial portion of the person's livelihood or for substantial financial gain."[26] The provisions that a blogger must regularly engage in newsgathering for livelihood or financial gain are aimed to address concerns of accountability and oversight – or put another way, to require the maintenance of basic journalistic ethics and values that generally come from being accountable to editors, readers, or advertisers. As a matter of securing enough votes among lawmakers who worry about overly broad definitions, this hybrid functional/status test emerged in the 110th Congress as the best compromise.

Yet another compromise centered on whether journalists should be able to argue that the "public interest" in their uses of confidential sources should be considered by judges in a balancing test. Allowing journalists facing jail sentences and stiff fines to argue in court that their news reporting and uses of confidential sources were in the public interest is a common-sense compromise between journalists who wanted absolutist protections and lawmakers rightly concerned about unusual cases and potential abuses. Neither side was particularly thrilled with the compromises. The behind-the-scenes compromises failed to produce a vote, however, and the federal shield bill once again died without passage when the 111th Congress adjourned.

With a federal shield law dead once again, the increasingly disparate rulings among federal circuits cry out for a resolution in the common law. As chapter seven showed, federal appellate courts are increasingly in disagreement about the scope of a federal privilege, and several circuits have recently overturned precedents in their respective circuits. The proper scope of the judicially created privilege in federal law remains contested, and this cries out for resolution.

ABSOLUTISM AND BALANCING IN ETHICS AND LAW

Historically, and perhaps understandably, the journalism profession has sought the most expansive legal protections available for confidential source protection while also recognizing the limitations of absolutism as a matter of ethics. A law affording journalists absolutist protections for confidential sources was sought in the 1970s congressional hearings, for example, while journalists could readily agree on extreme hypothetical cases in which they would feel compelled as a matter of ethics to break a promise of confidentiality. However, in the realm of ethical discourse, the privilege has never been conceived as absolute; journalists are largely in agreement that in some contexts, disclosure of confidential information is required as an ethical matter.

One recent example involves a case in which a journalist broke a promise of confidentiality to provide critical information that spared a potentially innocent man from a life prison sentence.

After listening to the opening statements during a criminal trial in which a former FBI agent was charged with four murders, reporter Tom Robbins of New York City's *Village Voice* was stunned.[27] The prosecution's case in the 2007 trial was almost entirely based on the testimony of Linda Schiro, the girlfriend of a legendary mobster who placed the FBI agent, Lin DeVecchio, in the middle of several mob-orchestrated homicides.[28] But during several tape-recorded interviews with Robbins and another journalist a decade earlier, Schiro told a very different story – consistently and repeatedly saying that DeVecchio was not involved in the activities about which she was now testifying.[29] She granted the interviews to Robbins and his reporting partner, Jerry Capeci, for a potential book, and the journalists signed a document promising to keep the information confidential prior to the book's publication. Nothing had come from the book proposal, and years later, after the opening statements in the DeVecchio murder case, Robbins dug out a box of materials from the failed book project stored in the back of a closet in his New York apartment. The journalist listened to the tapes and concluded "either she lied back then or she was lying on the stand. Both stories can't be true."[30] He knew that making the tapes public could very well save DeVecchio from a lifetime prison sentence.

The same information was also presumably in the hands of Capeci, described as the nation's foremost journalistic expert on the American mafia, when early on in the murder investigation, DeVecchio's attorneys issued a subpoena to Capeci for his notes and records related to his mob reporting.[31] Because of a state statute in New York affording journalists strong protections from revealing confidential information, a state judge tossed out the subpoena.[32] Now, Robbins and Capeci faced the bizarre situation of being legally justified in keeping their notes and recordings secret, and perhaps even legally required to do so under the *Cohen v. Cowles Media* precedent, but ethically torn over whether to make them public.[33]

What, and to whom, was Robbins' duty? Was it ultimately to his source, to whom his promise was explicit and in writing? Was it to the criminal justice system that was pursuing truth and justice? Was it to DeVecchio, a man whose livelihood and freedom was at stake?

Robbins decided he was ethically compelled to come forward and provide the tapes to the court.

Consider these questions through the ethical decision-making framework advanced by Professor Edmund B. Lambeth and discussed in chapter one. In *Committed Journalism: An Ethic for the Profession*, Lambeth proposed five guidelines for decision-making. They are: (1) identify the principle or principles and the probable consequences considered and how they are weighted in reaching a decision; (2) assess the stakes of the parties affected by ethical choice: sources, public, the journalists involved, peers, and the profession at large; (3) minimize the chance that choices are based on mere personal impression, style, or whim; (4) show, in cases of conflicting principles or ambiguous forecasts of consequences, what values guide ethical choice; and (5) create, in truly major cases, a record on which others can draw and reflect, so as to make the benefits of dialogue cumulative.[34]

When Tom Robbins broke his promise to his source by making his audiotapes public, resulting in the dismissal of the murder charges, Robbins prioritized his duty to truth and justice over keeping a promise. He talked with lawyers and journalist colleagues and settled on three primary justifications for providing the tapes to the prosecution and defense. First, he believed that after Schiro testified for the prosecution, her reasons for seeking confidentiality from Robbins a decade earlier were no longer controlling. Robbins said:

> I struggled with the idea of what do I owe her personally? Whatever I might have owed her, when she decided to become a public witness about the same events, I think they cancel each other out. If I was to come forward with something that she wasn't talking about publicly, that would be different.[35]

Robbins' second justification focused on the question of truth. He believed that his duty to keep a promise was somewhat mitigated by the fact that Schiro had either lied to him or lied in a public trial. The unstated compact between journalist and confidential source is that the information being passed along is true. A source who knowingly passes along false information is violating the ground rules, Robbins believed. The third consideration involved the high stakes involved. If Robbins remained silent and DeVecchio was convicted, Robbins would have been a participant in sending a potentially innocent man to jail for life.

"Lin DeVecchio is not a friend of mine. I owe him nothing personally," Robbins said in an interview. "If you ask me if I particularly like him I wouldn't know. Sitting in court I asked myself, am I going to put myself in a world of shit for this guy? But I didn't think I had much of a choice. If it had not been a murder case, maybe I wouldn't have done it. I don't know."[36] But, as he explained in a news story recounting the case, "Those are the kind of high stakes that take precedence over contracts and vows of confidence, no matter how important they may be to the business of reporting, and regardless of how distasteful it may be to violate them. The threat of a life sentence trumps a promise."[37]

An absolutist view of journalistic duty to protect sources in the Robbins case would yield a result in which the truth remained obscured, and justice would have been seriously perverted. In determining the "right" action, Robbins thought deeply about the functions of a journalist, the nature of promises, the motives of his source, and the implications of his silence.

Of course, one of the problems with reliance on ethical decision-making is the "fuzziness" of it all. Special Prosecutor Patrick Fitzgerald argued that the interests of truth and justice were perverted by Judith Miller and Matt Cooper's refusal to provide testimony about whether top officials in the administration of George W. Bush violated the law in intentionally leaking the name of a CIA agent in an attempt to discredit a critic of the administration's rationale for invading Iraq.[38] From Valerie Plame's perspective, the journalists were thwarting the interests of truth and justice by protecting the leakers' identities. In Robbins' case, the law allowed him to keep quiet but his sense of ethics required him to talk. In the Plame case, ethical claims led journalists to keep quiet, while the law mandated they talk.

The Robbins and Plame cases are extreme cases that show the problems with absolutist views of the privilege in ethics and law. They suggest that inherent in many privilege cases is a balancing of interests focusing on the public utility of journalism and confidential sources on the one hand, and the seriousness and centrality of the information to values of truth and justice on the other hand. The principle of source protection itself is an important value in itself. But the balancing for Robbins tipped toward disclosure because of the high stakes of a man facing a life prison sentence; in the Plame case, it was unclear whether the leak was an actual crime, allowing journalists to conclude that the interests of justice were important but not compelling enough to tip the scale. Determining where to draw the line – in ethics and in law – is complicated and inevitably imprecise.

Most journalists would sympathize with Tom Robbins' predicament, and can also agree with hypothetical cases in which they would reveal a confidential source. The research of the previous four chapters reveals a key normative question raised in cases where journalists' sources are sought: Who should decide when a journalist must reveal a confidential source? Reporters? Editors? Sources? Judges? Prosecutors? Grand juries? Each category of individuals assess the balancing differently, and thus it matters significantly who ultimately makes the decisions. As a legal rule, both judicial and statutory rules have generally reserved the court system's right to compel disclosure in situations where the interests of justice are significantly undermined by the journalist's refusal to cooperate. In both the ethical and legal realms, the competing interests are often framed as dueling public interests.

Not all leaks are the same. Journalists often make decisions about when to withhold particularly harmful or damaging information in a story. They are at their strongest when the disclosures can be justified as serving the public's interest.

DEFINING THE PUBLIC INTEREST

Historically, journalists have justified their need to protect confidential sources as a matter of public interest. Even in the earliest cases from the 19th century, journalists defended their uses of confidential sources as ultimately benefiting the public through the dissemination of information that otherwise would remain secret. Most articulations of the journalist's privilege principle are rooted in some conceptions of the public good. As a general proposition, the journalist's privilege enhances public debate by allowing journalists to reveal news and information to the public that otherwise would remain secret. The checking value and public-information theories of the First Amendment embrace this public-interest rationale. The *Branzburg* decision did consider the public interests in confidential sources as part of the balancing of the interests of the press and the interests of the judicial system. The Justice Department's own internal guidelines require prosecutors to "strike the proper balance between the public's interest in the free dissemination of ideas and information and the public's interest in effective law enforcement and the fair administration of justice."[39]

But the "public interest" has also just recently emerged as a central component in modern legal solutions, and these proposals for public-interest balancing will inevitably make journalism ethics and standards a more predominant feature in legal analysis.

Journalist shield legislation introduced in the past several Congressional sessions included a prong that requires an assessment of the "public interest." The House bill added an additional prong for determining when the qualified privilege can be overcome, requiring that the "public interest in compelling disclosure of the information involved outweighs the public interest in gathering or disseminating news and information."[40] The Senate bill added as an additional prong a judge's determination that "nondisclosure of the information would be contrary to the public interest, taking into account both the public interest in compelling disclosure and the public interest in gathering news and maintaining the free flow of information."[41]

The common-law proposal advanced by Judge David Tatel of the District of Columbia Circuit Court of Appeals also hinged on the public interest. In the Judith Miller case, Tatel argued that the framework for common-law privileges established by the *Jaffee v. Redmond* decision supported a common-law privilege for journalists.[42] Tatel argued "the court must weigh the public interest in compelling disclosure, measured by the harm the leak caused, against the public interest in newsgathering, measured by the leaked information's value."[43] In balancing the interests in the Plame case, Tatel concluded that the leak of Plame's identity had "marginal" and "slight" news value, and caused significant damage. Tatel argued that the vagueness of such balancing – whether the leak was more harmful than newsworthy – is not unmanageable for judges, who are often called upon to assess competing interests.[44]

The idea of the "public interest" standard places concepts of journalism ethics squarely into legal resolutions. Of course, deciding what is in the public interest is very much in the eye of the beholder, and because the public interest standard has just recently become an explicit element of legal analysis, few proposals exist that offer concrete guidance. One proposal advanced in a 2009 law review article in the *Columbia Law Review* concludes that judges should afford "more or less weight" to the public interest in protecting confidential sources based on the "extent to which a journalist's use of a confidential source adhered to procedural guidelines."[45] The proposal by David Abramowicz argued that adherence to "professional procedural ideals" should be used to assess the newsworthiness interests in the public-interest balancing in individual cases. Abramowicz argued that focusing on procedural analysis rather than substantive claims would provide more predictable outcomes, and therefore this approach can be contrasted with Judge Tatel's proposal that examines the newsworthiness of the leaked information and its potential harm. Under Abramowicz's proposal, a journalist's commitment to verifying information, deliberating with editors, and explaining to readers the reasons for confidential-source promises would weigh in the journalist's favor in legal cases.[46]

Under the Tatel and Abramowicz's proposals, the functions and principles of journalism are central components to legal solutions, although neither explicitly acknowledge the role that journalism ethics discourse is at play. As the public interest standard becomes more relevant in legal circles, journalism ethics can play a stronger role in providing solutions. Journalists will continue to have to justify their uses of confidential sources as being in the public interest, as a matter of professional practice and as a matter of law.

How might this work? A focus on the adherence to procedural guidelines supports an approach that finds a generalized public interest in confidential source protection as enhancing the free flow of information to the public. A substantive analysis that focuses on the nature of the specific leak or the news disclosure is another possibility. Here, judges may assess whether journalists are protecting a vulnerable whistleblower from retribution or are protecting a powerful leaker from accountability. A judge's assessment may also turn on the public value of the disclosure. Here, it may be that the disclosure of Valerie Plame's identity was of limited or no value, while the disclosure of the Bush administration's domestic spying program had significant public value because it disclosed potential violations of law. Legal arguments about public interest may be supported by affidavits articulating public good from the disclosures, such as Sen. Arlen Specter's praise of the newspapers domestic-spying stories in checking the power of the executive branch better than Congress. Another example is in the course of their fight to avoid revealing confidential sources, the *San Francisco Chronicle* reporters covering the baseball steroids scandal obtained affidavits from parents of kids who used steroids as explaining why it was important for a newspaper to publicize the steroid use of professional athletes as a way to shame Major League Baseball into getting serious about eliminating steroid use.[47]

JOURNALISM ETHICS AND THE BLOGOSPHERE

A second modern legal problem could also seek solution in the realm of journalism ethics discourse. The question of who is a journalist for the purpose of privilege protection is one of the most perplexing problems in the common law, constitutional and public policy debates over a journalist's privilege. Journalism ethics and professional standards are appealing in providing guidance to this legal problem.

Since *Branzburg* in 1972, academics, lawyers, judges, journalists, and members of Congress have struggled to articulate the best definition of "journalist" for purposes of the journalist's privilege.[48] Historically, newspaper reporters have been the most likely candidates to invoke the privilege, although judges and lawmakers have long recognized that a journalist's privilege should apply to television and radio reporters, investigative book authors, and established freelance journalists, among others.[49] Some scholars and judges, beginning with Justice Byron White writing for the *Branzburg* majority, have argued that the difficulties with defining journalists render the entire concept of a journalist's privilege suspect, and the growth of blogs has exacerbated these concerns. If Josh Wolf can be considered a journalist, couldn't anybody?[50] In *Branzburg,* Justice White noted that defining who qualifies for protection "would present practical and conceptual difficulties of a high order."[51] Appellate Judge David Sentelle emphasized the practical and theoretical definitional problems with the privilege in rejecting Judith Miller's First Amendment claim, suggesting no distinction could be drawn between professional journalists and the "stereotypical 'blogger' sitting in his pajamas at his personal computer."[52] During the 2007 and 2008 debates over a statutory privilege, the Justice Department argued that "(d)efining who is entitled to invoke a 'reporter's privilege' is a very difficult, if not intractable, problem," and predicted "bloggers and MySpace users" would flood the courts with journalistic claims to avoid subpoenas if Congress passed a law.[53] In recent debates over drafting a shield bill, several lawmakers expressed worry about the lack of accountability for bloggers, something that ostensibly exists for "mainstream" journalists who must be accountable to editors and executives of news organizations.[54] And Randall D. Eliason, a former federal prosecutor, has argued that "rapid technological changes in both the nature and quantity of information regularly made available to the public suggest that a reporter's privilege may soon have to be considered a relic of a simpler era – a relic that now is neither workable or necessary."[55]

Federal and state case law documents a long legal history of journalists' privilege claims by non-traditional journalists and suggests that the emergence of bloggers-as-journalists does not present a wholly new legal question.[56] Definitional problems should also not render the privilege doctrine unworkable. As First Amendment attorney Floyd Abrams argued in 1978 as several newsgathering-rights claims were being evaluated by scholars and judges:

> (I)t is difficult to comprehend why the difficulties in defining "press" should lead to the conclusion that no uniquely 'press' protections may be afforded. Nor are the definitional difficulties insurmountable ... (I)t is simply unacceptable to say that because a word in the Constitution is difficult to define, it should be afforded no meaning at all.[57]

Still, the cataclysmic changes to journalism and information dissemination brought by the Internet make it likely that bloggers will increasingly challenge both federal and state privilege interpretations. Because of worries expressed by both judges and scholars that bloggers may present intractable problems to the privilege, a coherent theoretical framework would be beneficial to the preservation of the privilege. A framework for resolving definitional questions is also relevant to public policy debates that are likely to continue in Congress,[58] as well as states that might enact statutes or revise current ones.

Several scholars have articulated characteristics that make journalism distinct from other forms of communication. One of the best is Bill Kovach and Tom Rosenstiel's *Elements of Journalism: What Newspeople Should Know and The Public Should Expect:*

> Perhaps, some suggest, the definition of journalism has been exploded by technology, so now anything is seen as journalism. But on closer examination ... the purpose of

journalism is not defined by technology, or by journalists or
the techniques they employ … (T)he principles and purposes
of journalism are defined by something more basic – the
function news plays in the lives of people.

For all that the face of journalism has changed, indeed, its
purpose has remained remarkably constant, if not always well
served, since the notion of "a press" first evolved more than
three hundred years ago. And for all that the speed,
techniques, and character of news delivery have changed,
there already exists a clear theory and philosophy of
journalism that flows out of the function of news. The primary
purpose of journalism is to provide citizens with the
information they need to be free and self-governing.[59]

Thus, the starting point for a definition of "journalist" for purposes
of legal protections should be a focus on the underlying rationale for
free press protections in the first place. Individuals who serve the
public-information and checking-value functions of the traditional
press, evidenced by their *purposes*, *process* and *product*, should be
afforded membership into the club that is "the press" when it comes to
evaluating access to special press rights generally and the journalist's
privilege specifically. Some people may be more "press" than others,
and as with any legal definitions, judges will invariably be confronted
with difficult cases. But the press should be defined, for purposes of a
journalist's privilege, by analyzing the purposes, process and product of
anyone seeking press protections.

This "comprehensive functional analysis" builds on the judicial
tests articulated in the federal case law that can be contrasted with
many of the "status" tests found in by state statutes. Status tests, such
as affiliation with newspapers or broadcast news organizations, may be
attractive for their clarity by providing a first tier of qualification, but
they are relics of an earlier era. Many of them do not account for the
dramatic technological developments that have transformed
journalism's delivery. The effects of the comprehensive functional
analysis should leave intact the privilege for journalists who need it
most while necessarily extending the privilege to others in cases where
rationales for the privilege is indistinguishable from cases involving
traditional journalists.

The comprehensive functional analysis draws from the common-law development of the journalist's privilege and emphasizes consideration of three factors that provide guidance to determine when an individual should qualify for a journalist's privilege:

Purpose. Individuals seeking to invoke a journalist's privilege must be able to demonstrate they intended at the beginning of any newsgathering process to disseminate their findings to a public audience. Their purpose must be related to the public-information or checking-value functions that underlie the philosophical rationales of a free press. Evidence of intention to disseminate could include statements to others, contracts with traditional news organizations or track records of publication.

Process. Individuals must be regularly engaged in traditional newsgathering behavior, perhaps best defined as a search for "journalistic truth." As Professor Thomas Goldstein noted in his brief in the Apple-bloggers case, journalists "gather, sift, analyze, verify, prepare and present information to an audience."[60] The process involves collecting "unorganized and fragmented bits of data, information and observation."[61] The process of newsgathering also involves the exercise and deliberation of editorial judgment, defined by Professor Randall Bezanson as a process of judgment that is "independent, audience oriented, and grounded in a reasoned effort to publish information (typically current or currently relevant) judged useful and important for the maintenance of freedom in a self-governing society."[62]

Product. The product of communication must be important to a public audience and the content at issue must be news, broadly defined as being in the public interest or provoking debate about public issues.[63] Because the privilege is rooted in the press's roles as public informers or watchdogs, the content must be factual in nature. Matters of fiction or pure entertainment would not qualify, as they are characteristics that separate journalists from other content producers.[64] This is consistent with several cases in which courts granted the privilege to non-traditional journalists based on the newsworthiness of the information.[65] Also, readers should be able to evaluate the credibility of the final product.

The body of judicial decisions examining the definitional question, and on which this comprehensive functional analysis is based, suggests that the adherence to journalism ethics is an important component of the calculus as to whether an individual is entitled to invoke the privilege. In case after case in which courts are presented with the definitional question, judges have implicitly examined the purposes, practices and product of individuals seeking journalistic protection and have extended protection to individuals whose principles and practices were similar to traditional notions of newsgathering. They have not explicitly framed their analysis in terms of ethical decision-making, but their rules invite consideration of journalism ethics as one component to constructing the boundaries of who qualifies for protection.[66]

In viewing the definitional question through a framework of journalism ethics, some bloggers and "citizen journalists" who practice journalism in a new medium are clearly deserving of protection, but other online publishers whose practices and purposes are not fundamentally journalistic in nature do not deserve protection. This is consistent with the both the legislative intent, at least in terms of Congressional history, and the policy goals of the common law.

In deciding whether an individual is producing "journalism," it is relevant to ask whether they are in fact "journalists," broadly speaking. Education, training, associations, and values are all relevant, if not determinative. But also critical to the analysis is a discussion of ethical standards, journalistic values and accountability. These have been implicit in decades of case law discussed in the previous chapter. For example, Mark Madden, the professional wrestling commentator, was excluded from protection in part because he lacked independence from his sources, he was not committed to the pursuit of truth, and there was no transparency in his interactions with his bosses who supplied him with the material. Andrea Reynolds, likewise, was not allowed to invoke the privilege in part because of her personal connections with the individuals, and because she did not have an intent at the outset of her process to publish the information she gathered.

The case law discussed in the previous chapter also shows that journalism ethics and values have been relevant to judicial decision-making, albeit implicitly. In rejecting Madden's claims, for example, the Third Circuit Court of Appeals emphasized Madden's failure to be ethically bound by traditional newsgathering conventions and a pursuit of the truth. In rejecting Andrea Reynolds' claims, the Second Circuit Court of Appeals emphasized her personal relationships with the principal actors and her lack of intent to publicly disseminate as important factors. On the other hand, judges extending the privilege to non-traditional journalists have emphasized an individual's mission of disseminating news in the public interest, the importance of investigative reporting and seeking facts, the significance of editorial judgment and independence, and the value in "activities traditionally associated with the gathering and dissemination of news."[67]

Certainly, there are problems with suggesting that journalism ethical canons should dictate legal protection.[68] But the legal tests emerging in common law and the values embraced by different statutory definitions suggest that standards of journalism have long been relevant in determining when bloggers may invoke a journalist's privilege, and one cannot separate definitions of journalism from conceptions of appropriate journalistic standards. Bloggers who toil in the realm of advertising, politics, entertainment, or public relations or who gather information for personal reasons would not be able to claim the privilege without demonstrating that their purposes, processes and product are "traditionally inherent to the press" – the sum of the tests articulated in *von Bulow*, *Shoen,* and *Madden.*

The comprehensive functional analysis outlined here builds on the work of several scholars who have supported and developed functional tests to the definitional question. Generally, these proposals support the proposition that individuals serving a "press function" are deserving of protection. For the most part, these scholars' proposals are simply restatements or distillations of the federal common law doctrine. They claim to extend the privilege to bloggers who practice traditional journalism in a new medium, but have barriers so not every Internet writer can claim privilege protection.

Professor Laurence B. Alexander uses the federal case law to develop a model statutory definition essentially embracing the three-part test from *von Bulow*, *Shoen* and *Madden.*[69] Alexander's model statute defines "journalist" as "any person who is engaged in gathering news for public presentation or dissemination by the news media" and defines "news media" as "newspapers, magazines, television and radio stations, online news services, or any other regularly published news outlet used for the public dissemination of news."[70] Similarly, attorney Kraig L. Baker argues that the *von Bulow* test is sufficient guidance to the definitional problem, and suggests that difficult cases may be resolved not by excluding questionable claimants from protection but by the subsequent analysis over the qualified nature of the privilege.[71] In analyzing whether the burden has been met to overcome the qualified privilege, Baker argues that judges analyze the "public concern" of the material, in part based on the nature of the claimant.[72] He argues that matters of entertainment, hobby, sport, or advertisement are not matters of public concern and therefore would not be protected by the qualified privilege.

Scholars taking a broader approach include Professor Linda L. Berger, who emphasizes that the privilege should protect "the work process of journalism" and identifies the "key components of the process of journalism," such as the reporter's past record of publication, the presence of internal verification measures, and the availability of information from which readers can judge the independence of the reporter or publisher.[73] Stephanie J. Frazee criticizes Berger's emphasis on past track records and instead focuses on the "effects" of the underlying speech that provoked the privilege claim, arguing that the privilege should be extended to a speaker "if information enhances freedom of individual opinions and beliefs and contributes to the free flow of opinion and reporting."[74]

Other scholars have offered proposals running the spectrum of protection. Provocatively, Professor Mary-Rose Papandrea proposes eliminating the concept of "reporter" from the journalist's privilege and argues that anyone who communicates publicly, regardless of function or status, has a qualified privilege from subpoenas seeking information about sources of information. She argues that to "continue to limit the reporter's privilege to traditional media outlets and professional journalists would unrealistically ignore how the public obtains its information today."[75] Daniel Swartwout critiques the implications of the outcome of the *Madden* case and argues that it invites judges to make legal decisions on the basis of content, which he argues is unconstitutional.[76] And Professor Clay Calvert has argued that in an age of media consolidation and the mixing of entertainment and news, the *Madden* test could prove impossibly ambiguous given the changing standards of news and entertainment.[77]

How might the comprehensive functional analysis apply in recent blogger cases? In the most significant judicial analysis to date on the blogger-as-journalist question, the California Court of Appeals in May 2006 conducted a functional analysis in determining that the bloggers reporting on Apple products were entitled to privilege protection under California's shield law, overruling a lower court's decision. The court framed the question as whether the blogs were functional equivalents of newspapers or broadcast news organizations. The court found no distinctions in the purpose, process, or product prongs between the bloggers and traditional trade publications. Among the criteria used was a commitment to accuracy, editorial oversight, transparency, authority, readership, intent, and past publication record:

> (W)e can see no sustainable basis to distinguish petitioners from the reporters, editors, and publishers who provide news to the public through traditional print and broadcast media. It is established without contradiction that they gather, select, and prepare, for purposes of publication to a mass audience, information about current events of interest and concern to that audience ... If their activities and social function differ at all from those of traditional print and broadcast journalists, the distinctions are minute, subtle, and constitutionally immaterial.[78]

The Josh Wolf case presented a more difficult set of facts, and his claim to be a journalist split the journalism community. While the Reporters Committee for Freedom of the Press paid part of Wolf's legal bills, Debra Saunders, a columnist for the *San Francisco Chronicle*, wrote, "I do not understand why newspapers – including *The Chronicle* – refer to him as the 'longest-imprisoned journalist in America ... (A) camera and a Web site do not a journalist make, any more than shooting a criminal makes a vigilante a cop."[79]

Applying the purpose, process and product tests to Josh Wolf's case, one can see that judgments need to be made that raise issues of journalistic ethics, norms and practices. Wolf's stated purpose in attending the protest was to "document and cover a demonstration that would have been neglected by the mainstream press" and post it on his blog, where he wrote commentary at least weekly and posted videos about once a month.[80] His intention to disseminate information to the public, before he started videotaping, distinguishes him to some degree from the individual who just happens to videotape an event that turns out to have news value.

Wolf's processes and product, however, make it less obvious that he was behaving as a traditional journalist. Wolf described himself on his blog as an "artist, an activist, an anarchist and an archivist" and was something of a participant-observer in the local anarchist movement.

To evaluate whether an individual's processes and product are the same as traditional journalists, courts have used prior work and work habits as a guide.[81] They have evaluated whether an individual was a participant in activities or if he "involved in activities traditionally associated with the gathering and disseminating of news."[82] One appeals court specifically used notions of "investigative reporting" as the standard. [83] Wolf's process could hardly be characterized as being similar to a detached investigative reporter. The most analogous case might be *In re Jeffrey Steinberg,* the case in which an appeals court rejected the claim by a political operative that his journals were protected from disclosure. The court simply determined that journaling was not a "journalistic endeavor."[84] On the other hand, if Wolf made a showing that his regular reporting on the local anarchist community was followed by a reader base and that he had established himself as a regular chronicler of events, the scales arguably tip in his favor.

The Wolf case also suggests that the definitional questions, while important, are not determinative. Wolf's subpoena was for non-confidential information and from a federal grand jury – two facts that make his claim more difficult to win regardless of whether he was a journalist or not. In fact, the legal system's treatment of his case – in ruling that even if Wolf was considered a journalist the qualified privilege had been overcome – shows that the definitional question, while important, is not the end of the inquiry. In fact, the Wolf case is a clear example of why blogger claims can be adequately handled by the legal system and do not present insurmountable problems to the future of the privilege.

CONCLUSION

The ethical and legal spheres of the journalist's privilege have developed to support and control an important journalism practice. This chapter has argued that the historical development of the journalist's privilege in practice supports the use of ethical principles to inform the law in three respects: in support of a qualified, rather than absolute, privilege; in the inclusion of a "public-interest" balancing prong that is currently included in statutory and common law proposals; and in determining who qualifies as a journalist for privilege protection.

Additionally, as a matter of professional practice, working journalists face a number of potential problems when they promise a source confidentiality. Professionally, journalists risk manipulation and a loss of credibility, while standing to gain important information they might otherwise be unable to obtain. These promises are plagued with ethical questions, and standards and policies have developed to provide guidance. Legally, journalists face vulnerability when third parties seek information for which confidentiality has been promised. Legal penalties for journalists are harsher today than ever before. The legal cases in the past decade show that when viewed through a broader historical lens, journalists are facing harsher consequences and more difficult choices when confronted with attempts at compelled disclosure of information. Jail sentences for journalists held in contempt have become longer – the three longest sentences in American history have occurred since 2001. Prosecutors have used waivers of confidentiality to pit reporters and sources against each other unlike ever before. Threats of huge fines have caused news organizations to turn over notes against the wishes of reporters and have also raised the possibility of personal bankruptcy for journalists. Gone are the days when a journalist spends a few days in jail, is treated well, and is released as a professional martyr.

Increasingly, journalism ethics will likely, and indeed should, play a role in developing solutions to problems in practice and in law. Ethically, journalists need to articulate standards of conduct in responding to subpoenas. Individuals need to know what to expect from their news organizations, which may well reveal deepening chasms between professional ideals and business imperatives. Journalists must think carefully about the meanings of their promises of confidentiality and the extent to which they are willing to bend those promises in particular circumstances, including when presented with waivers from sources.

Toward what additional research does this book point? A stronger articulation of the core values and factors of decision-making in journalistic practice may support more "procedural" forms of assessing public-interest standards, as proposed in the federal shield law. Additional historical research categorizing the types of cases in which journalists have revealed confidential sources as a matter of ethics, rather than in the face of legal compulsion, may shed further light on the competing interests in ethical discourse. Historical research could produce important evidence for legal development, especially in the area of common law, which looks to "reason and experience" for guidance. Legal analysis of the approaches to applying the three-prong test may reveal model judicial balancing standards to provide further clarity to journalists as to what the law will and will not protect. Professional discussions regarding the extent to which journalists are willing to violate final court orders, and under what circumstances, may develop a professional consensus that will be helpful to journalists facing difficult choices. Comparative research into the public policy goals of the other types of privilege, as well as their limits in their respective professions, might create new ways of thinking about the journalist's privilege. And in the realm of free-press theory, an articulation of the privilege as an example of a negative-liberty right that draws from the Supreme Court's press-clause doctrine might contribute to new formulations of the prior restraint/newsgathering rights dichotomy. Finally, this research suggests that First Amendment values can be instilled in law beyond the narrow category of Supreme Court-created constitutional right that journalists sought in *Branzburg*.

Confidential-source protection is an important part of modern journalism, and this research shows the practice has been important throughout American journalism history. The development of professional standards and justifications for confidential source use led to the recognition of the public interest in journalistic protection of confidential sources, which in turn influenced constitutional, common, and statutory law. In describing this history, the research shows a dynamic interaction between law, ethics and professional practice.

Chapter 8 Notes

---

[1] John Nichols and Robert W. McChesney, *The Death and Life of Great American Newspapers,* THE NATION, March 18, 2009, *available at* http://www.thenation.com/doc/20090406/nichols_mcchesney (last visited July 1, 2009).

[2] *Id.*

[3] *Decline in newsroom job slows,* American Society of News Editors, April 11, 2010, available at http://asne.org/annual_conference/conference_news/articleid/763/decline-in-newsroom-jobs-slows-763.aspx (last visited Dec. 1, 2010).

[4] *Id.*

[5] Walter Isaccson, *How to Save Your Newspaper,* TIME, Feb. 5, 2009, available at http://www.time.com/time/business/article/0,8599,1877191,00.html (last visited July 1, 2009).

[6] SCOTT GANT, WE'RE ALL JOURNALISTS NOW: THE TRANSFORMATION OF THE PRESS AND RESHAPING OF THE LAW IN THE INTERNET AGE (2007).

[7] *Id.*

[8] *Id.*

[9] *See generally* NEIL HENRY, JOURNALISM UNDER SIEGE IN AN AGE OF NEW MEDIA (2007).

[10] *See* chapter four.

[11] *See, for example,* the discussion of the Nugent case in chapter four.

[12] *See* the discussion of the Simonton case in chapter four.

[13] Joseph A. Mirando, *Lessons on Ethics in News Reporting Textbooks, 1867-1997,* 13 JOURNAL OF MASS MEDIA ETHICS, 26.

[14] WILLIAM R. ARTHUR AND RALPH L. CROSMAN, THE LAW OF NEWSPAPERS 257 (1940).

[15] See the discussion of the *Washington Times* case in chapter four.

[16] H.R. 215, Sec. 4 (2) 94th Cong., 1st Sess. (1975).

[17] H.R. 2102, Sec. 2 (a), 110th Cong. (2007).

[18] H.R. 985, 111th Cong. (2009) and S. 448, 111th Cong. (2009). *See* Lindsay Kalter, *Trying Again,* AM. JOURN. REV., October/November 2008, *available at* http://www.ajr.org/article_printable.asp?id=4633 (last visited Feb. 2, 2009). The Free Flow of Information Act of 2009 was introduced in the House of Representatives at the start of the 111th Congress and was identical to the bill passed in the previous term. *See* Reporters Committee For Freedom of the Press, News Media Update, *Shield Law Re-Introduced in House,* Feb. 11,

2009, *available at* http://www.rcfp.org/newsitems/index.php?i=9946 (last visited Feb. 13, 2009).

[19] H.R. 2102, 110th Cong. (2007).

[20] *See* Rem Rieder, *Brandishing a Shield,* AM. JOURN. REV., Feb./Mar. 2009, at 4.

[21] *Id.*

[22] *Id.*

[23] Charlie Savage, *After Afghan War Leaks, Revisions in a Shield Bill,* N.Y. TIMES, Aug. 3, 2010.

[24] H.R. 581, 109th Cong. (2005).

[25] Declan McCullagh, *So Who Should You Call a Journalist?* CNET NEWS.COM, Oct. 24, 2005, *available at* http://news.cnet.com/2010-1025_3-5907336.html (last visited Sept. 8, 2008).

[26] H.R. 2102, 110th Cong. (2007).

[27] Tom Robbins, *Tall Tales of a Mafia Mistress,* VILLAGE VOICE, Oct. 23, 2007.

[28] *Id.*

[29] Personal interview with author.

[30] *Id.*

[31] *Id.*

[32] *Id.*

[33] *Id.*

[34] EDMUND B. LAMBETH, COMMITTED JOURNALISM: AN ETHIC FOR THE PROFESSION 181-182 (1986).

[35] Personal interview with author.

[36] *Id.*

[37] Tom Robbins, *Tall Tales of a Mafia Mistress,* VILLAGE VOICE, October 23, 2007.

[38] *See Transcript of Special Counsel Fitzgerald's Press Conference,* WASH. POST, Oct. 28, 2005.

[39] 28 C.F.R. Section 50.10(a) (2007).

[40] Free Flow of Information Act of 2009, H.R. 985, 111th Cong. (2009).

[41] Free Flow of Information Act of 2007, S. 2035, 110th Cong. (2007).

[42] In re: Grand Jury Subpoena, Judith Miller, 397 F.3d 964 (D.D.C. 2005).

[43] *Id.* at 991.

[44] *Id.*

[45] David Abramowicz, *Calculating the Public Interest in Protecting Journalists' Confidential Sources,* 108 COL. L.R. 101 (2009).

---

[46] Id. at 130.

[47] *See* Affidavits of Denise A. Garibaldi and Donald M. Hooton, *available at* http://www.sfgate.com/cgi-bin/article.cgi?f=/c/a/2006/05/31/MNMOTIONDOCS.DTL#documents (last visited July 1, 2009).

[48] *See generally* Scott Neinas, *A Skinny Shield is Better: Why Congress Should Propose a Federal Reporters' Shield Statute That Narrowly Defines Journalists*, 40 U. TOL. L. REV. 225 (2008); Mary Rose Papandrea, *Citizen Journalism and the Reporter's Privilege*, 91 MINN. L. REV. 515 (2006); Joseph S. Alonzo, *Restoring the Ideal Marketplace: How Recognizing Bloggers as Journalists Can Save the Press,* 9 N.Y.U. J. LEGIS. PUB. POL. 751 (2006); Stephanie J. Frazee, *Bloggers as Reporters: An Effect-Based Approach to First Amendment Protections in a New Age of Information Dissemination,* 8 VAN. J. ENT. & TECH. L. 609 (2005); Linda L. Berger, *Shielding the Unmedia: Using the Process of Journalism to Protect the Journalist's Privilege in an Infinite Universe of Publication,* 39 HOUS. L. REV. 1371 (2003); Laurence B. Alexander, *Looking Out for the Watchdogs: A Legislative Proposal Limiting the Newsgathering Privilege to Journalists in the Greatest Need of Protection for Sources and Information,* 20 YALE L. & POL'Y REV. 97 (2002); Clay Calvert, *And You Call Yourself a Journalist? Wrestling With a Definition of "Journalist" in the Law,* 103 DICK. L. REV. 411, (1999); Daniel A. Swartwout, *In Re Madden: The Threat to New Journalism,* 60 OHIO ST. L.J. 1589 (1999); Kraig L. Baker, *Are Oliver Stone and Tom Clancy Journalists? Determining Who Has Standing to Claim the Journalist's Privilege*, 69 WASH. L. REV. 739 (1994).

[49] Seymour Hersh, for example, won a Pulitzer Prize for his reporting about the 1968 killings of Vietnam civilians in the so-called My Lai Massacre. Hersh was a freelance reporter working for an upstart wire service. *See* SEYMOUR HERSH, CHAIN OF COMMAND: THE ROAD FROM 9/1 TO ABU GHRAIB, ix-xi (2004).

[50] *See* discussion of Wolf case in chapter two.

[51] Branzburg v. Hayes, 408 U.S. 665, 703 (1972).

[52] In Re: Grand Jury Subpoena, Judith Miller, 397 F.3d 964 (D.C. Cir. 2005). As it relates to bloggers, Judge Sentelle wrote: "Are we then to create a privilege that protects only those reporters employed by Time Magazine, the New York Times, and other media giants, or do we extend that protection as well to the owner of a desktop printer producing a weekly newsletter to inform

his neighbors, lodge brothers, co-religionists, or co-conspirators? ... (D)oes the privilege also protect the proprietor of a web log: the stereotypical 'blogger' sitting in his pajamas at his personal computer posting on the World Wide Web his best product to inform whoever happens to browse his way? If not, why not? How could one draw a distinction consistent with the court's vision of a broadly granted personal right? If so, then would it not be possible for a government official wishing to engage in the sort of unlawful leaking under investigation in the present controversy to call a trusted friend or a political ally, advise him to set up a web log (which I understand takes about three minutes) and then leak to him under a promise of confidentiality the information which the law forbids the official to disclose?"

[53] Letter from Brian A. Benczkowski, Principal Deputy Assistant Attorney General, to Rep. Lamar S. Smith (July 31, 2007), *available at* http://www.usdoj.gov/opa/mediashield/odni-view-ltr-hr2102-092707.pdf (last visited Sept. 5, 2008).

[54] Declan McCullagh, *So Who Should You Call a Journalist?* CNET NEWS.COM, Oct. 24, 2005, *available at* http://news.cnet.com/2010-1025_3-5907336.html (last visited Sept. 8, 2008).

[55] Randall D. Eliason, *Leakers, Bloggers, and Fourth Estate Inmates: The Misguided Pursuit of a Reporter's Privilege,* 24 CARDOZA ARTS & ENT. L.J. 386 (2006).

[56] *See* chapter seven for a discussion of common-law cases regarding the definitional question.

[57] Floyd Abrams, *The Press Is Different: Reflections on Justice Stewart and the Autonomous Press,* 7 HOFSTRA L. REV. 564, at 581 (1978-1979).

[58] The Free Flow of Information Act of 2009 was introduced in the House of Representatives at the start of the 111th Congress and was identical to the bill passed in the previous term. *See* Reporters Committee For Freedom of the Press, News Media Update, *Shield Law Re-Introduced in House,* Feb. 11, 2009, *available at* http://www.rcfp.org/newsitems/index.php?i=9946 (last visited Feb. 13, 2009).

[59] Bill Kovach and Tom Rosenstiel, THE ELEMENTS OF JOURNALISM: WHAT NEWSPEOPLE SHOULD KNOW AND THE PUBLIC SHOULD EXPECT 17 (2001).

[60] Declaration of Professor Thomas Goldstein, Apple Computer, Inc. v. Nick DePlume, No. 1-05-CV-033341 (Cal. Super. Ct).

[61] *Id.*

[62] Randall Bezanson, *The Developing Law of Editorial Judgment,* 78 NEB. L. REV. 754, 760 (1999).

[63] *See* Rodney A. Smolla, *Will Tabloid Journalism Ruin the First Amendment for the Rest of Us?* 9 DEPAUL-LCA J. ART & ENT. L 2, (1998-1999) (showing how courts have occasionally fashioned tests around the idea of matters of public concern in areas of public-employee speech and libel). *See, for example,* Connick v. Myers, 461 U.S. 138 (1983) and Dun & Bradstreet, Inc. v. Greenmoss Builders, Inc., 472 U.S. 749 (1985).

[64] *See, for example,* In Re; Madden, 151 F.3d at 130 ("He was not gathering or investigating 'news,' … As a creative fiction author, Madden's primary goal is to provide advertisement and entertainment – not to gather news or disseminate information. It is clear from the record that Mr. Madden was not investigation 'news,' even were we to apply a generous definition of the word. … Fiction or entertainment writers are permitted to view facts selectively, change the emphasis or chronology of events or even fill in factual gaps with fictitious events – license a journalist does not have").

[65] *See for example* Von Bulow, 811 F.2d at 142 (upholding a district court's ruling that the privilege extends only to those "involved actively in the gathering and dissemination of news" and to who practice "investigative reporting"); Shoen v. Shoen, 5 F.3d 1289 at 1293 (saying the privilege protects those who "have historically played a vital role in bringing to light 'newsworthy' facts on topical and controversial matters of great public importance" and that the "critical question for deciding whether a person may invoke the journalist's privilege is whether she is gathering news for dissemination to the public").

[66] *See also* David Abramowicz, *Calculating the Public Interest in Protecting Journalists' Confidential Sources,* 108 Colum. L. R. 1949 (2008) (arguing that journalistic values and ethical codes should be legally relevant to public interest balancing in privilege cases).

[67] Von Bulow, 811 F.2d at 147.

[68] *See, for example,* Jeff Storey, *Does Ethics Make Good Law? A Case Study,* 19 CARDOZO ARTS & ENT. L.J. 467 (2001) and Todd F. Simon, *Libel as Malpractice: News Media Ethics and the Standard of Care,* 53 FORDHAM L. REV. 449 (1984).

[69] Laurence B. Alexander, *Looking Out for the Watchdogs: A Legislative Proposal Limiting the Newsgathering Privilege to Journalists in the Greatest*

Need of Protection for Sources and Information, 20 YALE L. & POL'Y REV. 97, 130 (2002).

[70] *Id.* at 130.

[71] Kraig L. Baker, *Are Oliver Stone and Tom Clancy Journalists? Determining Who Has Standing to Claim the Journalist's Privilege,* 69 WASH. L. REV. 739 (1994).

[72] *Id.* at 757-758.

[73] Linda L. Berger, *Shielding the Unmedia: Using the Process of Journalism to Protect the Journalist's Privilege in an Infinite Universe of Publication,* 39 HOUS. L. REV. 1371, 1412 (2003).

[74] Stephanie J. Frazee, *Bloggers as Reporters: An Effect-Based Approach to First Amendment Protections in a New Age of Information Dissemination,* 8 VAN. J. ENT. & TECH. L. 609, 639 (2005-2006).

[75] Mary-Rose Papandrea, *Citizen Journalism and the Reporter's Privilege,* 91 MINN. L. REV. 515, 590-591 (2006-2007).

[76] Daniel A. Swartwout, *In Re Madden: The Threat to New Journalism,* 60 OHIO ST. L.J. 1589 (1999).

[77] Clay Calvert, *And You Call Yourself a Journalist? Wrestling With a Definition of "Journalist" in the Law,* 103 DICK. L. REV. 411 (1999).

[78] O'Grady v. Superior Court, 44 Cal. Rptr. 3d 72 (Cal. Ct. App. 2006), *overturning* Apple Computer, Inc. v. Doe, No. 1-04-CV-032178 (Cal. Super. Ct., Mar. 1, 2005).

[79] Debra J. Saunders, *Josh Wolf – blogger – has no press pass,* S.F. CHRONICLE, Feb. 27, 2007.

[80] Alex Koppelman, *First Amendment martyr?* SALON.COM, Apr. 13, 2007.

[81] *Silkwood,* 563 F.3d at 436-437.

[82] *Von Bulow,* 811 F.2d at 143.

[83] *Shoen,* 5 F.3d at 1293.

[84] *In Re Jeffrey Steinberg,* 837 F.2d at 528.

Bibliography

Books

Abel, Elie. Leaking: Who Does it? Who Benefits? At What Cost? New York: Priority Press Publications, 1987.

Abrams, Floyd. Speaking Freely: Trials of the First Amendment. New York: Viking, 2005.

Arthur, William W. The Law of Newspapers: A Text and Case Book For Use in Schools of Journalism and a Desk-Book For Newspaper Workers. New York: McGraw-Hill Book Company, 1928.

Aucoin, James L. The Evolution of American Investigative Journalism. Columbia: University of Missouri Press, 2005.

Baldasty, Gerald J. The Commercialization of News in the Nineteenth Century. Madison: University of Wisconsin Press, 1992.

Bennett, Lance W. When the Press Fails: Political Power and the News Media from Iraq to Katrina. Chicago: University of Chicago Press, 2007.

Bernstein, Carl and Bob Woodward. All the President's Men. New York: Simon & Schuster, 1974.

Boehlert, Eric. Lapdogs: How the Press Rolled Over for Bush. New York: Free Press, 2006.

Bollinger, Lee. Images of a Free Press. Chicago: University of Chicago Press, 1991.

Buranelli, Vincent. The Trial of Peter Zenger, New York: New York University Press, 1957.

Chafee, Zechariah. Government and Mass Communications: A Report From the Commission on the Freedom of the Press. Chicago: University of Chicago Press, 1947.

Cohen, Dan. Anonymous Source: At War Against the Media, A True Story. Minneapolis: The Oliver Press, 2005.

Dicken-Garcia, Hazel. Journalistic Standards in Nineteenth-Century
    America. Madison: University of Wisconsin Press, 1989.
Dickerson, Donna Lee. The Course of Tolerance: Freedom of the Press
    in Nineteenth-Century America. Westport, CT: Greenwood Press,
    1990.
Ellsberg, Daniel. Secrets: A Memoir of Vietnam and the Pentagon
    Papers. New York: Viking, 2002.
Emery, Edwin. The Press and America: An Interpretive History of the
    Mass Media. New York: Prentice-Hall, 1954.
Fainaru-Wada, Mark, and Lance Williams. Games of Shadows: Barry
    Bonds, BALCO, and the Steroids Scandal That Rocked
    Professional Sports. New York: Gotham Books, 2006.
Frankel, Max. The Times of My Life and My Life with the Times. New
    York, Random House, 1999.
Fuller, Jack. News Values: Ideas for an Information Age. Chicago:
    University of Chicago Press, 1996.
Garry, Patrick M. The American Vision of a Free Press: An Historical
    and Constitutional Revisionist View of the Press as a Marketplace
    of Ideas. New York: Garland Publishing, 1990.
Gleason, Timothy W. The Watchdog Concept: The Press and Courts in
    Nineteenth-Century America. Ames, IA: Iowa State University
    Press, 1990.
Goldstein, Tom. Journalism and Truth. Evanston: Northwestern
    University Press, 2007.
Gordon, A. David. "Had Black ruled in Branzburg ..." in Dennis,
    Everette (ed.), Justice Hugo Black and the First Amendment.
    Ames, IA: Iowa State University Press, 1978.
Gross, Gerald (editor). The Responsibility of the Press. New York:
    Fleet Publishing, 1966.
Henry, Neil. American Carnival: Journalism Under Siege in an Age of
    New Media. Berkeley: University of California Press, 2007.
Hersh, Seymour. Chain of Command: The Road From 9/11 to Abu
    Ghraib. New York: Harper, 2005.
Hess, Stephen. The Government/Press Connection: Press Officers and
    Their Offices. Washington, D.C.: Brookings Institution Press,
    1984.
Hindman, Elizabeth Blanks. Rights vs. Responsibilities: The Supreme
    Court and the Media. Westport, CT: Greenwood Press, 1997.

Hocking, William. Freedom of the Press: A Framework of Principle. Chicago: University of Chicago Press, 1947.

Huntzicker, William. The Popular Press, 1833-1865. Westport, CT: Greenwood Press, 1999.

Iggers, Jeremy. Good News, Bad News: Journalism Ethics and the Public Interest. Boulder: Westview Press, 1998.

Isikoff, Michael and David Corn. Hubris: The Inside Story of Spin, Scandal, and the Selling of the Iraq War. New York: Crown Publishers, 2006.

Kennedy, George (ed). What Good is Journalism? Columbia: University of Missouri Press, 2007.

Knowlton, Steven R. and Patrick R. Parsons. The Journalist's Moral Compass: Basic Principles. Westport, CT: Praeger, 1995.

Kovach, Bill and Tom Rosenstiel. The Elements of Journalism. New York: Three Rivers Press, 2001.

Lakey, Thomas A. The Morals of Newspapermaking. Notre Dame: University Press, 1924.

Larson, Margali Sarfatti. The Rise of Professionalism: A Sociological Analysis. Berkeley: University of California Press, 1977.

Leonard, Thomas C. The Power of the Press: The Birth of American Political Reporting. New York: Oxford University Press, 1986.

Levy, Leonard. Emergence of a Free Press. Chicago: Ivan R. Dee, 1985.

Litchblau, Eric. Bush's Law: The Remaking of American Justice. New York: Random House, 2008.

Martin, Robert W.T. The Free and Open Press: The Founding of American Democratic Press Liberty, 1640-1800, New York: New York University Press, 2001.

Mayer, Jane. The Dark Side. New York: Doubleday, 2008.

Meyer, Phillip. The Vanishing Newspaper: Saving Journalism in an Information Age. Columbia: University of Missouri Press, 2004.

Mindich, David T.Z. Just the Facts: How 'Objectivity' Came to Define American Journalism. New York: New York University Press, 1998.

Miraldi, Robert. Muckraking and Objectivity: Journalism's Colliding Traditions. New York: Greenwood Press, 1990.

Nerone, John. Last Rights: Revisiting Four Theories of the Press. Champaign: University of Illinois Press, 1995.

Overholser, Geneva and Kathleen Hall Jamieson. The Press. Oxford: Oxford University Press, 2006.

Pearlstine, Norman. Off the Record: The Press, the Government, and the War over Anonymous Sources, New York: Farrar, Straus and Giroux, 2007.

Powe, Lucas A. Jr. The Fourth Estate and the Constitution: Freedom of the Press in America. Berkeley: University of California Press, 1991.

Rabban, David. Free Speech in its Forgotten Years. Cambridge: Cambridge University Press, 1997.

Risen, James. State of War: The Secret History of the CIA and the Bush Administration. New York: Free Press, 2006.

Ritchie, Donald A. Press Gallery: Congress and the Washington Correspondents. Cambridge: Harvard University Press, 1991.

Rosen, Jay. What Are Journalists For? New Haven: Yale University Press (2001).

Rosentiel, Tom and Amy S. Mitchell. Thinking Clearly: Cases in Journalistic Decision-Making. New York: Columbia University Press, 2003.

Roston, Aram. The Man Who Pushed America to War. New York: Nation Books, 2008.

Rothenberg, Elliot C. The Taming of the Press: Cohen v. Cowles Media Company. Westport, CT: Praeger Publishers, 1999.

Rudenstine, David. The Day the Presses Stopped: A History of the Pentagon Papers Case. Berkeley: University of California Press, 1996.

Sanford, Bruce W. Don't Shoot the Messenger: How Our Growing Hatred of the Media Threatens Free Speech for all of Us. New York: Free Press, 1999.

Schiller, Dan. Objectivity and the News: The Public and the Rise of Commercial Journalism. Philadelphia: University of Philadelphia Press, 1981.

Schoenfeld, Gabriel. Necessary Secrets: National Security, the Media, and the Rule of Law. New York: W.W. Norton & Company, Inc., 2010.

Schudson, Michael. Origins of the Ideal of Objectivity in the Professions: Studies in the History of American Journalism and American Law, 1830-1940. New York: Garland Publishing, 1990.

Schudson, Michael. Discovering the News: A Social History of American Newspapers. New York: Basic Books, 1978.

Schudson, Michael. The Sociology of News. New York: W.W. Norton & Company, 2003.

Siebert, Frederick, Theodore Peterson and Wilbur Schramm. Four Theories of the Press. Urbana: University of Illinois Press, 1956.

Siebert, Frederick. The Rights and Responsibilities of the Press. New York: D. Appleton-Century Co., 1934.

Smith, Jeffery A. Printers and Press Freedom. Oxford: Oxford University Press, 1988.

Stone, Geoffrey R. Top Secret. Lanham, MD: Rowman & Littlefield, 2007.

Thomas, Helen. Watchdogs of Democracy. New York: Scribner, 2006.

Ungar, Sanford J. The Papers & The Papers: An Account of the Legal and Political Battle Over the Pentagon Papers. New York: E.P. Dutton & Co., Inc., 1972.

Van Gerpen, Maurice. Privileged Communication and the Press: The Citizen's Right to Know Versus the Law's Right to Confidential News Source Evidence. Westport, CT: Greenwood Press, 1979.

Waas, Murray. The United States v. I. Lewis Libby. New York: Union Square Press, 2007.

Ward, Stephen J.A. The Invention of Journalism Ethics. Montreal: McGill-Queen's University Press, 2004.

Whalen, Charles W. Jr. Your Right to Know. New York: Random House, 1973.

Wheeler, Marcy. Anatomy of Deceit: How the Bush Administration Used the Media to Sell the Iraq War and Out a Spy. Berkeley: Vaster Books, 2007.

Wilson, Valerie Plame. My Life as a Spy, My Betrayal by the White House. New York: Simon & Schuster, 2007.

Woodward, Bob. State of Denial: Bush at War III. New York: Simon & Schuster, 2007.

Woodward, Bob. The War Within. New York, Simon & Schuster, 2008.

Woodward, Bob. The Secret Man: The Story of Watergate's Deep Throat. New York: Simon & Schuster, 2005.

Zerman, Melvyn Bernard. Taking on the Press: Constitutional Rights in Conflict. New York: Thomas Crowell, 1986.

Journal Articles

Abrams, Floyd. "The Press Is Different: Reflections on Justice Stewart and the Autonomous Press." Hofstra Law Review 7 (1978-1979): 564.

Alexander, Laurence B. "Branzburg v. Hayes Revisited: A Survey of Journalists Who Become Subpoena Targets." Newspaper Research Journal 18 (Spring 1994): 83.

Alexander, Laurence B. "Looking Out for the Watchdogs: A Legislative Proposal Limiting the Newsgathering Privilege to Journalists in the Greatest Need of Protection for Sources and Information." Yale Law & Policy Review 20 (2002): 97.

Alexander, Laurence B. and Ellen M. Bush. "Shield Laws on Trial: State Court Interpretation of the Journalist's Statutory Privilege." Journal of Legislation 23 (1997): 215.

Alexander, Laurence B. and Leah Cooper. "Words That Shield: A Textual Analysis of the Journalist's Privilege." Newspaper Research Journal 18 (1997): 51.

Allison, Marianne. "A Literature Review of Approaches to the Professionalism of Journalists." Journal of Mass Media Ethics, 1/2 (Spring/Summer 1986): 5.

Alonzo, Joseph S. "Restoring the Ideal Marketplace: How Recognizing Bloggers as Journalists Can Save the Press." New York University Journal of Legislation and Public Policy 9 (2006): 751.

Anderson, David A. "Freedom of the Press." Texas Law Review 80 (2001-2002): 429.

Anderson, David A. "The Origins of the Press Clause." UCLA Law Review 30 (1982-1983) 455.

Anderson, David A. "The Institutional Press and Professionalism: Defining the Press Clause in Journalist Privilege Cases." Free Speech Yearbook 34 (1996): 49.

Asner, Marcus A. "Starting from Scratch: The First Amendment Reporter-Source Privilege and the Doctrine of Incidental Restrictions." University of Michigan Journal of Law Reform 26 (1992-1993): 593.

B.K.K. "The Right of a Newsman to Refrain from Divulging the Sources of His Information." Virginia Law Review 36 (1950): 61.

Baker, Edwin C. "The Independent Significance of the Press Clause Under Existing Law." Hofstra Law Review 35 (Spring 2007): 955.

Baker, Kraig L. "Are Oliver Stone and Tom Clancy Journalists? Determining Who Has Standing to Claim the Journalist's Privilege." Washington Law Review 69 (1994): 739.

Banning, Stephen A. "'Truth is Our Ultimate Goal': A Mid-19th Century Concern for Journalism Ethics." American Journalism 16, 1 (1999): 17–39.

Bates, Stephen. "The Reporter's Privilege, Then and Now." Research Paper R-23, the Joan Shorenstein Center on the Press, Politics and Public Policy, Harvard University (April 2000).

Berger, Linda L. "Shielding the Unmedia: Using the Process of Journalism to Protect the Journalist's Privilege in an Infinite Universe of Publication." Houston Law Review 39 (2003): 1371.

BeVier, Lillian R. "An Informed Public, an Informed Press: The Search for a Constitutional Principle." California Law Review 68 (1980): 482.

BeVier, Lillian R. "The Journalist's Privilege – A Skeptic's View." Ohio Northern University Law Review 32 (2006): 467.

Bezanson, Randall. "The Developing Law of Editorial Judgment." Nebraska Law Review 78 (1999): 754.

Bezanson, Randall. "The New Free Press Guarantee." Virginia Law Review 63 (1977): 731.

Blasi, Vince. "The Newsman's Privilege: An Empirical Study." Michigan Law Review 70 (1971-1972): 229.

Blasi, Vincent. "The Checking Value in First Amendment Theory." American Bar Foundation Research Journal 1977 (1977): 521.

Bloom, Matthew. "Subpoenaed Sources and the Internet: A Test for When Bloggers Should Reveal Who Misappropriated a Trade Secret." Yale Law & Policy Review 24 (2006): 471.

Boutrous, Theodore Jr. "Retooling the Federal Common-Law Reporter's Privilege." Communications Lawyer, 17 (1999): 3.

Brewer, Paul. "The Fourth Estate and the Quest for a Double Edged Shield: Why a Federal Reporters' Shield Law Would Violate the First Amendment." University of Memphis Law Review 36 (2005): 1073.

Calvert, Clay and Robert D. Richards. "Journalism Sources as Trade Secrets: Whose Source is it Anyway?" Whittier Law Review 23 (2002): 985.

Calvert, Clay. "And You Call Yourself a Journalist? Wrestling With a Definition of 'Journalist' in the Law." Dickinson Law Review 103 (1999): 411.

Campagnolo, Theodore. "The Conflict Between State Press Shield Laws and Federal Criminal Proceedings: The Rule 501 Blues." Gonzaga Law Review 38 (2002/2003): 445.

Capocasale, Louis J. "Using the Shield as a Sword: An Analysis of How the Current Congressional Proposals for a Reporter's Shield Law Wound the Fifth Amendment." St. John's Journal of Legal Commentary 20 (2005): 339.

Carter, P.B. "The Journalist, His Informant and Testimonial Privilege." New York University Law Review 35 (1960): 1111.

Chemerinsky, Erwin. "Protect the Press: A First Amendment Standard for Safeguarding Aggressive Newsgathering." University of Richmond Law Review 33 (1999-2000): 1143.

Christians, Clifford. "Fifty Years of Scholarship in Media Ethics." Journal of Communication 27 (1977): 19-29.

Cronin, Mary M. "Trade Press Roles in Promoting Journalistic Professionalism, 1884-1917." Journal of Mass Media Ethics 8 (1993): 227-238.

Cronin, Mary M. and James B. McPherson. "Pronouncements and Denunciations: An Analysis of State Press Association Ethics Codes From the 1920s." Journalism and Mass Communication Quarterly 72 (Winter 1995): 890.

D'Alemberte, Talbot. "Journalists Under the Axe: Protection of Confidential Sources of Information," Harvard Journal on Legislation 6 (1968): 307.

Dalglish, Lucy A., and Casey Murray. "Déjà vu All Over Again: How a Generation of Gains in Federal Reporter's Privilege Law is Being Reversed." University of Arkansas Little Rock Law Review 29 (2006): 13.

Dennis, Everette. "Internal Examination: Self-Regulation and American Media." Cardozo Arts & Entertainment Law Journal 13 (1995): 697.

Denniston, Lyle. "From George Carlin to Matt Drudge: The Constitutional Implications of Bringing the Paparazzi to America." American University Law Review 47 (1997): 1255.

Desmond, Thomas C. "The Newsmen's Privilege Bill." Albany Law Review 13 (1949): 1.

Dicke, Michael. "Promises and the Press: First Amendment Limitations on News Source Recovery for Breach of a Confidentiality Agreement." Minnesota Law Review 73 (1989): 1553.

Drechsel, Robert E. "Media Ethics and Media Law: The Transformation of Moral Obligation Into Legal Principle." Notre Dame Journal of Law, Ethics & Public Policy 6 (1992): 5.

Drechsel, Robert E. "Media Malpractice: The Legal Risks of Voluntary Social Responsibility in Mass Communication." Duquesne Law Review 27 (1988): 237.

Drechsel, Robert E. "The Paradox of Professionalism: Journalism and Malpractice." University of Arkansas at Little Rick Law Review 23 (2000): 181.

Easton, Eric B. "Two Wrongs Mock a Right: Overcoming the Cohen Maledicta That Bar First Amendment Protection for Newsgathering." Ohio State Law Journal 58 (1997): 1135.

Edgar, Harold, and Benno C. Schmidt, Jr. "The Espionage Statutes and Publication of Defense Information." Columbia Law Review 73 (May 1973): 929.

Eliason, Randall D. "Leakers, Bloggers and the Fourth Estate Inmates: The Misguided Pursuit of a Reporter's Privilege." Cardozo Arts & Entertainment Law Journal 24 (2006-2007): 385.

Eliason, Randall D. "The Problems With the Reporter's Privilege." American University Law Review 57 (2008): 1341.

Elrod, Jennifer. "Protecting Journalists From Compelled Disclosure: A Proposal for a Federal Statute." New York University Journal of Legislation & Public Policy 7 (2003/2004): 115.

Ervin, Sam J. Jr. "In Pursuit of a Press Privilege." Harvard Journal on Legislation 11 (1973-1974): 233.

Eun, Eunnice. "Journalists Caught in the Crossfire: Robert Novak, the First Amendment, and Journalist's Duty of Confidentiality." American Criminal Law Review 42 (2005): 1073.

Evansen, Bruce J. "Journalism's Struggle Over Ethics and Professionalism During America's Jazz Age." Journalism History 16:3 (Summer 1990): 54.

Fargo, Anthony L. "What They Meant to Say: The Courts Try to Explain Branzburg v. Hayes." Journalism & Communications Monographs 12 (2010): 65.

Fargo, Anthony L. "Common Law or Shield Law? How Rule 501 Could Solve the Journalist's Privilege Problem." 33 William Mitchell Law Review 33 (2007): 1347.

Fargo, Anthony L. "Analyzing Federal Shield Law Proposals: What Congress Can Learn from the States." Communication Law & Policy 11 (2006): 35.

Fargo, Anthony L. "Is Protection from Subpoenas Slipping? An Analysis of Three Recent Cases Involving Broadcast News Outtakes." Journal of Broadcasting & Electronic Media 47 (2003): 455.

Fargo, Anthony L. "The Journalist's Privilege for Nonconfidential Information in States Without Shield Laws." Communication Law & Policy 7 (2002): 241.

Fargo, Anthony L. "Reconsidering the Federal Journalist's Privilege for Non-Confidential Information: Gonzales v. NBC." Cardozo Arts & Entertainment Law Journal 19 (2001): 355.

Fargo, Anthony L. "The Year of Leaking Dangerously: Shadowy Sources, Jailed Journalists and the Uncertain Future of the Federal Journalist's Privilege." William & Mary Bill of Rights Journal 14 (2005): 1063.

Ferre, John P. "The Dubious Heritage of Media Ethics: Cause and Effect Criticism in the 1890s." American Journalism 5 (1988): 191-203.

Fortner, Robert S. "The Journalist's Albatross: Objectivity, Critical Reporting and Social Responsibility." Journal of Communication Inquiry 6 (Winter 1981): 69.

Frazee, Stephanie J. "Bloggers as Reporters: An Effect-Based Approach to First Amendment Protections in a New Age of Information Dissemination." Vanderbilt Journal of Entertainment and Technology Law 8 (2005): 609.

Freedman, Eric M. "Reconstructing Journalist's Privilege." Cardozo Law Review 29 (2008): 1381.

Gallup, Earl H. Jr. "Further Consideration of a Privilege for Newsmen." Albany Law Review 14 (1950): 16.

Gleason, Timothy W. "Historians and Freedom of the Press Since 1800." American Journalism 5 (1988): 230-248.

Goldstein, Noah. "An International Assessment of Journalist Privileges and Source Confidentiality." New England Journal of International & Comparative Law 14 (2007): 103.

Gomsak, Mark. "The Free Flow of Information Act of 2006: Settling the Journalist's Privilege Debate." Brandeis Law Journal 45 (2007): 597.

Goodale, James C. "Branzburg v. Hayes and the Developing Qualified Privilege for Newsmen." Hastings Law Journal 26 (1974): 709.

Gordon, A. David. "The 1896 Maryland Shield Law: The American Roots of Evidentiary Privilege for Newsmen." Journalism Monographs 22 (May 1972): 1.

Graham, Elizabeth A. "Uncertainty Leads to Jail Time: The Status of the Common-Law Reporter's Privilege." DePaul Law Review 56 (2007): 723.

Hartman, Lynn Wickham. "Standards Governing the News: Their Use, Their Character, and Their Legal Implications." Iowa Law Review 72 (1987): 637.

Helle, Steven. "The News-Gathering/Publication Dichotomy and Government Expression." Duke Law Journal 1982 (1982): 1.

Hindman, Elizabeth Blanks. "First Amendment Theories and Press Responsibility: The Work of Zechariah Chafee, Thomas Emerson, Vincent Blasi and Edwin Baker." Journalism Quarterly 69 (1992): 48-64.

Hofer, Stephen R. "The Fallacy of 'Farber': Failure to Acknowledge the Constitutional Newsman's Privilege in Criminal Cases." The Journal of Criminal Law and Criminology 70 (Autumn 1979): 299.

Isralowitz, Jason P. "The Reporter as Citizen: Newspaper Ethics and Constitutional Values." University of Pennsylvania Law Review 141 (1992): 221.

Ivester, David Mitchell. "The Constitutional Right to Know." Hastings Constitutional Law Quarterly 4 (1977): 109.

Jennings, Marianne M. "Where Are Our Minds and What Are We Thinking? Virtue Ethics for a 'Perfidious' Media." Notre Dame Journal of Law, Ethics & Public Policy 19 (2005): 637.

Joyce, Daniel. "The Judith Miller Case and the Relationship Between Reporter and Source: Competing Visions of the Media's Role and Function." Fordham Intellectual Property, Media & Entertainment Law Journal 19 (2007): 555.

Katz, Alan M. "Government Information Leaks and the First Amendment." California Law Review 64 (1976): 108.

Kelly, Sean W. "Black and White and Read All Over: Press Protections After Branzburg." Duke Law Journal 57 (2007): 199.

Kielbowicz, Richard B. "The Role of News Leaks in Governance and the Law of Journalists' Confidentiality, 1795-2005." San Diego Law Review 43 (Summer 2006): 425-94.

Kirtley, Jane E. "Will the Demise of the Reporter's Privilege Mean the End of Investigative Reporting, and Should Judges Care If It Does?" Ohio Northern University Law Review 32 (2006): 519.

Knight, Denise D. "Charlotte Perkins Gilman, William Randolph Hearst, and the Practice of Ethical Journalism." American Journalism 11 (1994): 336–47.

Lange, David. "The Speech and Press Clauses." UCLA Law Review 23 (1975-1976): 78.

Langley, Monica and Lee Levine. "Branzburg Revisited: Confidential Sources and First Amendment Value." George Washington University Law Review 57 (1988): 13.

Larsen, Kara A. "The Demise of the First Amendment-Based Reporter's Privilege: Why This Current Trend Should Not Surprise the Media," Connecticut Law Review 37 (2005): 1235.

Laursen, Erik W. "Putting Journalists on Thin Ice: McKevitt v. Pallasch." University of Cincinnati Law Review 73 (2004): 293.

Lee, Douglas E. "Do Not Pass Go, Do Not Collect $200: The Reporter's Privilege Today." University of Arkansas at Little Rock Law Review 27 (2006): 77.

Lee, William E. "Deep Background: Journalists, Sources and the Perils of Leaking." American University Law Review 57 (2008): 1453.

Lee, William E. "The Priestly Class: Reflections on a Journalist's Privilege." Cardozo Arts & Entertainment Law Journal 23 (2006): 635.

Levi, Lili. "Dangerous Liasons: Seduction and Betrayal in Confidential Press-Source Relations." Rutgers Law Review 43 (1990-1991): 609.

Levy, Leonard. "On the Origins of the Press Clause." UCLA Law Review 32 (1984-1985): 177.

Lewis, Anthony. "A Constitutional Faith." Hastings Constitutional Law Quarterly 3 (1975): 769.

Lewis, Anthony. "A Preferred Position for Journalism?" Hofstra Law Review 7 (1978-1979): 595.

Lewis, Anthony. "A Public Right to Know About Public Institutions: The First Amendment as Sword." Supreme Court Review 1980 (1980): 1.

Lewis, Anthony. "The Right to Scrutinize Government: Toward a First Amendment Theory of Accountability." University of Miami Law Review 34 (1979-1980): 793.

Lewis, Anthony. "A Public Lecture by Anthony Lewis, The First Amendment in Perspective." University of Hawaii Law Review 29 (2006): 13.

Logan, David A. "'Stunt Journalism,' Professional Norms, and Public Mistrust of the Media." University of Florida Journal of Law & Public Policy 9 (1998): 151.

Lorenson, W.D. "The Journalist and His Confidential Source: Should a Testimonial Privilege Be Allowed?" Nebraska Law Review 35 (1955): 562.

Marcus, Paul. "The Reporter's Privilege: An Analysis of the Common Law, Branzburg v. Hayes, and Recent Statutory Developments." Arizona Law Review 25 (1983-1984): 815.

McDonald, Barry P. "The First Amendment and the Free Flow of Information: Towards a Realistic Right to Gather Information in the Information Age." Ohio State Law Journal 65 (2004): 249.

McKay, Floyd J. "First Amendment Guerillas: Formative Years of the Reporters Committee for Freedom of the Press." Journalism and Mass Communication Monographs 6 (Autumn 2004): 1.

McLean, Deckle. "Justice White and the First Amendment." Journalism Quarterly 56 (1979): 305-310.

Messer, Will E. "Open Season on the Journalist's Privilege: Do Recent Rulings Represent a Trend Against Assertions of the Privilege or Proper Applications of Existing Law?" Kentucky Law Journal 94 (2005): 421.

Mirando, Joe. "Lessons on Ethics in News Reporting Textbooks, 1867-1997." Journal of Mass Media Ethics 13 (1998): 26-39.

Morant, Blake D. "The Endemic Reality of Media Ethics and Self-Restraint." Notre Dame Journal of Law, Ethics & Public Policy 19 (2005): 595.

Murasky, Donna M. "The Journalist's Privilege: Branzburg and Its Aftermath." Texas Law Review 52: (1974): 829.

Murchison, Brian C. et al. "Sullivan's Paradox: The Emergence of Judicial Standards of Journalism." North Carolina Law Review 73 (1994): 7.

Nestler, Jeffrey. "The Under Privileged Profession: The Case for Supreme Court Recognition of the Journalist's Privilege." University of Pennsylvania Law Review 154 (2005): 201.

Nimmer, Melville B. "Is Freedom of the Press a Redundancy: What Does it Add to Freedom of Speech?" Hastings Law Journal 26 (1974-1975): 639.

Onorato, David Joseph. "A Press Privilege for the Worst of Times." Georgetown Law Journal 75 (1986): 361.

Osborn, John E. "The Reporter's Confidentiality Privilege: Updating the Empirical Evidence After a Decade of Subpoenas." Columbia Human Rights Law Review 17 (1985): 57.

Osiel, Mark. "The Professionalism of Journalism: Impetus or Impediment to a 'Watchdog Press?'" Sociological Inquiry 56 (Spring 1986): 163.

Papandrea, Mary-Rose. "Citizen Journalism and the Reporter's Privilege." Minnesota Law Review 91 (2006-2007): 515.

Plaisance, Patrick L. "A Gang of Pecksniffs Grows Up: The Evolution of Journalism Ethics Discourse in The Journalist and Editor and Publisher." Journalism Studies 6:4 (November 2005): 479-491.

Porter, Jaime M. "Not Just 'Every Man': Revisiting the Journalist's Privilege Against Compelled Disclosure of Confidential Sources." Indiana Law Journal 82 (2007): 549.

Portune, Buzz. "Media Relationships in the Post 9/11 World: Have Changes Impacted Newsgathering and Reporter Privilege?" Ohio Northern University Law Review 32 (2006): 529.

Praul, Tori. "Apple Computer, Inc. v. Does: An Unsatisfying Resolution to the Conflict Between Trade Secret Law, Journalist's Privilege, & Blogging." Berkeley Technology Law Journal 21 (2006): 471.

Puerto, Olga C. "When Reporters Break Their Promises to Sources: Towards a Workable Standard in Confidential Source/Breach of Contract Cases." University of Miami Law Review 47 (1992): 501.

Rodgers, Ronald R. "Journalism is a Loose-Jointed Thing: A Content Analysis of Editor & Publisher's Discussion of Journalistic Conduct Prior to the Canons of Journalism, 1901-1922." Journal of Mass Media Ethics 22:1 (2007): 66-82.

Rood, Leslye DeRoos and Ann K. Grossman. "The Case for a Federal Journalist's Testimonial Shield Statute." Hastings Constitutional Law Quarterly 18 (1991): 779.

Sack, Robert D. "Reflections on the Wrong Question: Special Constitutional Privilege for the Institutional Press." Hofstra Law Review 7 (1978-1979): 630.

Samaha, Adam M. "Government Secrets, Constitutional Law and Platforms for Judicial Intervention." UCLA Law Review 53 (April 2006): 909.

Schmid, Karl H. "Journalist's Privilege in Criminal Proceedings: An Analysis of United States Courts of Appeals' Decisions from 1973 to 1999." American Criminal Law Review 39 (Fall 2002): 1441.

Schoenfeld, Gabriel. "Has the New York Times Violated the Espionage Act?" Commentary, March 2006.

Semeta, Ramutis R. "Journalist's Testimonial Privilege." Cleveland-Marshall Law Review 9 (1960): 311.

Sherwood, Margaret. "The Newsman's Privilege: Government Investigations, Criminal Prosecutions and Private Litigation." California Law Review 58 (1970): 1198.

Siebert, Fredrick S. "Professional Secrecy and the Journalist." Journalism Quarterly, 36 (Winter 1959): 3-11.

Siegel, Leslie. "Trampling on the Fourth Estate: The Need for a Federal Reporter Shield Law Providing Absolute Protection Against Compelled Disclosure of News Sources and Information." Ohio State Law Journal 67 (2006): 469.

Simon, Todd F. "Libel as Malpractice: News Media Ethics and the Standard of Care." Fordham Law Review 53 (1984): 449.

Smith, David J. "News-Source Privilege in Libel Cases." Washington Law Review 57 (1982): 349.

Smith, Jeffery A. "Legal Historians and the Press Clause." Communications and the Law 8 (1986): 70.

Smolla, Rodney A. "Will Tabloid Journalism Ruin the First Amendment for the Rest of Us?" DePaul-LCA Journal of Art & Entertainment Law and Policy 9 (1998-1999): 2.

Soloski, John. "News Reporting and Professionalism: Some Constraints on the Reporting of the News." Media, Culture and Society 11 (1989): 207.

Spinneweber, Kristina. "Branzburg Who? The Existence of a
        Reporter's Privilege in Federal Courts." Duquesne Law Review 44
        (2006): 317.
Stamp, Heather. "McKevitt v. Pallasch: How the Ghosts of the
        Branzburg Decision Are Haunting Journalists in the Seventh
        Circuit." DePaul-LCA Journal of Art & Entertainment Law and
        Policy 14 (2004): 363.
Steigleman, Walter A. "Newspaper Confidence Laws." Journalism
        Quarterly 20 (Sept. 1943): 230.
Stephens, Kenneth D. "Note and Comment: Privileged
        Communicatoins – News Media – A 'Shield Statute' for Oregon?"
        Oregon Law Review 46 (1966): 99.
Stewart, Potter. "Or of the Press." Hastings Law Journal 26 (1974-
        1975): 631.
Stone, Geoffrey R. "Why We Need a Federal Reporter's Privilege
        Statute." Hofstra Law Review 34 (2005-2006): 39.
Storey, Jeff. "Does Ethics Make Good Law? A Case Study." Cardozo
        Arts & Entertainment Law Journal 19 (2001): 467.
Swartwout, Daniel A. "In Re Madden: The Threat to New Journalism."
        Ohio State Law Journal 60 (1999): 1589.
Ugland, Erik. "The New Abridged Reporter's Privilege: Policies,
        Principles and Pathological Perspectives." Ohio State Law Journal
        71 (2010): 1.
Ugland, Erik. "Demarcating the Right to Gather News: A Sequential
        Interpretation of the First Amendment." Duke Journal of
        Constitutional Law & Public Policy 3 (2008): 113.
Ugland, Erik and Jennifer Henderson. "Who Is a Journalist and Why
        Does it Matter? Disentangling the Legal and Ethical Arguments."
        Journal of Mass Media Ethics 22 (2007): 241.
Van Alstyne, William. "The Hazards to the Press of Claiming a
        "Preferred Position." Hastings Law Journal 28 (1977): 761.
West, Sonja R. "Concurring in Part and Concurring in the Confusion."
        Michigan Law Review 104 (2006): 1951.
Wirth, Eileen M. "Impact of State Shield Laws on Investigative
        Reporting." Newspaper Research Journal 16 (1995): 64.
Wright, Susan Webber. "A Trial Judge's Ruminations on the
        Reporter's Privilege." University of Arkansas at Little Rock Law
        Review 29 (2006): 103.

Zampa, Julie M. "Journalist's Privilege: When Deprivation is a Benefit." Yale Law Journal 108 (1998-1999): 1449.

Zelnick, Robert. "Journalists and Confidential Sources," Notre Dame Journal of Law, Ethics & Public Policy 19 (2005): 541.

Index